AMERICA'S TRIAL

AMERICA'S TRIAL

TORTURE AND THE 9/11 CASE ON GUANTANAMO BAY

JOHN RYAN

Skyhorse Publishing

Copyright © 2025 by John Ryan

All rights reserved. No part of this book may be reproduced in any manner without the express written consent of the publisher, except in the case of brief excerpts in critical reviews or articles. All inquiries should be addressed to Skyhorse Publishing, 307 West 36th Street, 11th Floor, New York, NY 10018.

Skyhorse Publishing books may be purchased in bulk at special discounts for sales promotion, corporate gifts, fund-raising, or educational purposes. Special editions can also be created to specifications. For details, contact the Special Sales Department, Skyhorse Publishing, 307 West 36th Street, 11th Floor, New York, NY 10018 or info@skyhorsepublishing.com.

Skyhorse® and Skyhorse Publishing® are registered trademarks of Skyhorse Publishing, Inc.®, a Delaware corporation.

Visit our website at www.skyhorsepublishing.com.
Please follow our publisher Tony Lyons on Instagram @tonylyonsisuncertain.

10 9 8 7 6 5 4 3 2 1

Library of Congress Cataloging-in-Publication Data is available on file.

Cover design by David Ter-Avanesyan
Cover image by Janet Hamlin

Print ISBN: 978-1-5107-7891-7
Ebook ISBN: 978-1-5107-7892-4

Printed in the United States of America

Contents

Chapter 1	Preparation.	1
Chapter 2	First Trip. September 2015.	9
Chapter 3	U.S. v. KSM. October 2015.	19
Chapter 4	Dirty Laundry. December 2015.	35
Chapter 5	Movie Day. February 2016.	47
Chapter 6	The 9/11 Attacks. May–June 2016.	67
Chapter 7	The Missing Black Site. July–August 2016.	79
Chapter 8	End of Year One—The Sodomy Files. October–December 2016.	91
Chapter 9	Trumpland. January–May 2017.	107
Chapter 10	Black Site Still Missing. August 2017.	121
Chapter 11	Transparency.	129
Chapter 12	Enter the FBI. December 2017.	135
Chapter 13	The Prohibitions. January–April 2018.	147
Chapter 14	Mic Drop. July–August 2018.	161
Chapter 15	Rich and Vivid Accounts. September–November 2018.	167
Chapter 16	Mic Drop II. December 2018–May 2019.	177
Chapter 17	The Never Ending Tour—Killing Time.	189
Chapter 18	Breaking Guantanamo. June–July 2019.	201

Chapter 19	Suppression. September 2019.	207
Chapter 20	What Makes a Black Site a Black Site? October–November 2019.	225
Chapter 21	Dr. Mitchell. January 2020.	237
Chapter 22	Dr. Mitchell v. KSM.	255
Chapter 23	The Long Goodbye. February 2020.	271
Chapter 24	Pandemic and Return. March 2020–August 2021.	283
Chapter 25	Twentieth-Anniversary Reboot. September 2021.	291
Chapter 26	The Silent Treatment. March 2022–September 2023.	301
Chapter 27	Suppression II—The "Flaming Bag of Crap."	315
Chapter 28	2024—Trifurcation.	329
Chapter 29	Fives Are Wild.	343
Chapter 30	End in Sight.	355
Chapter 31	Ghost Town.	369
Chapter 32	2025—Game of Inches.	385
Chapter 33	An "End."	399

Acknowledgments   411
Sources and Bibliography   413
Index   417

This town was never intended as a permanent place, it was merely part of a centuries-long journey.

—Ted Chiang, "Tower of Babylon"

CHAPTER 1

Preparation.

Over the years I've been tempted to blame David Nevin for the way things turned out, for setting me on the path to Guantanamo Bay becoming my second home. The legal affairs media company I helped start, Lawdragon, regularly profiles prominent lawyers, and sometime in the winter of 2015 I came up with the idea of profiling Nevin for his work as the lead lawyer for the accused 9/11 plot mastermind. Prior to taking on Khalid Sheikh Mohammed's defense in 2008, Nevin, whose litigation firm is based in Boise, Idaho, was a well-known and highly regarded defense attorney. He had had a number of high-profile victories, the biggest perhaps being his successful defense of Kevin Harris in a federal murder case arising from the 1992 Ruby Ridge standoff in Boundary County, Idaho.

Over a few emails we agreed to talk at 12 p.m. East Coast time on Friday, March 20. I was visiting my parents and called Nevin from my childhood bedroom in the Boston suburb of Needham, Massachusetts, using a foldup table as a desk in front of the closet where I still had some clothes and where my parents kept a plastic bin of my early journalism clips. We spoke for a good seventy-five minutes about standard profile stuff—his recent work on the 9/11 case, some of his past cases, and his formative years that preceded an interest in the law. Nevin, I learned, was something of a hippie in his youth, describing himself as a "child of the 'Sixties" who spent a lot of time "hitching rides, dropping in, and dropping out" before eventually getting an English degree and heading to Europe with his guitar. He was teaching English in a small town in Germany and playing in clubs at night when, one day, he happened to see some type of law journal at the US consulate in town. Paging through that journal is what first sparked the idea of pursuing a legal education, which eventually led him to the College of Law at the University of Idaho. This odd tale, which didn't quite add up—at least in its abbreviated form—generated at least a dozen follow-up questions that I decided to bypass to not miss talking about Guantanamo. I knew that Nevin could have made a lot more money in a big city, but he told me he wanted to remain close to nature. Ten minutes from his office, he explained, he could be biking in the mountains.

When I told Nevin that it was too bad I couldn't see him in action, he said something that surprised me: He thought it was actually pretty easy for reporters to attend proceedings on Guantanamo Bay. He told me to contact the *Miami Herald* and Carol Rosenberg, the acclaimed reporter who had been the public's eyes and ears for the US Naval Base since the Bush administration first sent war-on-terror detainees there in January 2002.

That's how it all started.

But when I think back on it, I must have used the Nevin profile as an entrée to at least consider doing a bigger article on Guantanamo Bay. My job had mostly turned into one of managing and editing, working with freelancers and vendors rather than on my own stories. More than a year had passed since I'd published my last major substantive work. That was a lengthy feature on the status of various justice efforts by Rwanda and the international community in response to the 1994 genocide, which I wrote in the months after a two-week research trip there with my wife. Visiting the court on Guantanamo Bay and writing something about it, I thought, could maybe fill a void in my life.

I prepared intensely for the interview by reading a mix of materials, some of which refreshed my understanding of the basic background facts. Among the most important: The five 9/11 suspects had been captured in Pakistan between 2002 and 2003 but did not arrive on Guantanamo Bay until 2006. In between, the Central Intelligence Agency (CIA) held them at secret overseas black sites for harsh interrogations, and this past abuse, I knew vaguely, was a big factor in their case. The Bush administration finally put them to trial in its second version of a military commission system in June 2008, a few years after the US Supreme Court ruled that the first attempt at commissions was unconstitutional. But Barack Obama won the election that fall, and the following year his administration put all commission cases on hold as it worked to reform the court.

His administration also decided to hold the 9/11 case in a federal courthouse not far from the fallen World Trade Center towers, even

Preparation.

as it kept the military commissions as an option for other detainees. I recalled well Attorney General Eric Holder's November 2009 announcement of the controversial decision to relocate the case; I had just recently moved to lower Manhattan myself at the time. Holding the "Trial of the Century" in that dense thicket of government buildings and construction seemed like a logistical nightmare to me, but I was still surprised by the extent of local and national opposition to the plan. The next year, Congress passed a ban on the use of federal funds to transfer detainees to US soil—a prohibition that remained in place at the time of my call with Nevin. The Obama administration recharged the 9/11 defendants in the reformed military commissions system, and the arraignment took place on May 5, 2012.

Parts of that history, maybe even most of it, I knew. Like most Americans, however, I really had no idea what had been going on since the second case began, and whether it was close to actually going to trial. The best book I read on the military commissions was *The Terror Courts: Rough Justice at Guantanamo Bay* by *Wall Street Journal* reporter Jess Bravin, but it came out in 2013 and basically ended with the start of the Obama-era cases. To fill the gap, I decided I should read an account of every day in court from the May 2012 arraignment onward. I had already read a bunch of Carol's stories for the *Miami Herald*, along with some of Bravin's for the *Wall Street Journal* and others by the Associated Press (AP) and the *New York Times*. I also found a great resource in the popular Lawfare blog, which for years did write-ups of each court day from the courtroom's remote viewing site located in Fort Meade, Maryland, which received a closed-circuit feed. Cutting and pasting these resources, I created a 242-page document with a clear chronology containing every day of court from the start of the second 9/11 case to my call with Nevin. Using this document, I was able to easily find transcripts of certain days of court on the commissions' website to supplement the written accounts.

By immediately jumping into the weeds, I had read about but failed to fully process what was surely the most important set of facts: In 2008, the five men wanted to plead guilty and embrace their martyrdom before the case was halted by the change in administrations. But now they were challenging the government's case. The only five-defendant death penalty trial in US history—for the biggest crime in US history—would have to unfold in a still new and untested court system, a hybrid of the military and civilian courts, in a remote location. The hybrid nature helped explain the odd assortment of characters I had read about. The chief prosecutor was an Army brigadier general overseeing other military officers as well as civilian prosecutors from the Departments of Justice and Defense. All the lead defense lawyers like Nevin were civilian criminal defense lawyers, but they had military lawyers on their teams, and all of them were overseen by an Air Force colonel serving as the chief defense counsel.

All in all, I understood the case as well as any interested person reasonably could from the outside looking in—which is to say, not very well. The case was odd, unlike any I had covered. Significant parts of the case's first three years dealt with a mix of ancillary issues and the ironing out of the case's protocols, such as the protective orders that would govern the handling of classified and other sensitive case information—much of it involving the CIA's now-disbanded Rendition, Detention, and Interrogation (RDI) program. The military judge, Army Col. James Pohl, issued a protective order over any description of the CIA's "enhanced interrogation techniques" along with the "observations and experiences" of the defendants while in CIA custody. Pohl also implemented a forty-second delay of the audio and visual feed reaching the viewing gallery, which is separated from the courtroom by three panes of glass.

In addition to the information protocols, the first three years dealt with a series of intrusions—perceived or real, depending on which side of the courtroom one sat—into court operations and into the functioning of defense teams. Among the dramatic early turns, in January 2013 the CIA remotely shut down the courtroom audio and visual feed to the viewing gallery. Pohl and the court security officer sitting to his right both had the authority to stop the feed to the gallery, which happens with the press of a button that sets off a flashing red light. But neither of them had decided to stop court.

In going to the transcript, I saw that the light went off as Nevin was presenting oral arguments on a defense motion related to the preservation of CIA black sites, which the defense teams wanted to have available for evidentiary purposes throughout the case. One of the prosecutors, Joanna Baltes from the Justice Department, told Pohl that she could explain what happened—but only in a classified court session, which is closed to both the public and the defendants. Nevin was understandably concerned, as was Pohl.

"Your Honor, on behalf of Mr. Mohammed I would like to know who has the permission to turn that light on and off, who is listening to this, who is controlling these proceedings," Nevin said.

"Got it," Pohl said. (I didn't need to read too many transcripts to learn that "got it" was Pohl's catchphrase to signify he understood where someone was coming from.)

Preparation.

Pohl eventually issued an order preventing any outside agency from interfering with his court, but there were other concerns. The defense teams discovered that the smoke detectors in the attorney-client meeting rooms at the detention facility were listening devices, and they also learned that the audio system at the defense tables in court could allow for eavesdropping. The prosecution team insisted that no illicit monitoring had or was occurring, but disputes over these events all played themselves out through dozens and dozens of pleadings, oral arguments, and witness testimony spaced over the case's early years.

All of those events paled in comparison to the case's most disruptive twist in April 2014. That's when James Harrington, the lead lawyer for one of the defendants, Ramzi bin al Shibh, discovered that the Federal Bureau of Investigation (FBI) had turned at least one member of his team into a government informant. The FBI was apparently concerned that Harrington's team and the other defense teams were improperly handling case information. This presented a massive conflict of interest, as defendants in any criminal proceeding are entitled to defense lawyers who are not under investigation by the same government also prosecuting the case. The five teams filed an emergency motion to abate the proceedings, and they argued the matter in the April 2014 hearing and throughout the remainder of the year.

In fact, the case largely shut down as the government tasked a special prosecutor from the Justice Department to update the court on the status of whatever investigations were happening. In the June 2014 hearing, Nevin told Pohl that the various unknowns about government investigations were preventing him from effectively representing his client.

"And there's a little bit of a feeling here like you're sitting around your campfire, and you hear the wolves howling out in the woods, and you think, surely there's nothing here they want, but on the other hand, you're extremely vulnerable," Nevin said.

He said that he would be "delusional" if he didn't have "a reasonable fear." He said he recently had canceled an investigative trip to the Middle East because his team felt under scrutiny.

"I am trimming my sails," Nevin said. "I am pulling my punches. I am being extremely careful about how I proceed."

Pohl initially decided to sever bin al Shibh from the case but reversed himself after a request by the prosecution team, which desperately wanted to have a single case instead of multiple 9/11 trials on separate tracks. But he ruled that the case would be on hold until the investigation into the bin al Shibh defense team was resolved—which would take a long while.

The special prosecutor's attempt to update the court in the February 2015 hearing led to another stranger-than-fiction twist. Near the start of court, bin al Shibh announced that the new interpreter assigned to his team and sitting at his table had been an interpreter at a CIA black site. The other defendants also recognized him. Somehow, someone who worked at a location where the defendants were held in abusive, incommunicado detention by the CIA had found his way to their side of the courtroom to work on their defense. The defense lawyers assumed that the CIA had engineered a blatant intimidation tactic, messaging to the defendants that they would never truly be free of CIA custody; the government denied any such intent. (As it would eventually turn out, litigation over this one event lasted another seven years.)

I spoke to Nevin in the middle of this madness, about four weeks after the interpreter scandal. Nevin wasn't exactly blasé about any of these issues. By this point in the case, he had already had to retain his own defense counsel multiple times in response to what appeared to be government scrutiny or investigations. But he had been dealing with these issues for years, and he was able to talk about them as facets of pretrial litigation.

While Nevin described as "Orwellian" the government's decision to classify his client's memories as top secret information—"If you didn't want people to know about the secret torture, you shouldn't have tortured him," he told me—he acknowledged that he and his colleagues were far freer to talk about torture than they had been. During the first few years of pretrial hearings, defense attorneys could tell reporters that their clients were tortured but could not mention any details they may have learned from their clients or their own investigative work. I saw this myself when watching some of the post-hearing press conferences on the court's website. A big change occurred in December 2014, when the Senate Select Committee on Intelligence (SSCI) released its summary of an investigation into the CIA program. The 6,700-page report and all the underlying information that went into the report remained classified, but the 500-plus-page findings and executive summary declassified an enormous amount of information about how the CIA detainees—including the five 9/11 defendants—were abused at the black sites.

"The Senate Torture Report," as it's commonly known, makes for some harrowing reading. Prior to my interview with Nevin, I used the search tool in Adobe Acrobat to read through all the references to his client in a PDF version of the SSCI summary—and there were many, as Mohammed was subjected to repeated bouts of waterboarding and other abuses that included prolonged periods of sleep deprivation, one of which lasted more than a week. Nevin did not go into much detail about his interactions with Mohammed, though he acknowledged the challenges of representing "a torture victim" who would naturally be distrustful of a defense team provided by the government that had tortured him. He also said that he wasn't especially hopeful that the government would provide detailed discovery about the torture beyond that included in the Senate summary.

"People who engaged in torture committed serious felonies," Nevin told me. "There's a strong instinct of people in power to protect them."

It was hard to tell what details might make their way into a lawyer profile. One topic I thought Lawdragon's readers would be interested in would be the effect the case had on his law practice and his partnership. Nevin first joined Mohammed's defense as a pro bono counsel in 2008, as the Bush-era law establishing the commissions only provided for military defense lawyers. His slot was funded by the American Civil Liberties Union (ACLU) and the National Association of Criminal Defense Lawyers, which had launched "The John Adams Project" to fund experienced civilian lawyers to help represent Guantanamo defendants. Among the reforms of Obama's 2009 act was to provide a "learned counsel" with capital experience for each commission defendant facing the death penalty. That meant for the second case Nevin was a Pentagon contractor earning the same rate as court-appointed capital lawyers in federal cases, which at the time was something like $175 an hour. That's a good wage, but it's far below what a prominent lawyer would charge a paying client. I tried a few different ways to ask about this, but Nevin held firm—he did not want to talk about money.

I followed his advice and emailed Carol at the *Herald*. She told me to contact the public affairs officer for the military commissions, then Army Lt. Col. Myles Caggins, who distributed media invites for journalists looking to attend proceedings. Caggins told me I would have a seat on the flight for the hearing scheduled for late April 2015. But the FBI investigation into the bin al Shibh defense team was apparently still unresolved. Pohl canceled the April hearing, then he canceled the late May–June hearing and also the session scheduled for August. It seemed like the 9/11 case might never get going again.

Frustrated, I decided to apply for the September 2015 hearing in the case against Abd al Hadi al Iraqi, an alleged senior al Qaeda operative accused of war crimes in Afghanistan, one of three military commissions in pretrial proceedings at the time. (Two other detainees had pleaded guilty and were awaiting their sentencing trials.) Carol told me that 9/11 case lawyers regularly used flights for other cases to travel to see their clients. Even if Nevin didn't go on the trip, I thought I might get some color for the profile by at least seeing where he worked. After all that I'd read about the place, I had to go at least once.

CHAPTER 2

First Trip. September 2015.

I took an Amtrak train from Penn Station in Manhattan to Washington, DC, on the afternoon of September 19, 2015, to stay overnight with friends before my journey to Guantanamo. Jeff, a former colleague from my first reporting job in Los Angeles, and Kristin, his wife, live near the Capitol by Stanton Park. Carol had told me that getting into Joint Base Andrews in Maryland, from where all commission flights depart, in the early hours can be confusing, as the base has multiple gates, so I decided to take a car to the hotel where she was staying early on Sunday. With her was the only other journalist making the trip, Janet Reitman, who was working on a feature story for *Rolling Stone*. We shared a car to Andrews and were met by the public affairs officer for the military commissions, at the time Navy Commander Gary Ross, who got us to the terminal.

A week earlier, Ross had me sign the "Media Ground Rules for Guantanamo Bay, Cuba" document, which was required for any journalist who wants to get to Gitmo. Lawyers for media organizations and Pentagon officials ironed out this version of the ground rules back in 2010. The rules limited the photography and video that attending journalists can take—most prohibitions were meant to protect the base's security infrastructures—and they required that media get approval of all visual material before any usage. The policies did not provide many limitations on what a journalist could report or write about court. The rules prohibited the disclosure of "protected information," which included classified information but also included other information that might "cause damage to national security"—which was somewhat vague. However, the forty-second delay of audio reaching the viewing gallery gave the judge and the government plenty of time to prevent a spill, so this appeared to be a nonissue at first glance. The rules said that media "will be urged to not use" any protected information inadvertently spilled, which was not a prohibition. I learned that these after-the-fact classification determinations are typically made much later—well after a story's publication—and often show up as partial redactions to public transcripts. I also noted the rule that alcohol "could not be stored or consumed" in or around the media center.

Holding court in a remote location meant that each military commission was essentially its own traveling court system that departed by chartered jet from Andrews. Some of the logistical, administrative, and security personnel who worked for the military commissions lived on Guantanamo Bay, but all the judges, their support staff, and the prosecution and defense teams did not. Most lived in the DC area, near where the court system kept its stateside offices in Virginia. Those who lived elsewhere (like Nevin) had to travel to the DC area at least a day before the flight to avoid the risk of missing it.

The Andrews air terminal had just a few dozen people in its waiting room. About an hour after checking in for the flight, an official in civilian clothes called everyone to attention to announce that the flight was postponed for a day, or, as the military says, "moved to the right." I found it strange that no one seemed to think this was strange; the sleepy group of passengers began gathering their things without complaint or inquiry. We later learned that the Air Force had scheduled an air show at Andrews but had neglected to tell the commissions personnel responsible for logistical arrangements. I texted Jeff that I'd be returning to his house for another night.

Cmdr. Ross suggested that we use the morning to have an on-the-record discussion in the terminal's distinguished visitors' room with the chief prosecutor of the military commissions, who oversaw all of the pending cases and any new ones that might be filed. I was looking forward to this. I had read quite a bit about Army Brig. Gen. Mark Martins as part of my research for the Nevin profile. Martins was the lone prosecutor to speak at the 9/11 case post-hearing press conferences that I had watched. I had also recently watched him in Lesley Stahl's 2013 segment for *60 Minutes* that addressed controversies with the Guantanamo Bay detention facility and also with the 9/11 case specifically, including the hidden microphones scandal. The Harvard-trained lawyer and former law classmate of President Barack Obama had long ago established himself as an effective, generally unflappable spokesperson for the Guantanamo tribunals despite their lackluster record—just seven convictions by that point, several of them overturned after the detainees were transferred out.

We shook hands and sat around a small table for about an hour. As looks go, Martins, dressed in fatigues and standing at what appeared to be an athletic 6'3" or so, was a striking, straight-out-of-central-casting version of a military officer. He was polite, serious, and eager to take questions, but also surprisingly prone to long answers that were hard to digest in a conversational flow. Of the two newcomers, Reitman asked about interesting topics—like why nothing on Guantanamo Bay, including the court cases, seemed to work very well. I settled on some of the more boring topics that interested me, such as the pretrial hurdle that the government was facing in the Hadi case. At some point, the government had to establish that he was an "alien unprivileged enemy belligerent"—which was the only category of person over which the Guantanamo court had any jurisdiction. Prosecutors would have to prove this by a preponderance of evidence before getting to a trial, a task that probably wouldn't be too difficult given Hadi's alleged work for al Qaeda in the war in Afghanistan. Still, it spoke to what Martins referred to as the "narrowness" of the commissions—that the court only applied to a relatively select number of foreign terrorism suspects, and that the federal courts were still the best option for most.

Martins appeared to have read my bio, available on Lawdragon or LinkedIn, which would have included that I earned a master's degree in human rights studies from NYU with a focus on justice mechanisms for mass atrocities. He referred to one of my lengthy Lawdragon articles on war crimes cases in the former Yugoslavia when elaborating on some of the jurisdictional issues tied to the military commissions.

"You can't use wartime authorities any old time," Martins told us, giving me a knowing glance.

On Monday morning, our flight left close to on time, around 10 a.m. The three-hour, ten-minute flight landed at the terminal on the mostly empty "Leeward" side of the US Naval Base, eventually stopping in the middle of a landing strip about seventy-five yards from the terminal. The experience of descending mobile stairs—which felt a little VIP to me, as I'm not sure I had ever done that before—was immediately soured by the thick wave of heat hitting my face and a vaguely unpleasant smell. Inside the terminal, we were met by public affairs staffers from the detention facility, who piled us into a van and drove us onto a ferry for a twenty-minute trip to the "Windward" part of the base, which has the Naval headquarters, the prison, the court complex in so-called "Camp Justice," and all the other facilities. We received security badges required to access the court, dumped our baggage at the nearby tents where we'd sleep, then set up our laptops in the media center and received an "operational security" briefing by the public affairs team on what we could and could not do and photograph on the base. Then we went to the base's big shopping center, the Naval Exchange or "NEX," to buy booze, snacks, and other supplies for the brief three-day visit before descending on the Irish bar, O'Kelly's, for dinner and then making our way back to the tents at Camp Justice for a nightcap. The day moved fast, and I was pretty wiped out.

Guantanamo Bay was not a prison compound. That was one of the basic facts I mastered before the trip, and it hits you pretty clearly once you arrive on Windward and begin driving around. It basically felt like a small beach town, with McDonald's and the NEX at its center. The base was already about a hundred years old before the Bush administration started sending war-on-terror detainees there in January 2002. When Obama campaigned on closing Gitmo, he was talking about the detention facility, not the Naval Base. Getting to the detention facility from the McDonald's at the center of town was a four-mile drive to the southeast part of the base, tucked away past some hills and overlooking the ocean. We did not go there on this trip, but Carol explained the general layout to Reitman and me as we drove around.

Much of the land portion of the base's forty-five square miles are low-lying, meandering hills on the south side of its main street, Sherman Avenue, a long road that more or less runs the length of the bay. I did a late afternoon hike up to the highest point overlooking Sherman with Navy Capt. Christopher Scholl, who served as the public affairs officer for the prison. We walked up the steep "John Paul Jones Hill" to the summit, which has four wind turbines—only a few of which had blades spinning. (They would eventually stop working.) I found the base surprisingly dusty and brown—not exactly un-tropical given the overwhelming humidity, but cacti and brush nestled in the hills far outnumbered the palm trees haphazardly dotting the streets. The base's population, at the time around six thousand people, was almost nowhere to be seen on the streets, at least during the height of the day's heat, and there weren't many people in uniform in the stores or restaurants. All of the service jobs are staffed by what the base calls "Third Country Nationals," or TCNs, mostly Filipinos and Jamaicans working low-wage jobs for a Pentagon contractor. Outside the court complex, TCNs were the most populous group we encountered, though O'Kelly's was fairly crowded at night.

I also knew before attending that I would not be going to Cuba, and that my lack of Spanish would not be a hindrance. Guantanamo Bay is not "in" Cuba even if it's "on" Cuba or part of the Cuban island. Members of the military often talk about liking Germany or South Korea or parts of Japan from their service at overseas bases, but they don't offer opinions about Cuba because they can't leave the base to visit it. The Marines still patrolled the fence lines that border Cuba on both the Leeward and Windward sides, as they did in Aaron Sorkin's *A Few Good Men*. Whether you're actually in another country is up to anyone's philosophical rumination; civilians need passports to enter the base and to return through customs at Andrews, which even in my first trip felt unnecessary given that we never left an area that was completely controlled by the US military and where only US law applied.

Karen Greenberg's excellent book, *The Least Worst Place: Guantanamo's First 100 Days*, explains how the Bush administration came to see Guantanamo Bay as the best option for holding detainees that coalition forces began accumulating in large quantities in the war to rout the Taliban, which began in October 2001. The United States had gotten ahold of Guantanamo Bay during the Spanish American War and entered into a lease agreement with Cuba in 1903. Later revisions to the agreement required its termination to be consented to by both sides—which left Cuba powerless to kick America out once we became enemies with Fidel Castro's rise to power. The United States did not want to put detainees in military bases in Europe, such as in Germany, because those governments would want some say in the treatment of detainees—who also might have access to the European Court of Human Rights. Placing detainees in US-controlled territories, such as in Guam or American Samoa, might give them legal access to US courts—another thing the Bush administration wanted to avoid. As Greenberg recounts, Gitmo was perfect because it was outside the United States and yet completely controlled by the US government.

As it turned out, in one of several seminal Guantanamo cases, the US Supreme Court ruled in *Rasul v. Bush* in 2004 that the detainees did have access to federal courts to challenge their detentions. The court would rule four years later in *Boumediene v. Bush* that detainees could file writs of habeas corpus even if they were determined by the administration to be enemy combatants. The US Court of Appeals for the DC Circuit, which reviews habeas cases filed in DC federal court, eventually made prevailing in these cases extraordinary difficult, but most of detainees were transferred out through administrative determinations made by both the Bush and Obama administrations. More than 780 detainees (mostly men, some boys) spent time on Guantanamo Bay. Starting in 2013, an interagency parole-like system called the "Periodic Review Board" began assessing detainees' suitability for release. By the time of the Hadi trip, the population was down to 115, and another transfer was made while we were there.

Camp Justice, which houses the court complex, was a two-mile drive from McDonald's in the opposite direction from the prison, culminating in the northwest section of the Windward side. It sat on a sprawling area on a former tarmac and airstrip elevated above much of the base. At the time, there were several dozen large military tents that were almost always empty. During court hearings, one or more would be made operational for journalists, with men and women kept separate. Plywood walls divided each tent into six living spaces with twin beds and dressers, with a common refrigerator, microwave, and ironing table set up in back. Loud generators powered air conditioners that cooled each tent down into the sixties in an unending battle against mold, and at night they powered giant floodlights illuminating the area. I quickly learned that the nearby latrine and shower tents had lost the mold battle long before my arrival.

A quarter-mile from the tent complex were tracts of FEMA-like trailers called containerized housing units, or CHUs, which housed the military personnel who worked on the cases, including Gen. Martins. (Most civilian lawyers and staff stayed in the hotels at the center of town or in town houses.) The CHUs sat across from the outer edge of the Expeditionary Legal Complex, or "ELC," named "expeditionary" as it was never meant to be permanent—a naming convention that was already evidencing a spirit of denialism. The ELC contained the large courtroom, which from the outside is a large metal box, and the attorney workspaces, also in trailers. Chain-link fencing, sniper netting, and razor wire surround the ELC in a large square that was completely off-limits to photography.

To any newcomer, I concluded, Camp Justice was a miserable place, visually unappealing and also potentially dangerous. I thought about doing sprints and bodyweight exercises in the vast expanse of tents until I recalled Carol saying that the base previously used this runway to dump fuel and that many people who have worked for the commissions over the years view Camp Justice as a cancer risk. The area's elevated position did not lend itself to as many breezes as one might hope. Not long into my second nightcap I was sweating through my clothes and unable to fend off unusually violent mosquitoes. Back in the tent, alone in the pitch black, I was freezing and scratched myself into a fitful sleep.

Camp Justice can also be beautiful, however. It is adjacent to the smallest and most pristine of the beaches, Glass Beach. On my second evening, the view westward over the depressing expanse of tents revealed a pink sunset that appeared comically fake. A magical version of that sunset, I would later learn, happens just about every day there.

I also quickly concluded that Camp Justice was a decent place to work. The Media Operations Center, or "MOC," was a quarter-mile from the media tents and across from the ELC's eastern edge. From the outside, it looked like something from a horror movie: a rusted-out, abandoned air hangar with wooden crates, stray cats, and the odd white owl. But the walled-off office within the terminal was comfortable and modern, with desks for a few dozen journalists and large HDTV screens that showed live broadcasts of the proceedings. The kitchen area had a full-sized fridge and a coffee maker and plenty of storage space for food, sunscreen, bug spray, and office supplies. There was no Wi-Fi at the time, but the internet connection by Ethernet—purchased from a military contractor at an obscene $150 per week—proved generally reliable, if not exactly fast.

We departed the MOC on the morning of September 22, 2015, for what was expected to be an uneventful, one-day hearing in the Hadi case. Getting into court required two TSA-like security screenings—one at the outer perimeter of the ELC and the other in the foyer immediately outside court. At this second juncture, visitors either veered right into the courtroom or left into the viewing gallery, which had four rows of seats for a seating capacity of about fifty. Uniformed military police guards staffed the security operations throughout the court complex, which for me enhanced the feel of the court as a military operation. I was used to the US Marshals in federal courts, but they never had as many assigned to one courtroom. Court rules posted on various walls prohibited electronics or any recording devices, including smartwatches and earphones. It was pen and paper only, with no sketching or doodling allowed, except by sketch artists who had to receive approval prior to the trip.

As with the trip overall, Hadi's hearing was a soft journalistic entry into the military commissions. The judge on the case, Navy Capt. J. K. Waits, used the occasion to grant Hadi's request for a new lead military defense lawyer. (Hadi did not face a death penalty, so he was not entitled to a "learned" capital counsel like Nevin.) Waits told Hadi that he did not see good cause to remove his current military team but that he was giving him "a free pass" because he had previously lost the lawyers he liked. Hadi's new lawyer did not yet have his security clearance, so the hearing had to conclude without any substantive progress—another Gitmo theme, I knew from my research. Hadi was transferred to Guantanamo Bay from CIA custody in 2007 but was not charged until 2014. He seemed mystified by Waits's suggestion that he was responsible for continued delays in the case.

"I stayed here in Guantanamo for seven years and six months without trial, and then after that, my case was sent to court," Hadi said in Arabic. "It took a long time."

The first thing you learn when attending a legal proceeding on Guantanamo Bay is just how long forty seconds actually is. Back in 2012, in the 9/11 case, Judge Pohl's approval of the forty-second audio-and-video delay came over the objections of the ACLU and a coalition of media organizations. Attendees in the viewing gallery all stand with the rest of the parties when the judge enters the courtroom, and we all sit when he sits. Then we wait for the judge to appear on the monitors located across the top of the gallery; it takes forever, almost as if there is a problem with the feed. Attendees then have to choose between watching the feed or live action through the glass that will be completely out of sync with the audio. I was also struck by how massive the courtroom was—maybe about a quarter of a soccer field—by far the biggest court I had ever been in. Hadi and his team, at the first defense table closest to the judge's bench, felt very far away from the gallery. The impersonal nature of the experience made watching the monitor that much more tempting.

On the night after the Hadi hearing, two lawyers from Khalid Sheikh Mohammed's team, one military and one civilian, came down to the media tents to share a bottle of scotch while catching up with Carol, who generously suggested I join. The lawyers had used the Hadi flight to come down and meet with their client as the 9/11 case seemed to drag interminably on hold. Despite all that I had read about the case before interviewing Nevin (he was not among the two who stopped by), I began to grasp how little I understood about the proceedings. Basic assumptions were undercut by a casual off-the-record chat, one that lasted not even two hours, and one limited by the fact that the lawyers knew they had a stranger in their midst. I can't share what these topics were, but I woke up with the reality that the trial operations of Guantanamo Bay made less sense to me than they had before the trip. This can be frustrating for a journalist, but also enticing. The

Mohammed lawyers also believed that the next hearing in their case—set to begin in about a month—would actually take place.

After the return to Andrews, an Uber took Reitman and me to Union Station in DC to get a train back to New York. Carol stayed in the car to go to her hotel room before flying back to Miami the next day. I tried to thank her for all her help, but she held her hand up and cut me off.

"Just come back," she said.

CHAPTER 3

US v. KSM. October 2015.

Early on Saturday, October 17, after a night with Jeff and Kristin, I shared a car to Joint Base Andrews with Carol and Ben Fox from the Associated Press, at that point the only truly regular Guantanamo reporter in addition to Carol. At Andrews we were met by Cmdr. Ross and also the journalist Laura Haim, who was working on a documentary for Canal Plus. Jeff and I tend to stay up late when we see each other, which left me in poor shape to deal with the chaos of traveling for the 9/11 case. Before too long, more than 125 people filled the waiting room: a mix of civilians and members of the military standing in line at the check-in counter, talking in small circles, grabbing seats, and competing for the limited number of power outlets. I should have anticipated the busyness, knowing that capital defense teams are often quite large. Each of the five defense teams, I was told, had fifteen to twenty members between the lawyers, paralegals, investigators, interpreters, information security officers, analysts, and mitigation specialists. Not all of them traveled for each trip, but those teams filled probably close to half the room. Carol introduced me to a bunch of people whose names and roles I quickly forgot.

In addition to the sprawling defense teams milling about, ten or so people, mostly men, formed a loose circle around Chief Prosecutor Martins in the far corner of the terminal. The court system also funds the attendance of victim family members, or "VFMs"; five are chosen by lottery, each of whom is allowed a companion to provide emotional support. That slate appeared to be mostly full, as did the group of about a dozen people representing nongovernmental organizations (NGOs) approved to observe proceedings. Judge Pohl was nowhere to be seen, presumably hiding out in the distinguished visitors' room or another private location. I saw people I later realized were part of the trial judiciary as clerks or court reporters, and others who did the real-time translation between English and Arabic during court. The Pentagon official who oversees the commissions system, called the "convening authority"—whose name I had forgotten—also has a staff, including legal advisors, some of whom were almost certainly present.

The 9/11 case was what the military calls "a large muscle movement," the implementation of which defines the hierarchy of the military commissions. Media left the terminal first for the bus ride to the chartered plane, and we sat in our assigned rows at the back by the bathrooms. We were followed by the NGOs, then the defense teams, then the prosecution, with the judiciary staff and the VFMs near the front or in first class. Of all the travelers, journalists are the only ones who paid for seats, at the time $400 round-trip. We had to show up with a $400 check or money order for Cmdr. Ross before getting in line to check in.

The Hadi flight was so small—maybe 15 percent full—that there was either no need for the strict ordering protocols or I hadn't noticed them. The 9/11 military commission was a true traveling court system, as if a federal judge in New York had decided to move a massive mafia case to whatever remote island hosted his beach home. It also felt like its own ecosystem and mini-economy. Its revival after months of false starts suggested that Judge Pohl was finally convinced that the case could move forward. Most likely, this meant that the criminal investigation into the Ramzi bin al Shibh defense team had concluded without any charges being brought. But I also knew the 9/11 case had been full of surprises up to that point. I was eager to get to court.

* * *

We arrived early on Monday morning, October 19, by about 8:25 a.m. Pohl had set a rule early in the case that the defendants had to show up for the first day of each session, so that he could read a script explaining their rights to either attend court or voluntarily waive their presence. This meant that all the defendants would be showing up for at least the first day. We watched as guards from the prison staff, called Joint Task Force Guantanamo or more commonly "JTF-GTMO," escorted each defendant into court, one at a time, with guards walking on each side of the defendant with a light touch or hold to both the shoulders and wrists until the defendant reached his table. The defendants were not shackled at either the wrists or ankles. During a tour of the Expeditionary Legal Complex on the Hadi trip, we saw restraint chairs in the sniper-netting-covered walkway between the holding cells and court that could be used for unruly defendants. The courtroom itself also had metal bolts in the floors under the defense tables that could be used for shackling a defendant to the floor, but these were not used.

I felt a heightened sense of anticipation waiting to see Khalid Sheikh Mohammed and four of his alleged coconspirators for the first time, but seeing them walk into court did not trigger an emotional response. As far as I knew, I had no direct connection to anyone who had either died or lost a close friend or relative on 9/11. It's also possible I had read so much about the case that it compartmentalized the defendants into "litigants"—parties to confusing proceedings removed from horrors I watched in real time on 9/11 and in each year since in the many documentaries and coverage that flood the airwaves on anniversaries, or in movies like Paul Greengrass's *United 93* or Oliver Stone's *World Trade Center*. I had a similar experience watching Radovan Karadžić, a notorious former Serb leader accused of war crimes, crimes against humanity, and genocide, in trial at The Hague in 2011. Karadžić, who represented himself, even cross-examined a prosecution witness on the day I attended. Some drama accompanied that day, but it also felt like just another day in court—as with the 9/11 case, one of dozens of days in court far away in time and space from the actual crimes. The experience was surely different for the victim family members, whose designated seating space was on the right side of the gallery behind the prosecution team; they could choose to pull a curtain across their side for privacy from other attendees. Several of them took turns coming over to our side to get a better look at the men before court.

My biggest first impression from the Guantanamo court was how pleased the defendants seemed to be to be there, both to see each other and at least some members of their legal teams. They began chatting animatedly among themselves and with team members who began filling the left side of the courtroom to near capacity as the clock approached 9 a.m. This seemed to be quality social time, like the bustle and chatter between colleagues and contacts that precedes the start of a conference in a hotel ballroom. The five defendants and the other "high value detainees," or HVDs, were transferred from the CIA black sites to Guantanamo Bay in September 2006. From that point, they had been held in the top secret and highly restrictive Camp 7 facility, kept separate from the other detainees. The conditions had loosened somewhat since the early days of mostly solitary confinement, but court was the only time these five could hang out together. They had gotten a taste of this benefit during the first commission, when they all attempted to represent themselves.

I noticed, as everyone does, that Mohammed, a citizen of Pakistan, had an orange beard. According to one news report, he dyed his beard using crushed berries, though there was also a rumor that his defense team was able to bring him henna. He appeared short and a little stout. The men, all between their mid-thirties and fifty, seemed to be in good spirits and also in reasonably good health—something that I knew to be factually incorrect. They all wore what to my uncultured brain was a similar type of non-Western attire, loose-fitting robes and tunics or tunic-style clothing, each with some type of headwear. Mohammed, the oldest at fifty, and the two defendants behind him, Walid bin Attash and Ramzi bin al Shibh, also wore camouflage jackets or vests, presenting a bit of a warrior or combatant look. (Their legal rights to wear certain clothing in court had been litigated earlier in the case.) Bin Attash, the youngest, a Yemeni who grew up in Saudi Arabia and was something of a child soldier when he joined al Qaeda, walked into court with a noticeable limp; he had lost his right leg from the knee down fighting the Northern Alliance in Afghanistan and wears a prosthetic.

Carol had helpfully informed me that the seating of the defendants in court followed their order in the charge sheet, which contained an eighteen-page narrative of the conspiracy behind the so-called "Planes Operation." Mohammed allegedly met with Osama bin Laden in 1996 to begin discussing the idea of using hijacked commercial planes as missiles. Bin Attash was alleged to have joined the plot in 1999, accused of training future hijackers in hand-to-hand combat and conducting surveillance of airport and flight security protocols. The third defendant, bin al Shibh, a Yemeni, was portrayed as Mohammed's key deputy in planning the 9/11 attacks through his work in the German terrorist cell that was critical to the plot; he also allegedly wanted to be a hijacker but failed at several points to get a visa for entry into the United States.

The remaining two, Ammar al Baluchi—Mohammed's nephew, who grew up in Kuwait, at the fourth table—and Mustafa al Hawsawi, a Saudi who sat closest to us by the viewing gallery, did not wear any paramilitary style clothing. They were the alleged money men of the operation, accused of sending the eventual hijackers money and other forms of assistance. Guards carried in a pillow for al Hawsawi and placed it on his seat. Even casual observers of the case knew this was because he felt constant pain while sitting due to rectal abuse he endured at CIA black sites.

The courtroom during the Hadi hearing felt unnecessarily large, almost absurdly so. Now it could barely contain the five capital defense teams. Initially, I was confused that the prosecution side of the courtroom was so empty, with just two lawyers, and neither of them Gen. Martins. But then I recalled that the first order of business was for the so-called "Special Review Team," led by Fernando Campoamor-Sanchez of the Justice Department, to update Pohl on the status of the investigation into the bin al Shibh defense team. After his lead lawyer, James Harrington, discovered the FBI infiltration into his team in April 2014, Martins decided that he and his team had to be "walled off" from this aspect of the proceedings. Discussions over the probe and any litigation about it might reveal the inner workings of the defense teams that the prosecution should not be privy to. Martins and his team waited elsewhere in the ELC.

Pohl walked in at 9:04 and called the commission to order for the first time in eight months. He began by asking each of the lead lawyers to identify who was in court for each team—something that happens every day—then he read his rights advisory to the five defendants, explaining their choice to either attend court or skip it. Pohl asked Mohammed if he understood his rights; Mohammed said "na'am" from the first defense table, Arabic for "yes," as an unseen translator explained in real time through the sound system. Pohl then asked the same question to bin Attash, who also responded in Arabic—notably high-pitched.

"Before I respond, I have some questions that are related to self-representation," bin Attash said.

And just like that, the 9/11 case veered off course again—before it even had a chance to right itself. Pohl was nevertheless unfazed. This hardly registered as a blip compared to the FBI planting a mole on a defense team or a former CIA interpreter sitting at a defense table.

"We will come back to that in a second, okay?" he promised bin Attash, before continuing his colloquy with the other defendants.

All of the civilian women on the defense teams wore head coverings out of respect for their client, which made keeping track of who was who somewhat more difficult. But bin Attash's lead lawyer, Cheryl Bormann, the only woman in the lead role among the five teams, stood out. She was the only woman to also wear an austere black abaya used by Saudi women, a full body cloak, leaving only her face visible. Facing questions by reporters after the May 2012 arraignment, Bormann said that she had never met her client in anything but the abaya. She portrayed doing so as an obvious move for any capital defender. Prior to her Gitmo life, the Chicago-based Bormann had been best-known for running Illinois's Capital Trial Assistance Unit, a state agency that assisted defense lawyers on death penalty cases. I knew from discussions with Carol that Bormann's attire and that of the other women was a source of annoyance and even anger among some observers, not least of all some of the family members. Having read about the challenges of attorney-client relationships over the years, particularly in death penalty cases, I didn't think twice about it.

Pohl told Bormann to speak to her client, but she said that bin Attash would not speak with her and wanted to address the court directly. Pohl asked bin Attash if he wanted to represent himself or to first discuss his concerns with his team before making a decision. Bin Attash responded again that he wanted to know "the procedures for self-representation." He added somewhat cryptically: "We have so many problems in the camp that take precedence over anything that they are discussing here in court. We are still in the black sites."

Pohl called for a thirty-minute recess so that bin Attash and his team could talk this over. When they came back on the record more than an hour later, Bormann took the podium to inform Pohl that bin Attash had lost faith in both her and the lead military lawyer, Air Force Maj. Michael Schwartz, who also had been on the case since the May 2012 arraignment. Bormann blamed the long list of government intrusions for the breakdown.

"He tells us that he doesn't know whether or not there is an FBI agent on his team," Bormann explained. "Why? Well, because there were FBI informants on other teams. He tells us that as he sits here today he has no idea if there is a CIA operative on his team. Why? Well, because in this bizarre setting that actually has occurred."

Bormann said that she really couldn't advise bin Attash on the process of representing himself in this case. In regular cases, a judge would likely grant the self-representation (called pro se) request but appoint lawyers to serve as standby counsel to provide assistance. At the detention facility, however, bin Attash would not have access to a law library and could not make phone calls to anyone on the team. When they were not on the island, defense teams communicated with their clients through an elaborate and secure courier system. Also problematic was the fact that the defendants could not review most of the classified information in the case, even though much of it pertained to what was done to them at the CIA black sites. They also couldn't attend classified sessions that were closed to the public, since attendance required the highest security clearances.

"This is like no other court," Bormann said. "So I can't possibly advise Mr. bin Attash of his rights because I, frankly, don't know what they are."

As Bormann spoke, Pohl saw a procedural problem: The prosecution still wasn't in the courtroom; it was just Campoamor-Sanchez and another member of the Special Review Team, Kevin Driscoll. The pro se matter was one that impacted "the regular trial team," Pohl said, so he recessed court again so that the prosecution team could come in. Ten minutes later, the right side of the courtroom was mostly filled with the large military and civilian team led by Martins, which included five additional prosecutors, several analysts and paralegals, and two FBI agents sitting in the back.

Pohl and the parties agreed that the judge needed to come up with a Gitmo-appropriate advisement to bin Attash that could apply to all the defendants should they raise a similar wish. Pohl said he would draft a pro se script—a warning, essentially, of how bad of an idea it was for a defendant to represent himself in this case—and send it to the defense teams and the government for input.

With that, court was over for the day. The case had immediately lived up to its reputation, and it did so again on Tuesday. That morning, James Connell, the lead lawyer for al Baluchi, raised a complication for the pro se advisement. He approached the podium from the fourth defense table. At age forty-four, just three years older than me, Connell already had a dozen years of experience working on death penalty cases, mostly in Virginia. While I was having trouble identifying the various players, I could distinguish Connell from the others with his shiny bald head; he had chatted with me amiably at the media center over the weekend. He told Pohl that there was a top secret program at Camp 7 that was relevant to whether a detainee living there could represent himself. Not everybody in court knew about this program. Having the highest clearance, a Top Secret Sensitive Compartmentalized Information, or TS-SCI, clearance, didn't mean you got briefed into every program, which is based on a need to know. Connell had been "read into" or briefed on this additional program, called an "alternative compensatory control measure," or ACCM, as had the prosecution team, but he didn't know about the other defense teams. As it turned out, Judge Pohl and his staff had not been briefed on the program.

Connell had a filing to inform the judge about it.

"Your Honor, could I double-wrap the document and submit it to the trial judiciary to be kept in a safe?" Connell asked. "You don't have a copy of it for the record right now, is one of my concerns."

"We will get to it when we get to it, but I don't want to take custody of a document I'm not authorized to read," Pohl responded.

It became clear that Pohl and at least some of the other defense teams that did not know about the program would have to be read into it in order to draft a fully informed pro se advisement for bin Attash. Court was again done for the day.

This all seemed very mysterious; it became less so when the parties assembled again two days later, on October 22, as Pohl worked to push the pro se script forward. The fact that some teams had not been briefed on the Camp 7 program was tied to one of the biggest disputes of the first three years of the case—Pohl's first protective order governing the handling of classified information. Defense teams objected to the terms of the order, which would prevent them from sharing classified information with the defendants—who of course did not possess security clearances. This provision, they contended, would prevent them from providing effective assistance to their clients in a capital case. Lawyers also criticized an overall lack of detailed guidance on classification issues provided by the government. But Connell had decided to sign the Memorandum of Understanding related to the protective order back in 2013 in order to begin receiving classified discovery, which meant he could be briefed on the ACCM.

One of the last two holdouts opposing the protective order, Nevin on behalf of Mohammed, had signed the MOU the day before, on October 21, with reservations attached to preserve his complaints on appeal, as Pohl had allowed the teams to do. Nevin's statement of reservation said that his signature was "conditioned" on the fact that Pohl might remove him from the case if he did not sign, and that the MOU did not "signify an ability or constitute an agreement to be bound by rules" that the government had not adequately explained to him. The next day in court, Pohl appeared at his wits' end with James Harrington, the final holdout, who finally agreed to sign it after having another conversation with bin al Shibh.

The last wrinkle was that Bormann wanted to discuss the issue with Marine Brig. Gen. John Baker, the chief military lawyer overseeing all the defense teams, who had not been read into the program. Because the next day was Friday, the holy day for Muslims, when the defendants often skipped court, Bormann asked that Pohl not address the pro se issue with bin Attash until the following week.

Court was done for the week—a total bust by almost any reasonable measure. To any legal affairs reporter, however, it was also completely fascinating.

A month later, Carol broke the story confirming what we all assumed to be the nature of the program—a surveillance system that eavesdropped on anything the detainees did in Camp 7. She did this by comparing Pohl's first draft of the pro se advisement with the final draft that included an additional warning that the defendants would not have any privacy in their holding cells or communal areas. I wished I had thought of doing that.

* * *

The AP's Ben Fox decided to depart after the uneventful first week. Cmdr. Ross received permission for the three remaining journalists to stay at a hotel for two nights, on Friday and Saturday, as Pohl had decided to schedule a rare Sunday-morning session to make up for lost time. Because the two hotels on the main part of the base were full, we took a Friday-afternoon ferry back to the Leeward side to stay at its Navy Gateway Inn & Suites, a two-story motel type place.

If life is slow on Gitmo, it is practically nonexistent on the Leeward side, which has the air terminal, the lodge, and a convenience store with souvenirs, snacks, and alcohol. You could go for days on Leeward and run into less than a few dozen folks. The setting recalled images in my mind of the nondescript desert areas previously used for testing nuclear explosions. It also has a nice beach and a cafeteria, or "galley" in Navy parlance. I had already become a fan of the galley on the Windward side: prepared entrées, a cooked-to-order grill, a salad and fruit bar, a sandwich stand, and trays of pizza, all for $6 or less, depending on the time of day. With its serenity, the Leeward galley was an even more satisfying dining experience, though it closed at 6:30 p.m., and I missed the Saturday-night dinner window.

On the first night, with a modest influx of guests, the hotel opened the limited bar space, but did not do so on the second night, so we brought our own drinks and sat along with a scattering of other would-be patrons latching onto the decent Wi-Fi connection. As Carol and I sat at the bar, an older man recognized her and pulled up a seat. It was David Remes, who was something of a Gitmo legend for taking on the representation of at least fifteen detainees over the years, initially in a pro bono capacity at the white-shoe law firm of Covington & Burling. Remes didn't represent detainees charged in the commissions, but instead those who were uncharged and seeking their release through habeas petitions in federal courts or the administrative review procedures set up by the Bush and Obama administrations. Remes made headlines in 2008 when he lowered his pants down to his underwear at a news conference in Yemen, attempting to make a point about the humiliating strip searches endured by his clients at Guantanamo. He left Covington & Burling shortly thereafter.

Remes was on Gitmo to visit a few clients but could not get a room in the main part of the base, so he was stuck with us. In one sense, Remes was unusually prolific in his pro bono work, but in another sense he was a typical "Guantanamo lawyer" in terms of his role—the vast majority of detainees have never been charged with crimes. As epic as the 9/11 case was and would continue to be, it was just a tiny sliver of the Guantanamo story, a fact that felt overwhelming to me when talking to Remes. *If I stay on this assignment*, I wondered, *will I want to also cover what's going on with all the other detainees?* So much of the Guantanamo story had preceded my arrival, but a lot of the story remained.

It was a fun night, but the combination of exercising in the heat, the lack of food, cans of beer, and the decision to switch to Carol's vodka after I went through my beer left my stomach in tatters. I was shaky on Sunday morning as we waited under the canopy at ferry landing. I vomited violently into a toilet in a nearby bathroom about ninety minutes before Pohl was set to call the commission back to order, and I cursed myself as I wiped my watery eyes walking onto the ferry.

* * *

The bin Attash drama was a sideshow to the main event. Finally, we would hear from Campoamor-Sanchez, the special prosecutor who had been keeping Pohl abreast of the investigation into the bin al Shibh team for a year and a half. On Sunday morning, he told Pohl that he had an ironclad guarantee from the Justice Department that any investigation into Harrington and other bin al Shibh team members was over, and that no criminal charges were filed.

"There is no investigation, therefore there can be no conflict," Campoamor-Sanchez said. "So we believe this issue can be, in fact, decided today by the commission with a finding of no conflict."

The defense side of the courtroom wasn't buying it. Harrington told Pohl that he was concerned by a caveat in the Justice Department filing that he was no longer under investigation "at this time."

"Unless there is a more firm representation that there is nothing pending and they have no intention of reopening this allegation, I still think that it hangs out there," Harrington said.

About three weeks earlier, Reuters reporter David Rohde had broken the news that a focus of the FBI investigation was a phone call made by a translator on bin al Shibh's team from Guantanamo Bay to bin al Shibh's brother in Yemen, which concerned some team members as a potential violation of security protocols. The message was of the innocuous "study hard in school" variety that the translator was relating to bin al Shibh's nephew through the brother, but the FBI was concerned for a time that it might contain a coded message.

During the downtime of the first week, Harrington had stopped by the media center to chat. He wanted to meet outside on the assumption that the media center "had ears," but swarms of mosquitoes pushed us indoors. Harrington was seventy, four years older than Nevin. The two of them were the lead lawyers with the most experience—the other three were a full generation or more behind. He told us that the phone call detailed in the Reuters story was an important part—but not the entirety—of the FBI's focus in its investigation; it was frustrating to him that he was still in the dark about much of it.

When it was his turn to talk in court on Sunday, Nevin displayed Rohde's story on the courtroom monitor and argued that the government had investigated defense counsel for doing their job.

"What we have been waiting for the last year and a half about is an investigation based on something we are required by law to do in this case," Nevin said. "We are required in the course of doing a mitigation investigation to reach out to the family, to maintain a relationship with the family, and to provide them information about our clients and vice versa."

It was good to see Nevin in action and get some color for the profile I was supposed to write, even though I saw now he was just one character inside a giant, slow-moving plot. I knew what he looked like from Lesley Stahl's *60 Minutes* segment and some news photos, but he looked smaller to me in person. Nevin was trim, a shade under 5'11", with short gray hair and matching glasses that he intermittently pushed up at the podium, giving him a scholarly flair. He had not returned my emails in prior months about doing a follow-up interview, so the article was on hold. He apologized when I finally met him at the media center; he said he had been busy.

The litigation over the FBI infiltration was unusually dense, even by 9/11 case standards, but it illustrated why following the proceedings had become so difficult. Lawyers generally did not refer to the pleadings, called "appellate exhibits," by their substantive title, but their "AE" number. So the hundredth motion in the case was AE100. Then each subsequent pleading within the series was given a letter, so AE100A was followed by AE100B and, when the series moved past Z, the next in line was AE100AA. Lawyers typically spoke the military phonetic of the letters, so AE100BB would be talked about in court as "AE 100 Bravo Bravo" or "AE 100 Double Bravo."

The initial motion to abate the case over the FBI infiltration in April 2014 was AE292. Since then, so many sub-pleadings, supplements, responses, and rulings had been filed that even Pohl was not entirely sure what was pending. The only lawyer in court who appeared to know the status of every filing was Connell, who I quickly discovered to be the case's explainer in chief—often to the visiting media and NGOs but also to the court. I was astonished by Connell's summary, though I understood basically none of it.

"Separately pending is 292 Quadruple Yankee (292YYYY), which is our request to unseal the long series of classified and unclassified but all under-seal pleadings by the Special Review Team," Connell told Pohl. "Connected to that, a sort of footnote to 292 Quadruple Yankee, is that the Special Review Team has filed 292 Quintuple Delta (292DDDDD), which was although styled as a notice, is really a motion to approve redactions without, in our opinion, complying with the requirements of Military Commissions Rules of Evidence 506."

Connell added that 292 Quintuple Delta "could be seen as an unauthorized supplement to 292 Quadruple Yankee, or it can be seen as its own issue." He told Pohl that the judge first needed to resolve those issues before moving on "to the question of resolving 292 Romeo Romeo (292RR), the government's motion to reconsider, and 292 Sierra Sierra (292SS), the defense motion to reconsider."

Connell continued, "Now, 292 Sierra Sierra, the defense motion to reconsider, contains within it essentially two components. One of those is the ruling in 292 Quebec Quebec (292QQ) regarding AE 292 Lima. . ."

It sounded absurd, of course, almost as if Connell was joking with us. The next day, on October 26, as oral arguments drifted onward, I became aware of the accompanying physical chaos of the defense side of the courtroom, what was almost a near-constant churn of bodies and activity. Staffers came and went from the packed defense tables, and others came and went from a sixth table right in front of the viewing gallery, which was used as overflow space. More surprising was that the defendants often talked among themselves in court, between the tables, apparently loudly at times; lawyers later told me that the din of ongoing conversation was a regular source of distraction. We could not hear any of this through three panes of glass. On this day, as Connell argued again at the podium, Pohl stopped him and looked over to the first defense table.

"Mr. Mohammed, I don't mind you discussing with your co-accused, but please keep your voice down," Pohl said, then waited briefly for some acknowledgment. "Thank you."

Pohl ran an accommodating courtroom. All the lunch and afternoon breaks were scheduled around the detainees' prayer time.

Despite the lingering concerns of the defense teams, Pohl had what he needed from Campoamor-Sanchez to rule. He gave an oral ruling before lunch, saying that he was convinced that the investigation was closed and that there was "no actual conflict or potential conflict of interest" for Harrington or other members of the team. However, he ordered Campoamor-Sanchez to provide discovery to Harrington's team on the details of the investigation and to other teams that may have been affected. This way, as Harrington learned more information about the infiltration, he could raise again the possibility that he might be operating under a conflict.

The details of the investigation, as they were passed on to Harrington from the Special Review Team over the next year, turned out to be quite troubling—multiple team members had given troves of defense-team work product to federal investigators. Harrington and his remaining team were already dealing with the fallout from having to replace the fired or departed support staff that had been compromised. The fallout would continue for years for the bin al Shibh defense and the entire Military Commissions Defense Organization. In the years ahead, the defense teams would discover additional investigations into their work from various arms of the government, leading to new lines of litigation that swallowed up precious court time.

But for now, the case could move forward and the parties could begin working their way through the many pending pretrial motions, of which there were about three dozen, according to a tabulation that Martins gave the media prior to the hearing. First, however, Pohl had to deal with the bin Attash representation issue. As it turned out, bin Attash did not want to represent himself. Instead, he wanted a new lead lawyer to replace Bormann. On Wednesday of the second week, Pohl held a private or ex parte meeting with bin Attash and his legal team to hear his grievances and other concerns. On Thursday, he ruled from the bench that bin Attash did not have a valid reason for changing lawyers. Pohl called a recess so that the defendant could speak with his attorneys about the decision. Bin Attash used the recess to pray, laying his rug to the side of his defense table while guards stood watch.

The chaos was difficult to track, and having only a pen and paper in court didn't help. Back in June 2001, I was in a serious car accident in Mexico that left me with eight back and pelvic fractures and a lacerated spleen. The least serious injury at the time—which I didn't even realize I had until my second week in a hospital—was nerve damage in my right shoulder, arm, and thumb. It improved somewhat in the months that followed, but my writing has remained incredibly illegible. I learned an important lesson during my first 9/11 trip: If I didn't type up my notes shortly after court, much of what I saw might be lost to history.

* * *

During this era of the commissions, the last day of each pretrial session ended with a formal press conference in a briefing room located near the media center within the abandoned air hangar. Defense attorneys, Gen. Martins, and victim family members all got their turn at the podium. Predictably, Martins praised progress in the two-week session while defense teams said it revealed why nothing ever gets done.

While journalists can stay for the entirety of a session, victim family members and NGOs rotate out weekly, with new groups coming in on the weekend. The government did not bring down family members for the second week, as no one knew if there was going to be much court. Two family members were allowed to stay on for the second week: Colleen Kelly and her mom, JoAnne Kelly. Their brother and son, William Kelly Jr., died in the World Trade Center's North Tower on 9/11. We learned from family bios given to us that Bill Kelly didn't even work at the World Trade Center and was only there for a one-day conference at Windows on the World.

Colleen Kelly, a nurse in the Bronx, was also a founding member of September 11th Families for Peaceful Tomorrows, which promotes non-violent solutions to conflicts. She knew Carol from past trips and hung out with us a few times at the picnic tables. The organization became one of the NGOs approved to observe proceedings, and Kelly would make several more trips with us as a family member and NGO.

On this Friday afternoon, Kelly said she was excited to see the case move forward. She wished that more people could watch the proceedings, which could only be viewed at Guantanamo or in closed-circuit screenings at some military bases. A handful around the country are available to VFMs, while only one—at Fort Meade in Maryland—was open to media and the general public.

"I wish the entire world could watch what's happening at Guantanamo Bay," Kelly told the mostly empty briefing room. "We have nothing to hide."

It was a clever line to give to three journalists spread throughout a room that had a capacity for thirty or so—and to a camera at the back of the room that was making a recording that probably no one would ever watch. I included the quote in my fifth and final article about the session. A few Lawdragon articles were the only ones covering a particular day of court or legal issue, even though this was the reboot of the biggest case in US history.

Being part of the large muscle movement in reverse, for the return travel, was a grind that culminated in the "customs" process at Andrews—with only a few Customs and Border Protection (CBP) officers to process the entire flight. Kelly and I ended up chatting on the train all the way back to Penn Station. It was a Saturday night, Halloween 2015. We hugged goodbye in the evening chaos of Penn, and I went to go find my wife at a friend's get-together in Brooklyn. The Gitmo bubble made me feel fragile in the frenzy of New York. I knew that of the pending motions, many of them—nearly twenty of them—dealt with various defense efforts to get more information about how the CIA tortured their clients at secret overseas black sites. Lawyers had told me that some of these would be argued at the next session, scheduled for early December. That, I figured, I may as well see.

CHAPTER 4

Dirty Laundry. December 2015.

To laypeople, it's not always obvious why the former CIA program became such a dominant issue in the 9/11 case. The Military Commissions Act of 2009, which reformed the Bush-era law of 2006, more strictly prohibited the use at trial of evidence obtained through torture or cruel, inhuman, or degrading treatment. For this reason, the prosecution could not use what the defendants said at the CIA black sites against them if a trial ever happened. Prosecutors did not and would not refer to the past treatment as "torture," but they would acknowledge that the CIA interrogations were "coercive." Instead, they planned to use incriminating statements that the five defendants made to FBI agents on Guantanamo Bay in early 2007, about four months after their transfer from the CIA black sites. The detainees were not read their *Miranda* rights, nor were they given access to lawyers. But the government claimed these were normal, interview-based sessions without any of the CIA's "enhanced" techniques—what the FBI calls its "rapport-based" approach to questioning suspects. From the government's perspective, these were "clean" statements free of coercion and completely admissible.

President Bush was surprisingly transparent about his administration's plans to clean up the CIA's past conduct in order to get some cases ready for trial. In a White House speech on September 6, 2006, Bush announced both the transfer of fourteen CIA high-value detainees to Guantanamo Bay, including the five 9/11 defendants, and his proposal to create a new military commissions system to prosecute them. Bush acknowledged that the CIA used an "alternative set of procedures" in the once-secret program but insisted that the "United States does not torture." He said that the CIA interrogators had mostly gotten what they needed from the detainees in terms of valuable intelligence, and now it was time to prosecute them so that the victims of 9/11 and their families could get justice.

But he also acknowledged that governing case law had turned against his administration and further called into question the legality of the CIA program. The Bush team proposed its new commissions system in response to the US Supreme Court's decision in the 2006 *Hamdan v. Rumsfeld* case, which invalidated the first attempt at commissions through executive order. In rejecting that system, the Supreme Court held that Common Article 3 of the Geneva Conventions—including bans on humiliating and degrading treatment—applied to the war against al Qaeda. Bush said in his White House speech that this "vague" language could be used by some people, including American judges, to conclude that CIA and military interrogators had committed war crimes. Common Article 3 also requires that captured detainees have access to "a regularly constituted court" before being subjected to any criminal sentences or executions. Whether the military court created in response to *Hamdan*, and later reformed in 2009, fit the description of "regularly constituted" was already one of the case's enduring disputes by the time I showed up and would remain one of the biggest.

The decision to create a court was not a foregone conclusion, or even necessary. Certain parts of the government and some associated with the CIA program had wanted to hold the high-value detainees in secret detention permanently, either to hide illegal conduct or keep them as a resource for anti-terrorism initiatives, or both. The prior year, however, in November 2005, Dana Priest, then with the *Washington Post*, had broken the news of the secret overseas detention program—that article and the follow-up reporting, along with investigations by human rights groups, would have made lifelong incommunicado detention impossible. Still, if forced to bring Mohammed and the others "into the open," as Bush said in his speech, the administration did not need to prosecute them. The position of the Bush administration (and later the Obama administration) was that detainees could be held legally for the duration of the war on terror, which had no end in sight. To comply with Supreme Court decisions, detainees merely had to be given a chance to challenge their detention. Most Guantanamo Bay detainees would never be charged.

Nevertheless, not long after Bush's speech, many of the FBI agents who had investigated the attacks in the months and years after 9/11 were assembled to form the "clean teams" that would get the presumptively clean confessions on Guantanamo Bay for use in the new court system. These statements became much of the government's most important evidence, the reliance on which was both absurd and legally unsupportable in the views of defense teams. These lawyers believed that there could never be any clean confessions following the years of torture and isolation that their clients suffered after their captures between 2002 and 2003. In a regular criminal case, if a suspect is roughed up in secret and later confesses on camera or signs a confession—perhaps to different interrogators than those who did the roughing up—the suspect's lawyer will want the details of the coercion to prove the taint and convince a judge to suppress the confession. The case against the 9/11 defendants and some of the other high-value detainees presented this scenario to a degree of intensity that was unprecedented in American history—confessions following three to four years of often brutal treatment, isolation, and relentless questioning. Defense teams wanted evidence of this past torture to argue for the suppression of the FBI statements and also to present a mitigation case against the death penalty in the event of any convictions. In their view, the US government had lost the moral authority to execute the defendants based on the scale of the government's illegal conduct and the punishment it had already inflicted on them.

The dispute over the admissibility of the FBI statements would have to come before any trial; it was, by far, the biggest pretrial issue the case would face. But preceding even that would be disputes over how much evidence and how many witnesses the defense would have access to in building their suppression cases, which would be exceedingly complicated given that so much about the CIA program remained secret. Martins's team initially had a narrow view of what it should turn over from the RDI program. The government's first determination was that the teams should only receive the statements their clients made in CIA custody that had anything to do with the 9/11 attacks, which in summarized form totaled several hundred pages. But by the start of the December 2015 hearing, Martins knew that Judge Pohl would not accept this position.

At the time, Pohl was also the military judge in the separate death penalty military commission for Abd al Rahim al Nashiri, another former CIA detainee who had been charged as a lead planner in the October 2000 bombing of the USS *Cole* in Yemen. In that case the year before, in 2014, Pohl ruled that al Nashiri's team was entitled to a far greater amount of discovery related to the defendant's time in CIA custody. Pohl came up with ten categories of discoverable RDI information, including the chronology of the different sites where al Nashiri was held; how he was transported between the black sites; his conditions of confinement at the sites, along with photographic and written documentation of these details; summaries of interrogations; the identifications and employment histories of interrogators, guards, and medical staff at the black sites who had contact with al Nashiri; and official documents related to the approval and use of the enhanced techniques at the sites, among other areas.

Critically, Pohl reasoned that the details of al Nashiri's CIA treatment would be relevant both to defense efforts to suppress his subsequent statements to the FBI and to mitigate against the death penalty. Seeing the writing on the wall, Martins was planning to submit an RDI discovery plan that used the same "ten category construct" for the 9/11 case. He would use Pohl's ruling in the al Nashiri case as a framework for consolidating the various pending motions in the 9/11 case.

As in the al Nashiri case, the government would not be dumping all of this information on the defense teams—something the defense lawyers pointed out was theoretically possible, given that their roles already required them to get the highest possible security clearances. Instead, the prosecution team would mostly be providing substitute and summary forms of evidence, as authorized by the Military Commissions Act. These provisions mirror those contained in the Classified Information Procedures Act, or CIPA, used in federal court cases to protect classified information. In his meetings with the media, Martins would often say that these CIPA procedures were "well-established in national security cases," which is true. It's also true that the CIPA process played a high-profile role in the only other criminal case brought for the 9/11 attacks, that against the suspected "twentieth hijacker," Zacarias Moussaoui, a French citizen indicted in US District Court for the Eastern District of Virginia in December 2001. (Moussaoui was arrested in Minnesota and never transferred to Guantanamo Bay.) In that case, after lengthy litigation at both the trial and appellate levels, the trial judge and the parties ended up fashioning substitute statements from potentially helpful witnesses for Moussaoui—including 9/11 suspects Khalid Sheikh Mohammed, Ramzi bin al Shibh, and Mustafa al Hawsawi—who were being held at CIA black sites. Moussaoui eventually pleaded guilty in 2005; a jury gave him life without parole instead of the death sentence sought by prosecutors.

Still, there was no precedent for the volume of classified information that would have to go through the substitute-and-summary process in the 9/11 military commission. In federal court cases, the government may need to summarize some number of documents or witness statements, or conceal the identity of a single witness—not millions of pages, not hundreds of witnesses. In the 9/11 case on Guantanamo, the government's effort to protect "sources and methods" prioritized maintaining the covert identities of CIA personnel as well as names of the countries where the United States set up its black sites. The latter obsession was somewhat curious given that work by journalists and human rights groups had revealed many of the host nations of the black sites, such as Thailand, Poland, Afghanistan, Lithuania, and others. But the government would never declassify this information and would endeavor to keep details about these relationships as secret at possible. The prosecution had already told Pohl that the government would accept dismissal of the case before providing the actual locations to defense teams as part of the discovery process. Defense teams understood the need for some secrecy, particularly with respect to covert agents. But they suspected that the CIPA-like substitute-and-summary process would be used to hide embarrassing details about the torture program and make investigating the abuse of their clients far more difficult.

The CIPA process would be enormously labor intensive for the government, which was obligated to go through all the known RDI information—the totality of which, one might surmise, was at least the six million pages that went into producing the Senate study of the CIA program. As the first step in the discovery process, members of the prosecution team would make a determination about what documents were relevant to the case—an opaque step that would forever concern the defense teams. The prosecution would then coordinate with "the original classification authority," or OCA, essentially the owner of the information, to summarize information and redact portions from the case-relevant documents to hide details. Thousands of CIA cables documenting the detainees' treatment, conditions, and statements would be rewritten in summarized form, without specific dates or identifying information related to personnel or locations. The most important OCA was the CIA, but the list included many other government agencies that had a hand in post-9/11 interrogations, the operations of the Guantanamo Bay detention facility, and the war on terror more generally.

As part of this system, the prosecution then had to submit the proposed summaries and substitute evidence to Pohl, who was tasked with comparing the substitutions to the original evidence. Pohl's role in this process—given the volume of classified material—would also be unique in the annals of American criminal history. Under the law, Pohl could only approve the substitutions and summarized evidence if he determined that they put the defense teams in "substantially the same" position as if they had the complete or original classified versions. To help make this assessment, Pohl would hold ex parte meetings with individual defense teams to hear their theories of the case so he could try to put himself in their shoes. Eventually, the defense would receive the discovery, the most important of which for RDI purposes would be CIA cables, reports, and other documentation of what happened to their clients at the black sites.

At the time, it was clear to me that Martins was confident he could manage the CIA's role in the 9/11 case and that the pretrial phase would move forward steadily, if slowly. I had no idea at the time whether this was naive, given that so much would be out of his control, which made him something of a middleman between the court and the intelligence community. But I knew his confidence was based in a career lined with achievement. He graduated first in his class at West Point in 1983; spent time at Oxford University as a Rhodes Scholar; and served in the infantry, becoming a judge advocate in 1990, when he received his JD from Harvard Law. Citing a consistently distinguished career as a soldier and lawyer, the law school awarded him its highest honor, the Medal of Freedom, in May 2011, a handful of months before his assignment to the commissions that came while he was serving in Afghanistan.

Among his many past assignments, Martins had co-led a task force on war-on-terror detention policies that worked closely with the Guantanamo Review Task Force, which assessed the status of detainees and their suitability for prosecution. He also played a role in drafting the 2009 version of the Military Commissions Act. Martins explained in an April 2012 speech at Harvard Law School that he had requested the chief prosecutor's role to be his last assignment in the military—and that he not be considered for a new job or a promotion thereafter—for the sake of continuity and to avoid any "suspicion of self-advancing motives." He was scheduled to retire in 2014 before he received a three-year extension. Martins was committed to seeing this through. By staying in his role, he would never be elevated beyond a one-star general.

* * *

That the 9/11 case was finally turning its attention to disputes over CIA evidence made the one-week hearing in early December 2015 historic, at least according to James Connell, the lead lawyer for Ammar al Baluchi. On December 11, Connell told Judge Pohl that anyone later studying the case would look back on this very day as the moment the case entered its "second phase" for finally addressing defense motions to compel information about the CIA's Rendition, Detention, and Interrogation (RDI) Program. The case had thus far been consumed with a litany of preliminary legal issues and, of course, the various intrusions into the defense teams, from the hidden microphones to the FBI infiltration.

The first CIA motion up for oral argument was one to compel the government to turn over correspondence about the RDI program between the White House, the Department of Justice, and the CIA. Connell said that the American torture program was different from those of earlier Roman, Spanish Inquisition, and Nazi periods—and from the more recent examples of Argentina and Chile—because of its heightened legalistic nature.

"This was not carried out by a rogue set of individuals or carried out in the dark of night with no information provided back to headquarters," Connell said. "Instead, this was a system well integrated into the American bureaucracy which involves lawyers, it involves security and interrogation professionals, it includes political leaders."

Less than a week after the 9/11 attacks, on September 17, 2001, President Bush signed a covert memorandum authorizing the CIA to capture and detain terrorism suspects. The following spring, the agency came up with a series of interrogation measures that would become known as the "enhanced interrogation techniques," which the Justice Department determined to be legal. The memos from the Justice Department's Office of Legal Counsel, and the associated input and memos from legal offices in the White House, CIA, and Pentagon, created a paper trail in the first few years after the 9/11 attacks that became known as the "Torture Memos" or the "Torture Papers," many of which were declassified. But defense teams wanted additional correspondence between the agencies, as well as the distribution channels showing which officials received which documents. Connell told Pohl that the nonlinear "feedback loops" between the various officials and agencies would provide important information about what the CIA did and what they were given permission to do at the highest levels of the government.

In just my second 9/11 hearing, it was easy to see that Connell and the rest of al Baluchi's team were the most media friendly among the five teams. Prior to the December hearing, they sent an "unofficial docket" to the media explaining the various motions up for argument. Connell also stopped by the media center after the scheduling conference that Pohl held after arriving on the base to write an updated "order of march" for the planned week on the whiteboard in the media center. The al Baluchi team also held an opening night barbeque for the NGOs at one of the town houses where team members stayed, which we skipped on this trip.

Keeping track of all the lawyers on the case was still basically impossible, but getting to know each team through its lead lawyer was helpful. Carol had told me that Connell was a Buddhist and that most members of the team were vegetarian, and they certainly gave off a positive vibe. Connell did not exactly look like a Buddha, but his fully shaved head and friendly disposition made for an easy association. Each team had their own media philosophy; most felt obligated, if not always comfortable, to engage with the press. Only one team, that for Walid bin Attash led by Cheryl Bormann, generally avoided us out of a belief that public comments would not contribute to the ultimate goal of preventing his execution. The al Baluchi team had long since arrived at the opposite conclusion, believing that any attention on the client, the case, or Guantanamo Bay generally—good, bad, or indifferent—was a net positive for the team's effort.

Connell and al Baluchi's long-serving lead military defense lawyer, Lt. Col. Sterling Thomas of the Air Force, would do as many interviews as journalists wanted, on camera or off. The team also had a new civilian lawyer, Alka Pradhan, who had previously represented Guantanamo Bay detainees in habeas cases at the UK-based organization Reprieve. She, too, would actively engage with the media and would eventually be the subject of a lengthy 2017 *New York Times Magazine* feature, "Alka Pradhan vs. Gitmo." With my article on Nevin on hold, I asked Connell to be the subject of my first Guantanamo lawyer profile. He agreed, and we set aside part of the December week's downtime for an interview. His effort to push forward litigation over CIA-related evidence would make the piece timely.

"From the beginning, the prosecution's approach to discovery has been delay, deny, and degrade," Connell told Pohl on December 11, as he continued his argument. "This is the third dodge that the prosecution has tried to make on the CIA discovery."

When he got to the podium, Gen. Martins took issue with Connell's characterization of the government's approach to discovery. He conveyed to Pohl what he told us in the prehearing media session: Now that all the teams had signed their MOUs related to classified information, the classified discovery process could begin in earnest. The government had already turned over about 300,000 pages of unclassified information to the defense teams related to the prosecution's case in chief—evidence it planned to use at trial related to the defendants' alleged roles in the 9/11 plot. But now it could start with the classified tranches, including evidence about the CIA program that the defense teams were entitled to receive to try to undercut the government's case.

He assured Pohl that the prosecution understood its discovery obligations and was "going to turn over a lot of stuff" related to the RDI program. The Senate's executive summary on the CIA program had already declassified large amounts of information; the prosecution was now in the process of going through the entire still-classified report and the underlying documentation to find more evidence to give to the teams.

"We have been working seven days a week trying to produce this," Martins said.

More importantly for this hearing, the prosecution's plan to use the ten categories of RDI information from the al Nashiri case—and to submit most of the evidence to Pohl in substitute or summarized form under the CIPA provisions—meant that Martins didn't want to argue Connell's motion this week, or apparently any time soon. He proposed holding off on arguments in favor of "a consolidated approach" that dealt with all eighteen defense motions to compel CIA evidence along with the nearly three dozen discovery requests that had not yet entered litigation. Pohl sided with the government, giving Martins two weeks to file a list of pending RDI discovery motions and a plan for handling them across the ten categories. The December hearing would not be as historic, or dramatic, as we hoped. But the case had still turned a page.

The week was also instructive on how many of the other pending motions were tied to the CIA program, even if they did not explicitly involve disputes over evidence. No issue riled observers of the case—to the extent they still existed—more than the motion by defense teams to prohibit the JTF-GTMO prison staff from using female guards to move the defendants to court and to their legal meetings, which involved some amount of unwanted touching. Defense lawyers claimed the use of female guards violated their clients' religious beliefs and also retraumatized them because of the sexual humiliation endured at CIA black sites. This was an example of what I soon learned was a common source of irritation on the defense side and, therefore, of occasional litigation—changes in prison protocols or to its "Standard Operating Procedures," or SOPs, which often shifted with new leadership or when a new guard force rotated in every nine months. The SOPs could include everything from how the guard force moves the detainees to what items legal staff can bring to client meetings. The rotations also changed the personnel who staffed the courtroom gallery, which could have a big impact on the level of stress associated with watching proceedings in person.

Pohl had issued a temporary restraining order against the use of female guards while the litigation played out. In what retrospectively seems like overkill, I wrote three stories during the week based on the testimony from current and former guards, who said the ban created morale and staffing problems. The best day involved some testy exchanges between David Nevin and Army Col. David Heath, who at the time ran the detention operations for JTF-GTMO. At one point, Heath acknowledged that male and female guards already had some different assignments with the detainees. For example, female guards did not perform frisk searches and they did not observe detainees when they were naked, which is something that happened at the CIA black sites. Heath said that the different tasks did not violate the principle of gender-neutrality and instead was based in "common decency" and "American values." He added gratuitously that, similarly, a female guard would not be allowed to see Nevin unclothed.

"It makes me a little uncomfortable that you imagine me as a detainee," Nevin said.

Several of us in the viewing gallery chuckled at this. Nevin did not.

* * *

At the end of the December hearing, Martins more or less quoted the entire CIPA-like provisions of the Military Commissions Act verbatim in his prepared statement to the media, a version of which was always distributed either before or after the chief prosecutor took his turn at the podium to answer questions.

"The prosecution will invoke these procedures for the small proportion of remaining classified information to provide the defense," the December 11, 2015, statement read.

Given that the defense teams believed they were still entitled to the entire Senate report and its underlying information—and a motion to compel the full report remained pending—Martins's characterization implied a profound difference of opinion regarding the government's remaining discovery obligations. The teams doubted that the government would willingly live up to its responsibilities under commission rules and *Brady v. Maryland*, the seminal 1963 Supreme Court case requiring the production of favorable evidence. During the press conference, defense lawyers who hazarded a guess predicted that a trial was five years out. Martins disagreed but declined to give his own prediction.

At that point, I didn't picture myself coming to Guantanamo Bay for many years to come. But I could feel myself becoming hooked on the story—that it was, in fact, filling a journalistic void. I've only had two journalism jobs over the years. Between 2000 and 2005 I was a reporter at the *Los Angeles Daily Journal*. I did well despite having no prior experience, winning multiple awards from the Los Angeles Press Club and three times being a "Print Journalist of the Year Finalist." And while it was a legal trade publication, I was lucky to be one of the few reporters to focus mostly on general interest issues that other papers were covering—immigration, the war on terror, the war on drugs, political corruption, or other high-profile criminal and civil cases. But I was still on the fringes of journalism, never having made it to the mainstream. I was beginning to suspect that this created a feeling of inadequacy that my time at Gitmo was helping to alleviate. After all, here I was holding down the fort for the media in the front row of the viewing gallery and at the press conferences on Guantanamo Bay.

I also hadn't been part of a newsroom since 2005, when I left the *Daily Journal* to help start Lawdragon. The company began operating remotely in 2014, with in-person work sessions largely limited to me discussing business over meals or drinks with Katrina Dewey, Lawdragon's founder, CEO, and publisher, whose enthusiasm and skillful editing of all my Guantanamo dispatches was as important as my own dedication to the work. Staying out at the picnic tables with Carol and a few other reporters, and maybe a few sources or some interesting folks from the NGO contingent, was great fun. I realized how much I missed this camaraderie, a satisfaction heightened by its formation in one of the strangest and most notorious places on the planet.

CHAPTER 5

Movie Day. February 2016.

Guantanamo Bay is best known for its prison, not its court system. For that reason, I jumped at the chance to attend a tour of the detention facility when a deputy director of public affairs for the prison operation at Joint Task Force—Guantanamo (JTF-GTMO) mentioned it to me. These tours, of course, never included a visit to Camp 7, the top secret location that held the defendants and the other high-value detainees. Still, I had read so much about the detention facility that I wanted to at least see the place. This meant I would spend most of the month away from Brooklyn, as February also had a two-week hearing in the 9/11 case.

The military operation in charge of the prison had hosted reporters since the day the Pentagon detention facility opened, in some eras running four- or five-day tours for the media. The current iteration was packed mainly into one day, with arrival on the island the night before. JTF-GTMO and the US Naval Base are under US Southern Command, or SOUTHCOM, which is based in Doral, Florida, so the trip originated from South Florida. I flew to Miami on Sunday, February 7, and stayed with Carol, who the following morning drove us to a small airport, called Landmark Aviation, on the outskirts of the city. Seven journalists boarded an Air Force–piloted propeller plane that, despite our close proximity to Cuba, would take two and a half hours to get there. We were given baggage weight limits of forty pounds each.

"We know you have many options when flying to Guantanamo Bay," the pilot deadpanned over the intercom, to great comic effect, as we approached the base. "We appreciate you choosing the United States Air Force."

The prison tours were a decidedly higher-class experience than covering the commissions, at least with respect to housing. Instead of the tents at Camp Justice, we were put up in spacious town houses. Much of the naval base is filled with suburban subdivisions that are short drives off the main roads, either Sherman Avenue, which runs along most of the base, or Kittery Beach Road, which connects the downtown area to the detention zone. Each subdivision has its own name—something like "Iguana Terrace" or "Caribbean Terrace" or, more counterintuitively, "Nob Hill"—with clusters of stucco houses heavy on pastel greens and blues, and plenty of beige. They often look like movie sets, straight out of *Edward Scissorhands* or some other version of a not-quite-real world. During my first trips to the base, when we drove around to kill time, I noticed that we'd never seem to see people working on their cars or cleaning their garages or enjoying coffee in their screened-in porches. For the tour, we stayed in "East Caravella," a more Soviet-inspired network of generously spaced out gray stucco town houses that were used for visitors on shorter stays. We had visited these town houses previously, as some members of the defense teams stayed here during court hearings.

Early on Tuesday morning, JTF-GTMO public affairs personnel picked us up in an oversized white van and drove us down Kittery Beach Road, eventually through the guarded gate to enter the detention zone. Carol and I knew most of the prison media team because they also provided support to the commissions; these were some of the same people who drove us around during the commission trips and monitored us during court. JTF-GTMO always had a chief spokesperson who would serve for a year or longer, but the support staff under that person was always a rotating public affairs unit from the Army National Guard, which changed every nine months. The unit then was led by Capt. Gregory McElwain, who in his normal life was a married father and teacher in Pennsylvania.

My first tour, well-managed within the obvious time limitations, was a total blur. The detention zone is basically one long road that curves along the shoreline, with trailers, offices, a cafeteria, and the actual detention camps spread across either side of the road. At the time, JTF-GTMO had approximately 2,000 people, roughly divided between 1,700 troops and 300 civilians. Of the 1,700 troops, about 1,200 made up the force that guarded the remaining detainees, which by this trip had shrunk to ninety-one. Most of them lived in Camp 6—a minimum-security facility with communal living—and Camp 5, a maximum-security facility for less compliant or noncompliant detainees. We spoke with the officers from both camps in an empty cell block of Camp 6, where we were also able to enter a sample cell.

The Officer in Charge, or "OIC," of Camp 5 said that the most common form of protest for her noncompliant population was "splashing," which involved attempting to hit guards with a mix of bodily fluids and waste, though she said this was rare. This officer and some of the other personnel could only be photographed from the neck down. That was the same policy for detainees, whom we were able to view and film from a rotunda in Camp 6 that had one-way glass looking into the communal area. There weren't many detainees milling about; a few were hanging out, preparing meals, and another turned on one of the satellite TVs in the corner.

We visited the medical center, where the head doctor there took questions on forced feeding of hunger strikers. What the military calls "enteral feeding" is done by flowing Ensure through a tube that is inserted into the nose and connects to the stomach. The doctor said that very few detainees were actively engaged in hunger strikes, though he did not provide an exact number. We also met with the OIC of "detainee programs" at the media library, a large trailer that had a collection of some 34,000 books, magazines, and DVDs. Detainee programs also included a number of courses on topics like personal health, finance, communications, and résumé writing. This is where I heard for the first time what I had read about previously: Detainees loved the *Harry Potter* books.

The tour included a few on-the-record interviews of senior personnel who could be photographed. It was good to see Col. Heath, the commander of detention operations, away from the witness stand; he was friendlier to us than he was to the defense lawyers who examined him over the female-guard dispute. Heath said that all the criticism directed at the detention facility from around the world could have a negative effect on morale if left unaddressed; he said it was his job to regularly remind them that "we're the good guys."

"These kids do a great job," he said.

The commander of SOUTHCOM at the time, Navy Adm. Kurt Tidd, was on the base at the time and also took questions. He said that JTF-GTMO had succeeded in its primary mission of providing for the "safe and humane" care and custody of detainees captured in the global war on terror. Now, he said, it was important to fulfill President Obama's policy to close the detention facility. By this tour, an additional thirty-six detainees had been approved for release by the administration's interagency parole-board process, called the Periodic Review Board. The task for finding nations to take in these detainees belonged to the State Department.

Between meetings, we got our versions of the same B-roll or establishing shots that have filled the newspapers and airwaves over the years—guard towers, the outside fencing of the detention camps, and the giant "Honor Bound" sign that is the centerpiece of the zone's main intersection near the entry gate. A few smaller signs along the road also get a decent amount of media attention, one with a rotating "Value of the Week" and the other with a number assigned to "Days Since Last Alcohol Related Incident"—a data point I failed to note down, unbelievably.

The public affairs team did the "operational security" review of our photos and footage at the air terminal on Tuesday night—which I wrote in my notes as having "generally proceeded amicably"—before a return flight that got us to Miami before midnight. I crashed with Carol again before catching a flight to DC, where I stayed with Jeff and Kristin for a few nights before taking an early car to Joint Base Andrews on Saturday, February 12. Four days after checking out of the town houses for prison visitors, I was back on the base, this time as a court reporter. Capt. McElwain's team drove us to Camp Justice to drop off our luggage at the tents and partake in another operational security briefing. As we approached the media center, I felt a sense of panic: It was dreadfully hot, and I was already physically drained and mentally sick of the place. I felt trapped. The December trip was a breeze, but I was reminded of the paradoxical nature of the two-week October trip. Court was endlessly confusing and exhausting, and I also had to keep up with all my other Lawdragon work. Yet filling time on the base, where almost nothing happens—where I had eaten at O'Kelly's four times before the middle of the first week—was a constant challenge.

I also knew that it would be another long stint of limited communications with my wife, Fiona. Back then, the base did not have commercial cell service. The only way to call home was getting a calling card from the Naval Exchange and using the landline phones in the media center, which did not offer much privacy except late at night. It was possible to latch onto Wi-Fi service at places like O'Kelly's or the bowling alley, which would allow for some texting and a few hard-to-hear phone conversations, but journalists spent most of their time in Camp Justice and had no internet access outside of the media center. On Gitmo I was both overworked and bored, not to mention bloated and unhealthy, while also being far removed from the most important people in my life. The panic eventually receded in the bustle of arriving-weekend errands and meetings, and as night fell on the base I was excited to hit up O'Kelly's again.

* * *

Movie Day. February 2016.

Later in the first week, on February 18, 2016, Judge Pohl double-checked with Gen. Martins that the government was committed to using the "ten category construct" for providing CIA-related information to the defense teams, which he had proposed at the end of 2015.

"I am not asking you to love it or embrace it, but you are not going to contest this framework and, as a start-up, you agree that's the plan we will use in this case," Pohl said.

"That's the plan we are proposing," Martins responded.

Martins promised Pohl that his team would work "seven days a week" to make sure he received their proposed substitutions and summaries of CIA evidence in about eight months, by September 30, 2016. The government would eventually have a massive team of dozens of lawyers, paralegals, analysts, and others working the summary-and-substitution process. Pohl sensed how much work was coming his way, and he pointed out the obvious by saying that the defense would not be receiving all the discovery on October 1, given his legal obligation to review the material for its adequacy. Clearly, this was going to extend well into 2017.

"If I don't approve them, and I send them back to you, then we have to revisit the adequacy of the summaries," Pohl said.

"Your Honor, we are very aware of that, with the back-and-forth that may be necessary," Martins said.

Facing arguments by defense teams who felt the categories were limiting, Pohl also said that the evidence—whenever it was approved—may not be the full scope of RDI information produced to the teams. He told Cheryl Bormann, arguing on behalf of Walid bin Attash, who still wanted her fired from the case, that the framework was a starting point and that they could file discovery motions that fell outside the ten categories.

"I will remind you of that somewhere down the line," Bormann responded.

As it turned out, James Connell reminded Pohl after lunch that day. In the afternoon, Connell walked to the podium to present his argument in support of a motion to compel the government to turn over communications between the CIA and the makers of the film *Zero Dark Thirty*, including the director Kathryn Bigelow and screenwriter Mark Boal.

"As far as I can tell, there is nothing related to these matters in the government's ten categories," Connell said, clearly to the chagrin of the right side of the courtroom.

Connell explained that the character "Ammar," who is tortured in several early scenes of the movie, was based on his client, Ammar al Baluchi.

In court, al Baluchi, then thirty-eight, was a tall and somewhat dashing figure, contrasted with his short and stout uncle three tables ahead of him. He often wore large sunglasses, which according to his team were not for stylistic purposes but to mitigate against crippling headaches. His torture included repeated bouts of "walling," or being slammed backward against a wall, which his lawyers said left him with a traumatic brain injury and a series of other ailments.

Zero Dark Thirty, which came out in 2012, dramatized the work of a CIA agent attempting to locate Osama bin Laden and a Navy seal team's invasion of his compound in Pakistan. I remembered mostly liking it. Among the defense teams and other human rights professionals, however, the movie was a shameless and dangerous piece of torture propaganda that helped the CIA push forward its narrative that the torture program worked. In the film, the character Ammar provides information that helps lead intelligence officials to target bin Laden's location in Pakistan. Connell told Pohl that the CIA, as part of this public relations campaign, "provided access to CIA facilities and personnel to the filmmakers," which meant they had some details and information not available to defense teams.

The lights dimmed so that Connell could show clips from the movie to illustrate his point. The torture scenes showing a beaten and sleep-deprived Ammar being water doused and crammed inside a coffin-like box felt less Hollywood and more documentary when watching them with five of the men who actually went through the abuse. Their backs to the viewing gallery, the defendants sat motionless and watched quietly as the court played a re-creation of their years of misery and isolation from which they probably felt they'd never escape. It was unsettling.

At one point, Connell stopped the movie after a scene in which Ammar is standing on a mat, pushed around by interrogators, and told he would be punished if he stepped off that mat. Connell told Judge Pohl that type of detail never came to his team from the government.

"The only way that these filmmakers would have known about that technique to include it in this film is by hearing it from these CIA officers because they certainly did not hear it from Mr. al Baluchi," Connell said from the podium.

Connell told Pohl that the communications between the CIA and the filmmakers could be another stream of information to help defense teams paint a more complete picture of the past torture.

"Okay, I understand," Pohl said. "Thank you."

Like the other lead defense lawyers, Connell had his own law practice and was a Pentagon contractor working for the Military Commissions Defense Organization. From my profile of him, which had just come out the prior month, I knew that he had defended many death penalty cases in the Virginia area. He also handled the failed habeas petition for "DC Sniper" John Allen Muhammad and attended Muhammad's execution by lethal injection in November 2009. As the prosecution got up to make its counterargument, Connell returned to the fourth defense table and sat next to his team's lead military defense lawyer, Air Force Lt. Col. Sterling Thomas, who is also completely bald. Though Thomas is black and Connell is white, from a darkened viewing gallery they looked like twins. Both attorneys had talked openly about the constructive and meaningful relationship, a friendship of sorts, that they and other team members had developed with al Baluchi over the years. One point of confusion for newcomers is that the prosecution and the judge, and the charge sheet for that matter, refer to al Baluchi as Ali Abdul Aziz Ali, or "Mr. Ali" in court, as it's his birth name. Connell said that he has gone by Ammar al Baluchi, an alias he used at one point, because it was the name used by his torturers at the black sites.

During one of our interviews, Connell explained to me that al Baluchi refused to talk to him for almost two years after the five defendants were re-charged in the Obama-era military commissions, in April 2011, which was about a year before the court arraignment. Connell wasn't surprised by the lack of trust: He was, after all, paid by the government that tortured his client, and half of his team wore military uniforms. A change happened in August 2013. Connell and other members from his team were the first to visit the Camp 7 detention facility that housed the fourteen former CIA captives—a right the defense teams secured from Pohl over the prosecution's objection. On the trip there, guards drove Connell and two team members in a van with the windows covered in circles for forty-five minutes to obscure its location. A prison combat camera photographer took hundreds of photos requested by the team, though was not allowed access to all areas. Eventually, the three team members sat with al Baluchi on the floor in his cell. Other Camp 7 detainees in the same tier had not eaten so that they could give their prison-issued halal meals to the visitors, enabling al Baluchi to properly host his team for dinner during the court-sanctioned twelve-hour visit.

"During that meeting, he said, 'You know, I think we could work together,'" Connell told me. "'Sometimes we'll agree and sometimes we won't agree but that's no different from any other relationship.' And from then on out we've had a strong working relationship."

Connell stressed to me, and to anyone who would listen, that most of what happens in the case happens outside of court. The hearings took place for only a week or two every four to six weeks, and they only addressed the motions that had been fully briefed and were ready for oral argument before the judge. His time at the podium was merely a ten-to-thirty-minute topper to a long process that preceded it. He was proud of the mix of military and civilian professionals who staffed the team.

Capital defense teams are ethically required to simultaneously build a trial defense as well as a mitigation case for sentencing, on the assumption that an execution is a possible outcome. In the 9/11 case, this effort had already taken defense teams around the world, in light of the sprawling nature of the alleged conspiracy—not to mention the many locations where the CIA was suspected of running black sites. Finding witnesses and putting together a complete narrative would take an enormous amount of time and work. The trips posed challenges. Connell told me a few anecdotes about arriving in a country (he could not say which) and being followed around by whatever allied government entity had been tipped off. Camp 7 personnel also seized DVDs that Connell's team had made of investigative trips to al Baluchi's former homes in Dubai and Kuwait, which were for mitigation purposes. The camp held on to them for two months, without any explanation, before finally returning the DVDs to al Baluchi.

To me, the Guantanamo court felt like a real court—maybe even "a regularly constituted" one—especially with the way Pohl ran things. If anything, he was more relaxed and more courteous than many federal and state judges I had seen in action. The Military Commissions Act created a court that was mostly based on the military's courts-martial system, with some elements of federal courts mixed in. But there were some big differences with the military commissions. One of the biggest and most-often cited was the much wider allowance of hearsay evidence that would not be allowed in a court-martial or federal prosecution. For Connell, the biggest difference was that he could not subpoena witnesses as he investigated the case and built a defense. The Military Commissions Act required that defense counsel have access to witnesses and evidence "comparable" to a federal court, but it was up to the prosecution team to produce or deny them. If the government denied the request, defense teams could file a motion to compel a witness with the judge. This set up many disputes over witnesses. Defense teams had to make requests for expert consultants to the convening authority, the Pentagon official in charge of resourcing decisions, and then could take these requests to the judge if denied.

Connell blamed the pace of the proceedings mostly on the government, due to the various intrusions that dominated the case's early years. But he also attributed the wide mix of legal disputes to the newness of the court system, with so many fundamental questions unresolved—such as the extent to which the Constitution and its due-process provisions applied to the military commissions. This was a military court with its own appellate court, the Court of Military Commission Review, from which appeals went to the civilian courts—the US Court of Appeals for the DC Circuit and eventually the US Supreme Court—and it was also a war court in which the laws of war were relevant. Court pleadings and oral arguments referred to a limitless mix of cases and precedents from domestic and international jurisdictions—the commission's own trial and appellate courts, federal trial and appellate courts, the US Court of Appeals for the Armed Forces and the International Criminal Tribunal for the Former Yugoslavia (ICTY). It was chaos. But Connell, who loved being a trial lawyer, enjoyed both the intellectual challenges and opportunities for creativity. His enthusiasm and energy were on display at the podium: Connell was the attorney most likely to be given the signal by the judge's staff to speak slower for the benefit of the courtroom English-to-Arabic translators.

The *Zero Dark Thirty* motion was an example of Connell's approach to the litigation; his team filed the most motions, and the other teams typically joined them. Earlier in the case, defense teams had to file motions to join the motions filed by other teams. Pohl saved a lot of paperwork by coming up with the rule of "automatic joinder," presuming that defense teams were joined to each other's motions unless they filed a separate pleading to decline joinder. Whether the teams had a formal joint defense agreement was a bit of a mystery and something the prosecution would unsuccessfully litigate to disclose. But it was clear the prisoners, who referred to each other as "brothers," were not going to turn on one another, and the five learned counsel had regular conference calls to discuss case strategy. A few defense lawyers told me that they'd never worked on a joint-defendant case where their clients were so united against the idea of pointing fingers at one another.

On the evening of February 18, Connell came by with Lt. Col. Thomas and other team members to say that he should have trusted his gut and advised al Baluchi to stay back at the detention facility rather than attend court to watch parts of *Zero Dark Thirty*.

"He was quite upset," Connell told us as we worked on our stories for the day. "The images and the feel of the torture room are so powerful; it had a big impact on him and I think everyone else in the room."

* * *

Movie Day was memorable, but it paled in comparison to the events of Week Two. One was relatively quick, when David Schulz, a renowned First Amendment lawyer, argued on behalf of a consortium of news organizations challenging the government's redactions of a public transcript from the prior October, when Camp 7 personnel testified in the female-guard dispute. By this point, Carol and I had agreed that at least one member of the media should be in the front row during proceedings to have eyes on the full courtroom. Quite often, it would be both of us, but it might just be me if Carol stayed back at the media center to live-tweet proceedings—effectively giving many people around the world a live "feed" from Gitmo. For the Camp 7 testimony, this meant that she had tweeted out some details that the government later redacted from the transcript, which the media claimed was unconstitutional censorship. Schulz and Carol had fought many battles over the years for journalists on Guantanamo, and it was fun to be around for one of them.

Because he did not have the necessary security clearances, Schulz could not be in court except to make his oral arguments, and he sat next to me in the gallery. When it was his turn on February 22, Schulz argued, effectively I thought, that the government "waived its right" to redact any of the proceedings because they already had become the "public's property" through the open session. But the best part was that, with the forty-second delay, Schulz was able to watch the last part of his own presentation on the video feed after he returned next to me in the gallery. That's all you need to know about the forty-second delay—it's really long.

But the bigger event was what Jim Harrington had planned. After getting to know Harrington over the first few trips—I was calling him Jim by now, like everyone else—I was surprised that members of his team had ratted him out to the FBI. From what I could tell, he seemed to be the most well-liked person in the commissions, much appreciated for a legendary irreverence and dry humor. Harrington is Irish, or Irish American, to the core; I had noted that his firm's website, for Buffalo-based Harrington & Mahoney, had shamrocks in the design. There are Ryans on his wife's side, and our first order of business was making sure we didn't have any familial relations. Carol had told him I was a runner, and he explained to me that he had once been a serious marathoner. He still exuded a healthy energy, even though his gut had gotten a little bigger over the years. Bad knees now made him a devoted morning walker.

The FBI infiltration had been devastating to the team for Ramzi bin al Shibh. Harrington and the lead military lawyer, then Army Maj. Alaina Wichner, basically had to rebuild the team from scratch after the fallout. But Harrington took it in stride. He told me that military officers and many contractors to the commissions believed that their professional livelihoods were based on their ability to maintain top secret security clearances. This was a sufficient, if somewhat cryptic, explanation for why some former team members might have viewed with concern his attitude toward the government's classification of information and the protocols for handling it, much of which he basically thought was ridiculous. He also thought it was idiotic that the government wasted eighteen months of the case investigating him and his team's operations.

Harrington, however, had another big problem on his hands with bin al Shibh, who was proving to be the case's most difficult client. Of the five defendants, bin al Shibh most clearly exhibited a mental-health fallout from his time at the CIA black sites. For nearly three years, Harrington had been attempting to convince Judge Pohl that the Camp 7 guard force—or some other entity—was subjecting his client to strange noises and vibrations to continue the torture from the black sites. His client was in a state of near-constant misery, another distraction that prevented the team from focusing on other pretrial matters. In what seemed like a risky move, Harrington in February 2016 decided to call bin al Shibh to the stand in support of his motion to end the alleged abuse and hold the guard force in contempt.

In his acclaimed book on the 9/11 attacks, *Perfect Soldiers*, author Terry McDermott portrays bin al Shibh as an affable and popular person who was critical to the successful formation of the German cell of the plot, which included several of the eventual hijackers. Bin al Shibh had lived in Hamburg with Mohamed Atta, who was the operational leader of the attacks in the United States until the hijacked plane he piloted, American Airlines 11, crashed into the North Tower. Harrington, too, regularly described bin al Shibh as intelligent and often very funny. His occasional smile in court, when talking to his codefendants and his lawyers, appeared to show a trace of an earlier personality that the CIA had mostly punished out of existence. Harrington would regularly tell us and Pohl that his client was tired and irritable from his constant lack of sleep. When meeting with the media,

Harrington wouldn't say whether he believed the noises and vibrations were actually happening, only that he knew bin al Shibh felt them. Harrington did tell me that he himself occasionally felt an odd vibrating sensation from the floor or table in his attorney-client meeting room with bin al Shibh.

This line of litigation put Pohl in a difficult position, as he would never really be in a position to know for sure what, if anything, was happening at Camp 7. In November 2015, Pohl issued an order directing the guard force to not subject bin al Shibh to noises and vibrations and to post a copy of the order on bin al Shibh's cell door. Harrington now hoped to convince Pohl that JTF-GTMO was violating the order.

Defendants seldom take the stand in their own case, whether in the trial or pretrial phase. On February 24, 2016, more than fourteen years after the 9/11 attacks, one of those accused of the "Planes Operation" would testify—perhaps the only time this would ever happen. The forty-three-year-old Yemeni walked to the witness stand without shackles and without guards holding his arms and elbows—the longest "free" walk he had had since before his capture on September 11, 2002, the one year-anniversary of the attacks. When he took the stand, bin al Shibh was calm. He spoke in heavily accented but clear English in testimony that lasted about two hours.

"Make all my life terrible, upside down," bin al Shibh said when Harrington asked him about the effects of the alleged disturbances. "You cannot concentrate, you cannot read, you cannot sleep, you cannot pray, you cannot do any of this because of living with this condition day and night, twenty-four hours a day."

Early in his testimony, at 10:14 a.m., bin al Shibh set off the courtroom's flashing red security light. The video monitors along the top of the viewing gallery switched to a "Please Stand By" message and white noise, and we were ushered out of the courtroom for a few minutes before open proceedings resumed. We'll never know what bin al Shibh said in the moments after the court security officer cut the feed. The last audio to reach the gallery involved bin al Shibh starting to compare structural characteristics of one of the black sites with Camp 7.

The testimony otherwise went smoothly for the well-prepared witness. Bin al Shibh said he knew the noises and vibrations were intentional because they so closely resembled techniques used at the black sites. Bin al Shibh said that the noises took different forms—from banging on the walls of his cell to buzzing—while the vibrations felt like "sitting in a car with the engine on." He said it was common for the guard force to wake him up after he appeared to fall asleep. He also said that disruptions occurred as he tried to work on his case, and that they got worse in the days before and during legal meetings and commission sessions. He said he had canceled legal meetings and decided not to go to court as a result of his sleep deprivation and anxiety.

Bin al Shibh testified that he had not voluntarily taken any drugs for emotional or mental health issues at Guantanamo Bay. He described the first psychiatrist he met after arriving on Gitmo as a "war criminal" and a "monster" for giving him injections of powerful sedatives that more or less kept him in bed at all times—all as punishment, he believes, for not cooperating with the government against his fellow detainees.

"Worst time in my life," he said. "Worse than the black sites."

He said he took pill versions of the medication only to avoid the injections and was allowed to stop altogether at some point in 2008. Bin al Shibh looked past Harrington toward the fifth defense table where Suzanne Lachelier, his military defense lawyer in 2008, now sat as one of the civilian lawyers for codefendant Mustafa al Hawsawi. He nodded in her direction and said that his past legal team had helped stop the forced medication—maybe not quite a thank-you, but close. During a break, Lachelier walked up to bin al Shibh and talked with him as Harrington watched—their first conversation in eight years. Lachelier later acknowledged to me that it was an emotional day for her in court. He had always resented her for raising his competency as an issue during the first military commission. It was Lachelier who asked Harrington to be bin al Shibh's lawyer for the second military commission, after she asked around with her contacts in the defense bar for a good fit. Everybody likes Jim.

Throughout the long paper trail of litigation, the government had repeatedly denied the disturbances were taking place. Prosecutors suggested that bin al Shibh may need medication again over the delusions, though Pohl the prior year had ruled that he was competent to stand trial. The task to cross-examine fell to Clay Trivett, the government's managing trial counsel, who in that role was the administrative team leader under Gen. Martins. Of all the prosecutors who argued in court, Trivett was the most boyish of the lot, without a trace of gray in his thick mane of black hair. He was, however, the longest-serving prosecutor on the commissions, having been assigned to court in 2003 as a Navy JAG (Judge Advocate General's Corps) lieutenant. He was now a prosecutor in the Justice Department's counterterrorism section, though he remained a JAG in the Navy Reserves.

Bin al Shibh rejected suggestions by Trivett that the sounds may not be happening or perhaps are natural sounds from pipes or other sources, such as construction. In his questioning, Trivett also raised the idea that bin al Shibh was lying to harass the guard force and to continue his jihad against the United States; the witness acknowledged that he still viewed himself as an enemy of the United States. He also acknowledged making abusive statements, such as calling female guards "sluts" and breaking security cameras. Trivett successfully elicited detailed testimony from bin al Shibh about the workings of the detention facility, which made his allegations seem something of a stretch. In the defendant's view, the facility was a giant machine that allowed guards to send noises and vibrations to almost any area, including cells, meeting rooms, and recreation areas. He said he did not feel them in court or on the van rides there.

At one point, Trivett asked bin al Shibh if he remembered his dreams when he slept. Bin al Shibh responded "sometimes."

"Do you ever dream about the people that were killed on September 11, 2001?" Trivett asked.

Harrington objected before bin al Shibh could answer; Pohl told Trivett to move on. The question earned a few groans in the viewing gallery, but bin al Shibh seemed to appreciate the move, showing outlines of that devilish, younger grin. Early in the afternoon, during a brief redirect by Harrington, bin al Shibh said that it might be the CIA instead of the guard force that was still torturing him; he said Camp 7 had lots of people coming and going and "nobody knows who they are."

"They could be CIA, they could be somebody else, North Korean people," the witness said. "Nobody knows."

* * *

Cmdr. Ross was a great guy, and we'd barbeque or eat dinner with him once in a while, but in my early Gitmo years the court's public affairs officers mostly left us to the support crew from the prison's media unit. We lucked out with Capt. McElwain and his team, who performed their job with the attitude that they should make our time on the base as comfortable as possible. They didn't care if one of us wanted to see a movie at one of the outdoor cinemas—the base has three, two of them outside the prison zone and thus available to us—while another worked out at the gym and another drank at O'Kelly's or ate at the bowling alley's Taco Bell. McElwain only got annoyed if he suspected that we were trying too hard to coordinate our plans to avoid inconveniencing his team.

By the end of the February trip, I had developed a few strategies for filling time and staying as healthy as possible. While some people said "they're not real beaches," I had taken a liking to the small, rocky beaches near Camp Justice, Glass Beach and Girl Scout Beach. My favorite activity was jogging to one of these beaches, jumping in and swimming for ten to twenty minutes, then jogging back for a latrine shower, which may or may not be scorching hot once the sun settled on the camp. The beaches are reachable from Sherman Avenue, heading on the main road in the direction of the Lighthouse, or from the opposite direction through a park that overlooks the ferry landing. I alternated my route but preferred running through this strange park, which has a narrow road that winds through canopies and grills before heading into an area of lush, tropical overgrowth. Turkey vultures always seemed to be swooping ominously above me on these runs, and I felt like I was in a truly remote area, maybe even the real Cuba, though I had no idea what that was like.

On the weekend between the two weeks of court, McElwain and two other team members rented a pontoon boat for the four journalists staying for the second week, which included me, Carol, Ali Watkins (then at Buzzfeed News), and Lou Dubose from the *Washington Spectator*. "Pelican Pete's Marina," as it's known, is a great spot on the base, with a large canopy providing shade for pool tables and chairs looking out into the bay. We departed from the marina and headed north toward Cuba, stopping at a popular island known as "Hospital Cay," where the British navy ran a medical facility in the 1700 and 1800s. This isn't the best place for swimming, but it has an elevated cement platform that allows for a twenty-foot jump into the water.

The real joy of a lazy day of boating is arriving at Conde Beach, which is across the bay from the marina. Conde has a long stretch of white sand that is usually completely empty because of its general inaccessibility. It feels like a non-touristy part of the Caribbean, empty and serene with clear water that was as warm as a bath. It made me think of the trips Fiona and I took to Puerto Rico. McElwain's crew anchored the boat fifty yards offshore so we could swim in the shallow water and stroll along the sands. We finished the day with some late afternoon snorkeling near Girl Scout Beach, where the rocky shoreline can provide a dazzling array of colorful fish.

One tradition that I started on this trip was suggesting a closing-night dinner at the Bayview, a civilized white-tablecloth restaurant with nice views of the water and decent cocktails and steaks. We took McElwain out on that Friday night as an appreciation for the genuine kindness he brought to his work. The evening illustrated the claustrophobic trappings of the traveling court system: Tables of the media, the NGOs, the prosecution, the victim family members, and a few of the defense teams were all within earshot of one another. This can happen at O'Kelly's, but the din of sports playing on the TVs and young soldiers drinking and talking provides more of a barrier.

Journalists were considered "officer equivalents" on the base, so we finished Friday night with drinks and games of pool at the adjacent Rick's, which is the officers' club. The place was almost entirely empty when we walked in, except for Trivett, who nodded hello and kept his distance. Someone from McElwain's unit got us back to Camp Justice, and we resumed the tradition that preceded me—finishing off any of the remaining booze in light of the ground rules that alcohol could not be stored at the media center.

I had been pestering Cmdr. Ross, who already had his next Navy assignment and just a few Gitmo trips remaining in his post, about doing a profile of Martins. Martins had done a good dozen on-the-record interviews with me in his formal meetings with the press corps and was overall very pro-transparency at the time. But Ross told me he was uncomfortable with a Connell-style profile, which was part of Lawdragon's "Lawyer Limelight" series—conversations with lawyers who are working on interesting cases or deals. Nevertheless, on the departing Saturday morning out of Gitmo, Ross got me a one-on-one interview in an empty room on the second floor of the air terminal. He must have gotten a whiff of the prior night's booze or seen a hangover in my eyes as we were heading into the room and decided to couch any of Martins's expectations about a productive interview.

"I think the media were up late last night," he said.

In his public statements, and to me, Martins touted the role of military commissions as appropriate to try some captured "alien belligerents," even in situations where the regular courts were available. This was a position held by the US Supreme Court in 1942. That year, the court rejected a challenge to the military commission set up by the Roosevelt administration to prosecute Nazi saboteurs who were captured in the United States. Previously, military commissions had mostly been used by the US military during periods of occupation or war, the most commonly cited early examples being the Mexican American War of 1846–1848 and the American Civil War. But for the Bush administration and other proponents, the 1942 case,

Movie Day. February 2016.

Ex Parte Quirin, was a greenlight for building a new military system after the 9/11 attacks to prosecute suspected foreign terrorists.

By the time I interviewed Martins on that February morning, military commission convictions included three during the Bush era (one by guilty plea) and four under Obama (all by guilty plea). Most convictions had resulted in short sentences or were reversed after the detainees were transferred to other countries. The biggest problem for the cases was that most detainees were charged with providing material support for terrorism—a common charge in federal terrorism cases but one that had not been among the established war crimes. The DC Circuit held that using this charge for the military commissions was an improper "ex post facto" application of the offense, as it hadn't been a war crime at the time of the alleged conduct. The DC Circuit did uphold a military commission conviction for a conspiracy charge despite a similar defense challenge. The 9/11 defendants had been charged with more established war crimes in addition to conspiracy, including attacking and murdering civilians, attacking civilian property, hijacking, and terrorism.

Martins always acknowledged that the federal courts had successfully handled many terrorism cases in the years before and after 9/11. Only one involved a former Guantanamo detainee, which happened when Ahmed Khalfan Ghailani was transferred in June 2009 to face trial in lower Manhattan federal court for his role in the 1998 embassy bombings in Kenya and Tanzania that killed more than two hundred and wounded thousands. His case was the ultimate Rorschach test for war-on-terror prosecutions, at least when it came to former Guantanamo Bay detainees who had been tortured at CIA black sites. In a major pretrial ruling, US District Judge Lewis Kaplan barred the government from using a key witness that had been discovered through Ghailani's CIA interrogations. The jury eventually acquitted him, in November 2010, of all but one of 285 charges related to the attacks. However, two months later Kaplan sentenced Ghailani to life in prison; he was at the supermax facility in Florence, Colorado, until his transfer to federal prison in Kentucky in 2019.

Supporters of the Guantanamo prison and court system saw the dangers of using the civilian courts; critics said the case proved that regular terrorism prosecutions worked well and generally led to longer sentences than the military commissions. While comparing cases with different facts and circumstances is tricky, I wasn't the only one to also think about the federal prosecution of the so-called "American Taliban," John Walker Lindh, who pleaded guilty in 2002 to fighting for the Taliban in Afghanistan. I wrote a lengthy article on the case for the *Daily Journal*'s weekly magazine. Lindh, an American who grew up in a wealthy California suburb and was defended by a large pro bono team led by famed litigator James Brosnahan, received a far harsher sentence in Virginia federal court—twenty years—than most of the Guantanamo detainees convicted by military commission.

Unlike with Ghailani, the Obama administration never physically transferred Mohammed and his alleged coconspirators to the United States, even after Attorney General Eric Holder's November 2009 announcement that the case was being transferred to New York. The plan lost political support within a small handful of months, well before the Ghailani trial began. A month after Ghailani's verdict, in December 2010, the Democratic-controlled Congress passed its ban on using funds to transfer detainees to US soil. In April 2011, just a few months before Martins became chief prosecutor, Holder announced that he was referring the 9/11 case back to the military commissions.

Martins contended that the commissions were better for certain terrorism suspects captured overseas in conflict zones where the governments may not be fully cooperative, or where US investigators faced other on-the-ground challenges. In his view, this is why the military commissions properly enjoyed a much wider admissibility of hearsay statements, including from individuals who did not receive *Miranda* warnings—evidence that would generally not be allowed in federal courts or courts-martial.

"There may exist voluntary but un-Mirandized statements that were taken properly and by special agents who were acting lawfully, and yet when the case comes to trial, those who made the statements cannot be compelled to testify or are otherwise unavailable because they remain overseas," Martins said.

This sounds sensible when thinking about law enforcement agents gathering evidence in difficult situations overseas, where they might not have complete control over how they conduct the investigations. But the biggest un-Mirandized statements in the 9/11 case occurred when the defendants were in US custody on Guantanamo Bay, in early 2007. Why couldn't they have been read their rights and offered lawyers before their so-called "clean" interrogations by the FBI? I didn't ask; maybe I wasn't as sharp as I should have been.

During the February trip, Obama had given a speech from the White House in which he again called for the closure of the Guantanamo Bay detention facility. He also called for Congress to make reforms to the military commissions system, which he criticized despite having largely adopted from the Bush era. Given the congressional ban on transfers, Obama's hopes for a closure before the end of his term was something of a pipe dream. From Martins's point of view, however, even an attainment of this goal would not end the commissions.

"Military commissions, like courts-martial, can be convened wherever you can securely hold a trial," Martins told me. "That can be many places."

CHAPTER 6

The 9/11 Attacks. May–June 2016.

Trivett's question about Ramzi bin al Shibh's dreams made a point unrelated to the defendant's claims about ongoing torture: This case was supposed to be about the attacks of September 11, 2001. Gen. Martins always sent out prepared statements by email to the media that included details about one or more of the attending victim family members. He also thanked them in his remarks at the closing press conference, and usually at least a few of the VFMs spoke. Still, for any observer of the pretrial proceedings within the courtroom, the 9/11 case did not have a whole lot to do with 9/11. Prosecutors had to find ways to bring the attacks back into court, often in small ways—but occasionally with a sledgehammer.

"Since the proceedings began in 2012, the word 'torture' has been used over five hundred times in this courtroom," prosecutor Ed Ryan told the judge on May 31, 2016. "By comparison, the phrase September 11, or 11 September, or 9/11, about two hundred times."

The prosecution team was stacked with current and former military lawyers, but Ryan was an outlier. He was a longtime federal prosecutor with twenty-five years of experience trying complex cases at the Justice Department. He was a trial lawyer's trial lawyer, completely at ease at the podium and champing at the bit to get the case moving faster. When interviewing Connell for his Lawdragon profile, he told me that Ryan was the one prosecutor in the courtroom he truly feared. Like most of the other members of the prosecution team who argued in court, other than Martins, Ryan had been on the case since the Bush era. He had split his career between US Attorney Offices in South Florida and North Carolina, which included a stint as the US attorney for the Western District of North Carolina. He also was experienced in truly massive cases, having led a RICO prosecution of Colombian drug cartels that netted more than a hundred convictions. His distinctions were plenty, including twice being awarded the Attorney General's Award for Distinguished Service.

Martins was the sole public voice of the government team, but I realized early on that Ryan was comfortable engaging in banter with Carol, and soon me. (We quickly established that we were not related.) In one of my first trips, he saw Carol and I buying booze at the Naval Exchange on the opening Saturday and remarked, "Ah, the fourth estate, I feel safer already." He also was comfortable wearing his heart on his sleeve. During the closing press conferences, Ryan sat in the back row. As victim family members spoke, I was surprised to see that the quiet sobbing behind me was coming from him.

As friendly as Ryan was outside of court, he could be an intimidating presence inside, maybe even something of a bully, with his tall frame and booming voice. On that day at the end of May, Ryan was at the podium hoping to convince Judge Pohl to allow the government to videotape the testimony of ten aging or infirm family members of the victims. Doing so would preserve their testimony for trial. Many victim family members were getting old and in poor health; two of the family members that the government had hoped to one day call as witnesses had recently died.

"Those events, those sad events, for us brought home very directly that these types of passages of life are happening and, in fact, they can actually happen quickly," Ryan said.

Defense attorneys objected to taking the testimonies, claiming that it would be prejudicial to their clients. Ryan disagreed. He explained to the judge that the prospective witnesses would all be "victim-impact witnesses"—those not called at the guilt-or-innocence phase of the trial but during the sentencing phase, in the event there were convictions.

"Our submission to you is that the testimony of people saying, 'My child meant the world to me,' or 'My husband meant the world to me,' and 'Their loss has devastated me,' that won't be anywhere near a point of jeopardizing a fair trial," Ryan argued.

He did acknowledge that one witness would have "a dual role" as both a victim-impact witness and as a fact witness to the attacks. That would be Lee Hanson, age eighty-three, whom the government planned to call as a witness to help document the horrors of 9/11 during the trial. Hanson lost his son Peter, daughter-in-law Sue, and granddaughter Christine—"the youngest victim of 9/11," Ryan said—when United Airlines Flight 175 crashed into the South Tower. Ryan explained that Lee Hanson had received a harrowing call from Peter during the hijacking.

"Stabbings of flight attendants, flying erratically, people screaming, hijackers claiming they had a bomb," Ryan recounted. "That phone call ended with Mr. Peter Hanson saying to his father, 'Oh, God, oh, God,'—and the plane crashed into the South Tower."

Ryan's delivery was a punch to the gut. Sobs could be heard as the curtain was drawn across the viewing gallery to give privacy to the family members on the right side of the room. He continued onward, lambasting one of the defense team's pleadings that contended that it was not necessary to take the testimony of these ten victim family members because the government had access to thousands of potential witnesses.

"In short, they want to benefit from having killed so many people," Ryan said. "In other words, 'You don't need these ten, you got lots more.'"

Nevin stood up to object, but he was clearly caught off guard by the blow.

"That's not a fair argument," Nevin contended. "That's not what we're saying. It's really not fair to say that."

"Objection is overruled," Pohl said.

Oral arguments continued into the afternoon. After Ryan finished his rebuttal to the defense presentations, Khalid Sheikh Mohammed spoke up, catching the courtroom completely by surprise. He spoke in Arabic, and one of the courtroom translators attempted a real-time translation in English. Mohammed told Pohl that although he had earlier been "neutral" in Ryan's argument, he now wanted to speak. Pohl was clearly taken aback: He told Mohammed to quiet down and threatened to remove him from the court, reminding him that he had defense lawyers to speak for him.

"He needs to know," Mohammed insisted, apparently referring to Ryan. "He needs to know that this is a nuclear bomb in the world."

The statement was followed by grumblings of confusion, and maybe a little fear, in the gallery; Pohl urged Nevin to get his client to quiet down. The two defendants behind Mohammed, Walid bin Attash—who often complained about his lawyer, Cheryl Bormann—and Ramzi bin al Shibh—who regularly complained about the noises and vibrations—had on a few occasions acted erratically and been removed from court. But never Mohammed. Nevin, closest to the podium on the right side of the first defense table, moved quickly over to its far left side where Mohammed sat under watch by the guards. He spoke for a few minutes with his client, who stayed silent, then walked to the podium.

Nevin reminded Pohl that his team hadn't had its courtroom interpreter in about a year. The defendants receive a live Arabic translation of the proceedings through an audio transmission, but they also have interpreters sitting next to them at the tables to provide additional assistance, given the complexity of the proceedings. For reasons that were still not exactly clear but extremely frustrating to Nevin, his team's interpreter had lost his security clearance and could not enter the courtroom. In fact, Nevin had unsuccessfully sought to postpone the proceedings until the interpreter was restored. (Prosecutors often point out that Mohammed seems to speak English pretty well. He earned a mechanical engineering degree from North Carolina Agricultural and Technical State University in 1986.)

Nevin explained to Pohl that the lack of a team interpreter contributed to Mohammed not fully understanding what was happening in court when Ryan, his voice at times breaking and trembling, was talking about the September 11 attacks. Nevin said that Mohammed also was bothered by the fact Pohl had overruled defense objections to some of Ryan's impassioned arguments.

"Well, that's the way the system works," Pohl said, still annoyed but somewhat placated by the explanation.

It was tough to ruffle Pohl. His ability to push forward the biggest case in US history, even if by one single inch at a time, was proving impressive to me as a relative newcomer. The day ended without additional drama.

After court, Nevin stopped by the media center to explain his view of what happened to the handful of reporters who attended the proceedings. Nevin said the nuclear bomb statement may have been a reference to US aggression in the world, such as the use of atomic weapons against Japan in World War II. More generally, Nevin said his client was bothered that Ryan seemed to be giving a closing argument in the case, and Pohl seemed to be helping him out by overruling the defense objections. He didn't fault Ryan.

"His argument was compelling and effective," Nevin said.

For a while, it seemed like this one-week session might not happen. The 9/11 case had a hearing scheduled for April, but Pohl canceled it after getting another filing from the Special Review Team, which was still tasked with keeping him informed on investigations related to any defense team members. We had no idea what this was about, or if the case would have to endure another long delay like that tied to the FBI infiltration. For this reason, I decided to attend the one-week hearing in mid-May for the Hadi case, the first commission I'd attended in September 2015. The hearing was limited to just one half-day as, once again, the judge dealt with Hadi getting new lawyers to his team, this time civilians. As it turned out, the SRT filing, whatever it was, became a nonissue once we learned that Pohl was going forward with the next session. This led to some hectic travel. By that point, my brother had given me his old car, and I was driving to and from DC, which enabled me to drive onto Andrews and leave the car there. After returning from the Hadi trip, I had just a week back in Brooklyn before having to drive back down again for the 9/11 case. I don't recall if on that pair of long drives I examined why I may have felt a sense of panic over the case having a delay.

* * *

The day after Ryan's arguments, victim family members stopped by for an on-the-record session with us at the media center. Not surprisingly, they loved Ryan's presentation for the witness depositions: Finally, they said, the proceedings had brought their focus to the 9/11 attacks.

"About damned time," said Kenneth Fairben, who attended with his wife, Diane.

The Fairbens lost their son, Keith, a twenty-four-year-old paramedic who died while helping victims in the South Tower. They set up a scholarship fund in his memory to pay for medical and paramedic training courses for applicants in Nassau County, New York—one of a countless number of charitable efforts launched by victim family members. Fairben said that most of his and his wife's friends were now becoming grandparents for the first time. But Keith was their only child.

"That's something we will never have," Fairben told reporters, his eyes watering a bit and his voice strained.

Over my first four trips, victim family members had proven to be a fairly diverse group. Most were middle-aged or older, having lost children, spouses, or siblings. While some, including the Fairbens, had attended the remote viewing sites to watch proceedings, more acknowledged being unfamiliar with the case's progress before coming to Guantanamo. Those who spoke on the record generally supported the Guantanamo Bay detention facility and the use of the military commissions, including its application of the death penalty for the defendants. These individuals tended to take critical views of the defense teams, bothered by their friendly socializing with the defendants during court breaks and what they saw as their endless litigation over peripheral matters. During most weeks of the commission hearings, one night was reserved for victim family members to meet with the defense teams in a conference room at one of the hotels. Lawyers told us that these meetings often went well but could also be tense and even confrontational; family members expressed the full range of emotion, from genuine appreciation for what the attorneys do to outright anger at them. The teams had working with them two leaders in defense-side victim outreach, Tammy Krause and Susan Casey, one of whom was always present on base during a hearing—and one of whom was always sitting a few rows behind Carol and me in court, providing great company in the mostly empty gallery. (The team for Mustafa al Hawsawi had its own victim-outreach specialist who sat with the team in court.)

In our media roundtables, some family members were critical of the commissions and found the defense teams' focus on torture entirely justified; I suspected more held these beliefs than voiced in our discussions. I knew some members of September 11th Families for Peaceful Tomorrows, the group cofounded by Colleen Kelly, were critical of the government even if they appreciated the dedication of the prosecution team. Competing views can create tension within the victim family group. At the closing press conference for the December 2015 hearing, my second trip, Phyllis Rodriguez, a member of Peaceful Tomorrows, thanked the defense attorneys for their work in exposing what she saw as a flawed system of justice. This enraged another victim family member, who called Rodriguez a liar when it was her turn at the podium—which then enraged Rodriguez's daughter, Julia, who also attended. Karen Loftus, who administrated the victim program, had to shut down the press conference as shouting commenced. The two VFM factions had to be kept separate for the remainder of the trip. A video of this press conference was never placed on the military commission's website. I later asked for the video a few times but was told it could not be found.

That Colleen Kelly hung out with us on her own, as she did on my first trip, was a rarity. The Victim/Witness Assistance Program, or VWAP, kept family members separate as true VIPs of the traveling court system. They typically always had a few minders or "escorts," a mix of military and civilian individuals, hovering nearby. Loftus and our public affairs officers had an informal agreement that they would coordinate a time for an on-the-record meeting, if the family members wanted one. The setup seemed to inhibit normal human interaction and to foster distrust and tension, though I well understood that the trips could be traumatizing for attendees, even without a media presence. The courtroom's blue curtain separating family members from the rest of the public—something I had never seen in another court—was another example of just how odd this court was.

Ryan's statistical claim about courtroom references to 9/11 versus torture might have also applied to the media's coverage of the case. In our meetings, victim family members occasionally expressed frustration for what appeared to be a journalistic preoccupation with the past torture of the defendants. This focus can be offensive to people who see torture as something that happened outside of the black sites—for example, being burned alive in an office, having a throat slashed open by a box cutter, watching a child's office building collapse on live TV, and reliving the agony on every anniversary of the attacks. One victim family member told me in one of my first meetings that she relived 9/11 twice a day, each time the clock showed 9:11. I started noticing this, too.

Fairben's line about never having grandchildren really stuck with me. I already understood, of course, that the damage caused by the 9/11 attacks had extended multiple generations, an incalculable tragedy that continued to ripple farther out as more first responders died from 9/11-related illnesses. But there was something about picturing Kenneth Fairben talking with a friend and being reminded of the murder of his son—and having to hold back tears—just because his friend did something natural like talk about one of his grandchildren. I wondered what Keith's kids would be doing now, if he had lived and had some more; they'd probably be elementary or middle school and eyeing the upcoming summer.

I realized after this VFM meeting how haunted I was from my first, in October 2015, by someone who did not speak at all. This middle-aged woman and her husband, who also attended, lost their son in the North Tower. The husband agreed to speak with us and joined the circle of reporters and family members in the media center; she declined and stood back against the wall. After exchanging the normal pleasantries, we began the process of everybody introducing themselves and explaining what brought them to Guantanamo. Within seconds, she began sobbing uncontrollably, her shoulders jerking as she brought a clenched fist to her mouth. She quickly exited the building, trailed by one of the victim's representatives provided by the Justice Department. She couldn't even make it ten seconds.

* * *

My tolerance for dark and depressing material, I had learned some years earlier, was high. In January 2008, I moved from Los Angeles to New York to attend New York University's Gallatin School of Individualized Study, where students at both the undergraduate and graduate schools develop their own courses of study. Over the next four years, while still co-running Lawdragon, I completed a program in human right studies with a focus on justice mechanisms for mass atrocities and other gross human rights violations, an interdisciplinary field generally referred to as "transitional justice." As part of my program, I made trips to The Hague, Bosnia-Herzegovina, Serbia, South Africa, and, shortly after I graduated, to Rwanda, each time producing a major feature article for Lawdragon in addition to whatever academic research I was doing. My interest was in accountability efforts in post-conflict settings, but there was no way to write about these mechanisms without becoming intimately familiar with the crimes that preceded them. I read a lot of this material—thousands of journal articles, advocacy reports, and journalistic works. When traveling, I also met with survivors and visited memorials and massacre sites.

I became mesmerized by the unending complexity of trying to account for some of the worst crimes in human history, a process that many people probably associate with the Nuremberg and Tokyo tribunals after World War II. My thesis was on the work of the War Crimes Chamber in Belgrade, Serbia. This court served as a complement to the International Criminal Tribunal for the Former Yugoslavia, or ICTY, based in The Hague, in prosecuting war crimes that followed the dissolution of Yugoslavia in the early-to-mid-1990s and from the conflict in Kosovo in the late 1990s. As a legal affairs reporter, I was particularly drawn to court processes like the Belgrade chamber and the ICTY, but prosecutions are just one component of "transitional justice." The field is vast, and the range of justice mechanisms includes truth commissions, reparations programs, government reforms, and the building of museums and memorials. Over four years of part-time study, I went down many rabbit holes; you could read fifty articles on a single truth commission or reparations program and barely scrape the surface.

The most important thing I learned was that most justice mechanisms, even the good ones, are doomed to fail in the eyes of many of the stakeholders they are designed to serve. Courts fail to charge the vast majority of war criminals, even those who planned the worst atrocities; truth commissions generally leave survivors without redress to the courts, even if they want their perpetrators prosecuted; reparations might only reach a narrowly defined "victim" population; institutional reforms will often fail to address the needs of the most marginalized; and museums might only document one side of the suffering. The best-intentioned accountability efforts can further divide a society or exacerbate tensions between nations, sowing the seeds for a conflict that might be worse than the one that recently ended. Beyond the good ones, ill-intentioned justice mechanisms might be established to cover up crimes or to secure power and condemn a society to decades of human rights violations. Deciding which type of mechanism you're reading about isn't always easy, and different stakeholder groups within each post-conflict setting will have competing opinions.

This material undoubtedly helped prepare me for covering the military commissions on Guantanamo Bay. It explains why I was drawn to—rather than put off by—the complexity of the proceedings in the 9/11 case, and why the dreariness of the subject matter did not turn me away. The process of seeking justice for the 9/11 attacks was proving to be satisfying to no one; virtually all the stakeholder groups had legitimate complaints about the court. Even high-functioning courts can't promise "closure" for horrible crimes, which for victims is a personal process and for a society is dependent on too many other factors. But the 9/11 case seemed to make a mockery of the concept of closure, having been in pretrial litigation in one form or another for eight years without a trial date on the calendar. Victims also had to wrestle with the possibility that it wasn't the court, or the defense teams, responsible for the pace of the case. It was the government's own conduct.

I learned from talking to family members that the pace of the case was made all the more frustrating by how quickly it was moving during the Bush era. During the first military commission, in 2008, the five men sought to plead guilty and wanted their executions to make them martyrs. But there were a few legal complications. The military judge, Army Col. Stephen Henley, was concerned over the mental competency of two of the defendants, bin al Shibh and al Hawsawi. Henley also had questions about whether, under the 2006 Military Commissions Act, a defendant could plead guilty to a capital offense, and whether a jury of military officers would first have to unanimously convict the defendant before imposing a death sentence. He asked for briefing on the issues; they were never resolved. Obama's election later that year and subsequent decision to try to hold the case in New York federal court ended up delaying a second case until 2012.

In our meetings, victim family members regularly cited a document from the first case that, in their view, showed that the defendants took great pride in the level of misery and devastation they inflicted on the world. This is the "Islamic Response," a six-page document that boasted that the US "intelligence apparatus, with all its abilities, human and logistical, had failed to discover our military attack plans before the blessed 11 September operation." The public court filing is a typed, translated version of the statement—which apparently one of the accused had written out earlier—with the names of the five defendants typed at the bottom; it's not clear who the initial drafter was or how the typed names arrived at the bottom. The government was still planning on submitting it as evidence of a confession for whenever the second case went to trial.

Family members would also point to Khalid Sheikh Mohammed's prepared statement on Guantanamo Bay in March 2007, in which he claimed responsibility for planning the 9/11 plot "from A to Z," along with many other crimes. He admitted this at his Combatant Status Review Tribunal, or CSRT, the review process set up by the Bush administration to determine if detainees were properly held as "enemy combatants." Before their capture, Mohammed and bin al Shibh also discussed the 9/11 plot with journalist Yosri Fouda, who included information from the interviews in the widely watched Al Jazeera documentary *Top Secret: The Road to September 11*, released a year after the attacks.

The Islamic Response and these other sources of information were, to many people, clear evidence of guilt, which made the length of the proceedings that much more absurd. Another absurdity, perhaps, was that the government would never release the defendants, even if a military judge dismissed the case or a military jury found them not guilty. The government would always maintain it had a legal right to hold enemy combatants who posed a threat. Regardless of whatever happened in the second case—if a trial ever took place—the men would not be set free. The 9/11 case was about something else.

The biggest difference between the two commissions was that, by the time I showed up, it was clear the defendants wanted to live. The second arraignment on May 5, 2012—a chaotic mess lasting about twelve hours—was a harbinger for the pace of the proceedings but less clear on the intentions of the defendants, who refused to enter pleas or answer any of Judge Pohl's questions, including whether they would accept their mix of civilian and military counsel paid for by the Pentagon. Each team's client relationship had gone through its own unique journey since then, some far more difficult than the others. But all the defendants eventually decided to work with their legal teams to challenge the government's case.

Even as torture-related health issues continued to mount, by 2012 the defendants were not as despairing as they were in 2008. While Camp 7 remained restrictive, the guard force had opened the cell-door slots for food—the so-called "bean holes"—in 2009, so that the men could talk to one another regularly. The detainees were able to see the sunlight and had gradual increases in rec and communal time; they also had a significant amount of human interaction with legal meetings. Above all else, they valued communications with family members and received letters, even if heavily censored. (They also later were able to engage in what was described to us as delayed video chats, in which a detainee would record a message that would be relayed to a family member after a security review and then receive a recorded message back.) I also assumed that getting a chance to reveal as many details about their past CIA torture was part of their changed attitude, though no one had told me this.

A few lawyers had also told me that Nevin deserved a significant amount of credit for the defendants changing their approach for the second case. During the gap, he continued to travel to Guantanamo Bay to meet with Mohammed, maintaining and improving the all-important attorney-client relationship. I knew Nevin would never discuss this on the record, but I figured I could find a way to work this into my profile of him, whenever I did it.

CHAPTER 7

The Missing Black Site. July–August 2016.

Long days in court—hours of arguments, questions, and answers all referring to scraps of information from mountains of documents—often hide big developments in plain sight. So it was back in the busy two-week hearing of February 2016 when David Nevin, arguing one motion for Khalid Sheikh Mohammed, made reference to a secret order the judge had given on a different motion. Nevin said he was not going to discuss the content of the secret order.

"But I will say we will be filing a motion to recuse the military commission and to recuse the prosecution in view of the events that transpired that led to the issuance of that order," Nevin added.

Anyone listening, meaning Carol and me, raised an eyebrow: Nevin had just announced, without any meaningful public explanation, that he would be asking the judge and the prosecution to step down from the case. But he and the other defense lawyers wouldn't answer questions about it outside court. Something was brewing; any reasonable observer assumed it had something to do with the CIA.

The process of producing substitute or summarized CIA information to defense teams conjures up images of government employees redacting details from documents, or summarizing one document into another, less detailed version in a Sensitive Compartmented Information Facility, or SCIF. That is mostly what happened. In the 9/11 case, that process was used more times than in any other case in US history. But criminal proceedings on

Guantanamo Bay against former CIA captives were bound to raise disputes over defense teams' understandable interest in accessing the black sites where their clients were tortured; the case would also present the accompanying inquiry into whether any substitute evidence of a physical black site would be adequate for the purposes of a death penalty trial. Four months after the May 2012 arraignment, the five defense teams filed a joint motion to "preserve any existing evidence of any overseas detention facility used to imprison" their clients and other potential witnesses, hoping to someday get their hands or eyes on important evidence that could help paint the picture of abusive conditions. Defense lawyers took every opportunity to remind the judge that any small detail about what the United States had done to the defendants could tip a capital jury's vote from death to life. By December 2013, Pohl had directed the government to preserve any facility "still within the control of the United States" unless given permission by him or another court.

It turned out that the government did have at least partial control over one former black site, referred to in court only as "Site A," which was initially preserved by Pohl's December 2013 order. What later shocked the defense teams was that Pohl, in a new order in June 2014, granted the government's request to "decommission" the site without any additional litigation—preventing the teams from making any arguments to keep the structure, and access to it, intact. What was even stranger, and more infuriating to the teams, was that they did not learn that the site was no longer accessible to them until early in 2016. Nevin and the other lawyers finally received the second secret order shortly before the February 2016 hearing—more than a year and a half after Pohl actually issued it. That's why Nevin made the cryptic remark to Pohl then. This turn of events would unleash a new wave of the litigation that became, by far, the most contentious in the case to date.

The first salvo was launched on May 10, when the Mohammed team filed the motion that Nevin had promised Pohl the prior February. Uncharacteristically for the media-cautious (if friendly) KSM team, it also held a telephonic press conference to announce their filing, which accused Pohl and the prosecution team of colluding to improperly destroy critical evidence in the case. In the motion, the lawyers recounted what Mohammed said when they informed him of the now-missing black site: "First they tell us they will not show us the evidence, but they will show our lawyers. Now, they don't even show the lawyers. Why don't they just kill us?"

The lawyers contended that the entire prosecution team should be removed from the case and that Pohl and anyone on his staff involved in the secret order should also be removed. The court filings were unusually bitter on both sides. Prosecutors accused the Mohammed team of a "scorched-earth litigation strategy," "shrill antics," and a "hatchet-job of a motion" unfairly maligning the prosecution team and Pohl, who had "served his country honorably for more than thirty-five years." They mocked the team's immediate calling of a press conference "to trumpet" how "the self-professed mastermind of the mass-murder of 2,976 people" claimed he now couldn't get a fair trial. In response, Mohammed's team wrote that prosecutors were predictably relying on "jingoistic histrionics" and had an "overarching priority of covering up the wide-ranging governmental conspiracy in criminal wrongdoing."

The bitterness carried over into court for the July 2016 hearing, with each side of the courtroom claiming the other was "despicable."

"We have lost our ability to put our hands on some of the most important evidence in this case," Nevin told Pohl on July 21.

At this point, Nevin was not actually requesting that Pohl remove himself and the prosecution from the case. Instead, he contended that Pohl must first recuse himself from hearing the recusal motion to begin with, claiming his impartiality had at least the appearance of being in doubt—that Pohl could not really rule whether he did anything wrong and possibly face disqualification. Nevin argued that another military judge should determine whether Pohl and the Office of the Chief Prosecutor acted in a manner that warranted their disqualifications from the case.

Nevin said the "destruction" order occurred six months after Pohl had issued his earlier "do not destroy" order. Since then, Nevin continued, defense teams had operated under the assumption that they would be notified if terms of the order were changed. Instead, they found out nearly two years later by receiving a redacted version of the June 2014 order.

In the unique phraseology of the system, Pohl's secret order technically granted the government's request to "preserve" the black site with "substitute" evidence through the CIPA-like process, in this instance with photographic renderings of the site—it was not clear to us whether it was a video or a series of photographs, or both. But the government's filing made it clear that all the teams had been provided with "the adequate substitute" after they signed their memorandums of understanding related to the handling of classified information. The teams, who had also received photos of their clients at the black site, did not know that the photographic evidence was a final substitution in lieu of ever accessing a black site in person.

The government's response fell to Robert Swann, another holdover from the 9/11 case of the Bush era. In fact, Swann, as an Army JAG colonel, was the lead prosecutor on that military commission before Obama scrapped it, and he also had served a stint as Chief Prosecutor between 2004 and 2005. Swann was now a civilian Pentagon lawyer who, according to a brief biography provided to the media, had more than a thousand courts-martial under his belt as either a prosecutor, defense counsel, or judge over the course of his long military career. Swann gave off a naturally disgruntled look that matched his exasperated approach to litigating discovery disputes with the defense teams.

In Swann's telling, the defense teams were now adding unfounded allegations of wrongdoing to their already unreasonable demands for discovery. He acknowledged that the failure to provide the second "decommissioning" order from June 2014 to the defense teams in a timely manner was "regrettable," which he blamed on miscommunication between the prosecution and Pohl as to whether the judicial staff or prosecutors were responsible for distributing the document. He said that the prosecution otherwise followed the CIPA-like rules of requesting and receiving judicial approval for substitute evidence of classified material.

Swann accused Nevin of "grandstanding" and "a perverse distortion of the facts," and claimed it was the defense that did not want to play by the rules.

"You have done nothing wrong, nor have we," Swann told the judge.

Nevin was incredulous based on what he viewed as the government's deception. He said prosecutors could have simply seen by the case's electronic docket system that the order had not been distributed to the defense.

"They go ahead and destroy it anyway without us being given notice, and we are going to be lectured about cheating?" Nevin fumed.

Two of the other defense teams, those for Walid bin Attash and Ramzi bin al Shibh, joined the motion to have both Pohl and the prosecution team removed from the case. Connell, for Ammar al Baluchi, supported the prosecution's removal but wanted to later question the judge in a voir dire session about the sequence of events to determine if his team would also seek Pohl's disqualification. Connell said he had hoped the facts uncovered thus far were not true.

"I do not want to believe them now because they are heartbreaking," Connell told Pohl.

Pohl, who seldom ruled from the bench, did so after the lunch break—denying that a different judge had to hear the recusal motion. However, he said he was open to being questioned by defense teams whenever the actual motion was being argued.

The Missing Black Site. July–August 2016.

"If you wish to have voir dire of me, I will permit it, assuming it's relevant," Pohl said. He said that some of it might need to take place in a closed session.

Gen. Martins stopped by the media center later that afternoon. He was clearly peeved when asked about the possible destruction of evidence, which he denied took place.

"Allegations that can be wild and extreme should not be confused with serious allegations," Martins told us.

Pohl set oral arguments over his and the prosecution's possible recusal for the fall. For the military commissions, however, that timetable was optimistic, given that arguments only take place after all the pleadings are filed. The black site decommissioning was, without doubt, one of the most dramatic and important disputes of the 9/11 case. At the same time, it showed why following the courtroom drama was basically impossible unless you went to all or most of the sessions. One facet of pretrial litigation such as this could stretch for very long periods of time, over multiple hearings, with associated disputes over discovery and witnesses lasting the better part of a year before the underlying motion was actually argued.

For many of the important motions, defense teams filed requests for discovery to learn additional facts known by the government, which the prosecution often denied in full or in part. Defense teams would then bring the matter to the judge by filing motions to compel discovery, and this "briefing cycle" needed to play itself out—eventually culminating in oral arguments just on the discovery dispute. The judge then needed to rule on the discovery dispute, which could take weeks or months. If the government was ordered to produce discovery, that new information along with ongoing investigative work by defense teams might lead to supplemental pleadings related to the initial motion. Another complication was that any evidence that the judge ordered the government to turn over could very well be classified, which might lead the government to file its ex parte motions with the judge requesting substitutions and summaries of the original evidence, initiating the CIPA process. Pohl then had to assess the adequacy of the substitute evidence and might order the government to provide more details, which would require the prosecution to coordinate with the CIA or other classification authorities.

A similarly lengthy process could happen if defense teams believed that witnesses were required to support their motion and the government disagreed—more motions and more oral arguments delaying actual arguments over the underlying dispute. Nevin would almost certainly be back at the podium later in the year over the missing black site, but not to argue for Pohl's and the prosecution's removal—but to ask for evidence and witnesses to support his case.

* * *

In almost every way imaginable, Pohl was the perfect military judge for this job. One of the inherent flaws of the military commissions system was that military lawyers, like Swann for example, tend to rotate between prosecution, defense, and judicial assignments, so that a perfectly capable judge might soon be called on for any number of other legal jobs. But Pohl, who was also the chief judge of the commissions, was a rarity, having become a judge in 2000 and remaining one since. Carol wrote an extensive profile of Pohl that the *Miami Herald* published shortly before the May 2012 arraignment, which was a month before Pohl turned sixty-one. As Carol explained, Pohl had been passed over for promotion from colonel to general but was still retained within the military, which meant "he's got nobody he has to please," according to one source.

Pohl continued his career long past the time when most officers retire, giving him a special employment status that required annual renewal. Pohl may not have previously handled a complex death penalty case—which almost never arise in the military courts—but he was the longest-serving judge within the entire military. Lawyers who spoke to Carol praised Pohl's temperament, humor, skill, and the egoless independence that characterized his work. He had previously presided over the courts-martial of soldiers charged in the various abuses of prisoners at the Abu Ghraib prison in Iraq. Early in that case, he issued a protective order protecting the prison from demolition so that it remained available as evidence. That particular act of independence might have contributed to the defense teams' disbelief over the fate of Site A during the July 2016 hearing.

Still, later in the same hearing, Pohl informed the courtroom—kind of randomly, as far as I could tell—that he was not satisfied with much of the government's proposed summaries and substitutions of evidence from the CIA interrogation program. The prosecution was working on getting all of this evidence across the ten categories of RDI information to Pohl by the September 30 deadline, and it had been giving it to him in tranches. Pohl's role was to assess the adequacy of the substitute evidence compared to the original—making sure it put the defense teams in "substantially" the same position—and he was apparently not rubber-stamping what he received. He said the government had provided him with about 50 percent of the total RDI evidence it was tasked with submitting by the deadline.

"Virtually all of it has gone back for additions," Pohl said.

In his meeting with the media at the end of the hearing, Martins said the CIPA process was meant to be "iterative" and "interactive," as Pohl had indicated, and that his team was still working twenty-four hours a day, seven days a week—including all holidays—to meet the deadline. It was clear that Pohl's review of the material would take litigation over RDI discovery well into 2017.

Pohl, it seemed by this point, was content to irk both sides. Defense lawyers said his rulings generally favored the government and assumed he would eventually side with the prosecution on the most important pretrial matters—such as admitting their clients' confessions to the FBI in early 2007, despite all the prior torture. But the prosecution was clearly annoyed at the pace of the case, which under one analysis resulted from Pohl's indulgence to the defense side of the courtroom. Pohl would hear oral arguments on any motion under the sun and let all five teams take turns at the podium—without any time limit. The prosecution would intermittently "rest on the pleadings," declining to provide any oral argument on motions they considered superfluous, but Pohl might call them up to the podium anyway for some Q&A. Then Pohl would ask the defense side if anyone had anything else to say based on what the prosecution had said, and a few more arguments would dribble in before it was time to go to lunch or before he called his afternoon recess for the defendants' prayer time.

Pohl could let a defense attorney carry on for twenty minutes before piping in with a question, leaving the gallery to wonder if he was as sleepy as we were; on another motion, he might pepper the attorney with a list of questions and create a real dialogue. He was almost unfailingly polite and open to a joke or two that never undermined the seriousness of proceedings. Martins may have outranked Pohl within the Army, but you wouldn't know it by how the courtroom dynamics played out. If anything, Pohl seemed more regularly annoyed by Martins's professorial tendency to long sentences that failed to deliver the clarity Pohl wanted. "General Martins, we are talking past each other," the judge would say every so often.

Pohl's lack of ego and laid-back approach to problem-solving came through again during the July hearing with his handling of Walid bin Attash, who still wanted to fire Cheryl Bormann and Michael Schwartz. By that point, Schwartz had left the Air Force to stay on the case as a civilian rather than rotate to another position in the military—a relatively common occurrence on the defense and prosecution teams. On Wednesday of the first week, Pohl denied again bin Attash's request to have his lawyers removed. The next morning, bin Attash reacted angrily when Bormann and Schwartz approached the second defense table, standing up and yelling "No lawyers at my table!" He could not be calmed, and the guards had to remove him from court. Bormann and Pohl decided that the best way forward would be for the entire team—except bin Attash's interpreter—to sit at the sixth table on the defense side of the courtroom, closest to the gallery, which was being used for overflow defense staff. Bormann's team would stay there going forward, far away from their client in the large courtroom.

According to Martins, by the end of the July hearing the parties had filed pleadings on 207 substantive legal motions, sixty-six of which had been argued in court. Whatever the differing views of Pohl might be between the various participants and observers, all would agree that he did not seem to be in any particular rush to get through them. Ed Ryan may have been correct in arguing that torture got mentioned a lot more than 9/11, but lots of other ancillary issues got mentioned a lot more than 9/11—which was among the drawbacks of a new court system. Prosecutors contended that the defense teams were using the litigation to extend the case as along as possible because, the longer it went, the longer their clients would stay alive. Defense lawyers contended their motions practice was dictated by the ethical demands of representing defendants facing the death penalty. They also put most of the delays on the government for dragging their heels on discovery and, above all else, the FBI infiltration debacle.

The pace of litigation in the 9/11 case is why most media organizations stopped attending, and the same can generally be said of the NGOs approved to send observers, who sit behind us in the gallery. There were notable exceptions. September 11th Families for Peaceful Tomorrows continued to send both founding members and eventually younger members who would have been very young or barely born on the day of the attacks. Dru Brenner-Beck, then the president of the National Institute of Military Justice, preceded my arrival on the commissions and attended regularly, as did George Edwards, a law professor who ran the observers program at Indiana University's Robert H. McKinney School of Law. Otherwise, while I overlapped with a smattering of mid- to senior-level representatives of Human Rights Watch, the ACLU, Human Rights First, and Amnesty International, along with some from bar associations and law schools, eventually law students became the most common type of NGO attendee, whether representing one of the organizations or their schools.

All of this contributed to the general public's, and even the highly educated public's, growing ignorance of what was happening in the military commissions. This, in turn, contributed to my interest in staying on the story. I wanted to help establish a journalistic record of the case with regular articles while also gathering material for a longer feature that could tie together some of the bigger themes. But even my coverage, along with Carol's, failed to include most of what happened in court. As much as I enjoyed the weeds of litigation, I experienced what Connell referred to as "Gitmo brain," the mental fog that thickens as a hearing dragged on, where it became nearly impossible to recall—without notes and a calendar—what motion was argued on what day, or even on what day a certain witness testified. At closing press conferences, I realized I sometimes had trouble determining whether a certain event in court was from week one or week two.

I hoped to remain on the case until it reached the anticipated disputes over CIA evidence and witnesses—which would follow the government meeting its discovery deadline later in the fall—but the July 2016 trip threatened to be my last. In COVID's shadow, it's hard to recall the significant level of panic caused by the Zika virus. As Fiona and I planned on trying to start a family in the coming year, continuing to come to the Naval Base seemed risky. We discussed the Zika dilemma prior to my leaving for the two-week July hearing. Then, during the trip, Carol broke the news for the *Miami Herald* that the base's hospital had reported a Zika case. Though the contractor had been infected on a trip to Jamaica, not on the base, it still added to the aura of danger. Fiona and I had a few tense calls during the trip, with me staying late at the media center to use the landline.

Carol and I began informing people that it would likely be my last trip, and we had a final night of shots at O'Kelly's with members of the team for bin Attash, including Bormann and Schwartz. On July 29, our table had a total of nineteen shots by 8:09 p.m., when Carol closed out and covered the tab for $80.75. I took a photo of the receipt for posterity. In the week or so after my return, however, Fiona and I talked ourselves out of halting Caribbean travel, at least for the time being, figuring that we could always reassess the situation as it progressed. For one thing, Zika was not prominent on the Cuban island generally. Second, the Naval Base was taking the virus seriously, conducting regular anti-bug fogging while also testing mosquitoes for the virus. Both of our doctors did not think that my traveling to Cuba was a serious risk, though they urged taking precautions. My doctor recommended the basics of using DEET and wearing long pants and long-sleeve shirts whenever possible.

All of this convinced me to keep my place on the next media tour of the detention facility, which was just a few weeks away. And just a few months after that, Fiona would accept a job as a director of the Clara Lionel Foundation, the charitable organization founded by Barbados-born Rihanna, which would involve a decent amount of travel to the region. For us, Zika sort of fizzled out. We would, in fact, never learn of another case occurring on Guantanamo Bay, though it's possible one or more did without us being informed.

* * *

My second prison tour, on August 13–14, 2016, had a dual purpose: The night before our flight on another Air Force–captained propeller plane out of South Florida I attended a book event for *Guantanamo Bay: The Pentagon's Alcatraz of the Caribbean*, a collection of Carol's articles published by the *Miami Herald*'s book division. The Friday evening event at Books & Books in Coral Gables was packed. Carol and I had by that point become good friends and traveling companions, well on our way to old-married-couple status where we started doing things like talking about meals on the flights down to the island. Knowing her pretty well, I was surprised to see her nervous as the crowd filled. No one in recent journalistic history owned an important story the way Carol owned Gitmo. I hate using the words "tenacious" or "fearless," both of which apply to Carol, but her overall steady and commanding professional presence was not something I associated with nerves. Of course, she's human. The evening went smoothly—she read part of a chapter, I can't remember which—and signed a lot of books, including mine.

Among the benefits of traveling with Carol's book was reviewing the staggering array of twists and turns that preceded my Gitmo life: the early detainee arrivals and controversies, the media's efforts to simply learn the names of the detainees (which the Pentagon fought), the movement of detainees to the more permanent camps, the arrival of the CIA prisoners from the black sites, the tragic periods of protracted hunger strikes and detainee suicides, and the stints of good commanders and bad commanders—and how all of this affected what had previously been a pretty quiet US military outpost. While it was no comfort to the detainees still held on Guantanamo Bay or their advocates, the detention facility continued to become a shadow of its former self. At the time of the August 2016 tour, the prison population was down to sixty-one—thirty less than during my first tour six months earlier. In fact, less than a month after this second tour, JTF-GTMO would close the maximum-security facility, Camp 5, to renovate it and consolidate all the low-value prisoners into Camp 6. (The fourteen former CIA prisoners remained at Camp 7).

Though she went on virtually all of the tours, Carol did not go on this one, which had a total of five journalists. On this trip, I was surprised by the lack of attendance by reporters from mainstream American outlets, other than Arun Rath, a radio reporter for WGBH in Boston and NPR who was also working on a documentary for the PBS show *Frontline*. Joining us were a reporter from Germany, Lena Kampf, and a photographer from Pittsburgh, Justin Merriman. The other attendee, who was not a journalist, was George Edwards, the regular NGO observer from Indiana University McKinney School of Law.

The August 2016 tour had a low-key "rinse and repeat" vibe to it, even though most of the senior personnel had changed over. Army Col. Stephen Gabavics, who ran the detention group at the time, talked to us in an informal session as we stood around an empty Camp 6 cell block. Like his predecessor, Gabavics said that detainees were held humanely in accordance with international law and that he was proud of his guard force. His boss, Navy Rear Adm. Peter J. Clarke, the commander of all JTF-GTMO, told us in a more formal press briefing that his force of two thousand personnel would be prepared to close Guantanamo—as Obama wanted—or bring in new prisoners, as then Republican nominee Donald J. Trump wanted.

At the medical clinic, an officer explained forced feeding—how a can of Ensure is administered by a rubber tube—while telling us that hunger strikes were increasingly rare. The soldier who ran the library told us that detainees still liked *Harry Potter* books and that they could take advantage of an array of language, arts, and skills-building courses. We went into the rotunda of the Camp 6 prison to see the prisoners hang out in small groups and pray. On this trip, I brought a video camera and captured a lot of quality footage, including the detainees praying. Eventually, I put together a twelve-minute documentary called *Guantanamo Bay: A Video Introduction*, drawing together a lot of the accumulated footage over my first year on the base, which I thought turned out pretty good.

I shared a town house in "East Caravella" with Rath, who had also gone on the two-week July trip in the 9/11 case. It was great having him for some of the 9/11 hearings. Same goes for David Welna, NPR's longtime national security correspondent who dropped in intermittently—and who like Rath had covered the commissions prior to my arrival in 2015. In my early years on Gitmo, we would sometimes pass the nights drinking and playing the Cards Against Humanity, the game where players have to fill in the blanks of offensive or risqué statements on one set of cards by choosing from equally offensive options from another set of cards. The game reaches more twisted heights when renowned radio reporters read the selections with the clarity and seriousness of a news report from the front lines.

After the second night of the tour, Rath and I asked a member of the public affairs unit to drive us to the base's biggest constellation of nighttime activity—an area that has a Jamaican take-out window, the Tiki Bar, the officers' club Rick's, and the Bayview restaurant. Rath's target was karaoke night at Rick's, which had maybe a dozen people milling about. I pulled out my iPhone as Rath took the microphone to the tune of "Folsom Prison Blues," hoping to get some blackmail for future use. But Rath's golden radio voice extends to the stage.

CHAPTER 8

End of Year One—The Sodomy Files. October–December 2016.

Seven members of the media showed up at Joint Base Andrews on the Saturday morning of October 8, 2016, for a one-week hearing in the 9/11 case. I was a little nervous for the socializing at Andrews as I had recently published on Lawdragon.com "Pretrial of the Century: The Sept. 11 Case on Guantanamo Bay," an eighteen thousand-word feature story with a few sidebars tacked on. I've had people dislike my stories, and I don't normally care, but I typically don't travel with those people to remote islands for a week or two at a time. I was experiencing what I had written about in the feature article—the claustrophobic trappings of the traveling court system. Running into court participants in the restaurants, bars, the gym, the galley, the outdoor cinemas, the beaches, and anywhere else was a regular part of life.

My favorite anecdote from Year One was seeing two of the feistiest lawyers, prosecutor Ed Ryan and defense attorney Walter Ruiz, engage in a mid-flight standoff as Ruiz made his way from the bathroom and Ryan headed back to use it. They glared at each other for several seconds, each refusing to budge in the narrow aisle, with Ruiz's face essentially conveying, "Come and try." I was contemplating hitting the flight-attendant call button when they eventually both laughed and skidded by each other with a pat on the shoulder. Later that night, as Jeff and I drank in his kitchen around midnight, we heard a "Hey, John Ryan!" from the street. We headed outside to see Michael Scwhartz, Bormann's deputy on the bin Attash team, walking his dog. He apparently lived just a few houses down, and Schwartz and his wife later became good friends with Jeff and Kristin. From about forty feet away, he had noticed the button-down short-sleeve shirt I had worn on the flight. At least my Gitmo work contributed that friendship to the universe.

My confidence in "Pretrial of the Century" being a fair and mostly comprehensive account of the case was bolstered by my business partner Katrina's patient editing and later by Carol's immediate reading of it after it went live on Lawdragon.com. All of us thought that "Pretrial of the Century" was pretty clever; I remain surprised that no one had used it. I received some complimentary emails from readers, as well as from some victim family members who appreciated it for what it was intended as—a good resource for a confusing case. It was solid clip, but I wasn't quite ready to walk away, figuring that I'd let a pregnancy or some other major life event be the thing to stop or slow my coverage. David Nevin, who was partially to blame for me coming to Gitmo in the first place, wasn't helping things. After I sent him a link to the article by email, he said that it made him think "it might be the first chapter or two of a forthcoming book."

This trip got off to a rough start. Army Lt. Col Valerie "Val" Henderson, who had replaced Cmdr. Ross earlier in the year as the commissions spokesperson, succeeded in getting us to the back of the plane in our assigned seats by the bathrooms. But she was called toward the front once it began filling up. Apparently, the weight of all the passengers, baggage, and equipment was deemed to be too heavy—something I hadn't thought possible in a chartered jet—and the favored solution was to remove the media and the NGO observers. Hungover from my night with Jeff the night before, I had already eaten the turkey and cheese sandwich that had been placed on our seats by the flight attendants before we filed in.

Henderson led us off the plane. Members of the defense teams photographed our sad walk from the end of the plane as possible evidence of the commissions' failure to hold a public trial. Back at the Andrews waiting room, personnel told us that our bags would be returned shortly—something that proved to be impossible when we watched the plane take off. I went back to Jeff and Kristin's and borrowed a change of clothes.

Wendy Kelly, the head of operations for the commissions, arranged for a jet to take us to Guantanamo Bay on Monday, with a separate plane secured for the NGOs. (Pohl did not hold court on Monday as he waited for the "public" to arrive.) Our plane was too small for all of the reporters, so one of us had to hang back. Jeffrey Stern, an accomplished book author and journalist, graciously offered to do so, as he lived in the DC area; he would have to wait a week for his suitcase. Our jet—the fanciest thing I've ever flown on—got us to Gitmo after a refueling stop at an executive airport in West Palm Beach with boxed sandwich lunches from Panera. The government's rotating contract with various airlines for the Saturday charter flights meant the quality of meal services for commission trips varied widely—from near-restaurant-quality hot meals to cheese sandwiches made by a four-year-old abandoned by his parents. The Panera meal was delicious—far superior to the mediocre sandwich I had eaten on Saturday morning. All in all, what started out as a humiliation turned into the most enjoyable travel day I had ever had to the Naval Base.

Later that Monday, Gen. Martins dropped by the media center to apologize for the inconvenience. He also told us that the prosecution team had, just a few weeks earlier, met its September 30 deadline of providing all of its discovery from the CIA interrogation program to Judge Pohl.

"There's going to be an undetermined period of time where the commission is reviewing the material we provided," Martins cautioned.

Over the course of the week, Pohl and the parties worked their way through another eighteen motions. The only one I had the energy to write about involved the long-simmering dispute over whether the Constitution applied to the military commissions, an open question that had become a sore spot for defense lawyers. Earlier in the case, the teams asked Pohl to issue a ruling that the Constitution was presumed to apply to the proceedings, and that the burden was on the government to carve out the specific circumstances when it did not. Pohl declined to issue what he termed "an advisory opinion" untethered to a specific legal dispute in the case, agreeing with the government that the matter was not "ripe for decision." But the judge added in his order, issued in January 2013, that any party could make arguments about the application of the Constitution to the proceedings so long as they were tied to "discrete legal issues" raised in the case.

James Connell thought he finally had one when it came to defense access to witnesses, given that Pohl had said in the months prior that he did not have the authority to order private citizens to testify in person on Guantanamo Bay. Connell filed a motion to have the case dismissed because the commission rules violated a criminal defendant's Sixth Amendment rights to obtain favorable witnesses, and also to confront witnesses in court. The prosecution opposed, claiming that the issue would only be ripe if the defense wanted a certain witness that was refusing to testify in person on Guantanamo Bay.

Connell was a bit peeved at the closing press conference, probably assuming—correctly, as it turned out—that Pohl would side with the government.

"After four and a half years, when do we get to know what the rules are?" Connell asked the six reporters sitting in front of him.

"I take exception to that," Martins said seventeen minutes later, when it was his turn at the podium. "The Constitution applies in Guantanamo. It applies to everything we do."

"So much for clarity," I thought to myself, declining to pursue the matter. This is what Carol termed "constitutional Whac-A-Mole," and I'd have other opportunities.

These events took place in even more of a black hole than normal, with the upcoming Clinton v. Trump presidential election. Other than Carol, the only other reporter from a major or semi-major outlet was Arun Rath, continuing to do work for NPR and WGBH in Boston. The start of the trip coincided with the release of the *Access Hollywood* tapes, in which Trump bragged about assaulting women and which all but guaranteed a Clinton victory. A Clinton presidency was generally seen as a positive among Gitmo advocates, at least compared to Trump's promise to load it with "bad dudes." It was widely assumed that a Clinton administration would allow the commission cases to continue, so nothing would immediately change for those of us tied to the traveling court system, but she'd continue Obama's policy of transferring out as many detainees as possible. The place would continue to shrink, no new cases would be filed, and the world would think about it less and less.

* * *

By the end of the year, I finally settled on why Pohl never seemed to be in too big of a rush. He had been waiting for the CIA discovery, and now he would have to sort through it—comparing summaries to more detailed cables of what was done to the defendants at the black sites to decide the adequacy of the substitute evidence. Some of that he had already been doing, as the government had been providing him proposed substitutes and summaries over the course of the year. The defense teams would need this evidence to begin mounting efforts to have their clients' confessions to the FBI in early 2007 suppressed, based on the severity of the past abuse. That forthcoming facet of the pretrial litigation, by one analysis, was all that mattered.

End of Year One—The Sodomy Files. October–December 2016.

But Pohl still liked to make use of the proceedings to avoid too many important motions piling up. That effort was threatened during the last hearing of 2016, a one-week session beginning December 5, by the health of Mustafa al Hawsawi. As with Ramzi bin al Shibh's perceived noises and vibrations, al Hawsawi's rectal discomfort was another example of how the consequences of the CIA program complicated the case. If bin al Shibh exhibited the greatest psychological fallout from the black sites, al Hawsawi was his counterpart on the physical side.

Al Hawsawi always showed up on the first day, as required by Pohl, but he was otherwise the most likely to hang back at the detention camp because sitting was so difficult for him. When he did come to court, he had to sit on a pillow and would eventually be given a larger medical chair with more cushioning. Even on the first day of a session, during the first midmorning break or lunch, he often requested to be transported back rather than finish the day in court. Al Hawsawi, then forty-eight, looked the frailest of the men on the short walk to the fifth defense table, moving gingerly with a loose-fitting white robe hanging off his rail-thin frame. Eating caused so much digestive discomfort that he often avoided the activity. By late 2016, he weighed less than 110 pounds.

Al Hawsawi's lead lawyer, Walter Ruiz, a former naval commander turned civilian, had told me over the weekend that he was going to attempt to convince Pohl to postpone the hearing. He believed his client simply wasn't well enough to participate. By that point, I had interviewed Ruiz many times. He would generally stop by the media center on the opening weekend, and he would often speak at the closing press conference, especially if we asked him to. Ruiz and I had bonded somewhat over exercise, as Gen. Martins and I had, but I wasn't in the same league with either of them—especially Ruiz. He was a serious triathlete who regularly competed in races. On the weekends when I would sit on the beach sipping a beer, Ruiz would occasionally emerge from the water in a wet suit, after swimming some ridiculous distance.

In his press briefings, Ruiz regularly lamented what he termed the "sodomy under the guise of medical care" that CIA personnel inflicted on his client at the black sites, which had caused lasting rectal damage. Ruiz often explained to reporters that his client had "a rectal prolapse" that required him to remove a part of his anus to have a bowel movement, and then to reinsert the tissue after finishing. That is why he ate so little.

Ruiz talking so openly about his client's colorectal problems was still a relatively new phenomenon, one only made possible by the December 2014 release of the Senate torture report and its declassification of many details of the past abuse. In fact, Ruiz had told me that the report also gave his team an opening to discuss al Hawsawi's torture with him. Al Hawsawi had been reluctant to discuss what had happened to him and did not volunteer recollections of his experiences. Page 100 of the summary noted that the CIA subjected detainees to rectal hydration "without evidence of medical necessity." The footnote below that stated that al Hawsawi "was later diagnosed with chronic hemorrhoids, an anal fissure, and symptomatic rectal prolapse." Page 154 stated "the CIA was forced to seek assistance from three third-party countries in providing medical care to al Hawsawi and four other CIA detainees with acute ailments," after the US military would not provide medical assistance in the overseas locations.

Ruiz often pointed out that, in the Senate report, a CIA interrogation chief concluded after just one session with al Hawsawi that he did not appear to be "a financial mastermind," yet his client continued to be tortured. Like many detainees, al Hawsawi spent time at the CIA's most brutal site, referred to as Cobalt or Location 2, a dungeon in Afghanistan that was a place of total darkness, freezing temperatures, constant loud music, and buckets for human waste. Captives were chained to the floor or wall, or hung from the ceiling if being subjected to protracted bouts of standing sleep deprivation. At this site, interrogators subjected al Hawsawi to a form of water torture known as "waterdousing," during which cold water was poured over him while he was naked and in a prone position. The report said that al Hawsawi "cried out for God" when this was happening. He spent nine months at Cobalt.

With the rectal damage, there had been one positive development recently: The JTF-GTMO medical team had arranged for al Hawsawi to have surgery on October 14 to alleviate some of his suffering. Ruiz was appreciative of this development, though he told me in an email a few weeks later that his client continued "to suffer excruciating pain during bowel movements and when cleaning the wound." In court on December 5, the first day of the hearing, Ruiz told Pohl that the situation had not improved.

"This man is really in pain," Ruiz said Monday morning.

Pohl acknowledged that he had a "conundrum" and that he had to put this motion at "the top of the docket."

"There were a lot of other ones that have been filed long ago, but the nature of this, it needs to be resolved quickly," Pohl said.

"I agree," Ruiz responded.

End of Year One—The Sodomy Files. October–December 2016.

Ruiz said that al Hawsawi was still experiencing severe pain, despite a regime of Motrin and the opioid Tramadol. (Percocet caused constipation and thus aggravated the problem with going to the bathroom.) Ruiz also expressed frustration on the limitations he faced in preparing for his argument to postpone the hearing; he had just received from the prosecution that morning the latest tranche of medical records that would be relevant to his arguing for a delay. Also, the Senior Medical Officer of Camp 7 had refused to even speak with Ruiz's team.

Pohl clearly did not want to postpone the proceedings until the next session, which was scheduled for January 2017, in the week after Trump's inauguration. He wanted to keep the momentum that appeared to be building, however imperceptible that might have been to any sane observer of the case. As he often did, Pohl split the difference: He recessed court for four hours so Ruiz could review the medical records recently dropped on his lap. And, when they came back, the Senior Medical Officer, the doctor who basically serves as the detainees' primary care physician, would take the stand so Ruiz could question him. The surgeon who performed the rectal surgery would also be available to testify, if needed. Outside court, Ruiz appeared satisfied and said he was confident he could make his case.

Of the five lead defense counsel, Ruiz was something of an outlier. He wore his Navy commander's uniform in court for the first few years of the 9/11 case, before returning to civilian life while remaining a commander in the Navy Reserves. People tend to assume that the lead lawyers in the commissions are civilians, which is mostly true, but Ruiz spent a stint both as al Hawsawi's "learned counsel" and lead military lawyer. After his initial military service, Ruiz spent more than a decade as a state and federal public defender in Florida before returning to active duty when the call came out that the military commissions needed lawyers. Like Connell sitting ahead of him, Ruiz was on the younger side, in his mid-forties, and beginning to sense that a single case might occupy this entire phase of his professional life—a time that many lawyers would consider the prime of their careers. Unlike Connell, who was bald, Ruiz had jet-black hair without a trace of gray and often kept an accompanying goatee. Like his client, Ruiz could appear a little too thin at times, with his suit hanging off him, depending on where he was with his triathlon training.

Ruiz also kept his team somewhat separated from the others. He would not join the opening night NGO barbeque, though he might meet with observers later in the week. His team also occasionally met with the victim family members separately. Ruiz participated in the intermittent conference calls between the learned counsel, but he was the only one pushing for his client to be tried separately from the others. His motion for severance would remain pending before Pohl for years. Ruiz wanted al Hawsawi as far removed from KSM as possible. As one of the two alleged money men of the 9/11 operation, along with al Baluchi sitting in front of him, al Hawsawi's alleged culpability for the attacks was far less. Ruiz was regularly annoyed that the prosecution team painted the entire defense side of the courtroom with the same brush, contending that it threatened the standard of "individualized justice" to which his client was entitled. As much as he wanted the December hearing delayed, Ruiz always maintained that severing al Hawsawi's case would move his at a much faster clip, which is what the client and the team wanted.

Ruiz was prone to colorful language, both in court and out. At the press conference in July, he criticized Martins for ignoring what for Ruiz was obvious: The government was flagrantly abusing the classification system—and willing to drag the case out as long as possible—to prevent a national embarrassment and conceal a vast "international criminal enterprise." In one of my first court hearings, Ruiz argued for dismissal of the case based on all the prejudicial statements made against the defendants by senior members of the Bush and Obama administrations. In doing so, he compared the 9/11 case to a toxic well.

"We should not drink from that well," Ruiz contended.

I suspected that Ruiz used exercise to grind out the aggression built up over long days in a court he considered a cheap imitation of American justice. But his frustration would occasionally show through in court, which made him the most likely to get under Pohl's skin. Looking back, the friction on this day (and there were many others) between the judge and Ruiz started before the witness—the Camp 7 Senior Medical Officer—took the stand. Ruiz began the afternoon session by asking for another ten-minute recess so he could discuss with his client the option of watching the proceedings from one of the holding cells outside court, which receive a broadcast feed of court and would be more comfortable.

"You couldn't have done this when we had the four-hour break?" Pohl asked, clearly annoyed.

The judge always planned an afternoon break for the scheduled prayer time, allowing the defendants to pray in court. One such break was coming in thirty minutes, Pohl said, so Ruiz and his client could discuss the option then. That wasn't good enough for Ruiz.

End of Year One—The Sodomy Files. October–December 2016.

"As I said, right now he is not feeling comfortable," Ruiz said. He added that it would only take the guard force ten minutes to transfer him to the holding cell.

"I am not giving you the ten minutes now," Pohl responded. "Go forward."

Ruiz then started taking slow laps around the court. It took a little while to figure out that he was passing out exhibits that he wanted to enter into the record, including an affidavit from his client (he was too frail to take the stand) and a pain chart that was used in monitoring his care., Because the courtroom is so large, paralegals would normally do the distribution of materials. But Ruiz was doing it—very slowly—handing out one exhibit at a time, before starting the lap over again.

Pohl was confused. He thought we were going to get a witness.

"What are you doing?"

Ruiz said he was passing out exhibits. Pohl said he had seen him do it twice already.

"How would you suggest I pass them out?" Ruiz asked.

"Have somebody else pass them out and give them four things at one time instead of making four separate trips," Pohl said.

Ruiz thought about this for a second. "Sure," he said.

He finished with the exhibits and called his witness. Like some of the other witnesses from the detention facility, the Army doctor testified anonymously under his job title, referred to in court and the transcript only as the "Camp 7 Senior Medical Officer" or "SMO." This was done to protect his security, though he did not wear a disguise. Ruiz scored some points on direct examination. The doctor acknowledged that when overseeing al Hawsawi's medical care he did not review any medical records from 2003 to 2006, during the brutal CIA years, in which the detainee's rectal damage had required some type of emergency surgery. This was important to Ruiz, who was trying to prove that the doctor could not fully assess his client's state of recuperation if he did not know the entire relevant medical history.

The SMO testified that al Hawsawi was still suffering, and that his pain was not limited to bowel movements. They stumbled over exactly what al Hawsawi's condition was. The SMO described the surgery as a hemorrhoidectomy, though he testified that the defendant had a prolapsing hemorrhoid, which he said meant "extruding from the anus." Even before the start of the session, when Ruiz met with reporters on Sunday, he was angry that the government was referring to the October surgery as a simple hemorrhoidectomy. Ruiz said he had a photo of his client's anus that showed the severity of the situation—"Seeing is believing," he said—but he couldn't share it with us. For some reason, he added, a picture of his client's rectal damage was "a matter of national security."

Prosecutor Robert Swann was ready to question the doctor, but first Pohl called for the prayer break and left the room. I also left, as most people in the gallery do, to defrost for fifteen minutes in the tropical sun. When we all came back, al Hawsawi wasn't there. That was a surprise to Pohl, who runs a pretty tight, if slow-moving, ship.

"Mr. Ruiz, did you have permission for Mr. al Hawsawi to leave?" Pohl asked.

"I'm sorry," Ruiz said.

Ruiz explained that, when the judge recessed for the prayer break, his instinct was to put his client back in a more comfortable setting, in the holding cell, so he could lie down.

"I will give you a one-time pass," Pohl said, starting to fume a bit.

Under cross-examination by Swann, the doctor was better able to downplay the severity of al Hawsawi's condition: It was not a colorectal repair surgery but the simple removal of a hemorrhoid, done on an elective, "outpatient" basis—an odd term to associate with a detainee confined to a location so top secret that even his lawyers didn't know where it was on the base. (Some defense lawyers, including Ruiz, had taken advantage of Pohl's earlier order allowing a visit to Camp 7, but its location was always obscured by driving in circles; attorney-client meetings were otherwise held in a cluster of huts off the main road of the detention facility.) The SMO testified that, while al Hawsawi would experience significant discomfort on occasion, he should have no problem sitting through court. The SMO also said that al Hawsawi was "pleasant" when discussing his ongoing recovery.

"In fact, when we were talking about the caliber and the consistency of his stool, we had the interpreter there trying to explain what we were trying to ask him, and I jokingly mentioned, 'Is your stool like hummus?'" The SMO recounted. "And he thought it was very funny and we both laughed."

Ruiz was ready for redirect. He felt that Swann had extended the scope of testimony by asking the SMO about al Hawsawi's medical records dating to 2014. Ruiz wanted to go back much farther to develop the argument that past abuse at the CIA black sites would complicate the recovery beyond what a normal patient would experience. Under questioning, the SMO acknowledged that understanding a person's medical history is important.

"Because if some other medical problem comes up, it could be a clue as to what's going on," the SMO acknowledged.

That cued up the next question—what Ruiz had been driving at all along: "And it is fair to say, isn't it, doctor, that your average individual hasn't been sodomized rectally?"

Swann objected before the SMO could answer, contending that the subject wasn't relevant. Pohl sought to clarify the issue, but he and Ruiz talked over each other, creating more tension.

"Mr. Ruiz, let me finish," Pohl said. "It works this way: When I am talking, you don't."

The judge sided with Swann. Going back to a few details in medical records from 2014, as Swann had, was not the same as going all the way back to what happened at the black sites. All Pohl wanted to know was whether al Hawsawi could sit in court, not what was done to his rectum by the CIA.

"What happened ten years ago is not what's before me," Pohl said. "What's before me is his current medical condition in the immediate preceding part and since it happened. So I don't want to go back."

Pohl said he was noting Ruiz's objection for the record. Also, the judge added, while the government's doctor had his opinion on al Hawsawi's current condition, Ruiz could present a contrary opinion from his own medical expert. In fact, he couldn't: Ruiz interpreted the strict guidelines in Pohl's protective orders governing the release of information in the case as preventing him from sharing such medical records with an outside consultant or potential witness, unless that person had been approved and paid for by the government. Ruiz hadn't had the time to set that whole process up.

"We have an order in place that we can't share records with another doctor to rebut his testimony," Ruiz said. "So no, I don't have that."

"Okay," Pohl shrugged. "You have what you have."

That was a tad sharp from the normally polite Pohl. Ruiz glared back from the podium.

"Great system, Judge," Ruiz said in a tone clearly dripping in sarcasm. "Great system."

That was a shock, even coming from Ruiz. One of the guards inside the court, sitting closest to us in the gallery, turned and raised his eyebrows in an amazed expression. Communication between people in the courtroom and the viewing gallery is prohibited and could get you reprimanded, potentially kicked out, so I remained stone-faced. It took me a few seconds to remember that we hear everything on an audio delay—this meant the guard was reacting to things we hadn't yet heard.

"You may not like this system, but you won't disrespect this commission on the record like that," Pohl said.

"Judge, I think this whole commission is disrespectful," Ruiz shot back loudly.

He wasn't backing down. Pohl said he did not want Ruiz's editorial opinion.

"It is disrespectful to our flag, and it's disrespectful to our system of justice," Ruiz said.

They spoke over each other as Pohl told him to sit down; the judge eventually raised his voice as loud as I've ever heard it.

"Sit down!" Pohl said. "You are done."

Actually, Ruiz countered, he wasn't done. He had more questions for the witness.

"You are done for now," Pohl said. "Sit down."

Ruiz smiled. He had one more remark for the road.

"I like the way this works," he said.

Ruiz glared for another second before taking his binder and making the long walk to his seat near the back of the courtroom.

If you look at the transcript of this day in court, at this point it says "[Pause.]"—which is accurate. Pohl didn't say anything for a few minutes. He pulled out a binder and, head down, began paging through it slowly. We all later assumed he had pulled out the commission rules and was looking for the section on contempt. However, the law still required that any defendant facing the death penalty have representation by a "learned counsel." If Pohl had Ruiz removed and sent to the brig or confined to quarters, the proceedings would stop until whenever Ruiz came back—good for al Hawsawi's recovery, but bad for progress in the case. In essence, that would be giving Ruiz exactly what he wanted.

Whatever meditation Pohl put himself through worked. Eventually, he asked prosecutor Swann if he had any other questions of the witness. Swann was brief, merely confirming that Tramadol would not have an impact on al Hawsawi's ability to pay attention in court. Pohl then looked to the far end of the courtroom, down toward Ruiz. It was obvious to anyone who followed the case that the judge was going to let Ruiz resume questioning the witness. It just would have been too un-Pohl-like to do otherwise.

"Mr. Ruiz, now you've had an opportunity to sit down," Pohl said, "I will let you continue your examination. But I expect you to conduct yourself appropriately."

"Very well," Ruiz responded and walked back to the podium.

Ruiz was calm, and he scored a few more points. For example, the Senior Medical Officer had testified that al Hawsawi should have no trouble sitting in court—but how could he really know? After all, as Ruiz prefaced in one of his questions, this was only the second time that al Hawsawi had even sat in a chair since the surgery.

"When he is in his room, in his cell, he sits on his bed with pillows and cushions and not in a chair," Ruiz said. "Were you aware of that?"

The SMO was not. And since the surgery, al Hawsawi had spent about 70 percent of his time in his cell at Camp 7.

"So you don't know what he does 70 percent of the time?"

"No," the SMO responded. "He is in his cell."

The SMO also reaffirmed that al Hawsawi would intermittently be in excruciating pain, especially if he went to the bathroom.

"Like I said, every time he has a bowel movement the wound opens a little bit," the doctor testified.

Ruiz was done a few minutes later, and the witness left the stand. The parties proceeded immediately to closing arguments. Ruiz went first and remained calm in making his final points. Though he didn't have his own medical expert, he had made a pretty good case: His client was going to experience excruciating pain until he recovered more fully, and he was not ready for long court days—not even close.

"Again, the word 'excruciating' is not my word choice," Ruiz told Pohl. "I have used it because it was in the medical records."

Al Hawsawi also made clear in his written declaration that he wanted to participate and was not trying to delay the proceedings. In fact, Ruiz reminded Pohl that his team's whole strategy was to sever al Hawsawi's case from the other four defendants, in part to move his case faster.

"It has never been a strategy of delay and defer," Ruiz argued.

When it was his turn, Swann contended that there was no reason to delay the case over mere "surgery for hemorrhoids." He wasn't trying to paint the situation as pain free, but hemorrhoids were a pretty common occurrence.

"Well, I'm sure I don't want to have hemorrhoids," Swann said, starting to ramble a bit. "I don't have those kind of problems. But he does. A lot of people do—"

A voice cut in—calm, but loud.

"You weren't sodomized."

The pronouncement from Ruiz's microphone came as something of a shock. It dangled in the air. Swann turned back to glare at Ruiz, his exasperation and disbelief somewhat elevated from his default levels.

"I'm sorry—what?" Swann bellowed.

In the second that followed, I pictured Pohl finally having had enough with Ruiz, enough with the sodomy—here he was crossing the line again. Then again, Pohl seldom took things personally. Ruiz had rattled him earlier, but the judge already had decided against contempt. And anyway, Ruiz had a point: Swann's lack of hemorrhoids didn't have much to do with al Hawsawi's fitness for court.

Pohl was siding with Ruiz on this one.

"If that is an objection, the objection is sustained," Pohl said of Ruiz's sodomy interjection. "Don't go into that, Mr. Swann."

Swann finished his brief argument, and Pohl ruled from the bench: The proceedings were moving forward. Of course, he added, under his existing rules al Hawsawi could choose not to attend the rest of the week so long as that waiver was voluntary. One may wonder, as Ruiz often did, whether his client's decision that week or any week was truly voluntary if he was staying back at Camp 7 because of intense physical discomfort.

Not long after court ended, Ruiz stopped by the media center along with a few members of his team. He was not in a good mood. Ruiz was born in Colombia and grew up in Georgia after his father moved their family to the States when Ruiz was eight. As he told me in one of our interviews, which became the basis for another "Lawyer Limelight" profile, Ruiz wanted to be a prosecutor in law school but joined the Navy and was assigned a defense-counsel role. He quickly became devoted to representing the underdog, and to being a trial lawyer; he eventually left the Navy to avoid a supervisory legal position that would have taken him out of the courtroom. That's how he became a public defender in Florida and handled enough death penalty cases to qualify as a "learned counsel." Ruiz used exercise to not only burn off frustration but also to build the type of stamina needed for a case that apparently had no end. On that early evening, however, he was worn down and dejected, having viewed the day's events and the treatment of his client as an insult to the uniform he wore for two decades.

"It's a really difficult conundrum," Ruiz told us in a discussion that lasted about forty-five minutes. "There's a part of you that says, 'You know what, I want to be done with this place. You know what, I'm sick of this stuff, sick of pretending, sick of banging my head against the wall and engaging with this system that's propped up to be something consistent with federal court.' It's such a joke, right?"

Ruiz said his team ran their defense on two principles: adherence to the rule of law and treating al Hawsawi with "humanity and dignity."

"That's our job," Ruiz said.

He explained that he felt no allegiance to the commissions system—that was pretty obvious to anyone who'd watched court that day—but he felt a personal and professional commitment to his client, with whom he had developed a relationship over several years. In this sentiment, Ruiz was not alone among defense lawyers and other staff on the five teams: concerned that he was helping to legitimize an illegitimate system but more concerned that leaving the case would put his client in a worse position. Ruiz said that al Hawsawi would understand if he wanted to leave the case. But he thought that doing so would be the coward's choice, the easy way out. Ruiz is nothing if not stubborn. He told me for my profile of him that he even finishes books he hates once he has started them; he can't help himself.

Still, Ruiz told us, maybe he would go forward with this particular protest and not show up to court on Tuesday, potentially forcing the judge to revisit the contempt question. He remained incensed that his team still could not show us a medical picture of his client's preoperative condition to rebut government claims that this was a simple outpatient, elective procedure.

"The picture of Mr. al Hawsawi's rectum and anus remains a threat to national security," Ruiz said bitterly. "Because someone in some office in Washington, DC, in the course of their daily work of classifying and declassifying information, decided this is still a matter of national security of the United States."

I asked him if the proceedings could go forward at all if he did not show up.

"I don't think so," Ruiz said. "That's a decision I really have to think through tonight."

Usually, reporters thank attorneys for stopping by after court to discuss the often-confusing events of the day. But this session was for Ruiz.

"Thank you for letting me rant," Ruiz said to us with a smile. "I feel much better now."

Ben Fox from the AP spoke for all of us when he told Ruiz it would be a much better story if the attorney ended up in the brig or confined to his quarters for contempt of court, instead of participating in another tedious day working through the dozens and dozens of pretrial motions.

"You owe me jail," Fox said, and we all laughed.

* * *

The prospect of minimal court time was enticing—a bit more beach time before heading back to the city's looming winter. The Trump-Clinton election had cast a pall over places like Brooklyn, and the base felt like an escape. December on the base brought a tropical and pleasant "Christmas in July" spirit, which was headlined by "Christmas Tree Hill." This is an annual light display that takes over an elevated tract of land near the center of town, with a few dozen light clusters forming various holiday images and characters culminating in a giant tree overlooking Sherman Avenue. Each year, the base has a holiday parade to celebrate the opening of the display, with base residents—including some of the 250 children attending the Pentagon-run school—throwing candy down the main drag of Sherman Avenue from floats.

I also saw the December hearing as prime shopping season for friends and family members hoping for some Gitmo-themed T-shirts, bottle openers, hats, towels, or other items. The souvenir shop outside of the Naval Exchange had the most options, but the least offensive to a wide audience—at least to non-Cubans—were items from Radio GTMO. Here the T-shirts proudly boasted about "Rockin' in Fidel's backyard." The station also had a forty-dollar Fidel Castro bobblehead, a good choice for VIP gift recipients. Other non-detention-themed gifts could be found at O'Kelly's, where the T-shirts carried the unsubstantiated claim that the bar was "The only Irish pub on communist soil."

On that trip, however, shopping would have to be done after court. The next morning, as I made my way into the viewing gallery at about 8:30, already dripping with sweat from the ten-minute walk to court, I saw Ruiz at the fifth defense table, prepping for the day's arguments. His client didn't come that day, but Ruiz wasn't going to absent himself in protest. He had his head down, staring intently at a pleading on the table.

CHAPTER 9

Trumpland. January–May 2017.

The trips to and from Guantanamo Bay are the layperson's definition of "unnecessary roughness" and an apt expression of the military's "hurry up and wait" approach to life. January 23, 2017, was somewhat more reasonable, arriving at Andrews at 5:15 a.m. for a scheduled 8 a.m. flight; we often had to arrive at 5:45 or 6 a.m. for a 10 a.m. flight that almost never left on time. Another difference was that it was a Monday flight instead of the normal Saturday departure due to the Friday inauguration of Donald J. Trump, which delayed the anticipated twentieth pretrial session in the 9/11 case by a few days.

Joint Base Andrews was dark, windy, and icy, the overall mood grim—a feeling likely enhanced for some by Trump's "American Carnage" speech. The flight was delayed for more than three hours to wait for some of the storms to pass and so that airport personnel could deice the plane, which is probably pretty common but sounded ominous given the blustery winds. The takeoff and ascent were exceedingly bumpy through walls of thick gray clouds and sheets of rain. The approach to Guantanamo and the eventual landing were much worse.

Some trips to Gitmo feel a little pointless on the return flight to Andrews, when it's not always entirely clear what was accomplished in court. The first Trump-era trip felt like it could end up that way before we even departed. Cheryl Bormann, the lead lawyer for Walid bin Attash, fell and broke her wrist on the day of the Women's March. Instead of coming to Andrews, she was on her way back to Chicago to have a doctor insert a metal plate somewhere in her wrist or forearm. That created a problem in light of the statutory requirement that all death penalty defendants be represented by learned counsel. Her team filed an emergency motion to abate the proceedings, but Pohl rejected it. Because the government opposed the motion, he apparently felt the parties should argue the motion in court in front of the defendants and figure out what could be argued without Bormann present, perhaps a few of the pending motions that did not directly involve her team.

This hearing carried an additional layer of significance. On the plane was Lee Hanson, then eighty-four, who had lost his son, daughter-in-law, and two-year-old granddaughter when United 175 crashed into the World Trade Center. The previous May, Ed Ryan had made his impassioned plea for Pohl to let the prosecution take pretrial depositions of ailing victim family members in public court proceedings on Guantanamo. Pohl had ruled that any testimony by Hanson related to the merits of the case—not the sentencing—would have to be in court, with the defendants given the option to be present, though the public would still be excluded. With VFMs in first class and media by the toilets, Hanson was not visible to us, but we knew he was on board to testify about watching the murder of members of his family on live TV.

The Caribbean wind off the shoreline is almost always strong during the daytime, even on a pristinely clear day like January 23, but it was especially violent this afternoon. The plane seemed to be skewing left as we approached the terminal, and it felt like it was going too fast. The right wing tilted so far up that it felt like the left wing would scrape the tarmac at a sharp angle. Carol and I often exchange glances during the landings, which are seldom smooth, but on that trip I looked out the window with genuine horror.

The plane leveled out enough before pounding the tarmac in a series of painful bounces and torqued zigzagging that caused a few screams, several "Oh My God!"s, and scattered curses—and for a moment it felt like we were going to skid uncontrollably—but the plane began straightening as the brakes took hold, with room to spare. We learned later that the air terminal staff had phoned the base's emergency medical personnel when they saw the unsteady plane approach the landing strip. Carol told me she had glanced at Colleen Kelly, the victim family member who was attending as an NGO observer with September 11th Families for Peaceful Tomorrows. Kelly hates flying and was gripping the armrests with her lips moving; thankfully we had one serious Catholic praying for us.

Every now and then, as I stand at the top of the mobile stairs and look down on the blistering tarmac waiting for my turn to descend onto the Naval Base, I feel something like regret and ponder all the stupid decisions in my life that brought me to such a particular place and time. That was one of those trips.

In court the next day, Ryan told Pohl that he could move forward with most of the docket, even without Bormann present. At the very least, Ryan contended, the parties had to take Hanson's deposition.

"I can't ask that good man to make that trip again," Ryan said the morning of January 25. "He has given enough."

* * *

Experience-wise, the Chicago-based Bormann was somewhat in the middle of her four counterparts. Nevin and Harrington had about decade or two on her as a lawyer, respectively, while Connell and Ruiz were a little less than a decade behind her in terms of court experience. Unlike Nevin and Harrington, who would be approaching a reduced workload or quasi-retirement at some point in the not-too-distant future (one hoped), Bormann, Connell, and Ruiz all had significant years of lawyering left. None knew with any certainty what working the 9/11 case full-time for a half-dozen or more years would do for their post-Gitmo careers, assuming that phase might someday arrive.

Bormann's impact in the area of death penalty law already was significant. Her work running Illinois's Capital Trial Assistance Unit was a key part of the coalition of lawyers and activists that convinced the state to abolish the death penalty in 2011. She told the *New York Times* in an article about the victory that maybe she would go to "another state" to fight the death penalty, perhaps not yet knowing she would soon be fighting its application in a place that was not a state but also not quite a country. From the vantage point of an East Coaster, Bormann oozed Chicago with her palpable accent and city pride—and it came as no surprise that she moved back to Chicago after a period in DC when she first joined the commissions. Bormann is a fantastic cook, something that benefited her team and also the five defendants during shared halal lunches on court days or in legal meetings at the detention camp. Her team often arrived at Andrews with the most prominent display of trunks and coolers of food and cooking supplies, though the meat selection at the Naval Exchange was ample.

One of the joys of sitting in the viewing gallery with an uninitiated NGO observer or journalist was being asked if Bormann is a Muslim; she is not. As mentioned previously, while all civilian defense team members wore head coverings when the clients were present, Bormann clearly drew the most attention with the black abaya, leaving just her freckled face visible. She also drew the ire of many during the May 2012 arraignment by criticizing the dress of women members of the prosecution team, one of whom wore a skirt that came above the knee. Bormann did not wear the abaya when the 9/11 suspects were not in court. This happened often on Fridays, the holy day for Muslims, when the defendants preferred to hang back at Camp 7 for prayers. The description of Bormann as "brash," which I've used myself, has a layer of sexism to it, though it might also be rooted in assumptions about Chicagoans. It's nevertheless accurate to say that she employed a grittier, plainspoken manner of argument rather than a more professorial style. That's not to say she was above lecturing, something she liked to do with Pohl when describing how "a real court" might operate.

During this phase of the case, Bormann's team still sat closest to us at the back of the courtroom at the sixth table, behind Ruiz's team for Mustafa al Hawsawi, while her client sat at the second table. The courtroom was built in 2007 to accommodate six defendants because the Bush administration also initially sought charges against Mohammed al Qahtani, a Saudi national who was suspected of being the missing twentieth hijacker. But Susan Crawford, the Pentagon official who oversaw the commissions in 2008 as its "convening authority," did not approve charges for al Qahtani because of clear evidence that he had been tortured during his earlier detention at Guantanamo Bay. (Evidence of early abuses at the detention facility on Guantanamo had come to light before those at the CIA black sites; the Senate report on the RDI program was still years away during Crawford's tenure.) Convening authorities, which for the Guantanamo cases have changed many times over the years, have significant power in military commissions as they do in the courts-martial: They make resourcing decisions, approve or reject charges sought by prosecutors, make plea deals with defendants, and get the final say on a jury's sentencing.

In January 2017, the absence of Bormann and her black abaya felt odd, like we were all doing something we weren't supposed to do given the learned-counsel requirement. A layperson might have taken the government's point of view that, while presence of learned counsel is important and should generally be mandated—certainly at the trial phase—a pretrial hearing could move forward on some pending motions given the team's other talented lawyers, some of whom actually had a decent amount of capital experience. Pohl had the same thought, at least when it came to the motions that Bormann had tasked other team members to prepare for and argue during the week.

"Unless there is a death-penalty-specific issue, why wouldn't having two months to prepare for appearing without her give you enough time to argue the legal motions at this stage?" Pohl asked Edwin Perry, a civilian lawyer on Bormann's team, who was at the podium asking for a postponement, on January 25. "Are you just saying, 'Well, because she's learned counsel, we're not competent to do anything without her'?"

The judge said Perry might be selling himself short. But Perry said that the requirements of the Military Commissions Act were clear, and that beyond that "it's hard to parse what could not be critical in a death case." He said a learned counsel needed to be in the courtroom in an ongoing supervisory role.

"Regardless of who initially drafts that pleading or regardless of who does the oral argument, she is present, and all of our counsel will always confer with her prior to sitting down and waiving the rest of their time," Perry said.

That was true for all five teams. Non-lead lawyers generally concluded their oral arguments or witness examinations by asking Pohl if they "could have a moment" and walking back to their table for a brief discussion with the learned counsel. They would just as often return to the podium to make additional arguments or ask more questions as they would to say "nothing further."

Pohl ended up kicking most of the motions down the road, but he scheduled Hanson's deposition for that Friday before the Saturday return—cutting the trip a week short. Pohl noted that the deposition was to preserve testimony, not to admit it, and that Bormann's team could always challenge its admissibility later. As it turned out, none of the defendants chose to attend that day. Defense lawyers refused to comment on the deposition from which we were excluded, other than to say it was an "emotional" day and that none of them chose to cross-examine Hanson.

Despite the novelty of the situation, the Bormann fall felt like its own "I told you so" moment. The Chief Defense Counsel, Marine Brig. Gen. John Baker, had been warning for more than a year about the problem of each team having only one learned counsel. He had filed multiple requests to the Office of Convening Authority for funding for a second learned counsel, but never received approval.

"Having just one learned counsel is a single point of failure for these proceedings," Baker told me when we met during this trip. Given all the downtime, I had gone up to his office to chat about the topic. His office was in a building on the Camp Justice hill that looked down on the court complex and the media center.

When we first learned that an injury to one of the lead lawyers might jeopardize the trip, my mind immediately thought of the triathlete Ruiz and the possibility of a biking accident. Once we showed up at Andrews for that trip, we saw that Connell was wearing a boot for an Achilles' tendon injury that he said was incredibly painful and would have kept him from attending if he needed surgery. At the time, the military commissions cost about $100 million per year. By one analysis, if the government was spending that much on a court system, it might make sense to spend a few extra million to prevent the biggest case in US history from shutting down if someone got the flu or had a fall.

Baker had many other problems with the commissions. I wasn't surprised by his frankness, but it can still be a little jarring to hear a lawyer in uniform describe the military court he works in as "ridiculous" or a "joke." I actually met Baker on my very first trip to cover the Hadi case, in September 2015, shortly after he became the head of the Office of the Chief Defense Counsel. One of his first acts was to rename the Pentagon organization to the Military Commissions Defense Organization, or MCDO, which he felt more accurately captured the entity by not putting the focus on him. Baker met with me, Carol, and Janet Reitman on that first trip but was extremely cautious about saying anything of substance, as he was so new to the job. But he quickly assumed his position as the military commissions' anti-cheerleader, opposite the generally positive Gen. Martins. Unlike Martins, Baker did not argue in court as a defense lawyer; his job was to oversee the teams and advocate for additional staffing and other resources from the convening authority. He would only get involved with team strategy or maintenance when lawyers sought his consultation. At the time, he had about 175 civilian and military personnel under him, a number that would grow to two hundred or so during his tenure.

I wrote a profile of Baker not long after the one Lawdragon published on Martins. I learned he'd been a supply and logistics officer in the Marines before attending law school at the University of Pittsburgh through the Marine Corps Law Education Program. Since graduating in 1997, he had served as a defense attorney, prosecutor, and judge. He said he found his true calling—managing defense lawyers—as the Regional Defense Counsel for the Eastern Region of the Marine Corps, a position he held from 2008 to 2010 before serving three years as Chief Defense Counsel. In that top job, he oversaw the establishment of the Marine Corps Defense Services Organization, which reformed how defense lawyers were supervised and assigned to cases.

Baker was unfailingly positive about his MCDO crew; like Connell, he enjoyed bragging about the paralegals and other support staff who didn't get all the attention in court. He was also in an ongoing state of disbelief over the government intrusions in the case, in particular the FBI infiltration that had derailed the case prior to his arrival. He told me that the bizarre FBI episode lingered "over his office every day," as did the government's refusal to provide the defense teams with comprehensive classification guidance for their cases. Baker would regularly refer to operating in this environment as an ongoing "chilling effect."

Even just filing pleadings—and there were thousands of them—could be a stressful endeavor. Defense and prosecution teams had to use either the Pentagon's secret communications network or its nonclassified network to file documents, depending on the classification of the material; not surprisingly, inadvertent spills were a regular part of life on Guantanamo. Staff from Washington Headquarters Services (WHS), the Department of Defense contractor that maintains information security for the case, would regularly have to wipe computers and laptops that improperly received classified information. Occasionally, though, WHS would refer a spill to a Pentagon administrative body that would review the mistake, which could jeopardize a person's security clearance—the loss of which could be a career-ender for people in the military or in certain contracting positions. I wrote one story about the tide of confusing litigation and testimony that followed a defense paralegal's use of the unclassified network to file a pleading that itself was unclassified—but which contained a classified attachment, and therefore should have been filed on the classified network. Two other teams had joined the filing, which meant three teams were either under investigation or administrative review for the spill. (This was another instance in which David Nevin had to hire his own lawyer.)

Baker also saw what he considered a big-picture absurdity: The commissions proceedings were so rife with problems that death sentences—if a unanimous panel of military officers serving as the jury ever handed one down—would never survive on appeal given the heightened scrutiny for capital cases. Any convictions surviving review by the convening authority and the Court of Military Commission Review would go to the US Court of Appeals for the DC Circuit and the US Supreme Court. Even if a death sentence had a chance at being affirmed, it would probably take more than a decade for that process to play out.

In addition to openly disparaging the commissions to any reporter or NGO observer who would listen, Baker was different than Martins in another way: He liked to hang out at night to talk about the cases and just about any other topic. In another instance of the system's claustrophobic trappings, the military defense personnel had their CHU (containerized housing unit) trailers in the same general area in Camp Justice as the prosecution CHUs, across from the court complex—though each side's rows of trailers were grouped together, to provide some separation. Starting in 2017, on most trips Baker would invite Carol and I to walk over for drinks on a slow night, sometimes with some meat to throw on a grill that sat near a large canopy on the far side of the CHUs. Occasionally he would have the entire media troop over for a more formal MCDO-hosted barbeque if Carol could assure him that each attendee understood "drinks on the table" meant everything was completely off the record.

This first year of the Trump era would be a big one for Baker. In fact, in his military career emerges the unlikely truth that the 9/11 case was actually the *normal* case on Guantanamo Bay. Also in protracted pretrial proceedings at the time was the death penalty case against Abd al Rahim al Nashiri, the former CIA captive charged as a lead planner in the bombing of the USS *Cole* in Yemen that killed seventeen sailors and wounded dozens of others.

Somebody working at the detention facility had informed Baker that there were "legacy" listening devices—meaning apparently no longer in use—in the attorney-client meeting room used by al Nashiri and his team, which was in a different location than that used by the 9/11 teams (who also had earlier discovered listening devices that looked like smoke detectors in their meeting rooms.) The al Nashiri team, led by Rick Kammen, a longtime death penalty lawyer based in Indianapolis, requested discovery on the listening devices as well as an evidentiary hearing with witnesses. The judge at the time, Air Force Col. Vance Spath, denied these motions, putting Kammen in a tough spot. Kammen explained to me (in a profile I later wrote on him) that he was ethically required to leave the case, a decision he made after consulting with a legal ethics expert. At the time, an odd rule in the military commissions gave the power to remove a defense lawyer from a case to the chief defense counsel, not the judge. Baker released Kammen and two other civilian lawyers from the case. (Congress later amended the law to give military judges the power to release counsel.)

During a hearing in October 2017, Spath ordered Baker to change his mind and reassign the attorneys to al Nashiri's defense. After Baker refused, Spath held him in contempt and ordered him confined to his Camp Justice quarters for twenty-one days—a dramatic act that signaled Spath's unpredictability and Baker's willingness to go to jail for his team. While I attended the other cases intermittently, I was not on the base for that hearing and had to follow Carol's reporting like everybody else. Her coverage of the event and the fallout from Spath's increasingly erratic behavior earned her a much-deserved Silver Gavel Award from the American Bar Association.

The convening authority freed Baker after two days, and the DC Circuit Court of Appeals later overturned the contempt conviction in June 2018. By that point, Spath had departed the commissions to take a job as an immigration judge, which is a position within the Department of Justice. The DC Circuit, in April 2019, vacated more than two years' worth of Spath's rulings in the al Nashiri case for a "disqualifying appearance of partiality" because he had been secretly negotiating for a job with a government agency that had lawyers on the prosecution team. The DC Circuit later made a similar ruling in the military commission against Abd al Hadi al Iraqi, after the judge in that case also left to become an immigration judge. Years later, by the time the military commissions resumed in mid-2021 after five hundred days of delays caused by the pandemic, both the al Nashiri and Hadi cases were still dealing with the fallout of those vacated rulings.

Say what you want about the 9/11 case, but that hasn't happened yet.

* * *

The January 2017 session may have been mostly a dud from a court reporting perspective, with Hanson's testimony having taken place in closed court, but I was happy I went, even with what felt like a near-death experience on the plane. The trip drew what had been the best media attendance in more than a year, with eight reporters joining Carol and me. The shock election of November 2016 provided a news hook—what Trump's tenure might mean for Guantanamo. As always, most outlets were interested in general update stories for their audiences rather than the weeds of pretrial litigation, so the lack of significant court time was not a major hindrance to their efforts.

Some attendees were prominent figures in Guantanamo or war-on-terror journalism from before my arrival in 2015, including Michelle Shephard of the *Toronto Star*, Margot Williams of The Intercept and former *Los Angeles Times* reporter Terry McDermott. McDermott was the author of two seminal post-9/11 books, *Perfect Soldiers: The 9/11 Hijackers—Who They Were, Why They Did It*, and *The Hunt for KSM*. He was there with Daniel Voll, an acclaimed journalist turned TV producer and showrunner, to gather color for a planned dramatic TV series about Guantanamo that would eventually have Oliver Stone attached. Ben Fox from the AP, David Welna from NPR, and Thomas Watkins from Agence France-Presse also showed up, as did, finally, Jeffrey Stern, another successful book author whose luggage only made it during his first attempt the previous October. (The *New York Times Magazine* would publish his feature on one of al Baluchi's team members, "Alka Pradhan vs. Gitmo," near the end of the year.) Much to Carol's and my benefit, Williams and McDermott would become quasi-regular attendees in the years ahead.

This was a fun group. I have often told friends and colleagues that if there had been fifteen journalists on my first few trips, I probably would not have kept coming. Looking back, I still think this is true: I'm not sure what a smaller, niche publication would have added to the journalistic record. But my decision to start another year of coverage wasn't entirely altruistic. The work was too journalistically satisfying to give up, and the camaraderie continued to buffer against some of the self-imposed assignment's more miserable elements. During the January 2017 trip, as I spent a lot of time answering questions from my colleagues about the proceedings, often late at night, I realized that I had become something of an expert. I could take some of the load off Carol and have a lot of fun in the process, even if in small bites: By the next trip, in March, the journalism contingent was down to three.

I also enjoyed the attention in my personal life, where my work was known within Fiona's and my fairly large circle of friends. I was regularly cornered at parties or bar hangouts, where friends or acquaintances would pepper me with an endless array of questions about how I had become one of just two journalists in the world to make Guantanamo Bay a second home. A lot of questions were about where we slept or drank, or how we got to Gitmo, or if we could spend a weekend in Havana. But I was surprised at how many good questions were asked about the status of the proceedings. People cared and were interested, even if they did not know much before the start of the conversations. They found it fascinating that the US government would torture people and then attempt to get them through an American court of law.

* * *

Trump's first year was an odd one for the 9/11 case. The prior fourteen months had been an intense blur, with several multi-week trips that packed in a number of consequential (and, just as often, inconsequential) oral arguments. With January 2017 came a slower pace of one-week hearings, with some scheduled for two weeks before the parties and Judge Pohl agreed they could cut it short. Occasionally, a prosecutor or defense attorney who was initially prepared to argue a motion would tell Pohl that "peace has broken out," and that the two sides were close to reaching a resolution on whatever the dispute was. Whenever scheduling and the idea of condensing a trip was discussed in court, Pohl would occasionally say "I don't do planes"—meaning he wasn't responsible for logistics. But his message, it seemed to me, was: "The reason I don't do planes is because someone else does, and that person should get the plane here a week early."

Much of the first year treaded familiar ground in court, as well, with oral arguments on motions that I dutifully covered for Lawdragon while a more important process happened largely behind the scenes—the defense teams receiving the government's judicially approved substitute evidence about the CIA program. But one bigger theme that started to emerge was whether Camp Justice and the Naval Base generally would ever be prepared to hold a massive death penalty trial that would last in excess of a year. These issues seemed to be getting under Pohl's skin. He called out a hypocrisy on the part of the US government, which referred to 9/11 as the "Crime of the Century" but then would haggle over resources that would allow multiple commission cases to operate effectively at the same time.

James Connell had filed a motion to abate the January session after the base unilaterally canceled hotel housing for civilian members of the defense teams, even though government travel regulations prohibited civilians from staying in CHU trailers. In his January 19 ruling, shortly before that first trip of 2017, Pohl declined to postpone the hearing after the reservations were reinstated. However, he pointed out some of the absurdities of having the progress of one of the most important cases in US history dependent on so many personalities outside of the court system. He said that it was the government that decided to hold the case on Guantanamo Bay and that it now had "the responsibility to provide adequate logistical support." He also touched on something that I often stewed over laying alone in my ice-cold tent during many sleepless nights—the silliness of having so much of the "Expeditionary Legal Complex" on Camp Justice be so "expeditionary," with tents, work trailers, and latrines that regularly had mold or other problems. Such austere conditions were not truly warranted.

"The Commission is convened at [Naval Station Guantanamo Bay], an active and relatively modern U.S. Navy base in existence since 1903," Pohl wrote. "The Commission is not convened in Iraq, Afghanistan or the Horn of Africa where the U.S. presence is truly expeditionary."

In the March hearing—another planned two-week session shortened to one—prosecutor Ed Ryan told Pohl that June 2018 was realistic for jury selection, a claim that the defense teams found laughable. But Pohl had already indicated a general support of the defense side's view that a trial date was pointless until the discovery process was complete, or much farther along. He also said he saw "a potential train wreck" with multiple cases moving forward at the same time. He was not enticed by Ryan's suggestion that the courtroom could host two proceedings during the same week by holding one case during the day and the other at night. Pohl said the solutions were obvious.

"They involve money and construction," Pohl said.

Ryan took a mocking tone about defense complaints that "it's just too hard down here" and said that the prosecution team would be ready for trial. Jim Harrington rose to make one final point from bin al Shibh's table, not seeing the need to walk to the podium.

"Ed Ryan has little sympathy for my advanced age," he said.

"None," Ryan confirmed.

Later, at the closing press conference, Connell told us that having "Night Court" for the 9/11 case would be undignified. Logistics and resourcing became a big issue again in the summer, when Pohl decided to cancel the entire July hearing. That happened after the judge was informed that the JTF-GTMO commander canceled the separate boat service that took Pohl and his staff across the bay after the arriving flights. Pohl believed the separate transportation was necessary to prevent "commingling" between the judiciary and the parties to the case on the twenty-minute ferry ride. This move drew some criticism, but it got the boat service reinstated.

The intervening session, in May, threatened to be the closest thing to a blockbuster hearing that the 9/11 case would have that year. This was due to bin al Shibh's continuing complaints about the Camp 7 guard force harassing him with noises and vibrations. Harrington was planning to call Abu Zubaydah, the camp's most high-profile detainee other than KSM, to testify in support of the team's motion to hold the guard force in contempt. As recounted in the Senate's torture report, Zubaydah was the test subject of the CIA's "enhanced interrogation techniques" after his capture in 2002. The CIA's work on him (and soon after on al Nashiri, the USS *Cole* bombing suspect) became the model for the interrogation program used on other detainees.

On Guantanamo, Zubaydah had become a cell-block leader and was one of the liaisons between the Camp 7 detainees and the guard force.

Zubaydah was never charged with any crimes, but his lawyers felt that the parameters for his testimony set by Judge Pohl—which would allow for cross-examination by the prosecution about Zubaydah's possible bias—were not fair. His repeated failure to testify over multiple hearings in which it was promised or plausible was a blow to the media, not least of all the AP's Ben Fox, who was beginning to tire of the case's lack of concrete news. As of this writing, Zubaydah has never been to a US court of law—either as a witness or to face criminal charges.

As he often did in his press briefings, Martins reminded the small traveling media troupe in May that the work of the military commissions continues regardless of what happens in court. The prosecution had now provided the defense teams with about 6,200 pages of discovery from the CIA's RDI program, most of it the substitute and summarized versions of classified evidence that Pohl had approved as adequate. That amount was more than a third of the total the government planned to turn over. By the start of the August hearing in 2017, this process was nearly complete. Of course, missing from those tranches of evidence was an actual black site.

CHAPTER 10

Black Site Still Missing. August 2017.

On August 24, 2017, David Nevin was in the awkward position of questioning a military judge about his role in what the attorney clearly viewed as an illegal destruction of evidence. The process of voir dire is typically used for questioning prospective jurors, or to ask a military judge about potential biases at the start of taking a case, but Pohl had promised the defense teams a year earlier that they could ask him about his role in whatever happened to Site A. Regardless of whether he punished the government, Pohl was unlikely to disqualify himself from the case, which meant that Nevin would be arguing many motions before Pohl for many more months to come.

This day of oral arguments came about fifteen months after Nevin's team filed its motion to have Pohl and the prosecution team disqualified, which is pretty fast for the 9/11 case. In weighing discovery motions, Pohl eventually ruled that the defense teams were entitled to some additional evidence related to the decommissioning. The government filed motions asking for time to comply with the order, then sought to provide substitute evidence, which Pohl eventually approved earlier in the year. In doing so, he granted a clarification sought by the government that the defense was not entitled to receive any communications between the prosecution team and the CIA over Site A's decommissioning—an interesting if predictable tidbit that you only got if you followed the litigation and waited for a public version of Pohl's order placed on the court's website. Over defense objections, there would not be any witnesses to this dispute, which made for a faster path to oral arguments.

In its court filings, the prosecution contended that the defense teams were not entitled to be notified if the black site preserved by Pohl's December 2013 order—the first one—underwent a change in status, which, in that situation, was a "decommissioning" that the defense termed a "destruction." When Nevin asked Pohl during the voir dire if he intended the defense teams to receive such notice, Pohl responded that he did. He expected the June 2014 order—which allowed the decommissioning—to be provided to defense teams, albeit in redacted form.

"Did you intend to—that we would be kept in the dark about the fact that the [December 2013 order] was no longer protecting that site?" Nevin asked.

"No, no, I wouldn't have," Pohl responded. "No."

Pohl said he became aware in late 2015 that a redacted version of his June 2014 order authorizing the decommissioning of Site A had never been sent to the defense teams. He then directed that it be sent out, and the government finally provided it to the teams in February 2016.

The CIPA-like process of providing substitute evidence of classified material to defense teams is covered by commissions' rule number 505, which leads to everybody in court referring to it as "the 505 process." Pohl echoed the government's position by stating that he intended to handle substitute evidence of the black site like any other piece of evidence going through the 505 process. The problem from the defense's point of view, however, was that the judge was required to compare the substitute evidence with the original material.

"Did you see the site before you issued that order?" Nevin asked.

"Did I actually visit it?" Pohl responded. "No."

Nevin wondered: "So how did you come to the conclusion that the substitution that was provided was an adequate substitute?"

As it turned out, Pohl had been given a longer, more comprehensive video representation of the site—that video, in his view, was the original evidence of Site A. The substitute evidence he approved was a shortened second video, which he viewed as adequate. Pohl elaborated that his reasoning in approving a video as substitute evidence was influenced by an earlier ruling in 2012 by US District Court Judge Emmet Sullivan, who held in a separate habeas proceeding in federal court that a video representation of a black site was an adequate substitution under the CIPA process. Pohl said he believed Sullivan's order was related to the same Site A. (This was later confirmed to be true.)

"I approved video number two as a substitute for video number one," Pohl said.

He added that the original video would still be part of the record of the case, as all original classified material is preserved for appellate review. That video, of course, was not the "original" evidence, which was an actual physical black site.

"The statute requires that the original will be preserved for appeal," Nevin said. "The original has not been preserved for appeal in this situation. It has been destroyed or decommissioned."

Pohl said he understood Nevin's position. He also said that he understood that the defense teams viewed the black site as important evidence for mitigating against the death penalty as the defense teams hoped to re-create the harsh conditions of confinement endured by the defendants.

"It doesn't take a particularly deep analysis to know that this is potentially mitigating evidence," Pohl said. "I've got it."

Nevin asked Pohl if the government had asked him to give secret orders related to other black sites other than Site A, but the judge's security officer told him that he could not answer the question in open court. Nevin then asked if Pohl had been informed of the actual location of Site A, but Pohl said he would have to wait to answer until the classified session closed to the public and the defendants.

Under questioning by Connell, Pohl revealed that he had engaged with the prosecution team in the iterative process of producing an adequate substitute by comparing the first video representation of the black site with the initial proposed shortened version made by the FBI—which he felt was not good enough because it had too many redactions. Pohl said he directed the government to produce a better second video.

"So what you've got in video number two, it's a more robust version of video number one," Pohl said.

Prosecutor Swann had no questions for voir dire, which resumed in a closed session the next afternoon.

The heavily redacted classified transcript is not too illuminating. During the session, Nevin returned to the issue of whether Pohl knew where Site A was located; while it's hard to tell with the redactions, it seemed as though Pohl did.

"Will you tell us where it is?" Nevin asks in one un-redacted section.

"No," Pohl responded.

Nevin wanted to know why. Pohl explained that the reasons were contained in the government's ex parte filing not available to defense teams.

"I don't know if I can give you a satisfactory answer without telling you things I am not authorized to tell you," Pohl said.

Nevin's next question—and perhaps an answer—are blacked out. But they prompted Gen. Martins to say he wanted to "assert the national security privilege." This is different than the classified information privilege, which identifies the classified evidence to be discussed in closed sessions. When the government asserts the national security privilege, it means that the information itself cannot find its way into the case at all—even in closed sessions. I didn't know then that, as litigation over other evidence and witnesses related to the CIA program continued in subsequent sessions, Martins's team would invoke the national security privilege more and more.

During his turn, Connell referred to elements of the video and other documentary evidence provided by the government that, in his view, revealed the inadequacy of the substitution. The specifics, however, are redacted as Connell refers to "the significance of certain details which we know are important but could only learn more about by physical inspection."

Once they reopened the session, the lawyers made their closing arguments. Nevin focused on the judge's approval of a substitute evidence without seeing the original—a clear violation of the CIPA or 505 principles.

"With all respect, Your Honor, you did not follow the rules when you approved a substitution of a substitution for this evidence," Nevin argued. "There is no such thing as a substitution of a substitution."

Nevin told Pohl that he was requesting his removal from the case with "trepidation," noting that the prosecution had attacked the defense for allegedly disrespecting Pohl's decades of military service. Nevin said he meant "with all due respect" literally.

"Mr. Nevin, I understand your position, and I don't take any of this personally," Pohl said—convincingly, to me at least.

Nevin said the issue went beyond CIPA or the commissions' 505 process: Pohl had no authority to hold a secret hearing on whether the government could destroy exculpatory evidence. Nevin also contended that Pohl was ultimately responsible for making sure that the defense teams received such an order, which would enable them to challenge it. If the defense teams knew the destruction was coming, they would have gone to the commissions' appellate court and, if needed, the Court of Appeals for the DC Circuit in the civilian system to stop it. The teams had hoped to call expert witnesses on the importance of physical evidence to help bolster their position on why the loss of the site was so catastrophic. The government opposed these plans, and Pohl had sided with the prosecution. Defense teams instead submitted affidavits by experts. Nevin told Pohl that the video substitution was "pretty close to a joke" compared to having a chance to portray the overall feel of a torture chamber.

"And that would have been something that we could have achieved by visiting the site ourselves, but more important, by visiting the site with experts," Nevin said.

In his closing, Connell argued that the FBI's photographic rendition was "not nearly as good as the average online real estate offering, much less a commercial video game." Connell's team was only pushing for the prosecution's removal, which he accused of acting in bad faith by exploiting an administrative mistake by Pohl's staff. It was Connell and his team that first discovered a possible ruling related to the status of Site A by seeing activity in the electronic "filings inventory" for the motion series. He made numerous inquiries by email to Pohl's staff, which then contacted the prosecution for clarification about the status of the defense teams' knowledge of the June 2014 order. Referring to emails turned over to the defense in discovery, Connell said that the prosecution suggested that the judiciary give him "a technically accurate but misleading answer" about the content of the order.

"It is clear that it knew that the defense had not been provided a redacted version and sought to use that information to its litigation advantage," Connell said. "We can tell that the government did not want the defense to know of the destruction."

Jim Harrington, as he often did in proceedings, put a folksy spin on the events, telling Pohl that the work of all trial lawyers really boils down to "storytelling." He then went into an anecdote about the cottage where his father lived until 1921 off the coast of Ireland. It had a thatched roof, no electricity, and just one room for the entire family. While Harrington had heard stories about it for many years, he did not fully grasp his father's upbringing until he viewed the decrepit structure with his own eyes in 1982.

"I say this to the court because that is what we were denied in terms of being able to do a physical inspection," Harrington said. He added that the FBI mockup was "lousy" but that even a better video rendition using the best technology would not be sufficient.

"We have been deprived of the ability to tell an important story to people who will decide whether our clients live or die," Harrington said.

Swann began his argument with characteristic bluster, taking offense that the defense teams would denigrate "American heroes"—but Pohl cut him off. He didn't need to hear it, reminding Swann that he was a judge and not a jury.

"If you've got a long part of that, skip over that and get to the substance of the matter here," Pohl said.

Swann contended that there was "no collusion" between the judge and the prosecution to hide the decommissioning order, and that its late arrival to defense teams was an honest mistake. He said the defense's "conspiracy theory" was "a work of fiction." He also returned to the semantics embedded in the CIPA process of "preserving" evidence through substitutes.

"Nobody destroyed anything, nobody disposed of anything," Swann said. "They have a judicially approved substitute. Nobody destroyed critically exculpatory evidence, which apparently has no definition in their world."

Nevin was infuriated in his rebuttal, arguing that if "nobody destroyed anything" then the past year of litigation was "a big waste of time."

"Because if it's still around, I'd like to see it, and I'd like to proceed to the matter of arguing that I should be allowed to go see it," Nevin said. "It was, in fact, destroyed. You can talk about the quality of the substitute that was approved if you want, but you cannot say that this was not destroyed. Words have meanings, and counsel for the government knows that perfectly well."

After hearing more from Nevin and Connell, Pohl asked the defense side of the room if anybody else wanted to be heard again. Harrington couldn't resist a chance to defuse the tension in the room. He stood and leaned toward the mic on his table.

"Judge, I will not describe my mother's house," Harrington said.

* * *

Relative to other pending motions, Pohl did not waste a whole lot of time in issuing his ruling. In January 2018, Pohl rejected all requests to remove either himself or any members of the prosecution team from the case. He blamed himself for a lack of clarity in his June 2014 order over whether the judiciary or the prosecution should have provided a redacted version to the defense. Otherwise, he didn't seem to view the events as a big deal: The evidence was not exculpatory or related to the charged offenses of the 9/11 attacks, he reasoned, but potentially mitigating for sentencing. He said again that the video produced to the teams was an adequate substitute for these purposes, and additionally, that the defense teams could call witnesses with knowledge of Site A and were already receiving documentary evidence about all the black sites from the discovery provided by the government. The defense teams were not prejudiced by the missing black site, he said.

Not surprisingly, that was not the last word on the matter. Pohl already had stayed any further dismantling of Site A—the status of which was known to defense teams, but not to the public—as the litigation was playing out. He would continue to issue further stays of dismantling as the defense teams pursued appeals to the commissions' appellate court, the Court of Military Commission Review, and then the US Court of Appeals for the DC Circuit. Those courts both held that the defense teams failed to show why the video rendition was not an adequate substitute; the DC Circuit's opinion came in March 2020, just as the pandemic shut down all proceedings.

In April the next year, the government filed a notice with the military commission that it was "proceeding with the completion of the dismantling of the remnants of Site A," regardless of the pendency of any litigation. Prosecutors said they would explain in an ex parte filing why the government had to take this step; the timing of the move suggested that the government would lose any ability to control the site following President Biden's plan to withdraw US forces from Afghanistan. The fate of Site A was finally sealed.

CHAPTER 11

Transparency.

Those who still had a stake in the Guantanamo Bay detention and trial operations wondered what Trump's election might mean for "the least worst place," and what might have happened with a different outcome. It's possible a Hillary Clinton presidency, if she ever had Democratic majorities in both houses, could have succeeded in lifting the prohibition on transferring detainees to US soil. But she probably would not have spent the political capital on such an effort. Instead, she would have just continued the detainee transfers following the recommendations of the Periodic Review Board, or PRB, which was Obama's version of the interagency assessments of the detainees' suitability for release. The population would have been whittled down to probably just the high-value detainees in Camp 7, along with Ali Hamza al Bahlul, a former aide to Osama bin Laden who is serving a life sentence for his 2008 conviction by military commission.

A specialized legal and diplomatic team within the US State Department handles the process of finding host countries for detainees cleared through the PRB. The real impact of Trump's election was that he gutted that State Department team, effectively halting all of its work. During Trump's term, only one detainee was transferred, and that was a Saudi—Ahmed al Darbi—who had pleaded guilty in 2014 with an agreement that included a provision for his return to Saudi Arabia to finish out his military commission sentence. However, Trump's campaign promise to not only keep Guantanamo open but to fill it with "bad dudes" went unfulfilled. The detention facility has not had a new detainee since 2008, before Obama even took office.

An astute observer might have noticed that, just a week after the January 2017 session, Trump appointed Gina Haspel to be deputy director of the CIA. It was known, though still technically classified, that Haspel had overseen the Thailand black site at which CIA interrogators conducted some of the earliest "enhanced interrogation" sessions, including those involving waterboarding. Haspel also played a role in the approval of the destruction of the videotapes of those sessions. Her position in the RDI program grew far greater attention thirteen months later, when Trump nominated her to lead the CIA. By then, defense teams had already begun to suspect that Haspel's ascendancy in the CIA had been playing a role in the pretrial litigation as it unfolded in 2017 with respect to their efforts to access witnesses and evidence from the interrogation program.

As for Trump's impact on the island as a place to live and to work as a journalist, that was initially hard to measure but eventually trended negative. Day to day, measuring hostility and its source of origin in a place like Gitmo is challenging. Sometimes when a group of reporters walks into O'Kelly's, everybody in the bar turns to glare at us; at other times, no one seems to care. Same for the bowling alley or the Tiki Bar. Occasionally people approach us to have a friendly chat; other times they stay far away or avoid eye contact when passing.

Even when it comes to actual policy, the amount of people involved in establishing the base's media conditions can complicate the process of determining motive or intent—at least for me, though I know Carol has a better sense of the players involved. The public affairs officer for the military commissions gets us to the Naval Base and in and out of court, and this person is responsible for us in Camp Justice and the courtroom. But outside of Camp Justice we are the guests of the base and its commander, a position held by a navy captain who generally serves a three-year tour. Media activities outside of Camp Justice—such as interviewing the base commander or getting photos around town—have to be negotiated with the base public affairs officer. And the detention facility, which leases its space from the Navy, has an entirely separate command structure and public affairs operation. In fact, if we want to take photos of the hospital or report on its work, we have to deal with yet another separate command structure and spokesperson.

Whether the public affairs officers and their superiors among the various entities get along plays a big role in what we can accomplish outside of court. Some people within the various chains of command have liked the media, and some have not, which has been true no matter who the president is. Still, access to the detention zone eventually slowed down, especially when it came to "windshield tours" of the facility that the court public affairs officer would occasionally arrange with the prison PAO on slow court days. Formal tours led by JTF-GTMO also would eventually dry up completely within a few years of Trump taking office.

One change that happened more quickly, in the first half of 2017, was that the media was barred from Rick's, the officers' club, even though we were still considered "officer equivalents" on the base. Rick's, which is adjacent to the Tiki Bar and part of the same building that has the Bayview restaurant, has a handsome wooden bar and a few pool tables, along with some great memorabilia dispersed throughout. With limited food and hangout options on the base, the burgers at Rick's came in handy, especially on the longer trips. I've always liked the Tiki Bar, but it is completely open air, leaving patrons at the mercy of the heat and bugs. The court's public affairs officer in 2017, Air Force Maj. Ben Sakrisson, who had replaced Army Lt. Col. Val Henderson, told us that the base no longer wanted us showing up, that we made people uncomfortable. It's hard to blame Trump for that, even if he would have appreciated the move.

Some of us surmised that the change might have had something to do with the Naval Base's biggest and still-simmering scandal of contemporary times: the January 2015 death of a Navy security employee, Christopher Tur, and the subsequent firing of the base commander, Navy Captain John Nettleton. He and Tur had fought after a night of heavy drinking that began at a secret basement bar below Rick's. The bloody brawl had something to do with Tur's concern that Nettleton was sleeping with his wife, and Tur was found floating in the bay a few days later. The criminal investigation was still pending a few years later, and Carol had continued to report on the story for the *Miami Herald*. (Eventually, Carol produced a must-read feature titled "Sex, Power and Fury: The Mystery of a Death at Guantanamo Bay" for the *New York Times* in January 2020.) Nettleton was never charged in Tur's death but was convicted in a Florida federal court of obstruction of justice for covering up the night's events.

Another change that Maj. Sakrisson informed us about during Trump's first year was that we had to wear our press badges at all times around the base, no matter where we were. The stated reason was "new security protocols," but it was pretty clear that base leadership wanted everybody on the island to know whenever we were around. This created something like a "Scarlet Letter" environment for media, even if we already stood out—and of course everybody knew who Carol was. From that point on, I started wearing my media badge everywhere, even on the walk from my tent to the latrines in the middle of the night. You just never knew who might be watching. I'm sure there's a video of me somewhere stumbling around without my badge as evidence of a violation.

Whether the Guantanamo court is a truly public court makes for an interesting discussion, sort of like debating whether the court is actually in Cuba. Attending in person is doable, if difficult, for media, approved NGOs, and victim family members, as is attending the remote sites, though there is only one site—Fort Meade, Maryland—open to the media and the general public. The court system earns transparency points for posting all of the court transcripts on its website, mc.mil, which for public sessions can often occur on the evening after court or the next day. The system is far from perfect, however. The CIA or other "original classification authorities" will often delay the release of a transcript—sometimes for weeks or months—to redact details, even though everything transcribed had happened in open court. Judge Pohl had sided with the government on this dispute, granting the government the power to redact transcripts of public proceedings, even if Carol has already tweeted the details.

For my first few years on the 9/11 case, classified sessions from which we and the defendants were barred were relatively rare. The judge and the parties always discussed in open court when those sessions would take place, and we would be informed about the length of each "806" session—named as such for its place in the commission rules—after they concluded. By the middle of 2017, Gen. Martins informed us in a written statement that the case had had a total of ten classified sessions constituting about 4 percent of the total court time.

The court system also posts transcripts of the closed "806" sessions after classified or other sensitive information is blacked out. While these are often opaque—with pages and pages completely blacked out—a close reader can pick up helpful information from the sentences or partial sentences that survive review. In his professorial and rose-tinted approach to analyzing the commissions, Martins would tell us that the posting of the 806 transcripts reduced the overall amount of "closed" court time based on whatever number of lines survived redaction. I understood what he meant, but that always seemed like a stretch to me—to characterize maybe a hundred lines of text out of fifty pages as contributing to the total amount of "open court." In 2017, both Carol and I noticed that the court had not posted several of the classified transcripts, even old ones, because they had not undergone security review. We made repeated requests to Martins and Maj. Sakrisson, as well as to Navy Cmdr. Sarah Higgins, who succeeded Sakrisson and became the fourth commissions' public affairs officer of my tenure. Eventually, the classified transcripts began arriving on mc.mil at a quicker pace.

The website can be enormously helpful, though that might depend on what era of the proceedings you're interested in. All public pleadings and rulings are posted on the site by their motion or "AE" number, but only after each filing undergoes a security review. Undoubtedly, the best way to prepare for any court hearing on Gitmo or anywhere else is to read the written pleadings on the motions scheduled for oral argument. But this has often been impossible when covering the 9/11 case because the relevant motions are not yet public, even though the court rules require the security review to take place within fifteen days of the filing date. The violation of this rule has led defense teams to intermittently argue that their clients are not getting a public trial. The prosecution and the judges have always acknowledged the problem, but it's never gotten fixed, rendering pre-trip preparation reading open to chance.

From a court perspective, the biggest blow to transparency during the early Trump era came in October 2017, when Sakrisson informed us that Martins would no longer meet with the media. Going forward, the Office of the Chief Prosecutor would not be making any comments on the record, including written statements. Sakrisson told us that for the prosecution to continue commenting on cases was becoming inappropriate as "the posture" of the cases moved closer to trial, a statement that did not need hindsight to raise an eyebrow. This change felt abrupt and came as a surprise to me. I loved discussing the case with Martins. I'm sure he was annoyed by us at times, especially when it came to the questions about torture, but he seemed genuinely interested in tackling both the "in-the-weeds" questions from me and Carol and the more foundational questions from newcomers. He could do big picture or small, displaying patience and even appreciation toward the journalists showing up. We suspected the change in media policy might have come from the new convening authority, a Pentagon official named Harvey Rishikof, who had been appointed to the position by Secretary of Defense James Mattis in April 2017. We had heard generally that Martins and Rishikof did not get along.

Having the prosecution's viewpoint was made more important by the fact that so many of the pleadings were also unavailable, which meant we often did not have a clear articulation of the government's position prior to attending court—and sometimes even then, if the prosecution decided to "rest on the pleadings" instead of providing oral arguments. James Connell, in his "explainer-in-chief" role for the case, would have to tell us in prehearing meetings what the government was contending in a particular dispute. Sometimes, if defense lawyers knew a government pleading was not classified, they would provide it to us before it was publicly available on the website. But that was a poor substitute for our wide-ranging chats with Gen. Martins. He remained friendly outside court—we could always talk about exercise, of course—but, as I started my third year of coverage, the 9/11 case had clearly entered a new and less-transparent era.

CHAPTER 12

Enter the FBI. December 2017.

"Your Honor, the United States calls Special Agent James Fitzgerald," Ed Ryan told the judge at 10:17 on the morning of December 5, 2017. With that line, the lanky prizefighter finally had his day. Not quite a trial, perhaps, but a genuine opportunity to bring the horrors of 9/11 into court and link at least one of the defendants to the crimes.

Fitzgerald was a fine witness to offer a taste of the government's case in chief. He did not quite look the part of a globetrotting FBI agent—more bookish and dad-like behind his glasses with a subdued voice—but he had the résumé as a former Massachusetts state trooper who had spent much of his two decades at the bureau working the 9/11 case in one form or another. He was now based in the Boston office. Fitzgerald told Ryan that he was in New Jersey when the planes hit New York on September 11, 2001.

"After the Towers came down, I was able to make my way into Manhattan," Fitzgerald said.

Fitzgerald soon became part of the formal investigative team called "PENTTBOM," named for the Pentagon, the Twin Towers (TT), and the explosive nature of the crime. Over the course of a few hours, Ryan led Fitzgerald through the basic outlines of the FBI's early attempts to piece together the staggering, world-altering attacks. In doing so, Ryan played videos of the crashes into the towers that became ubiquitous in the hours, days, and weeks after 9/11. The first was the video captured by Jules and Gedeon Naudet, two brothers and documentary filmmakers who were embedded with firefighters in lower Manhattan, showing American Airlines Flight 11 crashing into the North Tower. Shortly after the video began, the curtain in the viewing gallery was drawn to give the victim family members privacy.

Fitzgerald explained that many more videos existed of United Airlines Flight 175 hitting the South Tower because by then many news organizations and other onlookers had trained their attention on the World Trade Center. Ryan showed a handful of these, along with footage of the post-crash Pentagon devastation and the long-distance filming of the remains of United Flight 93 smoldering in a field near Shanksville, Pennsylvania. Ryan asked where Flight 93's data indicated it was heading.

"In general terms, the aircraft was flying towards the city of Washington, DC," Fitzgerald answered, reminding us all of what could have been.

Fitzgerald said he listened to the cockpit audio recording of Flight 93's final minutes, which Ryan did not play in court.

"At the end of the recording, you can hear Arabic voices and you can hear American voices," Fitzgerald said. "You can hear what appeared to me to be sounds of a struggle and shouting and banging noises."

He added: "It sounded like a life-and-death struggle."

Ryan played six minutes of an al Qaeda promotional video released after the 9/11 attacks that paid tribute to the hijackers. Fitzgerald said the names listed in the video matched the names of the men the FBI determined to be the hijackers as part of its early investigation, primarily using flight manifests. Ryan also played three pre-death martyrdom videos made by hijackers.

Ryan previewed portions of the government's document-intensive case, having Fitzgerald review a variety of documents displayed in court—visa applications, copies of passports, car rental agreements, phone records, and receipts to flight schools showing a sampling of pre-attack activities of the nineteen hijackers. As riveting as the videos were, Fitzgerald's testimony also revealed the trial itself would be a complex slog of paperwork.

This mini-trial was brought to the Guantanamo Bay courtroom courtesy of Mustafa al Hawsawi and his defense team, led by Walter Ruiz. Each defendant is entitled to challenge the government's "personal jurisdiction" over him, as the Military Commissions Act limits the commission system's jurisdiction to "alien unprivileged enemy belligerents"—or, in layperson's terms, a foreigner who engaged in or supported hostilities against the United States or its allies, or who was a member of al Qaeda. Al Hawsawi was the first to file his jurisdictional challenge.

The military commission is a war court set up to prosecute war crimes. At trial, the government would have to prove beyond a reasonable doubt not only that al Hawsawi played a role in the 9/11 plot but that the attacks took place during the context of an armed conflict—in other words, that the United States and al Qaeda were at war prior to 9/11. In the pretrial phase, facing a challenge like al Hawsawi's, the prosecution had to establish these elements by the lesser standard of a preponderance of the evidence. This set up something like a preliminary hearing that occurs in regular domestic criminal cases, where the prosecution has to prove to a judge that the state has enough evidence to take a case to trial. The other teams disagreed with Ruiz's strategy of filing the challenge now; they feared the implications of doing so while they were waiting for so much critical discovery from the government.

While torture may have been the case's dominant issue, the dispute over "hostilities" was also becoming a massive and widening one before Pohl—however esoteric it might have seemed. The government claimed that the war with al Qaeda began with Osama bin Laden's declaration of war against the United States in 1996, and that major pre-9/11 war events included the 1998 bombing of the American embassies in Kenya and Tanzania; the US response to the attacks by launching missiles against suspected al Qaeda sites in Sudan and Afghanistan; and the bombing of the USS *Cole* in October 2000—all during the Clinton administration. But defense lawyers contended that the vast majority of scholarship and relevant case law supported their contention that this type of intermittent hostility was not remotely close to establishing an armed conflict under the laws of war.

For most observers, this time-consuming dispute was another reason to roll their eyes at the proceedings. Would a judge really dismiss the biggest case in US history—the whole reason George W. Bush created the court in the first place—because he agreed with the legal conclusion that the United States and al Qaeda were not technically at war on the morning of 9/11? For me, however, the dispute became part of the churn of topics that made the case insidiously addictive. The issue was not only legally interesting, but it also forced the teams to make important strategic choices. Ruiz was taking a truly minimalist approach. Later in the week, he would call just a single hostilities witness, Creighton Law Professor Sean Watts, a lieutenant colonel in the Army Reserve who had taught the law of war at West Point and the Army's JAG school. Watts would testify that a war did not exist between the United States and al Qaeda until the invasion of Afghanistan in October 2001.

None of the other teams chose to participate at this juncture except the team for Ammar al Baluchi, led by James Connell, who feared—presciently, you might suspect—that if he ever wanted to make his jurisdictional case, he better get on the train that was moving. But he had a much different approach for his case: Connell wanted to call dozens and dozens of witnesses from the Clinton and Bush administrations to show that the US government viewed al Qaeda as essentially a criminal enterprise to be handled by law enforcement, not as an enemy of war. This strategy led to many discovery requests and subsequent disputes over evidence about how the two administrations handled the al Qaeda threat. Judge Pohl decided to tackle al Hawsawi's far more simplified jurisdictional case and kick al Baluchi's to some point in 2018.

Though it was his day in court, al Hawsawi did not show up for Fitzgerald's testimony. The frail Saudi skipped that day as he did most days due to his rectal pain and other health ailments, including chronic migraines, light sensitivity, tinnitus, and back pain. He was also absent the next day, when the government called its second witness, former FBI Special Agent Abigail Perkins. Her role on the stand would be to link al Hawsawi to the conspiracy that Fitzgerald had outlined and also to offer some support to the notion that the United States and al Qaeda were at war prior to 9/11. Unlike Fitzgerald, Perkins had left the bureau after twenty-two years and was currently a contract analyst with the Department of Energy.

Under direct examination by Clay Trivett, Perkins explained that she had also worked on the FBI's investigations into the 1998 embassy bombings in Kenya and Tanzania, videos of which Trivett played in court. Trivett had Perkins read from portions of the 1996 "Declaration of holy war" in which bin Laden criticized America's support of Israel in the conflict with the Palestinians, the presence of US troops in Muslim holy lands, and the US support of corrupt Arab regimes in the Middle East.

"As a terrorism investigator, what was the significance of that document to your investigations?" Trivett asked.

"It was a stated intention to target and kill Americans," Perkins said.

On 9/11, Perkins was in the FBI's office near the World Trade Center when the first plane hit the North Tower, shaking her building. She said that her office had CNN on and that agents ran down to the Towers after seeing the second plane hit.

"What agents from the FBI were involved initially in the investigation?" Trivett asked.

"Everyone," Perkins responded.

"All ten thousand FBI agents?" Trivett asked.

Perkins thought for a second, then repeated: "Everyone."

Perkins said that she was assigned to the part of the PENTTBOM tasked with the "financial aspects" of the attacks—and that al Hawsawi quickly became a focus due to the presence of his name on certain financial documents. Perkins said she traveled to the United Arab Emirates to get information on a bank account set up by al Hawsawi that he and some of the hijackers used. Trivett led Perkins through a long list of mail, financial, and travel documents—all displayed on screens in court and the gallery—that showed connections between the defendant and the hijackers. She testified that, in addition to assisting with travel arrangements, al Hawsawi received money back from hijackers in the days before September 11—a sign that the execution of the operation was near.

In light of her mastery of the material, Perkins conducted the formal interrogations of al Hawsawi on Guantanamo Bay in January 2007 and obtained what the government hoped would be the "clean" statements—free of the past CIA torture—to be used at trial. On the stand, Perkins described her sessions with al Hawsawi as "good, professional, respectful, cordial" over about thirty hours on January 11, 12, 13, and 16, 2007. She did not read him his *Miranda* rights, as the government's policy was not to provide detainees lawyers before charging them. However, using a protocol established prior to the sessions, Perkins told al Hawsawi that his participation was voluntary, that he could stop at any time, and that he would "not be returning to the custody of any of his previous custodians"—meaning he would remain in Department of Defense custody on Guantanamo and would not be returned to the CIA.

Perkins testified that she sat across a table from al Hawsawi, who was shackled at the ankles but not the wrists. Also in the room was Fitzgerald, who took notes, and a representative from the Department of Defense's Criminal Investigation Task Force, or CITF, which also had been involved in building criminal cases against detainees in early 2007. She said al Hawsawi was not under duress and participated voluntarily, and that she talked to him in English after determining that he understood her.

Perkins said she showed al Hawsawi many of the documents that Trivett had displayed in court, and that he confirmed it was his name on them. He also viewed photographs of the hijackers and confirmed the identities of the men he helped.

"Did you ask him specifically whether he helped support the brothers who hijacked the four planes, the September 11, 2001 Planes Operation?" Trivett asked.

"Yes," Perkins said.

She added: "He indicated that he was very happy to have been able to support the brothers who carried out the attack."

Perkins elaborated that al Hawsawi said he did not know the specifics of the operation but was pleased to learn of its success. She said she played for him an al Qaeda promotional video that showed al Hawsawi visiting with bin Laden in Afghanistan after the attacks, which Trivett also played in court. It was not hard to tell watching the monitors in the courtroom viewing gallery that the man in the video was also the man who often sat in front of us in court on a big pillow. Perkins said that al Hawsawi confirmed that he was in the video.

"How would you describe his demeanor while he was watching the video?" Trivett asked.

"He seemed to enjoy looking at it," Perkins responded.

By one measure, this was pretty damning stuff. The victim family members who traveled for the hearing and met with us that evening knew they had seen something special, with two important witnesses outlining the attacks. Of course, the flip side was having to relive 9/11 to a much greater extent than attending other sessions consumed by legal wrangling in oral arguments. One of the family members who spoke to us was Michael Salamone, who lost his brother, John, a thirty-seven-year-old stockbroker at Cantor Fitzgerald in the North Tower, who left behind a wife and three young children. Salamone spoke calmly to a half-dozen journalists as Welna from NPR and Rath from WGBH had their microphones extended to his face.

"As many times as I've seen those towers fall, number one, I cannot help but look even though I know it's coming," Salamone, then fifty-five, told us. "And number two, I can't help but get emotional and break down because I know that is the exact moment my brother is literally being killed."

* * *

But something else was afoot during that one-week trip. Al Hawsawi's lawyers had essentially called the government's bluff by requiring it to present in court two of the most critical witnesses against their client, perhaps the most important in Perkins. While the vast mountain of "hostilities" discovery was still out there, the government had to turn over discovery relevant to the testimony of the two FBI agents. On Monday night, December 4, 2017, after 9 p.m., just about twelve hours before Fitzgerald was set to take the stand, the al Hawsawi team hit pay dirt in the form of a twelve-page document.

Ruiz approached the podium the morning of December 5 to express to Pohl his outrage—if not disbelief—that he received critical discovery from the prosecution team so late. He said his team first requested the information on September 25, 2013, more than four years earlier. We didn't have the document, but Ruiz made it clear what the topic was.

"The relationship between the Federal Bureau of Investigation and the Central Intelligence Agency has been the subject of many, many discovery requests over the years, not only by members of Mr. al Hawsawi's legal team, but also by members of other defense teams," Ruiz said.

Ruiz also said he was still in the process of receiving un-redacted copies of the FBI's notes from the January 2007 interrogation sessions. He accused the government of engaging in discovery "by ambush" and said he might not be prepared to cross-examine Fitzgerald and Perkins during this session as his team worked to "digest" the new information.

"Okay," Pohl said. "Thank you."

Ryan then called Fitzgerald to begin laying out the 9/11 conspiracy.

That night, Ruiz stopped by the media center with his second-in-command, Suzanne Lachelier, the former navy commander who had been Ramzi bin al Shibh's military lawyer in the first military commission. Ruiz took his seat on the faux leather couch while Lachelier hung back behind the reporters. Ruiz had a document in his hand that went "to the heart of the relationship between the FBI and the CIA," he told us. The document wasn't yet posted on the commissions' website, but it was unclassified and would be discussed in open court during the week.

The document was an FBI memorandum issued prior to the January 2007 interrogations that stated that FBI interrogators would be given access to "CIA databases containing intelligence reports that were previously disseminated to the intelligence community." In other words, prior to re-interrogating detainees for the "clean" sessions, the FBI could review information learned from the detainees while they were being tortured or held in extreme isolation. The memo informed the agents that the interview sessions on Guantanamo Bay had to be documented "on a CIA-supplied laptop" and their notes sent to the CIA "for classification review." Agents had to create a separate documentation to note anything the detainees said related to their past abuse by the CIA, which would be kept out of the memorandum that would serve as the detainee's official statement for court purposes.

"We always felt they had unclean hands," Ruiz told us of the FBI. "This confirms that."

From Ruiz's point of view, the revelation effectively brought the CIA torturers into the FBI interrogation sessions. He described it as a "bombshell," and it was hard to argue. One of the enduring narratives of the post-9/11 era could effectively be boiled down to "FBI good, CIA bad"—that the FBI walked away from abusive interrogation sessions after learning what was happening at the CIA black sites. The torture program was, simply put, a CIA program, or so the story went. This twelve-page memo did not exactly turn that narrative on its head, but it linked the two agencies and provided a thread that defense teams could begin to pull on. Ruiz told us that he and his team were still assessing how the information should inform the cross-examinations of the two FBI witnesses, whether he did them that week or requested to do them later because he received the discovery so late. But the broader importance, he said, was that it would lead to many more discovery requests from the government.

"While only twelve actual pages, it's monumental in terms of the implications it has for how we continue to litigate from here on out," he told us.

At the time, I wondered if the production of this discovery would make the other four defense teams less angry at Ruiz for moving forward with his client's jurisdictional challenge. In the month prior to the hearing, I published a profile of Ruiz in which I asked him about his decision to move forward with the jurisdictional hearing while he was still waiting for discovery. He said his team already had what it needed "to win now." He also mentioned other "litigation strategies." Now, on the night of December 5, Ruiz sat back with a satisfied smile.

"You're starting to see some of those fruits," he told me.

Nevertheless, as he often was when talking about discovery, Ruiz was fuming. He told us it was ridiculous for the government to blame the pace of the case on the defense given the late production of discovery. He said it appeared clear the CIA did not want the case to move forward.

"This prosecuting team has a master that they're answering to, and that master has been slow-rolling information in discovery," Ruiz said. "It's the same master that we now identify by name in this unclassified document. And that master continues to be the CIA."

* * *

With Perkins on the stand, prosecutor Trivett focused on the financial and travel documents implicating al Hawsawi, along with videos that appeared to show the connections between al Hawsawi with at least seven of the hijackers, not to mention with bin Laden himself. But he knew he had to deal with the twelve-page memo that the government had turned over showing the CIA-FBI coordination. Even laypeople are familiar with the "fruit of the poisonous tree" concept: If the FBI used information elicited by CIA "enhanced interrogation techniques" to structure their own interrogations, these rapport-based interviews might not be so "clean" under the law. In what proved to be an awkward exchange, Trivett asked Perkins about her ability to access CIA databases in a secret facility in the capitol region.

"Did you use those materials in any way in preparing for your interview?" Trivett asked.

Perkins said that her "interest really wasn't to review what had been told to other people" but instead to get her "own information" related to the documents she had. Pohl jumped in, saying the answer wasn't "responsive to the question." He asked Trivett to ask again.

"Did you use any of the CIA statements specifically in preparing for your interview?" Trivett asked.

"I would say I wouldn't have relied on them to prepare my interview, no," Perkins responded.

Pohl now chimed in on his own: "Did you use any of them?"

"Review them, sir?" Perkins said, turning to the judge, who was now a little annoyed.

Pohl repeated: "Did you use any of the CIA statements in preparing your interview of Mr. al Hawsawi?"

Perkins stumbled a bit, saying she would have a hard time distinguishing between using and reviewing.

"Having them in my mind, sir, may have influenced me, so I can't disassociate completely," Perkins said.

"Got it," Pohl responded.

Ruiz decided to move forward with his cross-examination of both witnesses, which he conducted in quick fashion the next day, December 7. He confirmed another area of FBI-CIA linkage that the defense teams had suspected: Both Fitzgerald and Perkins testified that they and other PENTTBOM agents sent questions to the CIA for agency personnel to ask the detainees while they were at the black sites. Both agents wanted to do so in person but were denied access to the 9/11 suspects. Still, in one sense, the process of sending in what are called "intelligence requirements" meant the

FBI participated in the enhanced sessions remotely. This topic, too, would lead to many additional discovery requests that would become critical to defense efforts to suppress their clients' January 2007 statements.

The witnesses were hazy in their recollections of when and how they accessed CIA databases, and in what format the information came. Fitzgerald recalled accessing what he called a "closed system operated or owned by the CIA" at some point "circa 2007." However, he said he did not personally review information from the system in preparing for the interrogations of al Hawsawi, for which he was the notetaker, or for al Baluchi, for which he was the lead interviewer in separate sessions in January 2007.

Perkins said that she did, in fact, review CIA information, but she did not recall using a computer database at the CIA location.

"As I recall, in preparation for the interview, I had hard copy documents, hard copy printouts," Perkins said.

Ruiz briefly pursued another potential bombshell topic that could be damaging to the government's case. He asked Fitzgerald about two places in his notes where he said that al Hawsawi seemed to recognize his surroundings—signaling that the defendant had earlier spent time in Guantanamo Bay, when the CIA used a portion of the detention facility as a black site between 2003 and 2004. The fact that the government used the same location to conduct its "clean" sessions of detainees seemed like something that just couldn't possibly be true—and one that would lead to still more discovery requests. This information was even more problematic given that, according to the Senate report of the CIA program, the CIA maintained "operational control" of Camp 7 for a period of time after the detainees' transfer from the black sites. Prosecutor Ryan rose to say that any follow-up questions would have to take place in a closed session.

Under questioning by Ruiz, both agents confirmed the odd details of the January 2007 interrogation sessions. Normally, the FBI would write up its standard "302" reports, instead of having to draft a classified memorandum on a CIA laptop for the CIA to review. The witnesses recalled that at least three lawyers who eventually joined the prosecution team—Trivett, Robert Swann, and Jeffrey Groharing—were on-site and available for consultation during the sessions. Perkins said that she met face-to-face with Swann in preparing for the session. She said the interrogation sessions were not recorded but that other agents could watch a live feed in a nearby location—another new area of discovery.

At the closing press briefing for the December 2017 hearing, multiple defense teams referred to the memo as a case-altering development, even if they did not explicitly say that Ruiz's quick-fire jurisdictional challenge was a good idea. Connell said that, as the defense teams found more "links in the chain" between the two agencies, it would be impossible for prosecutors to effectively argue that "the FBI interrogations were independent of the CIA."

CHAPTER 13

The Prohibitions.
January–April 2018.

James Connell will occasionally meditate in court when he's listening to the prosecution side of the courtroom, tapping into his inner Buddha as a means of dealing with some of the Kafkaesque situations in which he finds himself. At other times, his sense of disbelief or anger on behalf of Ammar al Baluchi will be apparent on his quick rise from the defense table and brisk walk to the podium after a prosecutor returns to his seat. The latter better describes his mood on the morning of January 10, during the first pretrial hearing of 2018. The esteemed chief prosecutor of the military commissions system, Army Brig. Gen. Mark Martins, had just criticized the defense teams for attempting to investigate the past torture of their clients by the CIA. He accused them of running around like a "private attorney general, or whatever disembodied investigative authority they think they have outside the commission."

Connell was perhaps more stunned than angry as he replaced Martins at the podium. He paused for a second before beginning, speaking uncharacteristically slowly.

"A general in the United States Army just told you that the defense in a capital case should not be investigating," Connell said to Judge Pohl. "I just want to let that sit there for a second."

"I heard that, Mr. Connell," Pohl responded, using a tone that suggested he knew how his 2018 was shaping up.

Minutes later in his exchange with Connell, Pohl wondered what the sanction would be if defense teams did conduct investigations contrary to the government's admonitions. Connell responded: criminal prosecution. He asked Pohl if the judge should read him his *Miranda* rights right there in the courtroom.

"No, no, no, no," Pohl responded.

Connell and other defense lawyers did not believe they were overdramatizing the situation. In a long list of outrages, the government's latest move—blocking the teams from investigating critical parts of the case to prepare a defense—was finally going too far. From their point of view, this was becoming too much unlike a US court—"a regularly constituted court," as required by the Geneva Conventions—one in which it might become unethical to practice. In a way that even close observers of the case—myself included—had failed to grasp, this impasse had been building for months.

The defense teams already had lost the one overseas black site they hoped to access. Confronted with this reality in the middle of 2017, the teams moved forward with their motion to compel the government to provide the actual locations of all the former black sites, instead of code names like "Site A" or "Location 4" or "Cobalt." Oral arguments on this topic took place the prior fall, during the one-week session in October 2017. Alka Pradhan, a civilian member of Connell's team, told Pohl that learning the locations would help the defense teams find local witnesses in the host nations, learn physical attributes of the properties, and establish a chronology of their clients' time in CIA custody across multiple black sites. Journalists and advocacy groups had long ago identified the names of many of the host nations, but defense attorneys did not have confirmation of where the black sites were located, or what might be remaining in these locations.

"We want the tools to put on a defense—to put on a proper defense, as due process requires," Pradhan told Pohl, referring to locations as "the biggest piece of the puzzle."

Pradhan argued that Site A's unavailability—from its decommissioning or destruction—increased the importance of learning the actual locations of all black sites for defense efforts to reconstruct as best as possible the years of torture and interrogation endured by their clients.

This was, of course, a nonstarter for the government team. It would guard at all costs the actual black site locations—accepting even dismissal of the case before turning that information over. On this day in October 2017, Gen. Martins told Pohl that Pradhan's arguments were also legally unsound given that the judge already had approved the substitute forms of evidence, which in this instance included the code names for the sites and the video rendition of Site A. One big difference between the CIPA-like process in the military commissions and the federal courts is that legal teams in the commissions cannot file motions for reconsideration once a judge approves substitute evidence. While defense lawyers considered this provision unconstitutional—if the Constitution actually applied here, which remained an open question—it was nevertheless hard to argue that the motion to learn the site locations was anything but a motion for reconsideration barred by commission rules.

The same could arguably be said for pending defense motions seeking the blueprints, designs, work contracts, and other details of the black sites. In yet another motion, defense lawyers were also arguing for access to metadata—electronic information that can include time stamps, user identification, and GPS data—associated with the printed photographs the government provided of their clients at the black site locations. All of these efforts, the prosecution claimed, should be rejected because the judge had approved and would continue to approve summary and substitute evidence in the agreed-upon ten categories of RDI information—and this never would include the actual site locations. In a closed session during the October 2017 hearing, Pohl asked the prosecution to provide guidance to the defense teams on what could and could not be done with respect to investigating the black sites. In November, the prosecution issued a guidance telling the defense teams that they could not travel to suspected black site locations for investigative purposes, which from the government's point of view could have the effect of revealing or confirming classified information.

But what was even more egregious and oppressive from the defense point of view was another "guidance" that we, in the media, did not yet know about: A month before the October 2017 session, the prosecution sent a letter to the defense teams telling them they could not attempt to contact any CIA witnesses believed to be associated with the interrogation program. During the all-important jurisdictional hearing for al Hawsawi in December 2017, the new investigative restrictions were simmering on the back burner as the parties prepared their written briefs.

At the January 2018 hearing, the defense teams were finally ready to raise their objections to Pohl in court. Connell used the refrain he often turned to in explaining his work: His team is not a trial team that intermittently investigates; it is an investigations team that occasionally shows up to court to argue. He told Pohl on January 10, 2018, that investigating the case was the most important role of defense teams in a capital prosecution, and that not doing so would be "deficient performance" under clear legal standards set by Supreme Court case law.

"This prohibition on investigation by the government clearly interferes with the right to investigate and to prepare a defense, including the untrammeled access to prospective witnesses," Connell said.

The September 6, 2017, guidance letter barred defense teams from making any "independent attempt to locate or contact any current or former CIA employer or contractor, regardless of that individual's cover status"—something the defense teams had been doing as part of their normal investigative work on the case. Defense teams contended these were the most important sources of information and potential witnesses to paint a picture of their clients' torture at the black sites, which would be the foundation of their efforts to have Pohl suppress their clients' subsequent confessions to the FBI.

Lawyers also wanted this trove of potential witnesses to prepare motions to have the case dismissed for outrageous government conduct. Beyond that, in the event of a trial and any convictions, the defense teams viewed the past brutality inflicted on their clients at the black sites as the most powerful mitigation evidence against the death penalty to bring before a jury of military officers. A death sentence in the military commissions requires a unanimous vote by all twelve panel members; defense teams had to convince just one military officer that their clients had already been punished sufficiently, or that the US government lacked the moral authority to execute them—or even that, under the Convention Against Torture, the government actually had a legal responsibility to help rehabilitate torture victims rather than execute them.

Gen. Martins told Pohl that the prosecution stood by the letter "unapologetically" and that it was necessary to protect "very sensitive equities." Martins began his own refrain that he and his team would repeat in the months and years to come: The prosecution team had to balance the demands of due process with the obligation to protect national security. In its view, the government was striking the right balance by protecting covert CIA personnel while also having provided the defense teams with, by that point, about seventeen thousand pages of information related to the CIA program. Also, Martins explained, the defense teams could have access to CIA witnesses if they requested them through the prosecution team, as laid out in protocols contained in the September 6 letter.

Martins reminded Pohl that he had already approved the identification of CIA personnel involved in the interrogation program through the use of unique functional identifiers, or UFIs, such as "Interrogator A-C-4," as a substitute form of evidence. It is these witnesses that defense teams could request from the prosecution, under the new protocols. At that point, a CIA officer with an FBI agent present would reach out to the proposed interviewees to inform them that they were not obligated to talk to the defense teams but could do so if they wanted. Under questioning by Pohl, Martins said that the system should also apply to non-CIA personnel who may have been involved in the interrogation program.

David Nevin rose to echo Connell's sense of disbelief that the government would so severely limit a core defense function. He said that capital cases are regularly reversed by appellate courts when defense lawyers fail to conduct a thorough investigation for their clients. He said his team had a right to talk to the people who were present during Mohammed's torture.

"Not only a right, but an obligation to do it," Nevin said. "And it is not some odd species of desire on our part to do that. It is fulfillment of our obligation."

Oral arguments on the topic carried over to the next day, after Pohl stewed over the dispute and realized he had some additional questions—including what legal authority the government had to impose the restrictions. In response, Martins cited the Classified Information Procedures Act and the military commissions system's own CIPA-like provisions. In a line that would prove as memorable as it was strange, Martins added: "And the mere seeking of interviews with people and wandering up and ambushing people at the Piggly Wiggly is a serious thing."

One of the benefits of watching the courtroom monitors along the top of the viewing gallery instead of the live action is watching the expressions of people behind whoever is speaking at the podium. During any given afternoon, you might see an attorney beginning to doze off, and watching that person intently might prevent you from also dozing off. On this day, one of Cheryl Bormann's civilian lawyers, Edwin Perry, in view just to Martins's left at the second defense table, jerked his head up at the Piggly Wiggly reference with a stunned, confused look. *What the hell did he just say?* Members of the media had the same reaction. In the days, weeks, months, and even years afterward, Carol and I would occasionally ask members of defense teams if this statement had any basis in fact: Did an investigator from one of the teams locate a potential CIA witness from the black sites and approach him or her at Piggly Wiggly? People either said it didn't happen or they had no idea. The "Piggly Wiggly" remark became one of the case's enduring mysteries.

In any event, Pohl continued: "You're threatening them with criminal sanctions, aren't you, in your letter?"

"Well, it would get into prosecutions under the Intelligence Identities Protection Act," Martins said, referring to the statute that protects the status of covert operatives.

This response confirmed for defense teams that they would, in fact, be targeted for criminal prosecution for doing their jobs. When it was his turn to speak, Connell said that it was possible defense team members could also be prosecuted under the broader provisions of the Espionage Act. Connell told Pohl that the dispute over investigations seemed to blow up "out of nowhere" to consume most of the January session but really was "a long time coming"—a culmination of sorts: Now it was completely clear that the prosecution believed "there is no defense investigative function" in the Guantanamo proceedings.

"The position of the government today is mutually exclusive with a military commission that is adversarial in nature," Connell said.

* * *

I had no idea any of this was about to happen. My dad had died just a few weeks earlier, on Christmas Eve 2017, and the wake and funeral the next week had consumed all of my time and attention. My dad, who was eighty-five, had been ill and in a rehab center, but the turn of events was unexpected: The goal had been to get him home by Christmas, for good. Instead, with a sudden downward turn, we could only get him home for one day of hospice care. He had his entire family, including his wife of more than sixty years, in the house with him on what had always been our most important holiday. The day after Christmas, Fiona and I had to go shopping to buy funeral-appropriate clothes, as it had never occurred to us to pack them. My parents had me late; my dad was nearly forty-two when I was born. But I always assumed he'd get to hold my own kids, whenever Fiona and I succeeded in starting a family. It was devastating.

His passing had also prevented Fiona and I from traveling to South Carolina to see her family over New Year's and the days after, as planned. Instead, we finished up family time in Needham and drove back to Brooklyn, with a two-night pit stop at a hotel on Madison Beach in Connecticut, for a little bit of downtime. It wasn't an entirely easy call, but we both decided I should make the upcoming one-week trip for the 9/11 hearing. Gitmo had proven to be a mixed bag for us over the first few years. In addition to time apart, each trip created a mental and emotional fog that lingered well into my return to New York. We both noticed that I seemed to have a lot less energy to really engage with the city—fewer live music shows, movies, gallery openings, book events, whatever. By the time the fog lifted, another hearing was staring us down on the calendar, and each trip always took up two full weekends on either side with the long travel between Brooklyn and the naval base. Still, we thought that the January trip would be good for me, instead of hanging around the apartment and reading whatever Carol was tweeting or writing. Carol had told a few lawyers on the case what had happened, and they came up to me at the opening night NGO barbeque, held at one of the East Caravella town houses, to express their condolences. As I drank beers and listened to people talk about the case, I felt at home, or at least that I had made the right decision.

Once the week started, it became clear that the January 2018 hearing was one of the biggest in the case's long history. The arguments had clearly presented Pohl with a dense quandary. Defense teams in no way viewed the discovery they received on the torture program as lessening their ethical obligation to investigate the past abuse of their clients. In fact, while that obligation already existed, they now had a duty to investigate and explore every possible detail contained in the discovery, and they would have to do so on an ongoing basis. After all, as the lawyers often told us, a criminal defense attorney in a regular murder or assault case can't merely accept discovery from the prosecution without doing his or her own investigation on top of it—that invites a reversal for ineffective assistance of counsel. In this case, however, Gen. Martins portrayed the defense teams' investigative work as inappropriate efforts to get around the CIPA-like process of receiving classified evidence. In a sense, the prosecution was acting like the defense was cheating, or not playing by the rules, given that Pohl already had approved the substitute and summarized evidence that had gone to the defense teams about the RDI program. The two sides were as far apart legally as any two could be.

Keeping with the prosecution policy started in the prior fall, Gen. Martins did not meet with us for a closing press conference, which defense teams held January 11. Connell explained that his team had previously disregarded the September 6, 2017, guidance memo on the grounds that it had no legal basis, but that was likely to change given the clear threat of criminal prosecution.

"We will be seriously reconsidering our investigative strategy," Connell said, noting that he was often not the one knocking on doors of potential witnesses. "I can't simply be brave for myself. We have to think about all of the people who are involved in this system."

* * *

Connell did, in fact, halt his team's investigative work involving potential CIA witnesses, as he told Pohl during the next session held during the last week of February and early March of 2018. David Nevin went further by telling Pohl that he could not even participate in the current court session because the restrictions imposed an unworkable conflict: Either he did his job and faced criminal prosecution, or he failed to satisfy his obligations as defense counsel. Nevin said that he could only present oral arguments on motions related to the government's prohibitions, not on any other pending motions.

"If you are deciding to do that, that is your choice," Pohl told him on March 1.

"No," Nevin said. "I don't have any choice but to decide that."

As it turned out, Nevin spoke quite a bit that day because Pohl had tasked himself with sorting through the shifting guidances that had come from the prosecution. Pohl had come to share Nevin's view that the dispute over investigations was going to form an impenetrable roadblock to the pre-trial phase moving forward at all.

By that hearing, the government had withdrawn its prohibition on defense teams traveling to suspected black site locations, so long as they used open-source information to conduct their investigations and not any classified information learned in the case. Because the government had never given the defense teams the locations of the sites during discovery, this was not expected to be a significant hurdle. In ironing out this point, Pohl and the parties settled on the hypothetical example of Canada: If the *New York Times* published an article that Canada hosted a black site, defense teams could go there to investigate so long as they did not disclose any classified information when doing so. (The word "Canada" appears in the March 1 transcript thirty-two times.)

Nevin was not convinced this completely satisfied the defense obligations to investigate, given the policy's implied reliance on third parties, whether media outlets or NGOs.

"It's only when I get lucky enough to have some NGO come forward and on their own go and develop the evidence related to a black site in Canada that I can kind of glom on to that and use it as a stalking horse to get in the door to talk about conducting my investigation," Nevin said.

Still, the other four defense teams and the prosecution agreed that the withdrawal of that prohibition put the defense teams in roughly the same position as they were before the restriction was put in place. The real dispute now centered on whether defense teams could investigate the past torture of their clients by contacting CIA personnel or other individuals believed to have knowledge of the program. With this prohibition, the prosecution team was standing firm.

Connell portrayed the limitation as overbroad and completely unworkable. The government had identified about sixty-five UFI witnesses for which defense teams could request interviews through the prosecution team, but that was a small universe of potential witnesses from the RDI program. Defense teams had no way of knowing whether the people they wanted to contact based on their investigative leads were part of the UFI set, or if people identified by UFIs in the discovery knew they had UFIs.

In Connell's mind, oral arguments from earlier in the day had proved the necessity of talking to witnesses. In a separate motion, his team had sought additional details and underlying documents from the torture discovery based on errors and inconsistencies they saw between documents from the government and existing public sources like the Senate torture report. The defense teams had long had trouble organizing the RDI discovery, much of which were CIA cables that had been rewritten to obscure dates, locations, personnel, and some specifics of interrogation conditions and techniques. In fact, Connell had told me that he did not know after first receiving this discovery that they were actually CIA cables—or at least the versions of cables they were going to get—until he compared them with CIA cables released from Freedom of Information Act (FOIA) requests.

The prosecution had recently provided each defense team with a new "RDI Index" to help the teams sort through and match up details from the seventeen thousand pages of summaries and substitute evidence from the CIA program, but these indexes also had errors that did not match details in the summaries. Prosecutors had defended the discovery overall and said that the RDI Index was created to help the defense teams. However, they also acknowledged there were errors that would have to be fixed. Connell didn't reraise the matter to attack the government's work with the indexes, but only to point out that relying solely on discovery documents was inadequate, if not dangerous.

"Somewhere there's truth out there and a trial is a search for truth," Connell said. "The way that we get to that truth is by interviewing witnesses."

One of the odd flavors of the prohibitions was that they appeared to criminalize work that the defense teams already had been doing. Connell pointed out that many witness leads had come from public information, including from sources who published books or listed their past experience with the CIA on website bios, most commonly on LinkedIn.

"Because everybody lists 'I worked at Guantanamo,' 'I worked at the CIA,' 'I worked in a black site,'" Connell said. "They all list it on their LinkedIn profile. And so that's where we find witnesses. We're not, you know, trolling Piggly Wigglys looking for witnesses. We find them on LinkedIn."

What was particularly frustrating for defense teams was that they were already obligated by Pohl's earlier protective orders—and the law generally—not to disclose classified information. If defense teams wanted to discuss classified information with a witness, they would have to do so in a secured SCIF facility. Connell said that, as the holder of the national security privilege, the government can decide to withhold this access to witnesses from the defense, but it should only do so at a cost. The default, he argued, was dismissal of the entire case, though other types of remedies could be alternatives—such as suppression of the defendants' confessions to the FBI in early 2007.

The task of defending the restrictions fell to Jeffrey Groharing, the government's point person on CIA discovery and the prosecutor who appeared to serve as the primary interface with the agency. Like most of the lawyers on his side of the courtroom, other than his boss, Groharing's work on the 9/11 case dated to the Bush administration's first attempt to prosecute the defendants in 2008. Though he was now part of the Justice Department's national security division, Groharing remained a Marine reservist and kept an impeccable athletic appearance, sporting closely cropped hair and not an ounce of visible body fat.

Groharing said that the prosecution would provide the defense teams with a list of ten former CIA officers who could be contacted for interviews without going through the prosecution's new protocols, based on those officers' confirmed public connection to the RDI program. Obvious examples would be former CIA director George Tenet; Jose Rodriguez, the former head of the CIA's counterterrorism center who wrote a book, *Hard Measures*, about his work on the interrogation program; and Drs. James Mitchell and Bruce Jessen, the two contract psychologists who helped developed the program. Groharing said the prosecution would add names to this list as it made assessments about what was in the public domain.

(The list would grow to about twenty-five people.) But he said that identity of other CIA agents and contractors was "some of the most highly classified information" in the government's possession that demanded protection. He also explained that some agents who were not covert might have a connection to the RDI program that was classified and needed to be protected.

Groharing said that the defense teams already had plenty of evidence to "paint a very vivid picture" of their clients' past treatment. In his argument, Groharing unfurled what became his own catchphrase by telling Pohl that the government had no plan to challenge any portrayals of the past abuse so long as "they're tethered to reality." In other words, the defense teams could come up with basically any description of past mistreatment—whether to a judge or jury—and the prosecution would simply sit back and listen.

"We're not going to quibble," Groharing said. "We're not going to call witnesses and debate about whether Mr. Mohammed was waterboarded 183 times or 283 times. We, frankly, think that has little relevance to the commission and the issues before it."

Groharing suggested that the defense teams devote their resources to investigating facts related to the alleged offenses of 9/11 and not those surrounding the past treatment of their clients, which the government did not dispute. He also said that the defense teams had good sources of information about the defendants' past treatment by the CIA—their clients.

Jim Harrington had been mostly silent during oral arguments on behalf of Ramzi bin al Shibh, as he often was, choosing not to repeat points made by his colleagues. But he couldn't resist approaching the podium to tell Pohl that Groharing showed "a total ignorance of what capital law is all about." When it came down to it, this really is what irked the defense teams—that the government just didn't seem to have a clue about the law. As he and his colleagues would do repeatedly, Harrington also took issue with the suggestions that the five defendants were the best sources of information, given the torture's effect on memory and mental health and the risk of retraumatization.

"Torture affects the way that we get information from our clients," Harrington added. "It started in the beginning; it continues to this day. And the notion that we should go to our clients for getting information that we need to present a case to a jury in the trial is just preposterous."

At the end of the day, Pohl and the opposing sides at least agreed on how the case should move forward procedurally: In light of the defense teams' ongoing objections, the government would have to ask Pohl to issue a protective order formally binding the teams to the terms of the investigative restrictions. Pohl already had issued three protective orders in the case related to the handling of information, based on motions by the government. In fact, during oral arguments over the first protective order back in August 2013, a now-departed member of the prosecution team told Pohl that the defense teams were free to "interview any witness on any topic in any location on anything." Defense teams had relied on this guidance in investigating the CIA program until the landscape shifted four years later to trigger this latest dispute. They were left to wonder whether Trump's appointment a year earlier of Gina Haspel to the position of CIA deputy director played a role. One of the agency's most senior officials had earlier played an important role in the RDI program, and Trump nominated her to lead the agency prior to the next hearing.

"If we need to get a protective order from the court to get these procedures in place, we'll take that approach," Groharing said.

* * *

Finally, defense challenges to what would become "Protective Order #4" would settle the dispute for good, one way or the other. Groharing gave his defense of the requested protective order at the next hearing, about two months later in late April. He said the order allowed the teams "to conduct reasonable investigation without unnecessarily risking the lives of CIA personnel." This time, Groharing raised the stakes by painting a hypothetical scenario in which CIA agents were murdered after defense teams unveiled their covert status through investigative work. He said that a subsequent criminal prosecution or other sanction against a defense team member would "provide very little solace to a widow who lost her husband because of reckless actions taken."

"That's what's at stake in this motion, and that's why we are asking for this relief," Groharing told Pohl on April 30.

He again added that there was no limitation on defense teams talking to witnesses who saw the actual crimes of 9/11.

"There's no restriction for the defense to ask them about, you know, witnessing 2,700 murders that day," Groharing said.

Any drama he hoped to infuse into the day's arguments was impeded by their repetitive nature for anyone who had seen the prior two sessions. Defense teams once again acted like they were operating in a *Twilight Zone* version of a court.

"The idea that someone would say you can't go out and do the investigation is like saying everything you know is wrong, or two and two equals five," Nevin said.

Connell argued that the proposed protective order—which from the initial September 2017 guidance had gone through several different iterations—was "unbelievably expansive" by prohibiting the contact of black site witnesses and any individuals "affiliated" with them. He said that this basically shut down efforts to contact any CIA witness or anyone who knew any potential CIA witnesses. What was new in Connell's argument on April 30 was that his team, by then, had attempted to use the government's protocol by requesting twenty-eight UFI witnesses through the prosecution team. Connell began listing those who had refused, one by one, before Pohl cut him off.

"Would it be faster if you told me how many agreed to be interviewed?" Pohl asked.

"It would be more dramatic if I read you the list," Connell said, before reading Pohl's expression. "All right, sir: Zero. Twenty-eight out of twenty-eight declined to be interviewed."

Prior to the prohibitions, Connell said, his team had talked to "around twenty former or current CIA employers or contractors," six of whom had knowledge of the RDI program and others who knew people associated with the program. All of those leads were now cut off, Connell said, as his team could now not even approach witnesses with whom they already had met. Connell explained that the government's protocols prevented trained investigators from doing what they do best: Using background knowledge to approach a witness and make an initial assessment of his or her reliability; build rapport and trust by showing identification and addressing concerns over security clearances; and mentioning shared contacts, such as if the witness was suggested by another individual who had met with the defense team. By shutting this process down, Connell said, the prosecution had made its choice and now must bear the consequences.

"They have decided that it is more important to protect these witnesses than it is to prosecute the case," he said. "They're entitled to that view, and they get to enforce it."

All the defense teams echoed this position: The government could issue its restrictions or withhold information from the case, but it had to be punished in some way—ideally by the dismissal of the case, and a close second would be the removal of the death penalty as a sentencing option. Such a ruling, if it survived a likely government appeal, would put the case on the path toward guilty pleas and a sentencing hearing. A third option for a sanction would be the suppression of the FBI statements.

Groharing took the podium again to tell Pohl that the defense teams were wrong to say that the government had "to make a choice," or that it was having its cake and eating it, too. The whole point of the CIPA-like process of substitute evidence was conceptually the opposite: to find "creative solutions" that protected national security while ensuring "a fair trial." Groharing said the investigative restrictions—which still allowed access to CIA witnesses through the protocols—were "quite small."

As the arguments dragged on, the two sides continued to drift further and further apart. For the defense teams, the devil of torture was truly in the details and the presentation of them to judges and juries, a process that demanded unfettered access to witnesses and eventually some live testimony. Blocking this process would invite an appellate reversal of the case, they contended. You just never knew what details would lead a juror—and you only needed one—to vote against a death sentence. Bormann told Pohl that the defense needed "blow-by-blow descriptions," citing one example of hundreds in which her client was kept awake for a period of time.

"It doesn't tell me how the CIA kept him awake," Bormann said. "It doesn't tell me if they beat him, they doused him, they hung him from his hands, or did anything else. It doesn't tell me whether they swore at him, punched him, slapped him, dragged him down a floor to keep him awake."

CHAPTER 14

Mic Drop. July–August 2018.

Bormann was back at the podium in late July to continue pulling on the newer and still-developing thread of the CIA torture program—the FBI's role in the interrogations and its level of coordination with the agency. As Groharing had made clear in the prior sessions, the prosecution was not going to challenge the defense teams' portrayals of torture. Instead, it was relying on the presumed separation between that past abuse by the CIA and the defendants' subsequent confessions made to the FBI on Guantanamo Bay in early 2007. The jurisdictional hearing for al Hawsawi the prior December, however, had clearly put this "attenuation" argument in a considerable amount of legal jeopardy. Defense lawyers were no longer referring to the CIA torture sessions and what followed by the FBI as separate interrogations, but instead as one continuous process of extracting information from their clients.

"This was a long, singular, unified, coordinated effort by all agencies in the United States government to interrogate and torture these individuals," Bormann contended on July 23, 2018.

At that point, the defense teams were arguing for additional discovery on interagency coordination between the CIA and the FBI, as well as with the Department of Defense, which also had investigative agents in the 2007 "clean" sessions on Guantanamo Bay. Prosecutor Ed Ryan told Pohl that the government acknowledged the relevance of the material and would provide discovery to the defense teams in response to their new requests.

"A process is underway," Ryan said. "Some items have been turned over already; there is more in the works. I can represent that there's been a great deal of review going on as to this fairly broad subject matter."

Defense teams were incredulous, if not livid, that the prosecution would somehow consider this a new defense theory, given that they had made discovery requests on the topic as far back as 2013. Also odd was that some public materials—such as the Senate summary report on the CIA program—had mentioned the presence of FBI agents in early interrogations of captured terrorist suspects and the sharing of information between the agencies, which meant that the topic was not entirely a secret. Yet the FBI had been conspicuously absent from the government's discovery related to the CIA program. Beyond that, defense attorneys said that common sense would have led anyone to conclude at the outset of the case that interagency coordination was relevant. After all, the whole system created by the Bush administration for prosecuting high-value detainees on Guantanamo Bay was built on the process of re-interrogating them in "clean" FBI-led sessions.

"In this case, where the government knew going into this prosecution that they would be attempting to introduce statements taken in 2007 and 2008 by FBI, the idea that it took them until 2018 to understand that the relationship between the CIA and the FBI is important in that analysis is ludicrous," Borman contended.

Oral arguments continued a few days later with Judge Pohl peppering Ryan about what the government knew about the FBI's role in early interrogations. In his answers, Ryan gave what was now the government's position: Of course the FBI and the CIA—and for that matter, every other arm of the US government—coordinated after the worst-ever attacks on American soil. It would have been a massive, government-wide dereliction of duty to do otherwise.

"This was simply a nation acting properly to take on what it needed to do," Ryan said.

After Pohl continued to press for details, Ryan conceded that the FBI was involved in some interrogations prior to the detainees' arrival on Guantanamo. However, he said that the FBI was not involved in "face-to-face" questioning of the detainees.

"So you say they weren't the actual interrogators?" Pohl asked.

"While they were in CIA custody," Ryan confirmed.

This distinction would not necessarily prevent a taint. That the FBI sent questions into the CIA and later reviewed the material prior to doing their own interrogations of the detainees would call into question the admissibility of the early 2007 confessions. In addition, discussions in the closed session the following day, on July 26, 2018, revealed that Ryan's argument was not entirely accurate or complete when it came to the FBI's role in interrogations prior to the agents' meetings with the defendants on Guantanamo Bay in early 2007. Early on, Ryan rose to correct the record from the day before in open court. Redactions in the transcript make it difficult to understand Ryan's explanation for why he gave an incorrect answer, or why his statement might technically be accurate depending on how one parsed the language or described the scenarios to which he was referring at the time. Regardless, it wasn't good enough for the defense teams.

"I'm asking that the government fashion a properly worded response and apologize to the court in an open [session] and to counsel about misrepresenting the truth," Bormann said. "We should not in this court be left with the public—and those interested victim family members—being misled by government statements and then corrected in a closed session."

Ryan told Pohl that he could not correct the record in a public session because the explanation—if accurately stated—would "drift" into classified matters.

"Let's get real for just a moment," Bormann responded. "If they can talk about it in open court to deny that it occurred, then it's clear that the topic itself without the details isn't classified, right?"

Pohl did not decide on a remedy on the spot. Throughout the redaction-laden exchanges, it's clear that FBI agents were involved in interrogations of at least some of the defendants near the time of their captures in Pakistan before their transfer to the CIA. Ryan also described what sounded like post-rendition scenarios, including one where FBI agents questioned Mustafa al Hawsawi without telling him that they were from the FBI; this apparently meant that his defense team might have received discovery about early FBI interrogations without knowing it.

The waters were dark, and they were muddying. Even when it came to the CIA evidence that Pohl already approved in substitute form, the judge was beginning to have some doubts. When proposing substitute evidence, the prosecution has to provide a declaration by a government official—such as a senior-level CIA official—that the release of the original and complete evidence would pose a threat to national security. Among the many redactions and edits to cables from the black sites, the government replaced all specific dates of interrogations with the generalized notation of "early," "mid," or "late" of a given year. But Connell arrived at the start of the July session with an interrogation document that the CIA had released to a journalist as part of a FOIA request—and one that had a date on it, unlike the version of the same document provided to the defense through the government and Pohl. It was this type of specificity that defense teams contended could help them better construct the narrative of their clients' time in the black sites. Connell told Pohl that he should revisit his approvals of all the substitute evidence, in which six million pages of information that went into the Senate torture report became seventeen thousand pages of actual discovery.

It was unlikely that Pohl would take another look at all his prior approvals of substitute CIA evidence. But now he and the parties would be dealing with whole new tranches of discovery the defense teams would have to receive—related to the FBI's role in CIA interrogations—for which government would be seeking fresh new batches of substitute and summary evidence, triggering the "505" process again.

After Connell's FOIA example, Pohl was fuming as he turned to the prosecution side of the courtroom.

"Why should I have any faith in these determinations?" he asked.

* * *

Apparently, the judge had had enough. Unbeknownst to us, Pohl was cooking up a solution that would allow him to avoid the whole mess of CIA and FBI discovery. In fact, his solution would allow him to avoid even having a hearing to suppress the defendants' confessions to the FBI—which is what the entire pretrial litigation had been building toward.

In a true blockbuster ruling on August 17, 2018, Pohl preemptively suppressed the FBI statements as a punishment for the government's investigative restrictions in Protective Order #4. Pohl reasoned that the defense teams' case for suppression would hinge in large part on establishing the extent of CIA coercion or abuse that preceded the "clean" statements to the FBI. But the latest protective order, which Pohl adopted with some changes, would prevent the defense teams from being able "to develop the particularity and nuance necessary to present a rich and vivid account" of the defendants' time in CIA custody.

Pohl noted that the Military Commissions Act of 2009 requires defense counsel to have "reasonable" access to witnesses and evidence "comparable" to federal courts, and that "no party may unreasonably impede the access" to building a case. Pohl said that the government "vastly" understated its "intrusion" into the defense investigations through the protocols established in the protective order. He noted that, by the time of his ruling, only a total of five UFI witnesses had agreed to interviews by defense teams, and even these would have to take place by phone under the government's latest protocols.

"The protocol practically prohibits Defense Personnel contact with almost all CIA persons, and functionally precludes the Defense from independently conducting pretrial investigations involving the CIA RDI program and any other issue involving CIA persons," Pohl wrote.

The ruling was not a complete defense victory. He said that the defense teams were still adequately positioned to present a mitigation case at a potential sentencing phase, even in light of the investigative restrictions. This meant that he was not punishing the government by taking away the death penalty as a sentencing option.

That Pohl suppressed the FBI statements even before the filing of suppression motions—obviating the need for a suppression hearing—was perhaps a masterstroke of court efficiency. One wonders if Pohl, having seen all the original torture evidence when approving the substitutions, knew which way he was going to rule and decided it didn't make sense to waste a year of court time getting there. If the brutality of the CIA's torture and incommunicado detention were likely to lead to suppression, the still-emerging details about the FBI's role in the program were perhaps just the icing on the cake. Protective Order #4 gave him a way out of one of the case's giant messes, a hearing that would probably have lasted close to a year if not longer. The flip side to this analysis was that the government would likely appeal his ruling, a process that could take several months to resolve.

The ruling was a true shock, but it's possible it should not have been. One clue was a discussion that Pohl and Connell had on March 1, during one of the early rounds of oral arguments on the investigative restrictions. In one of his freewheeling intellectual exercises, Pohl was curious if evidence of CIA abuse would be necessary for the trial phase if, at some point earlier, he already had suppressed the FBI statements. Connell was blown away by the question, almost unable to answer it, as he hadn't even considered Pohl siding with the defense on this critical issue.

"Wow," Connell said.

"Judges can rule both ways," Pohl said with his characteristic trace of a smile.

"So I hear, sir," Connell said.

Either way, Pohl found another "out" about a week after his ruling. He issued an order announcing his retirement from the case. Pohl's sudden departure—without so much as a goodbye or even a warning—came as a surprise to many people, me included. Some observers tossed around the idea of foul play, that he may have been forced out after sanctioning the government. I personally assumed that Pohl felt he had gotten the case past its biggest pretrial issue, and now he could finally enjoy his retirement and leave the remainder of the mess to someone else. In his last act as chief judge of the military commissions, Pohl appointed a new judge to helm the pretrial of the century. Remarkably, when the proceedings resumed in just a few weeks in September, Pohl would not be in the courtroom. And the government would not have its most important evidence.

CHAPTER 15

Rich and Vivid Accounts. September–November 2018.

An era had truly ended with Judge Pohl's departure from the case. The new guy was nothing like his laid-back predecessor. Keith Parrella was a stern-looking, mostly unsmiling Marine colonel in the middle of his career. In fact, he already had his next assignment set for June 2019—an important and prestigious position to lead the Marine teams that protect embassies worldwide—which meant he would only be on the 9/11 case for about ten months. He had an impressive legal career with the Marine Corps, but only two of those years was as a military judge, the minimum threshold of experience set by commission rules. This again was a by-product of the military system that rotates service members to various positions throughout their careers, particularly if they hope to rise in rank. Pohl was the outlier, a lucky find for the commissions system.

During the voir dire on September 10, 2018, Parrella tried to cut short questions over his qualifications, given that he had met the two-year minimum. For him, that meant the matter was closed to discussion.

"We're moving out," the judge told David Nevin during his voir dire. I assumed that was a military way of signaling mobilization and may have hinted at Parrella's overall view of the pace of the case.

"But it's an extraordinary case," Nevin countered.

At the very least, he argued, the new judge should abate the proceedings until he had reviewed and understood the entirety of the substantive record in the case, instead of getting "up to speed" in real time while moving forward.

"It is not appropriate in a capital case," Nevin said.

On a separate topic, Harrington was bothered by Parrella's inability to describe, or even to remember, his reaction to the 9/11 attacks, even though he was in the Marines at the time.

"I will say that I probably felt similar to what everybody else felt in the country," Parrella said.

"I don't know what that means," Harrington said. "What does that mean? What did everybody else feel?"

Parrella, clearly annoyed, said that he doubted the relevance of his feelings nearly twenty years prior. He finally acknowledged that he probably felt "anger and just shock."

Later that night, Harrington saw Carol and me at the Windjammer Restaurant, which is in the same complex building as O'Kelly's and shares the same menu. If O'Kelly's is at capacity, or too loud for a conversation, the Windjammer is the fallback. He told us that he had seen Parrella earlier in the evening and nodded hello to him, but the judge walked by without any acknowledgment.

"I guess I did call him a liar a few times," Harrington said.

The bigger issue was that Parrella served between 2014 and 2015 in a Marine Corps fellowship program that assigned him to the counterterrorism section of the Justice Department's National Security Division, which has always had prosecutors on the September 11 trial team. During his voir dire, Parrella said he worked on terrorism cases during his stint at the Justice Department but did not work on the 9/11 case. He also acknowledged knowing one of the prosecutors socially for many years from his time in the Marines, though he said their interactions were infrequent. That was Jeffrey Groharing, who had taken center stage for the government with the disputes over access to CIA witnesses. While three teams moved for Parrella's recusal on the spot, two teams wanted additional time to research his connection to the prosecution team.

The next day was September 11, the seventeenth anniversary of the attacks. At the start of court, Gen. Martins told the new judge that the attending victim family members of the attacks—as well as one survivor from that day—would be coming and going from the gallery until 10:28 a.m., the time that the last hijacked plane crashed in Pennsylvania.

"Without in any way interrupting these military justice proceedings, they understandably wish to observe in relative quiet and privacy the different events of the sequence of the morning of September 11, seventeen years ago, as those impacts and moments of death occurred," Martins said.

"Thank you, Gen. Martins," Parrella said.

Not long after, Parrella rejected the first round of recusal motions but said that the teams could seek reconsideration if they found new grounds. In fact, the teams later argued in new pleadings that Parrella was not entirely forthcoming about his relationship with Groharing, which included the two of them competing together twice, in 2007 and 2008, in a four-person Marine team athletic event described as "an endurance challenge." Defense lawyers would pursue an appellate reversal of Parrella's refusals to recuse himself, even after he left the case for his embassy assignment, in the hopes of having all of his rulings thrown out.

For Pohl to appoint as his successor a judge who could only stay on the case for ten months felt a little odd, given that a trial date wasn't even on the calendar. But he probably knew the government would appeal his suppression of the FBI statements to the Court of Military Commission Review and then, if that failed, to the DC Circuit. That could chew up the better part of a year, which would make Parrella more of a placeholder judge dealing with administrative matters. After that, Pohl's replacement as chief judge of the commissions would appoint a new judge to take the 9/11 case forward through the conclusion of the pretrial phase and maybe even a trial.

It's hard to know what Parrella meant by "moving out," but he got a taste of running a case on Guantanamo Bay during hurricane season. With Hurricane Florence approaching, Parrella canceled the remainder of the first hearing so that we could all get a flight out on Wednesday, ahead of the storm. More than a hundred people associated with the 9/11 case gathered at Ferry Landing the next morning to take the big boat across to the air terminal. Before we did, an official with the commissions gathered together the sprawling group as best as he could and bellowed out that our plane never made it: Everybody would have to go back up the hill and should attempt to return to whatever housing they had previously. The next morning, as we were about to head to Ferry Landing, we learned again that the plane continued to have malfunctions and was still not coming to get us. Attempts to get a plane for Friday failed, and we ended up leaving Saturday as originally planned. It was logical to blame Parrella for the karmic unfolding of events, even if he couldn't have really known how things work with the military commissions. In the terminal, I voir dired Nevin about the wisdom of getting on a plane that had apparently experienced multiple crippling mechanical failures in recent days.

"That's a fair question," he said.

* * *

Living on a confined naval base like Guantanamo Bay, where you can't leave the base except by plane, contributes to the slow flow of island time. The Navy's "Morale, Welfare, Recreation" (MWR) department helps improve the quality of life by holding various events throughout the year, including many athletic competitions. Among them has been the 9/11 Memorial Run, which in my experience was less of a competition than a community event in which just as many participants walked. The 9.11-kilometer course started at the track complex in the center of town and curved past the entrance to Camp Justice for a long climb up to the lighthouse before circling back. Among my favorite unused photos from reporting on Guantanamo Bay is one I snuck of Gen. Martins and Nevin chatting amiably on the track in the minutes before the race. The lead prosecutor of the case for the worst-ever attacks on US soil and the lead defender of the accused mastermind of those attacks were showing us that, in the end, we are all in this together. Given the acrimony in court over CIA witnesses from the prior sessions, it also felt a little unsettling, like watching the MLB All-Star Game as a kid and seeing players from the Red Sox and the Yankees having fun together in the same dugout. I chatted with a mix of defense and prosecution staffers, including Groharing, the Marine reservist and Justice Department national security prosecutor.

Nevin and I kept roughly the same ten-or-so-minute pace during the run, while several lawyers took off like lightning. As I labored uphill to the lighthouse twenty minutes later, Groharing was already on his way back down, flying past me to be among the first handful to finish; he truly runs like the wind, gliding effortlessly. I thought of this when watching him at the podium a few months later, as the government's case hung in the balance. Groharing's courtroom style can be glacial, or stingy, as if he's holding on to words he just doesn't want to let go. His more plodding, cautious approach lacks the trial lawyer flair and steamrolling force that Ryan brings to the government's bench. On November 15, 2018, however, as he walked Parrella through the torture evidence the government had provided the defense teams, Groharing's presentation had an eerie effectiveness. His overriding argument was simple: Judge Pohl had acted prematurely in suppressing the FBI statements.

"Judge, the defense won the lottery without even buying a ticket," Groharing said.

With the theme set, Groharing tore into the reasoning behind Pohl's order for about eighty minutes—"respectfully," of course, he pointed out a few times—in the hopes that Parrella would reconsider the "clear errors and manifest injustice" of the premature suppression. Continuing the other theme of 2018—repetition—Groharing had to walk Parrella through the arguments he had made unpersuasively to Pohl. Chief among them was that Pohl had himself approved as adequate the substitutions of classified information going to the defense teams, including the discovery of material from the black sites that hid the identities of CIA personnel through the use of unique functional identifiers. If certain covert CIA witnesses identified by UFIs were later deemed to be necessary, Groharing said, a military judge should work with the parties on finding solutions. This could include the use of affidavits, written interrogatories, or secure testimony by video teleconference that protected anonymity.

Parrella was in a tricky spot. Pohl made his ruling after dealing with the torture litigation, in one form or another, for six years, and he had reviewed tremendous amounts of evidence, both in its original and substitute form. He also had wrestled with competing arguments over the implications of the government's investigative restrictions for close to a full year. Parrella had only been on the case for a little more than two months.

A core part of Pohl's reasoning was that the defense teams, limited in their interactions with CIA witnesses, could not paint the "rich and vivid accounts" of past abuse that would render any subsequent statements involuntary. But Groharing told Pohl that this was not the case—that the evidence turned over to the defense teams was quite vivid, so "rich and vivid," in fact, that it proved the government was not trying to hide disturbing material from the defense. To prove his point, he read from a sampling of the discovery, doing so uncomfortably slowly at points.

He began by reading a CIA cable documenting early interrogations of Khalid Sheikh Mohammed, in 2003, in which he was stripped naked and shaved before being subjected to multiple rounds of slapping, stress positions, standing sleep deprivation, and water dousing that caused him to moan, whine, and chant. Interrogators also punished Mohammed for refusing to drink water.

"When Mohammed again refused, he was taken back to the bathing room, placed on a plastic sheet, and medical officer rehydrated Mohammed rectally," Groharing read. "Mohammed clearly hated the procedure.

When he was returned to the interrogation room, he then complied and drank water."

Groharing said this cable was one of many dozens provided to the teams. He also read from several of the 185 statements that CIA personnel made to staff of the CIA's Office of Inspector General during the course of its investigation into an especially brutal black site referred to as Location 2, which was known to be in Afghanistan. One officer referred to Location 2 as "a disgrace" and "a nightmare," with freezing cold water used for water dousing and female personnel, like her, used to enhance the "humiliation" felt by detainees.

"The report was very critical of CIA actions at location number 2, and described it as what teenage boys would think of for a really bad prison," Groharing said.

Another officer described Location 2 as a "the closest thing he has seen to a dungeon."

"He said some of the detainees literally looked like a dog that had been kenneled," Groharing read from the inspector general report. "When the doors to their cells were opened, they cowered."

As he had argued to Pohl earlier in the year, Groharing told Parrella that the teams could combine this type of discovery with information both from their clients and open sources—such as the summary of the Senate's torture report—to create any account of past treatment that was "tethered to reality." At this stage of the litigation, the government was interested in reaching lengthy joint stipulations of fact with each defense team that would detail each defendant's course of treatment by the CIA. He said the prosecution would not dispute any accounts of past abuse because the case was about 9/11, not what the CIA did in the years after.

"It cannot be the focus of this case," Groharing said. "The CIA is not on trial."

He also challenged defense claims of a "chilling effect" from the government's protocols requiring the defense teams to request interviews of CIA personnel through the prosecution. Groharing suggested that the unwillingness of individuals to participate in interviews resulted from the fact that they already had participated in the investigations conducted by the Senate staff and the CIA inspector general.

"Moreover, the defense has referred to these individuals as torturers and criminals," Groharing said. "It's very understandable why someone who has been insulted in that manner would decline to speak with" the same lawyers who are now defending the people "accused of some of the worst crimes ever charged in history."

After the prosecutor sat, Connell urged Parrella to give preference to his predecessor's "reasoned decision," one reached after years of complex litigation—and one that also negatively affected the defense given that Pohl concluded that the investigative restrictions did not unduly impact their mitigation cases. That meant that a panel of military officers that would eventually serve as jurors in the case could impose a death sentence without hearing, from the defense teams' point of view, a full portrait of the past torture.

As effective as his arguments may have been, Groharing opened a can of worms by reading from the torture evidence and claiming that "it's hard to imagine a more rich and vivid description." Connell said that Groharing's reading of the "sanitized" government versions of events showed just how much detail was lost without having access to witnesses. He pointed out that the CIA cable documenting parts of Mohammed's interrogation didn't even say where he was hit or slapped.

"In his head? In his ear? In his stomach? In his scrotum? How many times did they hit him?" Connell asked. "How does he look after he gets hit? When they douse him in cold water, is there steam rising in the air? Is he shivering? Is he shaking? What kind of sounds does he make when he's in a cold environment drowned in cold water? Does he flinch? Does he wince? Does he cough? Does he beg?"

Connell said he would want to ask an interrogator what someone looks like hanging from chains and being subjected to such intense humiliations. His voice cracking for just an instant, Connell said that was the level of detail needed to re-create the feel of a dungeon that "looks like it was created by teenage boys who thought up the worst thing they could." He said that that human experience of the torture—both for the detainee and the torturer—was now completely off-limits to the defense teams. To truly paint rich and vivid accounts, defense lawyers would need to interview CIA personnel about "what it is like to drown another person or to anally rape another person," or to watch a colleague doing it. Prior to the restrictions, he said, interviews with CIA personnel revealed errors in the government's summarized evidence on interrogations along with new details they never imagined. That's why working on a stipulation from the government was inadequate.

"My imagination fails when it comes to how badly these men were treated," Connell said. "The things that these mental teenage boys did in this dungeon that they created defy my ability to imagine, much less to write into some sort of stipulation in dry legal prose."

Connell contended that Pohl's ruling was not premature, that it was simply acknowledging that the government could interfere with the defense's investigative function but that it had to do so "at a cost."

"And that cost is the exclusion of the January 2007 statements," Connell argued. "It should be, in my humble opinion, also the exclusion of the death penalty as a sanction. But I acknowledge that Judge Pohl ruled against me on that point."

Nevin rose to say that he "listened with interest" as Groharing was reading what was done to his client, which he said was a short summary of an interrogation that had lasted fifteen hours.

"You can read it in about ten minutes," Nevin said. "And so you think to yourself: What's not there?"

He said that the very first line of the account—that Mohammed "was stripped"—raised several questions about the exact details of treatment: "Did someone come up and unbutton the buttons and take them off or were they ripped off or did somebody take a knife or a pair of scissors like they do in an ambulance and cut them away? In what way, if any, was he restrained while that was going on?"

He had similar types of questions about every other part of the interrogation session, whether it was the shaving, the stress positions, the moaning and crying, the water dousing, and, of course, the rectal rehydration, which he said was "a polite way of saying rape."

"I'd like to know, how is it done?" Nevin continued. "I mean, does someone hold his legs apart? Is he lying on his face? Is he naked? Is he lying on his back? Is some kind of lubrication involved in this? How many people are there around? Who does the insertion?"

Nevin said that Pohl's ruling showed that the judge had understood the defense's obligation to use the summarized torture evidence as a starting point to conduct their own investigations. He said he had no interest in putting the CIA on trial, as Groharing said, but simply to put on an adequate defense. He said it would be a "walking" constitutional violation if he didn't do it by trying to talk to the witnesses who imprisoned and tortured his client.

Once again, the prosecution and defense sides of the courtroom drifted further apart in their assessments of what might constitute a fair trial.

In court, I thought, *Man, this is depressing*. The feeling lingered even after I finished my article for the day: "Attorneys in Sept. 11 Case Battle over Adequacy of Bleak Torture Descriptions," an appropriate title that my business partner Katrina came up with. To me, the day felt like the grimmest expression of America's split personality, its childish and arrogant insistence on having everything both ways—its casual and violent dismissal of the rule of law and its devotion to it. This was the end result. It was a sad affair, even something of a spectacle, though one without any fanfare—one mostly sealed away, doomed to Guantanamo's patented blend of repetition and irrelevancy, forgotten until some poor souls later read the transcript and let their imaginations wander, as mine had. But no matter, there was booze to be had.

In our discussion outside the media and NGO tents that night, each of us around the table pointed to a different detail as the most disturbing. This seemed to back the defense's position that it's impossible to predict what piece of information will convince a juror that enough is enough—that death is too much, given what the government had already done to the accused. Of course, that some of us were disturbed by Groharing's presentation supported the prosecution's position that it had given the defense teams some pretty persuasive evidence. For me, as apparently it was for Connell, it was the description of "teenage boys" coming up with a torture dungeon that got under my skin. Later that night, as I tried to sleep in my freezing cold tent, I realized that the line made me think of the graphic rape scene in the movie *Leaving Las Vegas*, and I couldn't shake the feeling.

Drinking is generally conducted with a degree of professionalism in Camp Justice, at least in the preponderance of situations, but there are exceptions. That was the situation on Friday night, as we labored to finish off the booze that could not be stored in the media center. I credit Carol and Dru Brenner-Beck, the regular observer from the National Institute of Military Justice, with quite possibly saving the life of a journalist I'll describe as a young male reporter from a niche publication. Both Carol and Brenner-Beck, a longtime NGO observer who often hung out with us, noticed the typically shy reporter getting noticeably more effusive as the night dragged on. They urged me to keep an eye on him after he stumbled off to the male media tent. I personally would not have flagged him as being in danger—legally drunk, for sure, but not approaching anything like blackout mode. Nevertheless, I dithered about in my living space later in the night, killing time by reading and listening to him breathe, when I heard him gurgle and vomit. I rushed in and saw that he was on his side—not choking, but maybe just barely. I was able to walk him to the tent showers to wash up, then bring him back into a fresh bed. I stayed up listening to him breathe for a while longer, just in case, as the long travel day approached. Even now, years later, thinking about that night fills me with panic.

CHAPTER 16

Mic Drop II. December 2018– May 2019.

On December 20, 2018, a man identifying himself as an Army counterintelligence officer called a former paralegal on the Walid bin Attash defense team and told him to report to Fort Hood, Texas, later that day. The Army paralegal had finished his service with the Military Commissions Defense Organization and was spending time with family in Texas before transitioning to a new assignment in South Korea. As he conducted his morning errands, the paralegal noticed two men following and photographing him from two separate cars. Upon his arrival at Fort Hood, the paralegal was taken to an interrogation room and questioned for two-and-half hours by two FBI agents. The topic: the activities of the bin Attash team led by Cheryl Bormann, as well as those of the other defense teams. They required him to come back the next day for a polygraph examination.

These and other details were in an affidavit by the paralegal filed by Bormann in a motion to postpone the one-week hearing scheduled to begin January 27, 2019, which was to be Judge Parrella's third pretrial session. Once again, the defense teams believed they were under investigation and needed to get to the bottom of what was happening before the case could resume. Otherwise, they would be operating under the type of conflict of interest that derailed the case for eighteen months once it became known in April 2014 that the FBI infiltrated the team for Ramzi bin al Shibh.

Once again, the prosecution team led by Gen. Martins was walled off from any issue tied to investigations into the defense teams, so the Special

Review Team rejoined the case to update the judge on what was happening. Apparently, the SRT filing before the trip convinced Parrella that nothing too serious was going on. In a somewhat odd procedural move, Parrella denied the defense motion for an abatement, had everyone fly down to Guantanamo, and then heard oral arguments on the issue, with the SRT participating by video from the DC area. By then, the defense teams had been provided with the review team's filing, which had initially been made ex parte to Parrella.

Bormann would logically have argued first but was suffering from flu-like symptoms so asked her colleagues to go first. Nevin told Parrella on the morning of January 28 that the review team's filing, which stated that defense teams were not currently under investigation, raised more questions than it gave answers. He referred to a part of his team's filing that recounted nine separate investigations that involved his team during his years representing Khalid Sheikh Mohammed. Several of those times, Nevin explained, he felt the need to get the advice of outside counsel.

"I don't believe that those are nine unrelated incidents," Nevin said. "I think they're all part of a continuing effort to intimidate the defense teams."

Nevin restated a position he had made in earlier phases of the case and would make intermittently again: Until the judge ordered the SRT to provide a comprehensive accounting of all past and present investigations involving all team members by any government agency, he would not "participate substantively in the proceedings." Nevin sat down, and the 9/11 case once again entered a strange phase, one that would have been a dramatic turn almost anywhere else but had become ho-hum on Guantanamo Bay: The defense team for the accused mastermind of the 9/11 attacks would not participate in the 9/11 case, except to present arguments related to reasons why it could not participate.

Jim Harrington told Parrella that he wasn't even sure he should take the podium given the "due process implications" of arguing a motion that had already been decided. Nevertheless, he did his best to explain to the new judge the devastating impact that the past FBI investigation had on his team, which he likened to a cancer in remission that eventually comes back. He paraphrased the oft-quoted line by Joseph Heller in *Catch-22* to make his point: Just because the five defense teams in the courtroom might sound paranoid, that doesn't mean the government isn't after them.

"There is a real basis for our paranoia," Harrington said.

Harrington recalled that, shortly after the FBI informant was found on his team in April 2014, the Special Review Team made many such assurances—that there were no pending investigations—that proved to be false.

The issue took up the entire day but ended with Parrella sticking to his determination that none of the defense teams were operating under a conflict. The remainder of the week was canceled, however, after Parrella informed the parties later that night that he had a medical emergency. It turned out to be a detached retina requiring surgery. The judge once again experienced Guantanamo-related travel headaches when, for reasons not entirely clear, the decorated Marine colonel could not get an emergency evacuation from the island for more than two days.

The biggest news of the brief hearing was that the *Miami Herald*, owned by the McClatchy Company, had offered buyouts of many senior reporters—among them, amazingly to me, Carol. For seventeen years, the paper had owned an important story for relative pennies on the dollar, given the affordability of Gitmo travel with Camp Justice tent living. The Pulitzer Center also provided funding for part of her work. The buyout offer created significant stress for Carol on the trip. She started communicating with outlets either genuinely or theoretically interested. In the end, the buyout was perhaps the biggest boon to Guantanamo transparency: By the next hearing, Carol would be at the *New York Times*, an immeasurably bigger platform where her work would go to new heights.

* * *

The litigation over Bormann's paralegal revealed that Parrella, even in his short time on the case, had to deal with some of the bizarre peripheral matters that consumed so much of Pohl's time. One of the biggest of such issues—involving possible "unlawful influence" over the proceedings—was one that Pohl had left Parrella to wrestle with. This dispute raised one of the case's most tantalizing "what if?" scenarios—the possibility that it could have ended by plea deals.

"Unlawful command influence" is a common legal concept in US military law, referring to problems that are unique to the fact the courts-martial are within the executive branch. The Uniform Code of Military Justice bars anyone subject to the code from attempting to influence a court-martial, the greatest threat coming from someone in a command position putting his or her weight on a specific outcome. The 2009 Military Commissions Act is somewhat broader in barring "unlawful influence" on the proceedings by any person, regardless of whether they are in a command position.

The five defense teams had seen unlawful influence creep into the case many times over the years—indeed, other than torture, this was probably the case's most common topic of dispute. In early 2015, for example, lawyers sought to have the case dismissed after the Office of the Convening Authority directed commission judges to relocate to the Guantanamo Bay Naval Base. This was a blatant power move to make the cases go faster. Pohl halted the 9/11 case until the order was rescinded, which it was in quick fashion. (Pohl often wondered why living on the base would speed up the cases, given that all the motions and discovery work was done stateside.) By the time I arrived that fall, the defense teams were finally giving oral arguments—after years of pleadings—in support of motions to dismiss the case for unlawful influence, given all the prejudicial statements made by senior officials in the Bush and Obama administrations about the defendants' presumed guilt. Pohl eventually decided against dismissal of the case but said that the defense teams would be given liberal challenges during jury selection, whenever the trial actually started. (Defense lawyers filed similar motions after President Donald Trump tweeted remarks about the pace of the cases on Guantanamo Bay.)

Allegations of unlawful influence could also coexist with, or become a part of, other litigation, as was seen with the female guard dispute. While that was pending, defense lawyers alleged unlawful influence after then Secretary of Defense Ash Carter and Joint Chiefs Chairman Joseph Dunford, in October 2015, criticized Pohl's temporary ban on the use of female guards to transport the defendants. Pohl sided with the government on the main dispute, but he left his ban in place for an additional period as sanction for the officials' "entirely inappropriate" comments.

But the biggest incident of alleged unlawful influence involved possible plea deals with the defendants. In February 2018, Secretary of Defense James Mattis fired the commissions' convening authority, Harvey Rishikof, and his legal advisor, Gary Brown. Defense lawyers claimed that the terminations were a response to Rishikof and Brown having opened plea discussions with the defense teams that would have removed the death penalty as a sentencing option. In the military commissions, all plea agreements and sentencings are the final decision of the convening authority, not the chief prosecutor or judge, though both would be involved procedurally as the agreements made their way through the court process.

That there had even been plea discussions was huge news when it first surfaced. Defense attorneys and other critics of the commissions, including some victim family members, had said for years that plea agreements were the only way to conclude the case within the lifetimes of anyone who cared about it. Rishikof, who had served in several senior legal positions in the government and was a former dean of the National War College, apparently saw the allure of plea deals not long after his appointment to the convening authority position in April 2017.

The defense and prosecution teams filed written arguments over evidence and potential witnesses associated with the firings throughout 2018, which meant Pohl could kick the matter to his successor. In his first session in September 2018, Parrella allowed James Connell to call one of his investigators to the stand to testify about what he learned about the Rishikof and Brown firings. As was fitting for the 9/11 case, this was not to support Connell's final arguments on unlawful influence, but instead to bolster his still-pending request to call twenty-two witnesses with knowledge of the firings.

The government considered this request absurd. Prosecutor Clay Trivett accused the defense of a "runaway train theory of unlawful influence" based on a mistaken belief that a convening authority could not be fired for any reason, even job performance. He told Parrella that the government already had provided declarations from Mattis and the other key figure in the firings, William Castle, who had been the Department of Defense's acting general counsel at the time. He said the firings resulted from Rishikof's management style and certain specific misdeeds, such as his decision to circumvent proper military channels by asking the Coast Guard to take aerial photography in support of a planned expansion of the Guantanamo Bay legal complex.

Connell's investigator, Navy Reserve Lt. Douglas Newman, testified to conducting eighteen interviews with witnesses that suggested other factors might have been at play. For example, Newman said that he learned that Trump's first attorney general, Jeff Sessions, made a phone call to Mattis to question him about why pretrial agreements were being considered in the 9/11 case. He also testified to tense relations between Rishikof and the chief prosecutor's office led by Gen. Martins.

"[Brown] painted the relationship as unhealthy and contentious," Newman said.

Rejecting Connell's plan to have twenty-two witnesses testify, Parrella allowed one witness for the next session in November 2018. That was Castle, the Pentagon's former acting general counsel, who testified by video feed from the DC area about his role in, and knowledge of, the Rishikof and Brown firings. This was my first (and so far only) time watching court proceedings in the 9/11 case from the remote viewing site for media at Fort Meade, Maryland. A friend's wedding on the prior Saturday had caused me to miss the commissions' flight, though I planned to fly to Gitmo midweek on IBC Airways, which at the time operated a limited commercial service from Ft. Lauderdale. A military escort met me at the Fort Meade gates to guide me deep into the base to watch the feed on a large screen in a classroom. I was the only journalist in attendance.

It was a weird experience: I was in a pressroom in Maryland; the judge and lawyers were in Guantanamo; and Castle was in some office at the Pentagon, with his testimony broadcast to the Gitmo courtroom and, by extension, to me. Beyond that, Castle's testimony, which began on a depressingly gray and bland Tuesday morning, was brutal. None of the lawyers could develop any rhythm with him, and he could not seem to answer any questions without a dozen "well"s, "um"s, "ahh"s, and assorted tics and self-interruptions. At one point, I stood up and paced in front of the screen, apologizing to my military minder and telling him I had to move to stay awake. He looked up at me confused and took out his headphones.

"Sorry," he said. "I had to tune this out a long time ago."

Castle, who was now a principal deputy general counsel, did confirm one of the more colorful parts of Connell's team's reconstruction of events—that he and Mattis were both pulled from a meeting at the Pentagon to deal with an angry call from Attorney General Sessions over plea deals. Castle didn't remember many details of the call, but he did say that it involved Sessions telling them that he did not want any plea deals.

"All I remember the attorney general saying is, 'No deal,'" Castle told Connell.

Mattis didn't know what Sessions was talking about, Castle testified, nor did he, which seems surprising at first, but isn't. As important as the case was from certain historical perspectives and among some stakeholders, the reality was that basically no one knew what was going on in the 9/11 proceedings or in the military commissions generally. Rishikof took what he probably thought was an obvious step in exploring plea deals, and he apparently did not make too much fuss about it. Perhaps he suspected that any attention to the negotiations might cause people to suddenly start caring about the case, which in the Trump era would almost certainly kill a resolution through plea deals.

After the brief call, Castle confirmed to Mattis that there was "no deal" but not because he knew what it referred to, only that he knew he had not made or approved any deal. Castle said that he later recalled that he had actually been previously briefed about Rishikof exploring plea deals in the military commissions, but that it did not immediately occur to him that this is what Sessions was talking about when the call came in.

Parrella kept the parties going into the late evening to finish Castle's testimony. Thankfully I missed the final ninety minutes or so in order to drive to long-term parking at BWI for the flight to Ft. Lauderdale. After a night in a cheap motel, I arrived on Guantanamo Bay Wednesday morning courtesy of IBC Airways to be greeted by public affairs officers who escorted me across the ferry and directly to the court complex. Back in court, I was able to watch closing arguments on the defense allegations of unlawful influence and ponder how life would have been so different for so many people if plea deals had been reached.

Compared to Pohl's pace, Parrella acted relatively quickly. Near the start of 2019, he rejected the defense motion, finding "beyond a reasonable doubt" that Rishikof and Brown were not fired over their pursuit of pretrial agreements with the defense teams. The teams did win a small victory, however, after noticing that the transcript of Castle's testimony was a little too smooth. Connell filed a motion for "a complete transcript," noting that Parrella had concluded in his ruling that Castle was a "highly credible" witness—a determination that the defense found, to say the least, unsupportable.

Connell argued that the transcript omitted "Mr. Castle's many pauses, filler sounds, and nonverbal vocalizations that may reflect on his credibility." Parrella ordered the prosecution to place an audio recording of Castle's testimony in the official record of the case.

* * *

Pohl had also escaped dealing with Connell's effort to hold a massive "hostilities" hearing for Ammar al Baluchi—with dozens of witnesses spread over several hearings, probably spaced over a year or so—to argue that the United States and al Qaeda were not in a state of war prior to September 11, 2001. This was a hearing I was looking forward to, though it actually taking place would likely push a trial a lot farther away. Unlike me, the prosecution didn't want it to happen.

In April 2018, about four months before leaving the case, Judge Pohl sided with the government in the jurisdictional challenge raised by Mustafa al Hawsawi. In doing so, he rejected the narrow hostilities argument that relied on just a single legal expert witness, Creighton Law Professor Sean

Watts. In some ways, this ruling was a bit of an afterthought. The move by al Hawsawi's team is what had gotten the government to turn over critical evidence about FBI-CIA coordination on interrogations. That had already proven to be one of the case's most important evidentiary turns. But the ruling was still important for the course of the case. In it, Pohl did not adopt the prosecution's position that the armed conflict with al Qaeda started with Osama bin Laden's 1996 declaration of war. He instead relied on judicial "deference" to Congress and two presidential administrations, which had passed the Military Commissions Act of 2006 and the 2009 reforms. He said the legislative and executive branches had determined "that hostilities existed as of September 11, 2001, and for at least some period before," which satisfied him for the time being. The prosecution would still have to prove its position at trial.

Connell still felt al Baluchi was entitled to present his own case on hostilities, as Pohl had repeatedly promised him. Connell told Parrella this in March 2019—that Pohl had only deferred his client's hearing. Trivett pushed back, contending that defense teams could challenge other elements of the jurisdictional requirements—such as the defendants' alleged roles in the attacks or membership in al Qaeda—but not whether a war existed.

"It can't be that we have an armed conflict with one of them and not the others," Trivett argued.

Parrella quickly sided with the government. On April 3, 2019, he ruled that Pohl's determination of a state of hostilities applied to all five defendants. To me, this was a great topic for an article. The word Kafkaesque is tossed around Guantanamo a lot, but this was a perfect example. As is said in the military, however, any interest in Parrella's hostilities ruling was "OBE," or overtaken by events. The same day, he ruled on the government's motion to reconsider Pohl's suppression of the FBI statements. In a bold reversal, he agreed with prosecutors that Pohl's suppression of the FBI "clean team" statements was "premature" and "a manifest injustice." The government's most critical evidence was back in the case—at least for now—and the defense teams would have to file their motions to have it suppressed.

In a confusing wrinkle, Parrella did not agree with the government that the defense teams were fairly positioned to present their "rich and vivid" accounts of past abuse by the CIA. In light of the prohibitions on contacting CIA witnesses, Parrella determined that this remained an open issue. He explained in his ruling that he (or a successor) might, in fact, agree with Pohl that the investigative restrictions were too severe. But he decided there was really no way to determine that without the defense teams at least first trying to bring their suppression cases. Parrella ordered the teams to file their motions to suppress the FBI statements by May 10—just five weeks later, even though they had been operating under the assumption that doing so would not be necessary.

Defense lawyers were dumbfounded by the order and expressed their concerns to Parrella at the start of the next hearing, on April 29, referring to the judge's plan as a "thought experiment" or "a trial run" of a suppression case. They were not particularly excited about the government's proposal to amend Protective Order #4 to allow the teams to send sealed letters to prospective CIA witnesses through the government, instead of having FBI and CIA personnel contact the individuals directly. They doubted this would help them achieve the level of witness participation they enjoyed prior to the prohibitions. By that hearing, the defense teams had received about twenty-seven thousand pages of discovery related to the CIA program. It was significantly more than the last time the government had said that discovery was essentially complete, but the teams were still pursuing an order to let them review the full Senate Torture Report and its six million pages of underlying documentation.

For most of the year, Nevin had not been participating in the proceedings because, in his view, his team had not learned enough details of the FBI's questioning of Bormann's former paralegal. But he chose to on that day, after Parrella finally ordered him to, and after Nevin consulted an ethics expert who gave him the go-ahead to participate. He told Parrella that his idea of a trial run for a suppression hearing was a bad one. Nevin argued that the judge would never know what could have resulted had the defense teams been able to exercise their constitutional rights to fully investigate the case.

"You may learn what we have been able to find as a result of working under Protective Order #4, but you will never be able to learn what we were not able to find," Nevin said. "You'll only know what the restricted process will produce."

The teams all eventually filed motions asking Parrella to reconsider his reconsideration of Pohl's order. But they differed on whether they would comply with it in the meantime. True to form, Connell told us that he would move forward with his suppression motion and his planned witness list. Outside court, Nevin said he had no idea what his team would do. Even before the hearing, Ruiz was defiant in his meeting with reporters. He said his team would not comply on the grounds that the judge lacked the authority to schedule a suppression hearing before the teams were ready. He described Parrella's reasoning as asking the defense teams to drink water that Pohl found unsuitable for drinking—to see if it really was poisoned.

"It's procedurally defective, particularly in a capital case," Ruiz told us. "We don't plan on doing anything."

Pohl had saved the case from witness-intense hearings that he knew would probably take at least a year. Parrella had put that process back in play, but he wouldn't be around to deal with the mess. The one-week hearing that ended May 3, 2019, was his last, and he soon went off to his next assignment for the Marines.

* * *

The last day of court was actually May 2, leaving Friday open for travel for anyone who wanted to leave early. While most court participants return on the Saturday flights contracted for the commissions, the base has flights coming and going from the military base in Jacksonville, Florida, on Tuesdays and Fridays. It was possible to get on these so-called "rotator" flights with some planning, even for media, which I did on that Friday. Fiona and I had a wedding that night in Brooklyn at a venue that was just a ten-minute walk from our apartment in the Carroll Gardens neighborhood. The connecting flight from Jacksonville to New York wouldn't get me there on time, but I'd arrive with the wedding reception still going. Our friends' wedding was, by far, the most convenient wedding to which I'd ever been invited.

Bormann, I soon learned, was planning on getting back to Chicago a day early, as well. We hung out at the air terminal's Subway with Mike, her information security officer and general jack-of-all-trades for the bin Attash team. Predictably, the terminal staff announced delays due to mechanical problems with the plane. Mike drove us to the galley for lunch, and we returned to learn about more delays. At this point, neither Bormann nor I would make our connecting flights out of Jacksonville, and we began searching for hotel rooms in the city. I would miss the wedding, but getting to New York earlier on Saturday would enable me to make the post-wedding barbeque on Saturday afternoon. We soon discovered, however, that virtually all hotel rooms in Jacksonville were filled due to the "Rockville Festival," a music event scheduled for May 3–5. Bormann got a room, but I did not. The air terminal staff, justifiably annoyed, took me off the flight manifest long after doing so should have been possible. Mike and I drove back to the ferry and returned to the Windward part of the base.

The consolation prize for completely missing the wedding events was being able to join my colleagues in finishing off the booze. By that phase of the case, the group of regular or quasi-regular media attendees included a few friends from academia. Lisa Hajjar, a professor of sociology at the University of California, Santa Barbara, traveled with the media because she wrote occasionally for the *Middle East Report* and *The Nation*. Kasey McCall-Smith, an Arkansas-born lawyer and lecturer at the University of Edinburgh Law School, in Scotland, was sponsored by *The Scotsman*. McCall-Smith was working on a law journal article, and Hajjar was working on a book project—what would eventually become *The War in Court*. Also on the trip was Leila Barghouty, a freelancer who wrote for a variety of outlets. This group of journalists and academics, along with author Terry McDermott and Margot Williams of The Intercept—who were not on that trip—formed the core journalist corps for a few years. (Ben Fox from the AP would still show up once in a long while.)

Later that night, McCall-Smith got a troubling news alert on her cell phone.

"Cheryl's plane just crashed!" she said, announcing that the rotator flight had crashed when landing at Jacksonville.

We decided to wake up Carol, who was in bed in her tent with a devastating sinus infection. Carol was able to get Bormann on the phone to confirm she was safe, then eventually arranged for her to speak live with CNN. The Boeing 737, operated by Miami Air, had skidded off the tarmac at the Jacksonville Naval Base, crashed into some rocks, and ended up in the Jacksonville River. Water and the smell of gasoline quickly entered the plane. Passengers had to make an emergency departure off the wing. Some of the 140 or so travelers and crew were injured, and all of the pets were killed. It was a harrowing experience that I was lucky to avoid, and I felt somewhat guilty about it.

The next morning, we arrived at the air terminal for the regular commissions' flight. We were, once again, met with news of delays. At first, it didn't sound too bad—departing at 10:40, which was only a forty-minute delay—until we were told that it was 10:40 p.m., not a.m. It turned out that the plane that was supposed to get us was the one sitting in the Jacksonville River, and the replacement plane had to come in from the Pacific Northwest. The media troupe and some members of the defense teams went immediately to the Leeward hotel to get rooms for the day. I was excited for this, since I had not stayed at the sleepy motel since the middle weekend of my first 9/11 hearing in October 2015. Connell and I walked to the convenience store to buy lots of booze, a blender, and frozen fruit, as we decided this was going to be a day for daiquiris. Gen. Martins ran into me during one of my several trips to the store to restock on beer. "Keeping busy, John?" he asked.

Against all predictions, the new plane arrived "on time" for a departure at 10:40 p.m., which got us back to Andrews at about 2 a.m., a disaster for anyone who didn't live in the area. Consistent with other predications, Customs and Border Protection personnel actually showed up to make us go through the customs charade late into the night. The inanity of Gitmo travel was getting old, both for me and Fiona.

CHAPTER 17

The Never Ending Tour—Killing Time.

Whatever it symbolized to the rest of the world, Guantanamo Bay by that point remained an endless mystery to me: a network of back roads, side roads, weapons bunkers from various eras, an abandoned restaurant, a secret marina, a miniature golf course that I never used, Cuban religious monuments, a charming thrift store whose hours I never properly tracked, "no unauthorized access" signs that appeared to protect hills of cacti, a variety of suburban subdivisions, and storage facilities—lots and lots of storage buildings and sheds, some old, some new, some grouped together in large lots and many others tucked away in the various inlets off the main roads. Storage facilities likely surely outnumbered the vast array of containerized housing units or CHUs, the trailer-like residences of various quality that house some of the foreign workers along with military members and civilian contractors of various ranks. These, too, seemed to spread like much of the base's mold, whether visible from the main roads, hidden off to the sides, or nestled into the hills.

History is everywhere but often obscured by the endless din and dust of construction projects in virtually every part of the base—fixing roads; building new housing, a new fire station, a new post office, and a new school; and not to mention the beginnings of serious workspace expansions in Camp Justice. Life on Guantanamo Bay was one of painful monotony, but parts of the base looked surprisingly different from trip to trip. I never seemed to guess correctly which of the roads off Sherman Avenue ran directly down to the water, where one day you might find a giant warship docked and later see the sailors cramming into O'Kelly's for tequila or Jell-O shots. In the weeks after heavy rains, the hills and even the vast expanse of the "Lateral Hazard" golf course assumed a vibrant green. At other times, the base was almost entirely brown, relentlessly breezy and dusty; even my pillowcase had brown stains from whatever got in my hair. Sometimes when I was on the verge of heat exhaustion hiking the popular Ridgeline Trail, I felt like I was in my past life, kicking up dust while hiking in the Hollywood Hills. On other pleasant afternoons, sitting in the concourse area of the Naval Exchange, the breeze and scent of this tropical small town took me back to one of the trips Fiona and I took to Puerto Rico—then a giant camouflaged Hummer driving down the main street would kill the memory.

The closest thing to Caribbean authenticity on base was "Rasta Hill," an outdoor food shack just down the hill from Camp Justice that is run by some of the Jamaican residents. That all the service jobs on Guantanamo are held by Filipinos and Jamaicans added to the depressing colonial flavor of the base. But here, at this "off-license" establishment where cash trades hands as "donations," the locals are in charge, serving curried goat, oxtail, fried chicken, jerk dishes, and fresh fish, depending on the day. Guantanamo is otherwise something of a food desert with entirely imported goods; the vast majority of items come in by barge, with fruits and vegetables arriving by plane. This has created the occasional shortage at the Naval Exchange, where your hopes for yogurt, fresh peppers, or your favorite potato chips might be dashed. You also might get to the bowling alley—where the food court has a grill and pizza shop ("Spinz") and an imitation Chipotle-type-place ("Bombers")—and be told "Sorry, no lettuce." For much of 2018, Carol and I experienced what I referred to as the "Great Club Soda Crisis" because the product never seemed to show up. When it returned, I started buying two six packs whenever I entered the NEX.

Passing time on Guantanamo Bay was a challenge, particularly during the day, and for me it was a process often festered with guilt. As the 9/11 case moved forward, however, increasingly consumed by disputes over CIA witnesses and evidence, more and more hearings began to have at least one and sometimes two days reserved for classified sessions closed to both the public and the defendants. I should have resented this, and a part of me did. But the other part of me, a bigger part, was happy to catch up on the varied responsibilities of my job and maybe relax a little or hit the gym, where you can end your workout in the sauna. After a day or two away, I'm generally happy to get back to court.

Journalists dropping in for just a week with no plan on ever coming back want to see as much of the base as possible, which is why our public affairs minders have done so many tours, driving newcomers around in vans for reporters to get "local color" and for broadcast teams to get their B-roll. Carol almost always joined on these tours to provide helpful facts, insights, and anecdotes; I generally joined to make sarcastic remarks and see how many absurd comments were taken at face value, which Carol then had to correct for the record, especially for the more literal-minded foreign press. I've done dozens and dozens of tours around the base—mostly by land, some by water—and have accumulated thousands of photos and videos on my iPhone or the video camera that I used to take on trips. Like my courtroom notes, most of these will serve no journalistic purpose or ever see the light of day. But I keep them: Plenty of shots are no longer allowed due to shifting operational security rules, and we still (as of this writing) are no longer allowed in the detention facility. It's also fun to share them with friends and family, who otherwise have no idea what spending between 25 to 40 percent of any given year on Guantanamo Bay is like. It's often quite boring, which is another reason why I tend to join the tours.

One of them, which is run by the Marines, is a great one to do if you're lucky enough to be on the base when it's happening. This is the "Northeast Gate Tour," named so because visitors are taken along the northeast border area with Cuba. The fence line separating the US Naval Base on Guantanamo Bay from Cuba is a desolate patch of concrete and grass down the hill from a former US Marine barracks. Maybe two hundred feet or so past the black chain-link fence is a single-story government building signed with "Republica De Cuba / Territorio Libre De America," with a lone palm tree rising above. Beyond that are tropical hills and stretches of land filled with mines. No Cubans, nor any signs of life, are visible from the American base. It's a little depressing looking.

On my first tour of the gate in July 2016, a handsome, dark-haired marine who served as our guide explained to the fifty or so base residents and visitors that he was himself born in Cuba and lived there until his family escaped Castro's regime. In decades past, he told us, Cuban soldiers would throw rocks on the roof of the barracks to disrupt marines attempting to sleep. The situation mellowed considerably with the election of Barack Obama. As our guide explained, the Cuban government and US Naval Base officials meet regularly throughout the year to discuss goings-on—no one wants Fourth of July fireworks to be misconstrued, for example. But they also talk about stuff like baseball. Tours led by other marines in subsequent years recounted the same basic set of facts, always with a smile, suggesting that the first election of Donald Trump did little to change the border dynamics there.

This reality makes the tension underlying *A Few Good Men* feel outdated, if not outright ridiculous. When I talk to people about my work, the most common association for anyone over the age of forty is the 1992 Rob Reiner film written by Aaron Sorkin, based on his 1989 play about a pair of marines accused of murder on the Naval Base after a hazing incident. Just about everybody recalls the famous "You can't handle the truth!" exchange between Tom Cruise, as navy defense lawyer Daniel Kaffee, and Jack Nicholson as Col. Nathan Jessep. (The court-martial itself actually takes place in Washington, DC). I was lucky enough to see the Broadway play during middle school on a trip to visit my oldest brother, Steve. The play starred two great if lesser-known actors: Tom Hulce, as the defense lawyer, and Stephen Lang, as the colonel. Oddly, growing up in Needham, Massachusetts, a kid named David Cox, who was friends with Steve, was later one of the marines at Gitmo who participated in the "Code Red" hazing incident that led to the murder charges on which the script is based. He was convicted of assault. (Cox himself was found dead under mysterious circumstances a few years later in Medfield, Massachusetts.) I had forgotten about this connection until my other brother, Mike, reminded me of it once I started going to Guantanamo.

The movie has significant staying power on the base, where the marines still guard the fence line with Cuba. Some of the T-shirts from the base's souvenir shops over the years have quoted the movie's most memorable lines, and O'Kelly's would eventually add a "Code Red Burger" to the menu. According to IMDb, the base scenes were filmed in military bases in California, but the movie does a decent job re-creating the look and feel of the base. The establishing shots of the early scenes capture the hilly and often brown terrain that makes up most of Gitmo. You also get a few glimpses of the base's more tropical settings, such as when all the main characters have lunch together. That scene, which has mostly tight shots, looks nothing like the outdoor dining area that is part of the Bayview—the base's nicest restaurant—and the adjacent officers' club, but of course I don't know what the base looked like then.

The Northeast Gate is as close as you'll get to Cuba, though the fence line area is so empty you could probably make a run for it. Otherwise, you'd get far more of Cuba in South Florida. (The Cuban sandwich at the Tiki Bar is a good sandwich, but not because it's authentic.) Still, the base shares more than beautiful sunsets with our neighbors. Ben Fox of the AP spent a lot of time in Cuba during his time covering the Caribbean and did reporting stints in Havana. (As of this writing, he is now an editor at *Politico*.) During one night drinking beers at the picnic table, Fox described how police in Cuba would approach him for questioning if they saw him with a camera or a notebook, or if he appeared to be doing any type of reporting.

"That happens here, too," he noted.

After the end of diplomatic relations in 1961, the United States and Cuba reached an understanding allowing some Cuban workers to come and go through the gate to keep their jobs at the Naval Exchange or elsewhere on the base. According to Karen Greenberg's book *The Least Worst Place*, the number of such workers was down to thirteen by 2000. Hundreds of other workers who defected from Cuba in the early 1960s opted to stay on the US base instead of relocating to the United States. These are called "Special Category Residents," the number of which has decreased from a height of about 350 to less than twenty by 2021. Most are in their eighties or nineties. They have access to a Cuban Community Center, and a dedicated community manager puts together social events for them. These folks and the iguanas—a legally protected species on the base—are the closest thing to Guantanamo Bay royalty, appreciated and respected by all.

Some of the Cuban residents will likely be buried in the base's cemetery, a fascinating and beautiful place filled with more than three hundred gravestones of foreign- and American-born visitors and residents dating back to the 1870s. This also is a great place to visit if you can find a way; it's not part of any formal tour, so our public affairs officers have had to seek special permission for us to go. (Carol informed me that the cemetery is open to the public one day a year, on Memorial Day.) On one Saturday morning, Carol, *Times* photographer Erin Schaff, and I latched on to a group of residents who were going to clean the gravestones, which apparently is one of the base's community activities. (Carol and Erin later produced a feature and photo essay on the cemetery in October 2021.) The road beyond the locked gate that leads to the cemetery connects to another road that, with the right vehicle, can take you down to a hidden area called "Blue Beach," another rocky beach and pristine area for swimming. For me, the cemetery followed by Blue Beach—a completely new experience after many years of coming to the base—was magical.

Less than a mile away from the Northeast Gate on the American side is the site of the former Camp X-Ray, where the United States held its first group of war-on-terror detainees after their arrival in January 2002.

These are the images many people associate with Guantanamo Bay: men in orange jumpsuits kneeling inside an open-air, chain-link prison complex. Remarkably, the small clusters of wooden towers and chained fences remains mostly standing even though the Department of Defense abandoned X-Ray after a few months in favor of a more traditional detention facility elsewhere on the base. Dozens of tropical storms and hurricanes have wreaked havoc since then, tearing away fortified military tents, damaging hard housing and ships, flooding fields and buildings. But X-Ray, nestled in an overgrown valley a half-mile from the road, is defiant, its purpose defined by whoever happens to be gazing down. James Connell, the lead lawyer for Ammar al Baluchi, has told reporters that he hopes that X-Ray will one day become "a site of conscience."

This is not part of the Marine tour, and instead is sometimes part of the B-roll tour led by our public affairs officers when court is not in session. Whether journalists can get their shots of X-Ray is constantly changing—it can either be enthusiastically encouraged, reluctantly allowed, strenuously prohibited, or a source of confusion. X-Ray is outside the detention zone, so it's sometimes unclear whether the decision is up to JTF-GTMO or the Naval Base. Even if filming is allowed, armed guards from the Marines or some other faction of base security might show up to ask what the hell is going on. I don't recommend journalists going there on their own to try to sneak in some shots. Cameras are everywhere on the base.

I give high authenticity marks to *Camp X-Ray*, the 2014 movie by Peter Sattler staring Kristen Stewart as a prison guard (Amy Cole) who befriends a detainee played by Payman Maadi (Ali Amir). Amir is apparently one of the early Guantanamo detainees, as we see him near the start of the movie in an X-Ray-like chain-link cell. The plot quickly cuts to "Eight Years Later," when Stewart is arriving for her nine-month tour as a military police guard. By this point, Amir is held in a traditional maximum-security facility that looks like the real Camp 5, which I have visited and photographed on JTF-GTMO-led tours. (The movie was shot in Los Angeles and in an abandoned detention facility in Whitter, California, according to IMDb.)

In some ways, *Camp X-Ray* takes place in a completely different world than *A Few Good Men*. After all, the prison did not exist at the time of the Code Red incident. *X-Ray*, by contrast, unfolds almost entirely in the detention zone, which is separate from the main part of the base, or in the barracks that probably would have been just outside the detention zone. In the movie, life in the guard force is a claustrophobic ecosystem within an already narrow base population, with socializing, drinking, and sexual encounters at the beaches and barracks taking place between an uncomfortably limited set of characters.

That Cole and Amir developed an intense relationship during her rotation is portrayed believably in the movie. So is the fact that Amir, throughout the movie, was always hoping to get the next book in the *Harry Potter* series—which, in our tours, prison staff would regularly tell reporters were among the most popular books. In 2018, when she was still at the *Miami Herald*, Carol wrote a great article about the friendship developed between a guard, Army Sgt. Steve Wood, and detainee Mohamedou Ould Slahi. Ben Taub also later won a Pulitzer Prize for his 2019 feature in the *New Yorker* that explored Slahi's ordeal and his relationship with Wood. Slahi is one of Guantanamo's most famous detainees for his memoir, *Guantanamo Diary*, which his lawyers helped him publish (with many redactions) in 2015 while he was still at Gitmo. The Obama administration's interagency parole board, the Periodic Review Board, approved him for release the next year and he eventually returned to his homeland of Mauritania. In 2017, the book was republished without the redactions.

The 2021 film based on the book, *The Mauritanian*, which was directed by Kevin McDonald, stars Jodie Foster as Slahi's lawyer Nancy Hollander. Carol knows Hollander well and has told me that Foster plays her perfectly. The movie, which was filmed in South Africa, provides convincing glimpses of the base's bizarre blend of over-the-top security and beach life—though I've never seen anyone actually surf on Guantanamo, which you can see in one of the background scenes. Even after hurricanes, the base doesn't get waves big enough for surfing. Hollander meets with Slahi, played by Tahar Rahim, in an attorney-client meeting room that is a passable re-creation of the real ones that we used to be able to photograph on prison tours.

Harold & Kumar Escape From Guantanamo Bay, a 2008 sequel to the *White Castle* classic, gets mixed marks on authenticity. The characters Harold Lee and Kumar Patel (played by John Cho and Kal Penn) get detained after a flight to Amsterdam when Patel's bong invention is mistaken for a bomb. In the subsequent interrogation, Homeland Security Deputy Security Ron Fox (Rob Cordry) tells them: "Where you guys are going, they have never even heard of rights." This otherwise great scene ignores the seminal 2004 *Rasul v. Bush* decision and others by the US Supreme Court that gave legal rights to Guantanamo Bay detainees—though there are surely many detainees and lawyers who would agree with the character's assessment. More importantly, Lee and Patel are US citizens (at least, as far as we know) and could not be sent to the detention facility, which was reserved for foreign terrorism suspects or "unlawful enemy combatants."

The brief prison scene on Guantanamo Bay, where the prisoners are all adjacent to each other in barred cells looking something like a county jail, misses the mark widely. It probably goes without saying that their relatively easy escape into Cuba after an attempted sexual assault by one of the guards understates the prison's security features. The geography is also off: To escape from the camps, you'd either have to jump into the water from the detention zone's southern shoreline or escape into the main part of the base—where you'd then have to escape again into Cuba through the border areas guarded by the marines.

But *Harold & Kumar* was prescient in its own way. About a year and a half after its 2008 theatrical release, on Christmas Day 2009, the so-called "underwear" bomber Umar Farouk Abdulmutallab attempted to detonate explosives on a flight from Amsterdam to Detroit. *New York Times* reporter Charlie Savage opens his epic 2015 book, *Power Wars: Inside Obama's Post-9/11 Presidency*, with an account of the incident and its aftermath. That the Obama administration treated Abdulmutallab like a criminal suspect—with *Miranda* warnings given by his FBI interrogators—outraged many Republicans and political commentators. In Savage's telling, the episode was a critical part of the emerging political climate that made closing Guantanamo Bay a near political impossibility, and it contributed to the hardening of Obama's war-on-terror policies. The next year, Republicans and Democrats joined together in passing the legislation that banned the use of federal funds to transfer Guantanamo detainees to US soil—which remains in effect to this day.

Another sequel, *Bad Boys II*, is also visually inaccurate but not without value in the cinematic dispersal of Gitmo info. In the movie's climatic scene, the characters played by Will Smith and Martin Lawrence drive a Hummer from a luxurious estate somewhere in Cuba to the Guantanamo Bay Naval Base, where they hope to be protected by American troops on "US soil, baby!"—though the soldiers shoot at both them and the car in pursuit. I'm not sure where they were driving from, but the base is so far in the middle of nowhere that my guess is that it would have taken a full day to get to Gitmo instead of ten to fifteen minutes. As with *Harold & Kumar*, the border area looks nothing like any border area I've seen on the base. But the antagonist's eventual explosion by a land mine in the ensuing shootout is at least based in the fact that Cuba has kept active mines on its side of the base. The Clinton administration finished demining the American side, but Cuba never demined its side. (In fact, Carol traveled to Guantanamo Bay in 1999 to cover the demining story for the *Miami Herald*. That made her a logical choice to go to Gitmo in 2002 to cover the arrival of the first detainees.)

I thought of *Bad Boys II* during one of the more memorable non-court reporting opportunities on the base—yet another chance for a tour—which came during the commissions trip scheduled for late February and early March 2018. Just a few weeks earlier, lightning strikes in Cuba sparked a wildfire that grew in magnitude when more than a thousand mines exploded, eventually threatening the Naval Base's residential neighborhoods closest to the Northeast Gate. The four journalists who traveled for a pretrial hearing in the 9/11 case got to meet with the base commander at the time, Navy Capt. David Culpepper, in an office at base headquarters to discuss the event. He explained to us how his fire department worked effectively with Cuba's fire brigade to put out the blaze. A Cuban helicopter dumped water on the flames, and Cuban firefighters came onto the base to fight the flames alongside base personnel.

We took a tour of the scorched earth with David Rose, the Department of Defense employee who at the time led the base's fire department, which was mostly staffed with Jamaican contractors. They doused the flames in this vast tract of land, a former minefield that was already a desolate moonscape before the fire. As it turned out, by keeping the flames at bay here, the firefighters had not only protected the closest residences but also Camp X-Ray, which once again survived to fight another day.

A few days after the fire reporting, we paid a visit to Radio GTMO for a tour of its operations. For many visitors, this is the best tour on the base. The military personnel who staff the station make the gift store in the lobby available most weekdays, and they are generally happy to show visitors around with some advance warning. The station has the military's largest collection of vinyl records, which are almost never used but kept as historical artifacts. You could kill a day going through the stacked card catalogs that contain the typed listings of the twenty thousand or so records.

I've never gotten my fortune read, mostly out of some vague feeling that it's better to live in ignorance. But I felt some deeper meaning pulling me toward the vinyl catalog on that March 2018 trip. I thought back to one night on the lower east side of Manhattan not long after I moved to New York from Los Angeles, in maybe 2009 or so, when I was drinking at a bar called Painkiller. As I left, a woman outside a small fortune teller storefront said she would read my fortune for ten dollars. When I declined, she offered to do it for five dollars; when I declined again, she told me she wanted to do it for free. I thanked her and moved on. As the years went on, that always felt like a mistake, like I missed an opportunity to learn a core truth about my life and what the future might hold. And that maybe I could have exerted some greater control over the direction of my life, if I had just known back then where it was all heading. For this reason, on that day at Radio GTMO, I told the assembled group that I would pick a card out from the vinyl catalog at random that would convey an essential truth about my life.

My song was "Where Lonely People Go," by Eddy Arnold.

* * *

Movies and photos can give you a glimpse, but the reality is that Gitmo is unknowable to anyone who doesn't live there full-time or part-time. It's a different world, and it frustrated Fiona that a huge part of my life was essentially off-limits because she could never go there. One positive development was that, by the end of 2016, T-Mobile had come to the base. Starting in 2017, I was able to use my iPhone by swapping out the SIM card; the following year I switched to T-Mobile full-time. This enabled a more regular and private means of communications, but the problems posed by separations can be insidious. Like many things, couples having their own lives is a real strength in a relationship until it isn't. Fiona and I used to smile at each other when noticing the bickering couple at the restaurant, or the boyfriend who had to leave the party at 10 p.m. because his girlfriend was leaving. But then at some point we began looking at each other like the joke had been on us.

Viewed one way, Gitmo is ridiculous, an "expeditionary" farce, a pretend front in the war on terror. There's no need to have a prison or a court here, certainly no need to have people living and working in trailers instead of in buildings and court houses, no need to have media and NGOs living in tents. As Judge Pohl said, this isn't some far-off base in Afghanistan; it's basically South Florida. The government ended up making the whole process difficult, surely out of inertia and some degree of incompetence but also just as surely out of a recognition that "out of sight" becomes "out of mind." I've taken part in the "expeditionary" fiction, pretending like I'm going to some far-off place, always taking longer to respond to emails or texts or deal with other parts of my life. Gitmo might just be a paradise, probably a false one, for anyone in their forties who wants to pretend like they're still in their late twenties.

People who like me portray me as loyal and committed, which is fair, but a more complicated assessment is that I just go with the flow, often in directions passively accepted. Fiona was proud and firmly supportive of my Gitmo work, but I also never really had an answer when she occasionally asked how long I planned on sticking with the coverage and the associated challenges of co-running a small business—which she knew was taking a toll on me. Having a kid, or at least getting pregnant, would have been a change in the forward flow, but that did not happen for us during the Pohl or early Parrella eras. By the middle of 2019, we put those efforts on hold to work on our relationship. Neither of us had an exact idea of when our relationship turned what appeared to be a troubling corner, but we were confident that my coming to Guantanamo wasn't the cause of the problems. We still both agreed that, at least for the time being, it didn't make sense to stop covering the 9/11 case.

I was, of course, curious to see what the third judge would do to get the case to trial.

CHAPTER 18

Breaking Guantanamo. June–July 2019.

From his first minute on the bench, Air Force Col. Shane Cohen exuded a friendly aw-shucks charm in sharp contrast to his marine predecessor. He actually seemed happy to be in the Guantanamo Bay courtroom when he first arrived on June 17, 2019, even appearing to enjoy the voir dire process as attorneys probed for biases, professional contacts, or any opinions that might reflect on his impartiality. He was potentially taking on a case that had been going on for seven years and still did not have a trial date set. The discovery process was incomplete, and several dozen motions had not yet been argued in court. In fact, even important legal issues—such as whether the Constitution applied to the military commissions—remained unresolved. But all of this just seemed like a really interesting opportunity for the new judge.

When he took the podium, Jim Harrington asked Cohen this very question: Did he think the Constitution applied here? Cohen said that he had been wondering about that ever since he had been assigned to the case. He said he had come to "no conclusions" and was hoping the parties could help him make the right call.

"Welcome to the sewer, Judge," Harrington responded with a smile.

This was the start of the case's thirty-sixth pretrial session.

It became clear pretty quickly that the Guantanamo court system was not going to do much better than Judge Cohen, who had served as both a defense lawyer and prosecutor and was now in his fifth year as a judge.

He was the Deputy Chief Circuit Military Judge of the Air Force's Eastern Circuit and would soon become Chief for that circuit. Though he had never presided over a death penalty case, or even a multi-defendant case, he had taken a course on capital litigation at National Judicial College earlier in the year. Unlike Parrella, Cohen also had never worked with any of the prosecutors on the case. (A defense challenge over Parrella's refusal to recuse himself was still pending at the appellate level.)

Perhaps just as important, the forty-seven-year-old colonel said he planned to be in the assignment for at least two years and was not facing retirement for a total of nine years. He said he expected the Department of Defense and the Air Force to understand that both sides of the courtroom deserved "continuity" in the case. The message was clear: He could be here for a long time if he made it through any challenges after voir dire.

Harrington's questioning produced the oddest exchange of that Monday morning. He said that the case had "political aspects" and asked if Cohen had developed any opinions about Israel and its "conduct in the Middle East." Cohen responded by saying that, even though his last name was Cohen, he was not Jewish but instead a member of the Church of Jesus Christ of Latter-day Saints.

"I believe that all people, men and women, should be able to worship how, where, and what they may," Cohen added. "I have no affiliations with the State of Israel, nor do I harbor any ill will towards the religion of Islam."

Harrington was caught off guard: He had been asking about the judge's opinions on regional tensions that contributed to the motivations behind some terrorist attacks, not about Cohen's own religion.

"I wanted to just put that aside because I do realize it is a very Jewish name," Cohen explained, a line we later chuckled about.

Harrington asked him if he felt any pressure to speed up the proceedings.

"Zero," Cohen responded.

If Cohen lacked what defense lawyers saw as Parrella's arrogance, he also lacked Pohl's more polished disposition and quiet wit, not to mention his deeper bench experience. But Cohen was convincing that he could make up for experience with dedication and hard work. While he gave the defense teams and the prosecution until Wednesday morning to decide whether to make any challenges to his taking the case, the extra time proved unnecessary. All parties decided on the spot that they would accept Cohen. The general sentiment was that the 9/11 case had its new judge, at least for the remainder of the pretrial phase—and perhaps for the trial, too.

The proceedings hadn't exactly moved on from the Parrella era, however, or even from the Pohl era. Cohen's first task was to decide whether he agreed with Pohl's decision to preemptively suppress the FBI statements or Parrella's decision to reverse him and to start suppression hearings later in the year. In his first week, Cohen became the third judge in less than two years to hear oral arguments from defense teams challenging the prohibition on their ability to independently contact CIA witnesses. Over several hours on Thursday, the five defense teams and prosecutors revisited their arguments pitting the constitutional obligation for defense counsel to investigate versus the government's obligation to protect national security. All five defense teams urged Cohen to reverse Parrella and reinstate the exclusion of the FBI statements, or at least to come up with a remedy that allowed for better access to the CIA witnesses.

"The longer I have been here, the more this is like *Groundhog Day*," Walter Ruiz told Cohen, speaking for many of us. "As I'm somewhat envious of you because this is the first time you've heard these arguments."

The arguments also made clear to Cohen that he was dealing with six different litigants as opposed to merely two sides of a courtroom. Ruiz hadn't yet filed a motion to suppress, nor had the team led by Bormann. Among the quandaries, Bormann explained to Cohen, was that after Pohl's ruling foreclosed the need for suppression hearings, the convening authority decided against funding experts who could support suppression motions. She told Cohen that his predecessor's schedule for filing suppression motions was "implausible." The other teams had filed theirs. But whereas Connell had filed a motion totaling nearly a thousand pages of narrative and exhibits for al Baluchi (all classified and unavailable to the public), Nevin's team for Mohammed had filed a quick ten-page motion to comply with Parrella's May 10 deadline and to simply assert that it was the prosecution's burden to prove the FBI statements were made voluntarily.

Prosecutor Clay Trivett told Cohen that the government was ready to start the suppression hearings in the three-week session scheduled for September. He urged Cohen to stick with Parrella's regime and use the hearings to determine, at long last, the admissibility of the FBI statements.

"We want to get this done and we want to know, up or down, do we have these statements available to us," Trivett said. "And then we want to seat a jury and try this case."

Cohen thanked the parties for walking him through the long history of the litigation and said he would consider the matter carefully.

"I want to make the right decision in this case," Cohen said. "Period."

Among those decisions, the judge noted the next morning, was scheduling. He asked the government and the defense teams to provide input on how he should fashion a series of deadlines leading to a trial date. The theoretical September suppression hearing revealed the challenges of creating deadlines, as well as the potential scope of the hearing—about which defense teams and prosecutors had widely divergent views, both in terms of number of witnesses and length of anticipated testimony. Trivett's initial plan was to hear testimony from eight or more witnesses in three weeks. But Connell told Cohen that his team might need three full days just with one witness, James Mitchell, the CIA contractor who helped develop the interrogation program.

"Wow," Cohen responded.

Thinking out loud, Cohen said that four other defense teams and the prosecution would also want to question Mitchell, which meant that "one witness, particularly an important one, could take an entire week or more."

"Yes, sir," Connell said.

Cohen seemed more excited than annoyed.

"This is great," he said. "This is great feedback."

Other defense teams told Cohen that an additional six months would help them continue to investigate and be better prepared for suppression hearings. The delay would also enable the five teams to participate more or less on the same schedule, instead of moving ahead piecemeal with Connell's suppression motion for Ammar al Baluchi on the faster track. Ruiz reminded the new judge one last time on Friday that he could avoid this whole issue by merely adopting Pohl's ruling that punished the government for the investigative prohibitions in Protective Order #4.

"This issue can and should be moot," Ruiz said.

* * *

Cohen was firmly grounded in the reality that he needed to be educated by the lawyers before him. He also seemed genuinely nice, even saying "Thank you, sir" to each defendant after they answered affirmatively to the scripted colloquy of whether they understood their right to attend court or stay at the prison. Defense lawyers nevertheless shared with me and Carol their fear that he might be one of those judges who kill the defense with kindness while siding with the government. On the initial dispute, one factor that later emerged was that Cohen loved court—the action of court, which for him meant witnesses. You learn things with witnesses, after all, and maybe even see areas for additional discovery. Cohen could either study the record of the 9/11 case for months and move cautiously, or he could do his best to catch up while also moving the proceedings forward. He adopted the latter: He wanted witnesses; he wanted a suppression hearing.

Cohen used the next hearing, in late July 2019, to toil with some of the pending motions and to continue the process of setting a more detailed litigation schedule, beginning with the September suppression hearing but ending with an actual trial date.

"I am trying to put order to a process that I did not create," Cohen said on July 26, the concluding Friday.

Ed Ryan, whose passion had been simmering in the background for much of the prior hearings, was the logical choice to hammer the new judge into setting a trial date. Ryan told the judge something that is almost certainly true—that dates drive action in the government. If Camp Justice and the 9/11 case in particular needed more money and resources, the one way to get "to the head of the line" was to give the government deadlines.

"You have been and will be deluged with the talk from the parties to my left of the needs, the wants, and the rights of these five self-avowed enemies of the United States," Ryan said. "Our client, this nation, deserves a reckoning. The families of 2,976, which include people who honor us by their presence seated behind the glass, deserve justice."

Ryan said that June 2020—less than a year later—was a realistic date to begin jury selection. The defense teams considered this preposterous, given the lack of adequate workspaces and dedicated housing for a capital trial that could last a year or more, not to mention a lack of funding for experts and consultants, all of whom would need security clearances. Connell told Cohen that if his true intent as a defense lawyer was to forever delay an actual start of a trial then he would support Ryan's proposal.

"I would agree to their plan because it would break Guantanamo," Connell said. "It would break it."

While none of the defense teams wanted a trial date set, Connell told Cohen that, if he was inclined to set one, October 2021 was more realistic. Pohl had always held off setting a trial date while discovery was pending. The government's position was that the discovery process was essentially complete, including the close to thirty thousand pages of information from the CIA program. But defense lawyers had heard that refrain before—only to get more discovery, including still-arriving tranches of evidence of the FBI's previously concealed coordination with the CIA. Just that week, in fact, the teams had received CIA-specific discovery in the form of instant-messenger chats between CIA personnel involved in the interrogations at the black sites. Defense lawyers could not elaborate because the material was classified. Connell could only tell us that some of the communications were "depraved."

Nevin reminded Cohen—or perhaps alerted him for the first time—that among the critical motions still pending was the defense request to have access to the full Senate report on the torture program, which included the 6,700 pages of the report and the six million pages that Senate investigators reviewed to produce it. He also said his team was still grappling with a recent discovery update from the government involving all the medical personnel who treated the defendants at Guantanamo Bay over the years, whom the defense teams wanted as witnesses. These individuals were only identified in documents by pseudonyms, and the government acknowledged that it could not locate or even determine the actual identity of many of them.

"Hundreds of witnesses have utterly disappeared," Nevin said.

In a long day, this line by Nevin—a showstopper in some courts—was something of a throwaway. Cohen ended the day thanking the parties for their input.

"I have some tough decisions to make, but that's what they asked me to do," Cohen said. "And I will do so."

Pulling a page from Pohl's playbook, Cohen split the difference between Ryan's and Connell's proposed dates. He set jury selection in the 9/11 case for January 2021. But that's several lifetimes away in the military commissions. All that mattered was September, when the suppression hearing would start.

CHAPTER 19

Suppression. September 2019.

On the early morning of Saturday, September 7, 2019, members of the media and NGOs began passing through the TSA-like security screening from the main waiting room at Joint Base Andrews into a smaller waiting room, where we waited for a bus to take us to the chartered plane located down the tarmac. Greeting us in the second room was an airman in his late twenties or so, a lanky fellow with a friendly smile who had been around the terminal on other trips.

"Catalina Wine Mixer?" he asked us, referencing the climatic event from *Step Brothers*, the comedy starring Will Ferrell and John C. Reilly. "This is nonstop to the Catalina Wine Mixer."

As grueling as travel days can be, the airman had somehow made the whole operation worth the effort. He repeated the joke destination a few more times as defense lawyers trickled in. Cheryl Bormann smiled and gave a quick raspy laugh in spite of herself.

"It might be too early in the morning for humor," she said.

This was a promising start for the suppression hearing, which was to be the 9/11 case's first-ever three-week session. Given that the prior one had concluded with arguments over the preparedness of Camp Justice and the entire Naval Base, the three-week blockbuster was widely viewed as a serious stress test for the court system. I was excited, if tired, as I hopped on the first bus to take us to our plane. After about ten yards, it broke down. We had to walk back to the terminal and try another bus.

* * *

Judge Cohen could not immediately dive into witnesses. This was not going to be like any other suppression hearing in light of the vast amount of classified and other sensitive information involved; certain protocols had to be worked out for both the public and closed sessions. Since the last pretrial hearing, prosecutors had provided the defense teams with tens of thousands of pages of additional discovery. The government had also recently declassified pieces of information that were relevant to the hearing. One was that the FBI had "detailed"—or assigned—some of its agents to the CIA's interrogation program. This declassification showed just how far the narrative had shifted from the earlier storyline that had the FBI walking away from the CIA-led program in protest over the so-called "enhanced interrogation techniques."

Another important declassification was that the CIA had previously used a part of the Guantanamo Bay detention facility as a black site between 2003 and 2004—which had not been confirmed. In fact, the location of the former black site was the same portion of the detention facility where FBI agents later interrogated detainees in January 2007 to obtain their "clean" statements for use at a subsequent trial. This would undercut the government's attenuation arguments for the two defendants, Ramzi bin al Shibh and Mustafa al Hawsawi, who had spent time there when it was a black site. Journalistic reporting had earlier revealed that the CIA planned to use a Gitmo black site as a permanent home for detainees, and nicknamed it "Strawberry Fields," for the Beatles song. The CIA renditioned them to other black sites in 2004 with the *Rasul v. Bush* decision pending before Supreme Court, which would soon grant Guantanamo detainees access to habeas counsel. The Bush administration decided to move the CIA captives before any of them got legal rights. Now Guantanamo was the first (and so far only) black site location officially confirmed by the government. It was the same part of the facility long since used for attorney-client meetings.

"Those are big declassifications," Connell told Cohen on the opening Monday, September 9.

The defense's suppression arguments had two overlapping components. One was that the severity of the past torture by the CIA rendered the defendants' confessions to the FBI involuntary—even if the FBI did not use coercive techniques—because the defendants had been brutally conditioned into telling their interrogators whatever they wanted to hear. The other was that the FBI's cooperation with the CIA created a taint because the FBI had relied on or benefited from information extracted during the earlier torture sessions when structuring its own interrogations. The recent declassifications were particularly important for this later theory, not to mention timely (or implausibly late), given that the first witnesses for the suppression hearing were FBI witnesses.

Connell and his colleagues were otherwise displeased at the limitations placed on them by the prosecution. The prior week, they received a new twenty-five-page classification guidance that set forth what defense lawyers could and could not say when eliciting testimony from the upcoming witnesses. Connell told Cohen that the government had invoked the national security privilege over significant amounts of information relevant to suppression, including the identities of CIA personnel, dates of certain events, and locations of black sites. As in past sessions, this was different than merely requiring the defense teams to cover certain topics in classified sessions closed to the public; invoking the national security privilege meant that the information was completely off-limits—as Connell complained to Cohen, it was removed entirely from "the judicial process." While the defense teams never expected to learn the actual identifies of covert agents, Connell said the dates of certain events were important to understand how and when FBI agents interacted with the CIA program.

"There's an enormous amount of information that's just being taken off the table," Connell said.

Clay Trivett pushed back, noting that the government previously had asserted privilege over CIA identities, dates, black site locations, and sources and methods of intelligence gathering. He said it was obvious that defense lawyers could not ask questions about these topics.

"The rules didn't change," Trivett argued.

Cohen was not merely presiding over a suppression hearing; he was also simultaneously tasked with assessing whether the defense teams were fairly positioned to argue for suppression, given the restrictions they faced in presenting their case. The hearing was even more complicated because Cohen was also using the suppression hearing as a broader evidentiary hearing for a wider range of pending motions, including the jurisdictional challenges that four of the accused—other than al Hawsawi, who had lost his—were entitled to make. This meant that lawyers could question witnesses about matters not directly tied to the voluntariness of the 2007 confessions or the impact of Protective Order #4.

The biggest restriction facing the defense teams was clearly the prohibition on independently contacting CIA witnesses, but another was the inability to ask certain questions of witnesses who would actually take the stand. As a result, the defense teams needed some way to establish a clear record of the limitations. Cohen suggested that defense lawyers submit to him a list of questions they were prevented from asking the witnesses. Connell said his preferred method was to ask the questions to the witnesses and let the government object by citing the national security privilege, at which point Cohen could sustain the objection. Before asking each question, Connell would have to caution the witness not to answer until prosecutors had a chance to object.

"Now, is that going to be the most beautiful cross-examination that I've ever conducted or the most interesting one that the military commission has ever presided over?" Connell said. "I doubt it."

Trivett said the government's primary concern was not spilling classified information. However the defense or the judge wanted to establish the record of what could and could not be asked was fine with him.

"We want them to be able to make their record," Trivett said.

Another complication that highlighted the unwieldy nature of the suppression hearing—one that was expected to last close to a year, over several pretrial sessions—were pending disputes over witnesses, along with the fact that each defense team was planning its participation somewhat differently. This first session was largely focused on Connell's client, Ammar al Baluchi, whose team had coordinated with the government on what witnesses would testify first, even though the two sides remained worlds apart on what the eventual scope should be. Connell wanted at least fifty witnesses, and maybe up to a hundred, between CIA and FBI personnel, JTF-GTMO witnesses, and other Bush administration officials. The government was only agreeing to about twenty witnesses, give or take, a number that would shift somewhat over time. Connell agreed to table his motion to compel additional witnesses until the parties got through the agreed-upon cache. At that point, they could assess the lay of the land and argue over what additional testimony was needed.

The judge would still have to hold suppression sessions for the other four teams, while also dealing with their accompanying disputes over witnesses. The five suppression cases were not completely separated procedurally, however. The other four teams were planning to participate in questioning witnesses for the al Baluchi–focused hearing who had overlapping relevance to their clients. The most obvious were Drs. James Mitchell and Bruce Jessen, the two former CIA contract psychologists who played lead roles in designing the interrogation program and were scheduled to testify in January 2020. These were the only two CIA witnesses agreed to by the government. Several critical FBI witnesses would come first.

* * *

The suppression hearing formally started the next Monday, September 16. In his opening remarks, Connell described the proceedings as "historic" for being "the first public adversarial inquiry into the decision" of the United States "to use torture as an instrument of policy and investigation." Referring to the family members sitting to our right in the gallery, Connell said that the FBI witnesses would also testify about "the mass murder" of 9/11 that caused the suffering of many. He suggested that a national healing could only take place through an understanding that both narratives of the case—the horrors of 9/11 and the torture of the five defendants—were true.

"Our nation suffered a grievous wound, and it failed to live up to its principles afterward," Connell said.

The prosecutor helming the government's case was Jeffrey Groharing, who told Cohen he didn't have any opening remarks. Under the rules of evidence for the commissions, the government has the burden of establishing the voluntariness of the statements by a preponderance of the evidence. The former marine wanted to get straight to his first witness to support this position—FBI Special Agent James Fitzgerald, who conducted what the government considered its "clean" interrogations of al Baluchi in January 2007. Fitzgerald had testified in December 2017 during al Hawsawi's jurisdictional challenge about his role as the notetaker during those interrogations, which were led by his colleague, Abigail Perkins. With the al Baluchi interrogations, those roles were flipped: Fitzgerald was the lead and Perkins took notes. Groharing began by having Fitzgerald make the formal identification of al Baluchi to the court.

"He's towards the back of the court on the right-hand side," Fitzgerald said, meaning the left-side for us and anyone else facing the judge. "He's wearing some sort of head wear, and he's looking at me right now."

Fitzgerald said that al Baluchi—whom he referred to as "Mr. Ali," as the government does—became a person of interest almost immediately after the 9/11 attacks because his name was on financial documents uncovered early in the investigation. Groharing and Fitzgerald walked the courtroom through a painstaking map presentation prepared by the FBI's "Laboratory Special Projects Unit" that showed apparent connections through wire transfers from the United Arab Emirates, where al Baluchi lived, to locations in the United States. Al Baluchi's passport was used to open an account at a UAE bank called the Wall Street Exchange Centre from which money flowed to confirmed hijackers, Fitzgerald explained. At the time, al Baluchi—a Microsoft-certified software engineer—worked at a company called Modern Electronics Centre, which was a short drive to the bank.

This type of testimony was expected. One unexpected tidbit was that al Baluchi filled out a visa application to travel to the United States from September 4 through September 11, 2001. It didn't make sense to me for al Baluchi to be a hijacker—the others had arrived much earlier to prepare, and al Baluchi did not have the profile of the hijackers—but perhaps he was there to offer some other type of on-the-ground assistance.

Fitzgerald said he learned at some point in 2003 that al Baluchi was in CIA custody, and acknowledged that there would have been "a back-and-forth" between the CIA and the FBI on information coming from detainees at the black sites. But he said he was not aware of any statement made from the black sites that helped the FBI get evidence to be used in the case against al Baluchi. He also downplayed the significance of his accessing a CIA database with information learned from the black sites prior to traveling to Guantanamo Bay for the January 2007 interrogations. He began visiting the secret CIA location the previous October, though he did not recall many details of this process.

"What role, if any, did any statement made by Mr. Ali to the CIA have in your interview preparations?" Groharing asked.

"To the best of my knowledge, none," Fitzgerald said.

The government's theory on the voluntariness of the confessions was a simple one: Before each session, agents told the detainees they did not have to participate and that they would not be punished for choosing not to do so. Fitzgerald testified that he started the interrogation as instructed by his FBI superiors, giving the "modified rights advisement" to al Baluchi that did not involve *Miranda* warnings or the right to a lawyer. It focused instead on the detainee's understanding that the session was voluntary and that his time with the CIA was over, no matter how he answered the questions.

"He indicated that he understood he would not be going back to the custody of the CIA," Fitzgerald said.

In fact, Fitzgerald recalled that it was al Baluchi who said "Let's get down to business" once they went through the formalities, and the agent began showing him the documents of wire transfers, bank records, and ID cards, as well as photos. Over the course of four days—for a total of about thirty hours with breaks for lunches from McDonald's—al Baluchi confirmed details of wire transfers of money and other assistance he allegedly provided to the hijackers, according to Fitzgerald. He said al Baluchi was not under any duress or experiencing any pain or discomfort.

"How would you describe your rapport with Mr. Ali over the course of your interviews?" Groharing asked.

"I would describe it as courteous, professional, respectful rapport," Fitzgerald said.

The next morning, Groharing used the witness to drop a major evidentiary bombshell. He had Fitzgerald read English-language transcripts of secret recordings made in the Camp 7 detention facility for the high-value detainees. We assumed that surveillance like this existed based on earlier litigation over secret Camp 7 programs, which defense lawyers could not discuss in any detail. In addition, Daniel Klaidman wrote about the recordings in his 2012 book *Kill or Capture*, though his reporting suggested the government had earlier decided against using them in court proceedings against detainees. We didn't know it at the time of Fitzgerald's testimony, but the prosecution had informed the defense teams years earlier that they planned to use some of the recordings at trial. After Pohl suppressed the FBI statements in August 2018, the prosecution told the teams that they intended to use dozens more of the recordings. Though Parrella had put the FBI statements back in play for the time being, the Camp 7 recordings would help buffer against a possible loss of the suppression dispute.

On September 17, Fitzgerald read from parts of transcripts in which al Baluchi discussed with a fellow detainee whether he should plead guilty, at one point reading parts of his draft guilty plea. In another section, he expressed surprise at the amount of evidence the FBI had against him and allegedly told his confidant: "three-quarters of the money for the operation was sent through me." One of al Baluchi's defenses at trial would be that, even if he moved money for his uncle, KSM, he did not know the purpose of the transfers. In one section of the transcripts read by Fitzgerald, however, another detainee mentioned this type of defense to al Baluchi, to which al Baluchi allegedly responded: "No, I did know." Still, much of what Fitzgerald read was filled with redactions, so it was hard to get a full sense of the context or meaning. After court, Connell wasn't too concerned and thought that parts of the conversations involving his client could be exculpatory.

* * *

The expectation for cross-examination was that Connell would probe Fitzgerald's hazy memory of accessing CIA databases prior to interrogating his client—all in the hopes of better establishing the FBI's reliance on torture-derived material. He did some of this over his two days of questioning Fitzgerald, but Connell was on to bigger and more elaborate connections between the two agencies. In recent months, the defense teams had received a trove of discovery on the FBI's role in the black site interrogations. These were so-called "intelligence requirements" or "FBI requirements"—lists of topics and questions that FBI agents investigating the 9/11 attacks wanted the CIA to ask the detainees at the black sites. The defense teams had received close to eighty such requirements in which the FBI had requested CIA personnel to ask the detainees hundreds, perhaps thousands, of questions.

Connell had these in binders on the witness stand for Fitzgerald to refer to, starting with FBI requests for information in 2002, before al Baluchi was even captured. Groharing objected early in the questioning, claiming that the information was not relevant.

"The questioning should focus on what happened after Mr. Ali was captured," Groharing said on September 18.

Connell countered that the investigation of his client started well before he was captured and that torture-derived evidence played a critical role in that process. Beyond that, he wanted to paint the picture of a yearslong collaboration between the FBI and the CIA that was so thorough it was impossible to view the 2007 interrogations as separate from the CIA or as clean from its taint. Connell wanted to show the "feedback loops" between the agencies.

"This is our core point, that the FBI and CIA were tightly integrated throughout the course of this investigation," Connell said. "It's like a river that ultimately leads to the January 2007 interrogation, and the feeders to that river involve multiple defendants."

Cohen sided with the defense. Connell then began showing Fitzgerald many of the intelligence requirements he and his fellow agents had sent into the black sites. Fitzgerald testified that the FBI used a secure cable system to send in requested questions, and that the CIA would eventually distribute information learned from the detainees in cables to the broader intelligence community. The FBI had to sift through this reporting before coming up with follow-up questions. Fitzgerald testified that his questions weren't always the best ones to elicit cooperation from the CIA, and that he eventually learned that his lists of questions annoyed the agency. But the feedback loop clearly existed.

Suppression. September 2019.

On Thursday morning of the hearing's second week, Connell walked Fitzgerald through the various topics of his "clean" interrogation of al Baluchi in January 2007. For each topic, Connell had Fitzgerald refer back to an earlier CIA cable that produced information on the same topic—all based on questions submitted by the FBI.

"Are there, in fact, any topics about which you interrogated Mr. al Baluchi that the CIA had not previously interrogated him?" Connell asked.

"I don't know precisely," Fitzgerald responded.

The dramatic crescendo came when Connell walked Fitzgerald through a document the agent sent by cable to the CIA in October 2003 that contained hundreds of questions for black site personnel to ask al Baluchi and three of the other 9/11 defendants about planning for the attacks. Connell began reading each question, to which Fitzgerald responded with a "yes" to confirm that he had sent the question in to the CIA.

"Sir, when you drafted those hundreds of questions, did you have any idea how much these men would be tortured to get answers?" Connell asked.

Groharing objected. He said the question assumed "facts not in evidence" and called for Fitzgerald to make "a legal conclusion."

Connell said he would rephrase: "Did you think they would ask nicely?"

"I certainly wouldn't use the word 'nicely,' no," Fitzgerald responded.

He said he couldn't recall if he knew at the time how the CIA was treating the detainees during the interrogations at black sites.

"Perhaps I did," he allowed. He said he knew that the CIA was not using the FBI's "law enforcement approach" to interrogations.

"Sir, at this time, in 2003, you had been a law enforcement professional for more than ten years," Connell said. "Why were you willing to participate in something like that?"

"There were three thousand dead people, and there were multitudes of threats and unknown information," Fitzgerald said forcefully. "I considered the actions I took at that time to be reasonable."

After Connell finished, Judge Cohen drilled down on the extent to which Fitzgerald reviewed the CIA material before interrogating al Baluchi himself in 2007. But the witness remained foggy.

"I may have seen a cable; I don't have a specific recollection," he said.

Cohen tried again: "I guess the question I would have is for purposes of this criminal trial: What did you do with the information obtained via the CIA interrogations with respect to Mr. Ali or any of the others?"

Fitzgerald asked back: "In other words, sir, if I'm understanding, did I, say, take a statement that they may have made in CIA custody and then use the substance of that information in my interview or interrogation?"

"Correct," the judge said.

"I have no recollection of doing that, number one," Fitzgerald said. "And number two, I knew that that was not the design or the intent of these interrogations."

Still, Cohen wondered: What steps did he take to make sure information from the CIA did not make its way into his questioning of al Baluchi?

"I tried to keep the interrogation focused on documents, things where I could present a document or a photograph, what I considered essentially a neutral item, and ask questions about that," Fitzgerald said.

In a brief redirect examination on Friday, Groharing attempted a little cleanup.

"Do you have any recollection of using any statement that you may have read from [Mr. al Baluchi's] time in the RDI program during your interview?" Groharing asked.

"I do not have any recollection of using any statement," Fitzgerald said.

Connell had another witness to testify about the FBI's accessing CIA reporting from the black sites. Nearly two years earlier, in December 2017, former FBI Special Agent Abigail Perkins had been a somewhat difficult witness for Walter Ruiz, recollecting few details of her preparation for the January 2007 interrogations of al Hawsawi. She was a different witness this day, perhaps enticed by the thought of moving quickly through her testimony in a single day to be done in time for the Saturday flight off the island—instead of having to stick around for the third week. She recalled in much greater detail the process of spending about two months going to a CIA location in Virginia before the January 2007 interrogations to prepare.

In her prior testimony, Perkins recalled mainly reading hard copy printouts of information. She now described accessing a computer system that had "buckets"—one folder for each of the high-value detainees with "CIA reporting that had been disseminated out about a detainee or from a detainee." Once she was in a bucket, she could click on any document related to the detainee, mainly CIA cables about interrogations. Perkins testified that she read less of the CIA reporting on al Baluchi because she was not the lead interrogator for him, but did so for al Hawsawi and other detainees for whom she would be doing the interviewing. Perkins said she reported to the CIA location daily, and that Fitzgerald was there at a workstation as the lead agent on al Baluchi. She now recalled the printouts she testified about in December 2017 as likely being printed materials from computers that were captured in raids, not printouts of CIA cables.

Groharing performed a brief cross-examination to once again paint the portrait of a voluntary session. Perkins said that al Baluchi was not nervous or under any physical duress, other than mentioning some stomach discomfort.

"He seemed very relaxed," Perkins said.

She also said that al Baluchi seemed to enjoy their lunches together and talking about TV shows—she thought maybe *Seinfeld* was a topic of conversation—and other elements of Western culture.

"I would describe the conversation like you would have almost with anyone, a lunch conversation, a friend you were going to meet," Perkins said, though surely most of her lunch dates were not shackled at the ankle to the floor.

She said that al Baluchi did not mention his prior treatment by the CIA, and the agents didn't ask about it. That would have required permission from the CIA, Perkins said, and they did not seek such permission. She said they were attempting to draw a separation between the CIA and FBI, to build a new relationship, and that "dredging up old memories" was not the best way to go about it.

* * *

The three-week September session was a watershed for another reason: David Nevin, Mohammed's longtime lead lawyer and team "learned counsel," was stepping down from that role. On the other teams, all of which had only one lawyer to qualify as "learned," this would have been a giant wrench in the all-important suppression hearing. After all, Bormann's broken wrist on the day of the Women's March rendered the first Trump-era hearing mostly void of oral arguments. But the Mohammed team was stacked with capital talent. One of the longtime lawyers on the team was Gary Sowards, a renowned death penalty lawyer, then living in New York. Among his many cases, Sowards represented "Unabomber" Ted Kaczynski through a guilty plea that resulted in a life sentence. The team also had another prominent figure in the field, Denise "Denny" Leboeuf, a lawyer based in New Orleans and longtime leader of the John Adams Project—the joint effort established by the ACLU and the National Association of Criminal Defense Lawyers (NACDL) to fund pro bono civilian lawyers for Guantanamo defendants during the Bush administration. More recently, the team had added Rita

Radostitz, a lawyer who had handled a significant amount of death penalty cases in Texas. The ACLU was still funding a few pro bono slots on the KSM team, including Sowards and Leboeuf. Sowards and Nevin were now trading places, with Nevin returning to his pro bono role from 2008 and Sowards becoming the government-funded learned counsel.

Judge Cohen began the three-week hearing by noting he had received the filing from the Mohammed team that requested the switch. Cohen confirmed with Mohammed that he agreed to the change, asking if he needed to discuss this further with members of his team.

"No, I'm okay," he responded in English.

Sowards briefly put his qualifications on the record, noting that he had handled forty-five death penalty cases during his forty years of practice, including the Kaczynski case—and none had resulted in a death sentence. At sixty-nine, he was about a half year younger than Nevin. During the first break, Nevin came up to Carol and me under the tent outside court to say that his client wanted people to understand that it was not Mohammed's initiative. In fact, Nevin said, it was largely a logistical and practical issue related to the case's unprecedented amount of classified information. The only way Nevin could review such information in his faraway world of Boise, Idaho, was for a special courier to bring it to him, or for Nevin to travel to the commission offices in Virginia. Nevin had to use a secure facility in Idaho to review the material once it was brought to him. The chief defense counsel, Gen. Baker, had hoped to set up a terminal at this location that would allow for the electronic transmission of classified information, but this effort failed. Nevin portrayed the endless travel and use of couriers as expensive and exhausting. Sowards would have an easier time of it going to and from New York.

Even if Nevin wasn't going anywhere, Sowards now spoke for the team in court. I may have been the only one in the viewing gallery to note down the truly historic moment later that afternoon when Nevin walked out of court while oral arguments were happening. Lawyers and other staff on both sides of the court do this all the time, but learned counsel have to remain present. Nevin now got to take a bathroom break without waiting for a recess. He shot Ruiz a smile as he passed the fifth defense table, a look that seemed to ask: "Jealous much?" Ruiz confided to me later that he was, in fact, quite jealous.

Nevin had met with reporters regularly over the years, generally stopping by the media center when asked and occasionally doing so on his own initiative. So did the team's lead military lawyer, Marine Lt.

Col. Derek Poteet, who had been assigned to Mohammed's defense in 2011. Poteet, a very friendly guy, and Nevin began sharing duties as the public face for the team long before my arrival. Poteet was a rarity by staying on the case for so long as a member of the military, instead of becoming a civilian to do so. (He would finally take a new assignment for the Marines in 2020 by becoming a judge.) Sowards quickly changed the team's approach to media relations, avoiding almost any public comment and adopting a more standoffish approach. Like most people involved in the commissions, however, he was friendly outside court and game for conversations that did not include the case. He cut a striking figure at the podium, standing north of 6'2", mostly bald with a thick white beard. He was the only civilian male attorney not to wear a tie with his button-down shirt and coat, though that was apparently not a career practice, as he could be seen in a tie during coverage of the Unabomber case.

We were not expecting Sowards to do much in the September 2019 session given that the suppression hearing focused mostly on witnesses related to al Baluchi's case. On that opening Monday, however, Sowards rose to express his dismay over the government's twenty-five-page guidance and ground rules for conducting witness examinations related to suppression.

"This is an instance which very much demonstrates to us the point that torture is only always in the room," Sowards said.

That was the first time he used what would become his catchphrase: "Torture is only always in the room." He would say it often. That morning, Sowards said that the entire discussion the judge was having with Connell and the prosecution on how to conduct the proceedings and establish a record was bending to the government's efforts to cover up the torture program. That, he said, was the "virtually exclusive purpose" of this whole exercise. Cohen appeared a bit taken aback, with something of an "ouch" look on his face.

Sowards sat silently during the week-two examinations of Fitzgerald and Perkins but was eyeing with interest a government witness during the third week. On Tuesday, September 24, the prosecution attempted to bolster its case that al Baluchi was in sound mental and physical shape in 2007 by calling Bernard DeLury, a judge on the New Jersey Superior Court. In 2007, DeLury was a reserve navy captain with a security clearance and served as president of a three-member Combatant Status Review Tribunal, or CSRT. The Department of Defense established the tribunals to determine whether

Guantanamo detainees were being properly held as "enemy combatants" under the law of war; those who were not deemed enemy combatants could be released in coordination with foreign governments.

All of the defendants in the 9/11 case except Ramzi bin al Shibh went before a status tribunal, which took place in the months after the FBI interrogated the defendants in January 2007. The government was using DeLury to support its claim that the defendants' overall demeanor in their hearings showed that they were not in a state of "learned helplessness" from CIA torture. In fact, under direct examination by Ed Ryan on Tuesday, DeLury testified that al Baluchi did not show any signs of emotional or physical distress. He said that al Baluchi even put up a defense by denying membership in al Qaeda. The government did not plan on using these statements at trial against al Baluchi, they were merely using his CSRT to support the voluntariness of his behavior in early 2007.

Prosecutors did, however, intend to use CSRT statements against the other defendants, including Mohammed. In his written statement for the tribunal, Mohammed claimed responsibility for planning the 9/11 attacks "from A to Z," among other crimes. In the spirit of what is often referred to as "judicial economy," Ryan questioned DeLury about the demeanors and behaviors of the other defendants to avoid having to call him back whenever the suppression hearings focused on the other defendants. DeLury testified that none of them appeared to be experiencing any duress, including Mohammed.

"He appeared to be alert and interacting with the tribunal," DeLury said.

Sowards couldn't let this go unchallenged. With an Aircast on his foot, Sowards ambled up slowly to the podium as an intense thunder-and-lightning storm began to intermittently shake the prefab courtroom. This created the oddest audiovisual experience I've had in court. The video feed going into the courtroom's viewing gallery trembled, and the forty-second audio delay meant that we heard thunder in real time and then later through the gallery monitors. I had trouble determining which thunder was past or present.

Sowards had to stop at one point to let the thunder pass.

"The gods are angry," he surmised with a smile.

At first, Sowards engaged in a friendly colloquy with DeLury about his extensive experience as a criminal judge and the rigorous attention he gave to ensuring that a defendant's guilty plea or incriminating statements are voluntary. His tone sharpened as he asked DeLury if he had ever had a defendant arrive in his courtroom after being physically and psychologically tortured for more than four years.

"It hasn't happened in front of me," DeLury testified.

"Excellent," Sowards said, his eyes drilling into DeLury like a laser. "You're lucky."

Sowards began a hypothetical: What if the judge had been informed that a defendant appearing before him had "been stripped naked, hung from the ceiling of his cell, and deprived—"

Ryan objected. He wasn't going to let Sowards go through a long torture description to ask a simple question. But Cohen allowed Sowards to rephrase.

"If at the time Mr. Mohammed appeared before you, you had been informed that he had been in continuous government custody for approximately four years, during that time, in order to coerce him into making statements which were—the substance of which were going to be repeated in the CSRT tribunal before you—had been held by government officials who had stripped him naked and had hanged him from the ceiling of his cell for approximately a week and twelve hours—"

Another objection, this one much later, from Ryan. Once again, however, Cohen allowed Sowards to get his question out. This time in phrasing the hypothetical, Sowards added new details—that Mohammed's captors left him "in his own defecation and urine; they had deprived him of sleep over seven days and twelve hours; that he was also anally raped by his jailers; that his jailers subjected him to 183 mock executions, meaning procedures which put him in imminent fear and the belief that he was about to die; that the police had kidnapped and abused his children and threatened to kill the children if Mr. Mohammed did not confess."

All agree that Ryan is a great trial lawyer, but the objections backfired. It's a long view from the gallery to the prosecution table, but I felt him fuming.

Would all of that past treatment, Sowards finally wondered, play into an assessment of whether the statement was voluntary?

"I would certainly take it into consideration," DeLury, who knew exactly what was happening, said dryly.

"And would it be a neutral factor or would it cause you concern?" Sowards asked.

"It would be causing me concern," DeLury responded.

DeLury testified that he engaged in a discussion with Mohammed about his past abuse by the CIA. He said he did not feel compelled to determine whether Mohammed was suffering the continued effects of his CIA custody during the CSRT hearing. He did, however, recommend Mohammed's allegations of torture to his higher-ups for investigation. DeLury testified that he had no professional training related to torture victims that would enable him to identify the signs of learned helplessness or other aftereffects. Sowards had made his point and sat down.

Later that evening, I ran into Nevin outside of the gym and asked him about the DeLury cross-examination, which surprised me given the general silence from the Mohammed table during the hearing. Nevin was also surprised.

"We had no idea he was going to do that," Nevin said.

It occurred to me on the short walk to O'Kelly's that I never did my profile of Nevin. The only reason I first attended the military commissions in 2015 was to see him in action, to get color for the piece. Now 2020 was staring us down, and Nevin was no longer even the lead defense lawyer on the case. On the one hand, this felt a little embarrassing. On the other, it probably confirmed that I was the right reporter for this job—I never quite saw the rush with any of this.

Whether the gods were indeed angry or not, the storm took its toll on the legal complex. The trailer bathrooms outside the court all overflowed, creating what Bormann called a "poop river" on the walkway to court from the outer security tent. Personnel put a wooden ramp over the deepest part of the brown flow so we could leave with minimal damage to our shoes. Several women using the trailer bathrooms outside court experienced waste spurting up while they were sitting on the toilets. These were rich and vivid additions to what was already a toxic wasteland.

The first-ever three-week session ended a day early, on Thursday, with the defense and prosecution teams renewing their arguments over scheduling issues. Rita Radostitz, one of the newer Mohammed attorneys, urged Cohen to reconsider his plan to hold twenty-two weeks of hearings in 2020, which encompassed thirty weekends because of travel days. She said that the schedule would make it extremely difficult for her team to file all the motions they felt were necessary. As a civilian lawyer, Radostitz was staying at the motel lodging on Guantanamo, which she acknowledged was better than the tents or the CHUs in Camp Justice. But she told Cohen that she awoke earlier that morning to brown water leaking on her bed and found her entire bathroom floor covered in brown water. She added that the storms twice caused electrical outages that interrupted work for several hours. The weather also contributed to outages in the detention complex where attorneys meet with their clients, which led to cancellations of those meetings.

Radostitz said that while these inconveniences were minor in isolation, collectively they presented a challenge to a fair trial.

"It has a cascading effect on our ability to litigate," she said.

The judge acknowledged that he had learned in his first three sessions—particularly this one—that running a massive case on Guantanamo presented unique challenges.

"I share with you the issues that are down here," Cohen said.

Ryan was less sympathetic. He told Cohen that the prosecution was completely committed to the planned schedule. He said the best email blast the prosecution ever sent to the victim family community was the one alerting them to the January 2021 trial date set by Cohen.

"We don't want to go backward," Ryan said.

Glancing over at the five lawyers sitting to his left at Mohammed's crammed table, he also assailed what he termed the "ridiculousness" of Radostitz's complaints.

"I know there's a joke in there someplace about how many lawyers it takes to file on time," Ryan said. "I would submit that the punchline is less than five."

If Ryan wanted revenge over the DeLury exchange, perhaps he had it. He also told Cohen that his argument from earlier in the year—that dates drive actions—was proving to be true in terms of the resources now flowing to the commissions in anticipation of a trial. Earlier in the year, more workspaces were added at the legal complex, with each defense team and the prosecution team receiving new work trailers—large, prefabricated structures that looked like oversized shipping containers where legal teams could read and produce classified documents. Ryan's argument rang true to anyone who visited the legal complex: It was still "expeditionary," one supposed, but its footprint was growing. The dust in the air surely contributed to the overall toxicity of Camp Justice, but it also seemed to offer visual support for the idea that the government was committed to holding a trial there.

Of course, even sealed containers are not immune to health hazards, and tales of mold, moisture, and leaks accompanied the start of the next hearing in late October, scheduled to last two weeks. Nevin told Cohen that, in the Mohammed trailer, "a very troubling looking and smelling brown liquid is oozing up between the tiles." He said he was still clearing his throat after having only been in there trying to work for about a half-hour.

Cohen said that the commissions could probably prioritize some work orders and "have someone look at that right away."

CHAPTER 20

What Makes a Site a Black Site? October–November 2019.

September was a productive start to the suppression hearing, but it had a long way to go. The pretrial hearing would, on its own, be longer and more intense—and more procedurally complicated, given all the classified information—than almost any actual trial in US history. Only three reporters decided to attend the second suppression hearing, set to last two weeks beginning October 28, compared to the dozen who showed up for the start in September. In addition to me and Carol, the other attendee was one of the other semi-regulars, Kasey McCall-Smith from the University of Edinburgh Law School. The flow between the two sessions suggested what I assumed would accompany a trial: Many reporters would show up for the start of jury selection, which, while not always exciting in itself, would nevertheless signal—at long last—the start of the 9/11 trial. Then just about all the reporters would leave. Jury or "panel" selection of the military officers who would decide the case was expected to last two-to-three months, with the commission flying in troves of potential jurors in groups of fifty or so every few weeks. Whenever that finished, opening statements would then probably draw the biggest group of reporters, just about all of whom would leave once the slog of witness testimony began.

The trial itself was expected to last close to a year, maybe more, depending on how the judge scheduled breaks. For much of that, it would just be Carol and me, though I had not fully thought through or discussed with Fiona in significant detail how we would handle a trial. It was assumed that the judge would come up with a schedule like four or six weeks in court, followed by one or two weeks off, with people free to return during the off times. Still, a defense lawyer who worked on one of the other cases told me that the prospect of having a yearlong trial on Gitmo was dangerous. He thought people would snap, that you'd have mental breakdowns and fights.

Under any schedule, the front row of the viewing gallery would mostly be empty, with most journalists dropping in for certain witnesses. That's why the October 2019 hearing had a paltry media presence. Clearly, most reporters were eyeing the January 2020 session that was scheduled to feature Drs. Mitchell and Jessen, the former CIA contract psychologists. People wanted to see the accused torturers in the same room as their victims. Testimony involving the FBI's still-emerging role in black site interrogations was fascinating—and historically important—but harder to explain to a public that had mostly forgotten about the case.

Even the September media showing was somewhat misleading, as several journalists stayed for a week or less. During the first week, Carol came with Wendy MacNaughton, an acclaimed illustrator, to collaborate on what became "Inside America's War Court: Clothing and Culture at Guantanamo Bay," published in December 2019. This is easily the best exploration of the topic, with great sketches of Gen. Martins—in his characteristic wide-legged seating position, with his fingers forming a steeple in front of his chest; the women defense team members in varying head coverings and Sowards in prayer with his client's nephew, al Baluchi, among other subjects.

One of the reporters for the second week was NPR's Sacha Pfeiffer, who had recently produced an investigative segment on Guantanamo Bay that came out near the start of the hearing. Pfeiffer, who had also come for a week of the prior session in July, marked a solid return for public radio, after a long break without having either David Welna or Arun Rath on base. Earlier in her life, Pfeiffer was part of the *Boston Globe* "Spotlight" team that won the Pulitzer Prize for its investigative work on the Catholic Church sexual abuse crisis. (She is played in the 2015 movie *Spotlight* by Rachel McAdams.) Her radio piece, which contained criticisms of the perceived waste associated with the prison and the military commissions, caused a bit of a stir within the traveling court system at the start of the massive suppression case. Pfeiffer interviewed Gary Brown, the former legal advisor who was fired along with the former convening authority, Harvey Rishikof. Brown backed up earlier claims by the defense teams, saying that they were fired for pursuing the greatest cost-saving move imaginable—ending the cases by plea agreement.

Pfeiffer's story listed the cost of the military commissions at about $60 million annually. The number that I received from the commissions' spokesperson in 2018 and intermittently since was $100 million. In all of my reporting on the commissions, I have not focused much on costs. My attitude resulted, in part, from spending loads of time researching other large justice mechanisms around the world, and from being generally familiar with the budget of the Pentagon. I'm not sure how much costs matter, even if it's always good to point out instances of waste and fraud. The commissions barely took up one-tenth of a percentage point of Pentagon spending. As time has dragged on, however, I've come to see this thinking as flawed. There are more important factors that have shaped the course of proceedings on Guantanamo Bay, but that many people and entities get money from the commissions is part of the puzzle—a significant part to some critics, who see the Guantanamo court as a New Deal–like jobs-and-work program.

During the third week, we were joined by Terry McDermott and Daniel Voll. Showtime had stopped moving forward with their show *Guantanamo* because it was a project of the Weinstein Company, but the project was not entirely dead. Voll and McDermott had with them Assaf Bernstein, the acclaimed Israeli writer and director who was a creative force behind the show *Fauda*, in which Israeli agents track Palestinian fighters. Bernstein was attached to possibly direct *Guantanamo*, now that Oliver Stone had dropped out. During our nights at the picnic table, the creative trio succeeded in breaking two of the four scotch glasses I had purchased from the base's thrift store for $2, perhaps my greatest-ever find on the base. Still, it was great fun having them around. McDermott had a local contact on the base, a Filipino contractor helping him with some journalistic legwork who also had a pontoon boat. We spent a lazy afternoon getting a boat ride around the exterior of the base to help Bernstein get a visual sense of where all the drama unfolds.

Even a modest uptick in journalists seemed to strain the functioning of the system's media apparatus. The media operations center or "MOC" was two adjoining rooms connected by a kitchen, with each side having a screen to broadcast court. You could fit maybe eight or ten reporters comfortably on each side, though not all the ethernet cables worked, and broadcast teams would take up more space with their equipment. (It remains amazing to me that more than fifty journalists showed up for the May 2012 arraignment.) Rains also led to occasional ceiling leaks and the ongoing threat of mold, especially between hearings when the air-conditioning units were turned off.

Whether the aircraft hangar that contained the MOC was officially condemned remained a point of confusion for a surprisingly protracted period. During parts of 2018 and early 2019, Carol and I wore hard hats on the walk through the hangar to the trailer bathrooms, due to falling debris, either because we were ordered to or decided to on our own. In early 2019, however, the hangar was finally condemned, and we could no longer walk through it to enter the MOC. Ron Flesvig, who had replaced Cmdr. Higgins as the court's public affairs officer the prior fall, told us before the March 2019 session that the media center was "unavailable until further notice." We spent that session working in a small replica of the MOC built inside a large military tent on the dirt and grass outside the hangar. The constant flow of contractor trucks through Camp Justice made hearing anything impossible, which created annoying delays when attempting to interview lawyers. Even more troubling was that heavy rains gave the floor the feel of an unsteady waterbed. As Carol, in her first session as a *Times* journalist, aptly stated, the media operations "lacked dignity" that week.

Because the MOC was its own structure with its own roof on one side of the hangar, we could continue using it if someone carved out an emergency exit on the exterior wall of the building and sealed the hangar-side access. That happened before the next session, and we had our office back, though we permanently lost the separate briefing room that was fully within the hangar. Another annoyance, however, was that the trailer bathrooms had long since stopped having any air flow, a problem that dated to the prior year. Using the bathroom for any period of time during the day was borderline dangerous given the heat, and sitting on the toilet for a while would often mean sweating through your clothes. Flesvig and I started coordinating when each of us would use the larger handicap trailer for longer bathroom breaks so we could prop the door open several inches and still have some privacy.

With Flesvig, the fifth public affairs officer of my Gitmo life, the public affairs position became a full-time civilian role, which meant he would not automatically rotate out to a new assignment. (He was also a commander in the Navy Reserves at the time.) During his first year, the court mostly lost the assistance it had been receiving from the JTF-GTMO media operations. This support, which included soldiers from the prison public affairs team taking us to court and driving us around the base, began dwindling during Higgins's tenure and was fully withdrawn without warning by the September 2019 hearing—right when we were about to need it most, with the amped-up suppression hearings. Flesvig would soon hire civilian contractors to drive us around in vans provided by the commissions. We won a small victory during this session when the director of commission operations on Gitmo bought us a gas grill for the wood hut that sat halfway between our tents and the media center, which diversified our dining options and reduced the nightly need for drivers. Flesvig had inherited from Higgins a folder called "Grill Drama," which documented Carol's and my long-pending grill efforts, though the contents remained something of a mystery.

The media won a bigger victory prior to the start of the suppression hearing. In the weeks before, the naval base's public affairs office—separate from the court's or the prison's—attempted to push through a new set of draconian ground rules for media to sign before coming to the base to report on the commissions. These went beyond the rules that media organizations and the Office of the Secretary of Defense agreed to in 2010 and had remained in effect since. Among the new provisions, journalists would need a public affairs officer present for all reporting work, which meant a public affairs representative would have to sit in for all interviews, regardless of where and with whom they took place. Audio recordings also had to be submitted for review. The regular journalists who learned about the proposals forcefully opposed them. I wrote a few different memos in opposition, including a lengthy one with a bulleted list of how unworkable the changes were, and Carol consulted the *Times*' lawyers. In an article by The Intercept on the proposed changes, Flesvig also backed up our position, saying that the Office of Military Commissions did not agree with the naval base's position that a public affairs officer had to sit in on interviews and review recordings.

"I'm not going to enforce that rule," Flesvig said.

On September 6, 2019, the day before our flight, he informed us that the naval station had suspended its requirement to sign the new rules. As the late October–November hearing approached, no one had mentioned them again.

* * *

During that two-week session, Connell continued his strategy of linking the FBI to the CIA black sites through cables and "intelligence requirements." Two more FBI agents from the PENTTBOM team acknowledged on the stand that they and their colleagues sent in questions for the CIA to ask detainees. The first witness, former FBI Special Agent Adam Drucker, was a little difficult to see among the binders stacked at the witness box.

He was good-natured, however, over two days of public testimony before shifting into a closed session at the end of the week.

Drucker worked on bank fraud cases until the September 11 attacks, at which point he shifted his responsibilities to investigating the financing behind the operation. Connell walked him through cables sent to the CIA—including ones that the witness himself drafted on topics related to al Baluchi—seeking information from detainees. Drucker testified that the process of sending in questions began in 2002, in the months after the capture of Ramzi bin al Shibh, the first 9/11 defendant to be apprehended. In February 2004, the FBI detailed Drucker to the CIA's Counterterrorism Center to serve as a liaison between the two agencies. He said he was aware that the FBI had drafted questions to be posed to detainees in CIA custody through 2006.

For me, Drucker added a new and intriguing layer to the broader topic of how the fruits of CIA interrogations went beyond the agency's efforts to stop future attacks. Connell played for the court a video of a younger Drucker testifying before the National Commission on Terrorist Attacks Upon the United States, the independent bipartisan body that produced the widely acclaimed "9/11 Commission Report." In his 9/11 commission testimony, Drucker referred to information coming from "detainee reporting," including details that came from the interrogations of Mohammed. This meant that, fifteen years earlier, when the existence of black sites was still largely secret, Drucker testified in a public session about information elicited during CIA interrogation sessions that made its way into the "9/11 Commission Report." In fact, we would later learn that the 9/11 Commission also sent questions to the CIA to ask detainees—its own "requirements." Defense teams would seek additional discovery on that, as well.

Drucker said that, given his expertise in the financial side of the attacks, he was considered for the role of lead interrogator of al Baluchi in January 2007. But he said his time at the CIA proved to be a hindrance, again alluding to the government's desire to separate the FBI sessions in 2007 from the CIA.

"I was too much CIA to be FBI," Drucker said on October 30. "And frankly at the CIA I was too much FBI to be CIA. That's kind of the sum total of my existence for five years."

Instead, Drucker watched the January 2007 interrogations of al Baluchi and other detainees from a monitoring room in the detention facility. Under cross-examination by prosecutor Ed Ryan, Drucker testified that the sessions took place without any threats or raised voices and that the detainees did not exhibit any fear—confirming the earlier accounts of his former colleagues, Fitzgerald and Perkins, that the sessions were voluntary from the FBI's view. Drucker also confirmed that he obtained bank records and other financial documents related to the 9/11 investigation "fairly quickly" after the attacks, before any of the defendants were captured and sent to CIA custody.

Once again, Gary Sowards couldn't leave the "voluntary" portrayal alone, and once again he did so over Ryan's objections, asking Drucker if he was aware of the many abuses—rapes, mock executions, threats to children—that Mohammed had been subjected to prior to his arrival on Guantanamo Bay.

"That's the first time I heard that," Drucker said.

The FBI-CIA overlap became even more explicit during the second week with the testimony of FBI Supervisory Special Agent Michael Butsch, who led the January 2007 interrogations of Ramzi bin al Shibh. It was, in many ways, a repeat exercise, with the prosecution using the agent's testimony to paint the FBI-elicited statements as voluntary, and Connell using it to flesh out more "information loops" between FBI investigators and the CIA. At one point, in responding to a prosecution objection to the repeated questioning, Judge Cohen told Connell that he was ready to issue "a finding of fact" that interagency information-sharing existed between the CIA and FBI. Butsch also testified that, like Perkins and Fitzgerald, he accessed the CIA database in Virginia prior to conducting his interrogation of bin al Shibh in January 2007.

Unlike the other FBI witnesses, however, Butsch testified on November 7, 2019, that he was present at a secret overseas site in 2002 to observe the questioning of bin al Shibh, in the early days after his capture on September 11, 2002, in Pakistan. (The other four defendants were captured in Pakistan between March and late April of 2003.) This was a major revelation, though one that was particularly excruciating to sit through given the classified nature of the details. With the other FBI witnesses, Connell approached many topics that either had to be saved for a closed session or that could not be asked at all because the government had asserted its "national security privilege." Establishing this record was fairly boring, not only because the witnesses could not answer but because Connell often huddled with the prosecution team prior to asking his questions—just to confirm what could and could not be asked, or potentially answered, even if in general terms. With Butsch's presence at an overseas site in 2002, Connell spent less time questioning the witness than he did chatting away from the microphone with prosecutors.

Butsch could not name the entity in control of the building where he attended the interrogation, nor the country where it was located—he could only refer to it as "Location #5." Answering mostly "yes" or "no" questions asked by Connell, Butsch testified that he met people at the building, gave them information, then observed the questioning of bin al Shibh from a room in "close proximity" to the debriefing room. The questioning of bin al Shibh lasted several days, Butsch testified. He said that he took notes from the sessions that were the basis for cables sent to the FBI. The next day, Butsch testified that he did not consider the building in "Location #5" a black site, which intrigued Connell.

"What makes a site a black site?" Connell asked.

"I don't know," Butsch responded. "That's a good question."

The agent testified that he did not believe FBI personnel were allowed at black sites, and he was allowed to be at the building in "Location #5"—hence it was not a black site, as he interpreted it. He added that his understanding was that "enhanced interrogation techniques" were used at CIA black sites, and he did not observe any during the bin al Shibh sessions. However, under additional questioning by Connell, Butsch confirmed that he returned to his hotel after leaving "Location #5" in the afternoon and did not know what transpired overnight. This access was a one-time deal for Butsch, who never again was allowed to visit a location with any suspected 9/11 conspirators. From then on, Butsch had to send questions in to the CIA like the rest of the PENTTBOM team.

Over this and the prior hearing, Connell had elicited an interesting, if confusing, set of facts. FBI agents leading the 9/11 investigation could not access the main suspects at CIA black sites and instead had to rely on an inefficient cable system and "feedback loop" of communication. But the FBI also eventually had agents detailed to the black sites—which meant, apparently, that PENTTBOM investigators did not have direct access to their own colleagues at the CIA locations. This raised a number of questions. I wanted to know whether the FBI agents detailed to the black sites were off limits to defense teams as potential witnesses, if they were considered "CIA" witnesses as part of Protective Order #4. Connell, as always, generously stopped by the media center after each day of court, taking questions on topics that straddled the line of what he could and could not tell us. Quite often, he would pause for several seconds, look up at the ceiling or at his colleagues, and eventually say: "I can't comment."

The last hearing of 2019 would benefit from more judicial economy. Butsch was the government's key witness in establishing the voluntariness of bin al Shibh's statements in January 2007, and Harrington decided to cross-examine him rather than have to recall him at a later date for his suppression case. He did so for about two hours on the last Friday. Mostly, Harrington sought information on the agent's knowledge about bin al Shibh's mental and physical condition at the time of the January 2007 interviews and what had been done to him earlier at the black sites. Butsch expressed almost total ignorance about bin al Shibh's condition and the specific "enhanced" techniques used earlier by the CIA. He said that he had not read the Senate's report of the CIA interrogation program and could not recall any of the news coverage accompanying its release in December 2014.

Butsch testified that he did not know bin al Shibh had been prescribed a cocktail of Haldol, Ativan, and Benadryl and had been on "self-harm watch" at the detention camp prior to the January 2007 sessions. He also did not know that bin al Shibh's hair and beard had been forcibly shaved off a week before the interviews, and that this was also done at the black sites. Clearly, this undercut the government's attenuation argument. As with al Hawsawi, attenuation was further compromised by the fact that bin al Shibh had been held at Guantanamo Bay when it was a black site.

Harrington asked Butsch if he believed interviewing bin al Shibh in the same interrogation room he had earlier suffered abuse would constitute "re-traumatization."

"If there were traumatic things that happened to him in the location and then we interviewed him in the same location, it could, sure," Butsch said.

Harrington then asked whether Butsch had known about bin al Shibh's treatment at the black sites, which included exposures to long periods of light, darkness, cold temperatures, sleep deprivation, stress positions, and nudity. He was doused with water and threatened with waterboarding and "rectal rehydration." He was put on a liquid diet, slapped, and slammed into a wall. Butsch said he had not known of the prior techniques used.

"Do you know that he was told if he . . . said certain things that people wanted him to say, that those techniques would stop?" Harrington asked.

"No," Butsch responded.

The next morning, in the air terminal before our departure, I saw from my company's site analytics that at least some people were reading my story on Butsch's testimony. At one point, I looked up and saw that I was sitting kitty-corner from Butsch, and that he was looking at me and the giant press badge sitting on my chest.

* * *

In between Drucker and Butsch, the government called a particularly tantalizing witness—the first commander of Camp 7, the portion of the Guantanamo Bay detention facility reserved for the "high-value detainees" previously held by the CIA. He testified in open court to support the prosecution's claim that the defendants' early confinement on Guantanamo Bay was sufficiently attenuated from the CIA black sites. The witness testified in civilian clothes under the pseudonym "First Camp 7 Commander." He served in that position from shortly before the detainees arrived in September 2006 until March 2008. Carol knew the Camp 7 commander in his current position, and so was surprised when it was decided his name would be protected. Because the timing of his testimony was flexible—no one seemed too concerned about the exact day or what might happen if he needed to be called back—we assumed he still worked on the island, or at least came regularly.

Under direct examination by prosecutor Robert Swann, the commander testified that he had informed the fourteen new detainees upon their arrival in September 2006 that they were now in the custody of the Department of Defense and would be treated consistently with Common Article 3 of the Geneva Conventions, which included the right to meet with representatives of the International Committee of the Red Cross. The commander testified that, months later, the detainees voluntarily chose to attend the FBI interrogations starting in January 2007—though they were not told beforehand that they would be meeting with the FBI. Nevertheless, he testified that the detainees also voluntarily chose to attend subsequent sessions with the FBI agents.

Swann read briefly from page 160 of the Senate torture report that stated the CIA had "operational control" of Camp 7 after the high-value detainees arrived. The commander disagreed.

"As a commander, I had full responsibility and authorities over those forces," the witness said on November 1. "They responded to my orders consistently. I believe that to be the case."

"Okay," Swann said. "I will ask you for your reasons in the closed session."

Under cross-examination by Connell, however, the former commander acknowledged that an "interagency" group controlled some high-level decisions about Camp 7 policies. Connell also asked him about the members of Camp 7's internal guard force, who wore military uniforms.

"Were they, in fact, military?" Connell asked.

Swann objected, contending that the question called for "a classified response." Judge Cohen encouraged the defense and prosecution to confer, after which Connell got to ask again: "Were the guards military?"

"No," the witness responded.

"And we'll take up the rest in the closed session," Cohen said.

Once again, the defense teams were outraged that the government elicited an opinion in open court—this time about who controlled Camp 7—that could not be fully explored through cross-examination until a closed session. The next month, in ruling on a defense motion, Cohen agreed that the prohibition on cross-examining the witness on this topic in open court was not consistent with the defendants' right to a public trial and undermined "public confidence in commission proceedings." He said he would strike the former commander's opinion from the record if the government did not come up with a plan to allow for additional cross-examination in public. Litigation over this dispute would last several more years.

CHAPTER 21

Dr. Mitchell. January 2020.

Dr. James Mitchell showed a predictable degree of controlled hostility toward the defense side of the courtroom once his testimony began on Tuesday, January 21, 2020. He was the star attraction in a suppression hearing that had consumed four weeks of testimony in 2019 and was expected to last for most, if not all, of 2020. James Connell, as the lead lawyer for Ammar al Baluchi, began by thanking him for showing up in person. The commission was still operating under the assumption that a military judge could not order a civilian witness who was not a government employee to travel to a foreign military base, though it could compel his presence at a video teleconference site in the continental United States.

"Well, thank you," Mitchell replied. "I actually did it for the victims and families, not for you."

No one could be blamed for thinking this day would never happen. Even when we sat in the waiting room at Joint Base Andrews the prior Saturday and heard that Mitchell and his former partner in the interrogation program, Dr. Bruce Jessen, were somewhere in the air terminal waiting for the same flight, it all felt very tenuous. The CIA had exerted such control over the release of information in the case that pulling Mitchell and Jessen back at the last minute felt plausible, if not likely.

Seen another way, however, allowing Mitchell and Jessen to testify was the best way the CIA could maintain a significant level of control over evidence and testimony in the case. Everybody already knew who they were, as they had become the public face of the program. They had never even been CIA employees; they were two former contractors who had finished with the interrogation program after its disbandment in the early days of the Obama administration in 2009. And Mitchell already had put much of what he was allowed to say in his 2016 book *Enhanced Interrogation*, which was written with former CIA spokesperson Bill Harlow and published after review by the CIA's Prepublication Review Board. More recently, Mitchell had talked with author Malcolm Gladwell for his 2019 book *Talking with Strangers*.

The defense teams wanted dozens and dozens of CIA witnesses—interrogators, analysts, medical personnel, psychologists, psychiatrists, guards—who would have knowledge of what happened to their clients at the black sites. Most of those people would be actual current or former CIA employees, not contractors. Prosecutors rejected all of these witness requests, claiming that Mitchell and Jessen could speak for the entire program. Connell was still content with moving forward with the testimony of agreed-upon witnesses while a motion to compel additional witnesses remained pending before Judge Cohen. Connell, like Cohen, believed in the practical benefit of starting witness testimony—you might develop an interest in new witnesses you hadn't even thought about, and you might conclude you no longer needed other witnesses once deemed necessary.

As with the prior witnesses, the five defense teams—all of whom were planning to examine Mitchell and Jessen—would face limitations in what they could ask. In fact, three teams sought a delay in Mitchell's testimony so they could better study the last-minute classification guidance provided to the teams. Before Mitchell entered the court Tuesday morning, a clearly frustrated Gary Sowards told Cohen that receiving a new classification guidance from the prosecution always felt like "buying an iPhone" right before the next version comes out. He said he was not as "nimble" as Connell and that it was dangerous to move "on the fly" in a capital case.

Walter Ruiz, scheduled to go second, said he agreed with Sowards but that he could get up to speed on the guidance while Connell did his examination, expected to last three days. He referred Cohen to a motion that Pohl had rejected nearly three years earlier, one in which his team contended that a fair trial was impossible in light of all the "national security considerations" that engulfed the case. Ruiz told Cohen that the tension between national security and due process had only heightened since then.

"This is not the way to run a capital trial," Ruiz told him. "At some point, there must be some finality in the guidance, and the defense must be in a position where we understand the rules of the road and we can abide by them."

We all knew that Connell was eager to get going, regardless of any new guidance. After all, Mitchell was right outside the courtroom doors, and you never know what could happen in the space of another delay. As with the suppression witnesses in 2019, the prosecution would be asserting the "national security privilege" over information that the government believed could reveal (or help someone piece together) certain classified information, most importantly the identities of covert agents, the locations of the black sites, and the roles of at least some non-covert agents or officials whose relationship to the black site program was not yet known. Continuing the scheme from the prior year, lawyers would establish a court record of what information was prohibited by confirming with the witness that he could not answer a question on a particular topic. For reasons I could not fully grasp, even some of these questions—those which could not be answered—would have to be asked in a closed session.

After Mitchell took the oath and sat in the witness box, Cohen handed him a top secret document that contained a key identifying CIA personnel by real or covert name alongside a code of random numbers and letters, the "UFIs," for unique functional identifiers. The key also contained a list of the true location of each known black site alongside the number that everyone in court had to use. That way, Mitchell would know what he was being asked about and could respond in the coded fashion approved by the intelligence community. The coded system was well familiar to anyone associated with the case or who followed it, but for Mitchell it was new. If a lawyer asked him about "Location 2" or individual "NZ7," as required by the government's classification guidance, he would need to check the document to confirm the actual location and person. The prosecutor who would be cross-examining Mitchell, Jeffrey Groharing, told Mitchell that because the government had invoked the national security privilege over the entire document, he should cover it up if Connell ever approached the witness box. Defense lawyers were not entitled to see the key.

"Would someone remind me if that comes up?" Mitchell asked.

Oddly, the new guidance from the government prevented defense lawyers from asking Mitchell about certain details published in his book, including some physical descriptions of CIA personnel and buildings along with pseudonyms or nicknames of agents. In early questioning by Connell, Mitchell confirmed that no one from the government had ever told him that his book contained unauthorized disclosures of information that could damage national security. Connell asked him what his reaction would be if someone told him that now.

"My reaction would be: Buy the publication rights and take it off the market," Mitchell said.

With his book and various media appearances, Mitchell, then in his late sixties, was something of a public figure. He looked familiar to me with his healthy, mostly white head of hair and matching beard. But he looked older than I expected, wrinklier in the face. The acclaimed sketch artist Janet Hamlin, who had intermittently captured court scenes in Guantanamo Bay over the years, sat to my right and got to work. But the media contingent was not as big as expected; it included most of the semi-regulars, along with Pfeiffer from NPR and a few newcomers. Julian Borger, who had attended once the prior year, was a welcome return from *The Guardian*, which has intermittently done excellent reporting on the proceedings.

Connell has an "open book" style of witness examination and prefers to meet with witnesses before they testify to discuss everything he intends to ask, leaving "gotcha" moments for TV shows and movies. With Mitchell, Connell reminded him that he had talked briefly with his two lawyers, who now sat in the back of the courtroom behind the prosecution team. These are the lawyers who represented Mitchell and Jessen in the civil suit brought by the ACLU on behalf of three former CIA detainees; the case, filed in federal court in Washington State, settled on the eve of trial in August 2017. Prior to Mitchell's travel to Guantanamo, Connell offered to go over with the lawyers an outline of his examination and the classified documents about which he intended to ask. Mitchell said that it was his decision to reject the offer, and Connell wanted to know why.

"You people have been saying untrue and malicious things about me and Dr. Jessen for years—for years," Mitchell said in his deep Southern drawl. "So you shouldn't be surprised that I don't want to spend a lot of time with you, and I'm not particularly interested in looking at things that you have to present."

Once Connell got into the substance of the testimony, it became clear that this day was not about his client, at least not directly. Mitchell testified that he recalled meeting Ammar al Baluchi a few times over the years at CIA black sites but only after he was cooperating and no longer going through enhanced interrogations. He said that al Baluchi was not an important figure to him during these years, between 2003 and 2006, and he did not remember the details of the meetings.

Connell had bigger plans for Mitchell, whose testimony could help paint the broader narrative of the US government's turn toward torture after 9/11. As much as he may have distrusted the defense attorneys, Mitchell found in them true allies for the public airing of what he considered an important, fundamental truth—that the program went far beyond him and Jessen, and that something like it would have been implemented with or without them. The CIA reached out to Mitchell and Jessen for advice on interrogations because the agency had already contracted with them on certain projects, which included producing a paper on terrorist resistance methods to interrogation techniques. Both had many years of experience as psychologists and instructors with the Air Force's "Survival, Evasion, Resistance and Escape" or SERE program, which prepares service members for possible capture by hostile forces. Mitchell and Jessen would base the CIA's interrogation techniques on those used during SERE trainings.

The triggering event for their involvement came in late March 2002 with the capture of Abu Zubaydah after a firefight in Faisalabad, Pakistan. Zubaydah was suspected of being a high-ranking al Qaeda operative. An operational psychologist at the CIA invited Mitchell and Jessen to attend an early April 2002 meeting at the CIA's Counterterrorism Center (CTC), during which participants discussed how to elicit valuable intelligence from Zubaydah. The prior September, less than a week after the attacks, President George W. Bush had signed his covert Memorandum of Notification authorizing the CIA to capture and detain terrorism suspects. Now they had a live body, though just barely, as Zubaydah was badly injured in the capture and kept alive only by sustained medical care.

Under questioning by Connell, Mitchell testified that he later learned the Pentagon's Joint Personnel Recovery Agency, or JPRA—which oversees all SERE programs—had already been communicating with the CIA about interrogation strategies and had assisted in the interrogation of another senior al Qaeda operative. But Groharing, the prosecutor, prevented Connell from asking about the presence of a JPRA official at the April 2002 meeting. Connell told Cohen that he was intending to show that Mitchell was not "a rogue actor" but instead a small, if important, part of a much larger infrastructure that was already taking shape. Groharing eventually asserted the national security privilege over information relating to the attendance of the JPRA official at this meeting, even though the JPRA official was only identified in court by a UFI. (The UFI was also later redacted from the transcript.)

In an odd wrinkle to this whole exchange, Jessen was in a leadership position at JPRA at the time and was forced to leave the April 2002 meeting because Department of Defense employees were prohibited from attending—all of which led me to conclude that the JPRA official Groharing was so concerned about was no longer with the JPRA at the time of that meeting. As for why I dwell over these details, your guess is as good as mine. In any event, this meant that Mitchell would be without Jessen for his first foray into CIA interrogations.

Other parts of the April 2002 meeting were fair game for Connell. Jose Rodriguez, who would become the CTC's director the next month, chaired the meeting. Mitchell testified that senior-level participants used the phrase "the gloves are off," and that the message was clear: The CIA had let America down by failing to stop the 9/11 attacks, and now it needed a tougher strategy to prevent future attacks—one potentially involving weapons of mass destruction, maybe even a nuclear weapon. That night, Mitchell joined an interrogation team on a flight to the country that hosted a black site referred to as "Location 3." While the name of the host country remains officially classified by the government, reporting by journalists and NGOs had long established that it was in Thailand. Mitchell testified that his role was as a contract operational psychologist to assess any resistance methods employed by Zubaydah; he was not hired to build an interrogation program, or even to do any interrogations himself. At the time, Zubaydah was being held and treated at a private medical facility. Mitchell said that FBI agents Ali Soufan and Stephen Gaudin were already there by the time he arrived, and that they and CIA agents took turns questioning Zubaydah while he drifted in and out of consciousness.

"Is it fair to say that the effort to obtain information at the hospital from Abu Zubaydah was a joint effort between the FBI and the CIA?" Connell asked.

"That would be true," Mitchell said.

Mitchell said that the two agencies continued their joint effort once Zubaydah arrived at "Location 3," the actual black site, from the hospital. During this phase, interrogators did not use any enhanced interrogation measures, or EITs, as the Justice Department had not yet approved them. Mitchell nevertheless said that the around-the-clock interrogations would not fit the "rapport building" method typically used by the FBI. Also, unlike most other FBI interviews, these sessions were video recorded.

Mitchell said that Rodriguez called him back to the CTC for additional meetings in July, after Zubaydah had stopped cooperating. At one critical meeting, Mitchell recommended that the CIA employ SERE training techniques if it intended to use what he called "coercive physical pressures" during interrogations. Mitchell said his concern was that the CIA would use dangerous, untested techniques that would prove counterproductive in interrogations. In a life-defining turn, Rodriguez asked Mitchell to lead the interrogations of Zubaydah instead of remaining in his roles of observer, psychologist, and consultant. Mitchell's eyes began to water when recalling his reluctant decision to accept.

"I just tear up when I think about this, and it slows me down," Mitchell said.

Mitchell said he agreed to do it because he felt he had a "moral obligation to protect American lives." Once again, he said he was not agreeing to build a "program" at the time but to exploit a single individual who was viewed as the "linchpin" to getting to other al Qaeda operatives.

"And let me tell you, just so you know, I'd get up today and do it again," Mitchell said.

The next day, Connell and Mitchell transitioned to discussing his interrogations of Zubaydah. Not long after Mitchell returned to Thailand in August 2002, this time with Jessen, the Justice Department's Office of Legal Counsel had approved a list of EITs that included waterboarding, walling, sleep deprivation, slaps, and the use of confinement boxes, among other techniques. Mitchell and Jessen used all of these on Zubaydah, though without the involvement of the FBI. Weeks earlier, Mitchell had been at a meeting in which FBI Director Robert Mueller told CIA Director George Tenet that the FBI would not be participating in sessions using enhanced techniques.

"He said, 'We don't want to do it. We're not going to have our agents there,'" Mitchell, who portrayed himself as a "straphanger" at the meeting, recalled.

This decision apparently set the course for an interrogation program that would be controlled by the CIA with diminished FBI involvement, at least compared to the early co-interrogations of Zubaydah by the two agencies. It was clear in Mitchell's testimony, as it was in his book, that he liked Gaudin and intensely disliked Soufan, who, in his own book *Black Banners* and other public statements, had long since become the public face of the FBI's principled stand against torture. The FBI's more involved role in the CIA program was still emerging as a result of the ongoing suppression hearings; it was unclear at this point if Soufan would testify. (He left the bureau in 2005 and is the head of the Soufan Group, a security consulting firm.)

Mitchell testified that he believed the EITs he and Jessen employed on Zubaydah, including many waterboarding sessions, produced valuable intelligence. They came to believe, however, that he didn't know anything about imminent attacks within the United States, which was the agency's primary concern. Mitchell and Jessen wanted to stop the EITs, but CIA headquarters overruled them with a directive to "stay the course." The Location 3 interrogation team even produced a video compilation of the waterboarding sessions in a failed effort to convince headquarters that EITs were no longer necessary. After two senior CIA officials came to Location 3, Mitchell and Jessen agreed to waterboard Zubaydah one last time to convince them to stop—and this time they succeeded. He said that he and others who were present during the final waterboarding session were tearful, though he added that he personally cries at "dog food commercials."

"Understanding that you cry at dog food commercials, why were you crying at the waterboarding of a human being?" Connell asked.

"I felt sorry for him," Mitchell acknowledged. "I thought it was unnecessary."

* * *

By this point, it was clear that Mitchell liked to wink. He did it occasionally when answering, sometimes when looking at Connell and sometimes toward the prosecution side of the room, though it was not clear to whom those winks were directed. It was also clear that the proceedings were adopting Mitchell's language and program-specific vocabulary. Mitchell highlighted a number of errors he saw in the top secret key that identified personnel by UFIs. He said several were incorrectly identified as "interrogators" when they were instead "debriefers." In his view, interrogators were people who actually employed the EITs on the detainees, while the debriefers would be analysts and experts who were on-site either to feed questions to interrogators or to ask questions themselves during more conversational meetings.

At various points, Mitchell took issue with the phrase that came to characterize the intent behind the entire CIA program—the purported goal of putting detainees into a state of "learned helplessness." He said the CIA used the term incorrectly in its cables and communications. Learned helplessness, in which a person has lost any hope over controlling his situation, is counterproductive for interrogations, Mitchell explained. The goal was, in fact, to condition a detainee like Zubaydah into understanding that he could improve his situation considerably by answering questions, to fully "graduate" from the EITs into "debriefing mode." Mitchell said he also preferred the term "coercive physical pressure" over "enhanced interrogation techniques," but EITs eventually won out. He said a formalized program of EITs with properly trained personnel was key to avoiding "abusive drift," the possibility that interrogators would lose control of their violence and begin to dehumanize detainees.

Mitchell spoke of rivalries at the CIA between contractors and career employees. Mitchell and Jessen were "green badgers," for the color of their badges, in contrast to CIA "blue badgers" for employees. Mitchell said that officials in CIA middle management and some personnel at the black sites resented him and Jessen, the men who actually did waterboarding, often calling them "pussies" for being too soft on detainees. Nevertheless, the pair were tasked to lead the interrogations of a second high-value detainee—Abd al Rahim al Nashiri, the suspect in the October 2000 bombing of the USS *Cole* in Yemen, who would later be charged in his own military commission. In November 2002, Mitchell traveled to the United Arab Emirates, where al Nashiri had been arrested, and accompanied him on the trip back to Location 3 in Thailand.

Connell elicited from Mitchell some chilling details on the one-night stopover he and al Nashiri had at Location 2, or "Cobalt," known to be in Afghanistan, before traveling on to Thailand. Mitchell described Cobalt as "poorly run" and staffed by "indigenous guards," with detainees chained in what appeared to be "horse stalls" in total darkness without adequate heat. Later that month, one of the detainees, Gul Rahman, died of hypothermia, leading to an internal CIA investigation and report that documented many problems with the facility. Mitchell would never return there. Connell showed Mitchell several photographs of Cobalt provided to the defense teams in discovery, but the witness did not recognize them as the Cobalt he saw—the place had apparently been prettied up somewhat for the photos. One photo showed a heater, which Mitchell did not think was present at the site.

"Thank you, that is helpful," Connell said.

Mitchell said he and Jessen did not expect to become program leaders, even after their perceived successes at interrogating Zubaydah and al Nashiri at Location 3. In fact, Mitchell testified that the agency had already started an employee-run program to train prospective black site interrogators by November 2002. An agent identified in court by the UFI "NX2" led this effort, with some level of input by the JPRA. As he did in his book, Mitchell portrayed NX2 as his chief nemesis during this early phase of the black site program. NX2 was at Location 4 or Blue (known to be in Poland), when Mitchell arrived there from the Thailand site with Zubaydah and al Nashiri.

NX2 greeted Mitchell at Location 4 by telling him that "there's a new sheriff in town," and that the contract psychologist was there to watch, not to participate in any way. Mitchell testified that NX2 and his "acolytes" used techniques on detainees that had not been approved by the Department of Justice. Among them was an unauthorized version of a stress position in which a detainee kneels on the ground and is forced to lean backward at a painful angle. Mitchell said that NX2 had his team put a broomstick under al Nashiri's knees and push him back so hard that his shoulders touched the ground behind him.

"And he was screaming," Mitchell testified. "And I was concerned that they were going to dislocate his knees."

Mitchell also complained when interrogators stripped al Nashiri and rubbed his "balls and ass" with a bristle brush and then rubbed his face with it. His complaints were ignored; at one point, NX2's team even threatened to restrain Mitchell if he didn't leave the interrogation room. He said he was not allowed to leave Location 4 or have any means of communicating with the outside world after he told staff on-site that he wanted to talk to headquarters.

Eventually, Mitchell was able to make complaints in-person at CTC, and he did so again after watching an April 2003 training course (he did not say where it was held) in which NX2 demonstrated the broomstick method of the stress position. Not long after, the CIA removed NX2 from his role. He died later in 2003, as did one of his top "acolytes," referred to in court as MA2, who had put together the training program with him. From Mitchell's point of view, this turn of events—NX2 trying but failing to force him and Jessen out—contributed to the CIA turning to him and Jessen to design and lead a formal program.

NX2's legacy was lasting, however, as Connell established when finally turning Mitchell's attention to al Baluchi's treatment, which he did over parts of the second and third days of testimony. Mitchell was a less-than-ideal stand-in for other CIA witnesses, as he was not involved in the interrogation sessions of al Baluchi at Cobalt in the spring of 2003. Connell led Mitchell through a lengthy explanation of the proper SERE-based "walling" method in which an individual is slammed backward against a wall that is constructed out of plywood, with some give to it. Mitchell explained that an interrogator should use a rolled-up towel to create a collar for a detainee, who was usually naked, and push him against the wall at an angle so that the shoulders, not the head, bear the brunt of the force. The walling makes a loud noise, but the effect is meant to be more startling than dangerous or painful. He acknowledged that the captive's head can hit the wall if it's done wrong.

Dr. Mitchell. January 2020.

"It's not a deliberate thing to do," Mitchell said on Wednesday.

"Under proper techniques," Connell responded.

"Under proper technique," Mitchell confirmed.

The next day, Mitchell said he later learned that NX2 used interrogators recently graduated from his own training course—and some interrogators still in training—to practice enhanced techniques on al Baluchi. Connell and Mitchell discussed summaries of al Baluchi's interrogation sessions, which included many bouts of walling and one in which he was slapped twenty times—an excessive amount, in Mitchell's view.

"It looks like they used your client like a training prop," Mitchell said.

Connell read from a report by the CIA's Office of Inspector General that said all of NX2's trainees practiced "each of the measures" on al Baluchi "in order to gain their certification." Mitchell said that this was clearly improper: In SERE courses, instructors and students practice on themselves, not on actual detainees. At one point, Groharing objected to the questions, pointing out that Mitchell was merely being asked to state "what a particular sentence means" in a report or cable he did not write or even recall seeing before, given his lack of interaction with al Baluchi. Connell was flabbergasted, reminding Cohen that the government agreed to only two of the more than fifty CIA witnesses his team asked for. It was the government's fault that Mitchell and Jessen were "supposed to carry the weight of thousands of pages of documents" they mostly "had nothing to do with."

"So my first argument is: He's all we've got," Connell said.

* * *

While Walter Ruiz can occasionally look a little thin for his suit in court, depending where he is with his triathlon training, that was not the case on Friday, January 24, 2020. He showed up in a well-fitted black suit, charcoal gray shirt, and black tie. With his jet-black hair and trimmed beard, Ruiz looked like an assassin. He moved quickly at the podium, completing his often-testy questioning of Mitchell in one day. Mitchell was annoyed at times with Connell but eventually approached a rhythm with him, at least at times, a comfort that he never reached with Ruiz. The witness, portraying himself as a steward of precise language, was not a fan of certain questions.

"Could you put that in English?" Mitchell asked Ruiz at one point.

Whereas al Baluchi stayed back at the detention camp during the parts of Mitchell's testimony that dealt with his abuse, Mustafa al Hawsawi was the lone defendant to attend court Friday morning, though al Baluchi and Ramzi bin al Shibh would later show up in the afternoon.

"I see you glancing to the back of the courtroom," Ruiz said near the start of his examination. "Do you see Mr. al Hawsawi back there?"

"I can't really tell because he's got a lot of stuff on his head, but I think he's toward the rear," Mitchell responded.

In his meetings with reporters Thursday evening, Connell told us that NX2 or the "New Sheriff," as Mitchell referred to NX2 in his book, appeared to run a secondary or peripheral program separate from the one run by Mitchell and Jessen. That NX2 and his acolytes implemented a program of unapproved torture techniques would support defense efforts to have their clients' confessions suppressed, as well as their motions for dismissal of the case for outrageous government conduct. At the time, Ruiz's team was the only one to have filed its outrageous government conduct motion, which it did the previous month, referring to the RDI program as "a vast international criminal enterprise." The other teams were waiting to file their motions after more witness testimony and, presumably, after receiving additional discovery that always seemed to be trickling in.

With Ruiz, Mitchell once again highlighted what he saw as an important distinction—that NX2's interrogation program came first chronologically, as he and Jessen were only initially contracted to consult on or perform interrogations of individual detainees, starting with Zubaydah and al Nashiri. Even when Mitchell and Jessen arrived at Location 4 or Blue and began interrogating Khalid Sheikh Mohammed in March 2003, he still viewed their work as interrogating an individual detainee.

"Dr. Jessen and I weren't training people, so there's only one training program, and it was his [NX2's] training program," Mitchell testified on Friday morning.

Though he wasn't present for it, Mitchell said that he would have known in 2003 that al Hawsawi spent time at the nightmarish Location 2/Cobalt, a period that turned out to be nine months. Ruiz showed him a medical evaluation of al Hawsawi at the time he entered NX2's custody in March 2003 that showed no medical problems, and certainly not the rectal damage that would eventually include a prolapsed anus. During this exchange, Mitchell insisted that CIA detainees got "better medical care than" US citizens or service members—a claim that sounded preposterous after Ruiz reminded him that medical staff did not intervene to help detainees at Cobalt, including Gul Rahman, who died from abuse and neglect.

At the site, NX2's team subjected al Hawsawi to its version of EITs, including walling, sleep deprivation, ice baths, and an unapproved stress position in which a detainee leans his forehead against a wall for extended periods. After reviewing photos that were not shown to the gallery, Mitchell confirmed that al Hawsawi, like al Baluchi during his time at Cobalt, was put through what many people would consider waterboarding but which the witness characterized as "water dousing." Mitchell said that the proper SERE-based method of waterboarding involves tilting a detainee back at a forty-five-degree angle before pouring water over a cloth placed on the person's face. NX2's team didn't do it this way.

"My recollection is there was a lot of water involved in it, they sort of poured it all over him, and some was on his face," Mitchell explained.

Mitchell said he discussed al Hawsawi's past treatment with him during numerous meetings on Guantanamo Bay from late 2003 into mid-2004, back when the CIA had a black site on the grounds of the detention facility. By that point, Mitchell said, al Hawsawi had transitioned into full debriefing mode; in fact, he said that no enhanced interrogations were ever done at the CIA black site on Guantanamo, which was reserved exclusively for debriefings in a facility that some people at the agency hoped to be a permanent home for the incommunicado detainees. Mitchell said he met with al Hawsawi both on his own and at other times with another CIA debriefer.

Ruiz asked Mitchell at length about a psychological assessment he and Jessen conducted of al Hawsawi on Guantanamo Bay in December 2003. In this report, they noted that al Hawsawi complained of medical problems, including the prolapsed anus, but was otherwise deferential, amicable, and "eager to please." Ruiz asked him why the assessment did not make any reference to al Hawsawi's past torture and its likely psychological impact. Predictably, Groharing objected to the use of the word "torture," but Cohen let the exchange continue.

"Did it matter in your assessment that Mr. al Hawsawi had been tortured in these many, many ways?" Ruiz asked.

"First off, I reject your characterization as the use of EITs as torture," Mitchell responded, adding that the president, the National Security Council, Justice Department, and CIA director all approved the techniques. He also said that a physician and a psychologist would have been on-site during the EIT sessions to intervene if necessary.

"If you did the same thing today, would it be torture?" Ruiz asked.

"I'm not going to get into that," Mitchell said.

He explained that al Hawsawi's prior experiences would have "factored" into his psychological assessment, but that he did not need to detail them in the document because they would have been included in other CIA reporting. Ruiz wouldn't let it go, however, asking again why someone's previous systematic torture would not make its way into a psychological report. Cohen finally became annoyed with Ruiz after Groharing objected again: Ruiz's insistence on using the word "torture" was clearly going to muck up the examination, making it much longer than it needed to be. Ruiz and Cohen bickered over exactly how he should phrase his questions, with Ruiz frustrated that everyone wanted to avoid the "dirty word."

"I'll say it all day long with you, counsel," Cohen said.

"Is it torture or not?" Ruiz asked.

"Well, ultimately I guess I'll have to rule on that, won't I?" Cohen replied. He told Ruiz that using the word "torture" was only delaying him getting the information he needed from the witness.

"I'll tell you what, Judge, I'm not going to sanitize this for their convenience," Ruiz said.

Ruiz moved on, however, and the tension fizzled out. Following lunch, Cohen allowed him to ask Mitchell if he avoided using the word "torture" because it constituted a crime that could lead to his prosecution. After Mitchell denied it, Ruiz cued up a video. He played on the courtroom monitors part of Mitchell's November 2018 YouTube appearance on the *Mike Drop* podcast, in which he discussed enhanced interrogations with the host, former Navy SEAL Mike Ritland.

"We never used the word 'torture,' 'cause torture's a crime," Mitchell said in the clip.

* * *

That Friday night, the media met with the victim family members who attended the first week. For more than an hour, we sat interspersed with them in a large circle in the conference room of the Navy Gateway Inn & Suites, the motel complex not far from the Tiki Bar and the Bayview. Over the years, most VFM meetings have followed relatively mundane days in court, with family members regularly expressing frustration with the pace and opaqueness of the proceedings. This group, which included four repeat attendees along with several newcomers, saw one of the most exciting and consequential weeks in the case's long history.

All of the eight family members who met with us were fans of Mitchell and Jessen. While the Senate torture report is damning, it is far from the dominant narrative. In addition to books by people like Mitchell and Jose Rodriguez, several US senators on the Senate Select Committee on Intelligence published minority views that criticized the main report. These senators were convinced that the RDI program produced valuable intelligence. The CIA itself published a lengthier rebuttal to the Senate report. While this response acknowledged that the agency was unprepared to create the RDI program—and admitted to many flaws in its operations—it also maintained that the program produced intelligence that saved lives.

One of the new victim family members sitting immediately to my right asked for my views on the RDI program, whether or not it was the right thing to do after 9/11. I told her I was not an opinion writer and generally did not share my views on issues that I'm writing about, which was true in these settings—my wife and friends certainly knew my views. Kenneth Fairben, one of the semi-regular attendees, said he appreciated Mitchell's statement that he traveled to Guantanamo Bay for the victims and the families, not for the defense lawyers. Fairben said he wanted to "hug the man" after hearing that line.

Much has been made about the money the US government gave to Mitchell and Jessen. Their company, Mitchell, Jessen & Associates (MJA), received $81 million from the US government starting in 2005, which came on top of the payments for contract services in the three years prior. (In his testimony, Mitchell explained that most of the $81 million went to personnel and other costs, as MJA eventually provided most of the interrogators and guards at the black sites.) Many people consider this money extremely well spent. During several parts of his testimony, Mitchell succeeded in establishing the context of his work for the CIA: The world was terrified after the 9/11 attacks, and he was asked to help prevent something worse from happening.

Marc Flagg, another semi-regular visitor, told us that the EITs described by Mitchell did not constitute torture. His parents, retired Navy Rear Admiral Wilson Flagg and Darlene Flagg, were on board American Airlines Flight 77 when it crashed into the Pentagon.

"I think it's fantastic what both Dr. Mitchell and Dr. Jessen have done for our country," Flagg said. "America really does not understand what they have done to protect our country, and we as a country owe them a debt of gratitude."

His wife, Michelle Flagg, was a first-time visitor to the Naval Base. She told us that a resolution of the case might help victim family members move on from the attacks. Though she added that she doubted that would ever happen.

* * *

The first week felt especially long due to some of the late nights at the picnic table outside our tents. Hanging with friends and colleagues was a welcome morale boost for me: In the days before the January trip, Fiona and I had agreed that we should try a separation in the coming months to see if a "reset" would help. I thought my two articles from week one were good, but I was distracted. Several of the journalists who showed up were not exactly known for pulling themselves away from the table at a reasonable hour, with perhaps NPR's Pfeiffer being an exception. In fairness, at least a few of them were working on longer projects and did not have to worry about writing news stories on the proceedings. I had no such excuse, nor did Terry McDermott, who on that trip was writing articles for his former employer, the *Los Angeles Times*. Jerry Dunleavy out-produced us all with his flurry of articles for the *Washington Examiner*.

Lisa Hajjar was gathering material for what would be the final chapters of her excellent book, *The War in Court: Inside the Long Fight Against Torture*, which would come out in 2022. A newcomer for the media, at least since my time coming to the base, was Cathy Scott-Clark, the coauthor with Adrian Levy of (among other books) *The Exile*, an account on the movement of the bin Ladens and other inner al Qaeda members after the 9/11 attacks. At the time of that hearing, Clark and Levy were still working on *The Forever Prisoner*, which focused on Mitchell's interrogations of Zubaydah. The book, which also came out in 2022, followed the Alex Gibney-directed HBO documentary of the same name that would feature Mitchell prominently, along with his early FBI counterparts in Thailand, Ali Soufan and Stephen Gaudin.

When also factoring in Margot Williams, who was there for The Intercept, the accumulated war-on-terror knowledge from this group was impressive. One might have expected our nightly conversations to produce valuable insights about the week's events, and I'm sure we covered some important ground. But soon enough most conversations at the picnic table veered toward increasingly emphatic discussions about music, TV, books, and movies, and also the bars and restaurants associated with the cities in which we lived and occasionally overlapped.

On the first Friday night, I stuck mostly to beer and headed into the tent shortly after midnight in preparation for a half-marathon scheduled for early Saturday, one of the many athletic events organized by the base's Moral, Welfare, and Recreation (MWR) team. The prior December, Fiona and I took a mini-vacation to Kiawah Island, South Carolina, for my first-ever full marathon at age forty-six. The training for that, which included several long runs on Gitmo, nearly killed me a few times on the base. A fourteen-mile run during the November session nearly ended in catastrophe as I struggled to make it to the media center on my return to Camp Justice around 11 a.m. I panicked that I would not remember the passcode on the door and would end up dying on the burnt grass outside. Once inside, I grabbed as many water bottles as I could and stepped outside, propping the door open, and poured them over me to cool down. I remained confused and somewhat irritable for the rest of the day. Ed Ryan told me outside court the next Monday that he saw me laboring through the edge of town and considered stopping to offer a drive back to Camp Justice; I told him to do that next time.

Once completed, however, the Kiawah event allowed me to coast into the January 25 run with relatively ease. I awoke at 5 a.m. and rode Carol's bike into town to the track complex, where the race began in the pitch dark with maybe sixty or so runners. I pinned my press badge over my race number, sticking with the Trump-era base regulation to self-identify as an enemy of the people. The initial four-mile jog toward the Detention Zone, heading southeast, was almost dangerous in the dark. But by the time we turned off to take the hilly and winding road to Windmill Beach, the sun was beginning to rise. As miserable as Guantanamo Bay can be, it is almost always beautiful at dawn and dusk. The loop around the beach's canopies and parking spots was a brief reward before reversing course uphill just as the morning's heat was intensifying. The route back took us through one of the base's residential neighborhoods before dropping us on Sherman Avenue for the final push down Main Street.

Other runners were doing the course twice to hit 26.2 miles; I was completely spent and could not even ride the bike back to Camp Justice. I called Flesvig to pick up me up. Hours later, I sat with a few colleagues at O'Kelly's, combining a Blood Mary with four Advil to dull my arthritic pain and any thoughts I might be having about the next week's testimony, or life in general.

CHAPTER 22

Dr. Mitchell v. KSM.

Back in 2008, David Nevin knew that agreeing to represent the man accused of plotting the worst-ever attacks on US soil would present certain complications for his personal and professional life. But he never could have guessed the case would last for so long, or that the most important week in court for Khalid Sheikh Mohammed would arrive some twelve years later.

That would have been a great way to start a profile about Nevin, if I had ever gotten around to it. In fact, my waiting more than four years—even though Nevin was no longer KSM's lead lawyer—might have paid off, as this was truly one of the most dramatic events in the case's long history. When he took the stand on Monday morning, January 27, 2020, Dr. James Mitchell was maybe twenty feet from the man he'd waterboarded 183 times. He smiled as he focused his gaze to the podium, where Nevin greeted him with "good morning."

"Glad to be here," Mitchell said. "I've been looking forward to this."

Nevin acknowledged to reporters before court that his examination would be shorter given the work of his two colleagues the prior week. Connell, in particular, covered important historical ground that Nevin did not need to retread. While the teams' different strategies occasionally created a low-grade tension, they acknowledged that Connell and the rest of the team for Mohammed's nephew often did much of the heavy lifting.

In his first week on the stand, Mitchell had cut a fascinating figure, displaying the full range of human emotion from the outset—starting with anger at defense attorneys for allegedly slandering him and then declaring he was there to help them with their case. He was rude and evasive but also gave answers beyond the scope of a question and would return from a break with another recollection he thought might be relevant. He snapped in anger but also smiled and continued to wink when giving certain answers, leaving people to wonder whether it was a tic or a tactic. Sun-damaged and heavily wrinkled with gray hair and a beard, Mitchell at times looked like he might collapse in his seat and at other times was bursting with energy and good humor. He was reserved when discussing the techniques he himself used on helpless detainees, occasionally smiling at a memory of interacting with one of the defendants, then teared up when recalling the horrors of 9/11 and his life-defining decision to help the CIA with its interrogations. He proudly took ownership of his work in building the program but also regularly deflected blame to an endless array of other characters: Bush administration lawyers for approving the techniques; rogue agents for using unapproved abusive techniques; Obama for ending the program; and now the CIA for "diming" him and Dr. Jessen out as the key figures of a program that involved literally hundreds of participants, thousands of decision points, and tens of thousands of documents and cables. His deflection of blame was frustrating to defense attorneys but ultimately supported their contention that this was a vast government operation, not a two-man program, and that they might be entitled to many more witnesses who tortured their clients or at least saw what happened.

Mitchell, of course, knew all five defendants, but he claimed to have relatively little interaction with some of them in his senior position at the RDI program. In various parts of his testimony, Mitchell portrayed himself as a frequent flyer shuttling between black sites on a schedule that was understandably somewhat hazy to him now. Mohammed, as one of the CIA's most prized possessions, was an exception. They spent lots of time together, though Mitchell was not at the first black site—the Afghanistan site referred to as Cobalt or Location 2—where Mohammed was first tortured. Among other techniques, personnel at Cobalt under NX2's command rectally rehydrated Mohammed when he was not being compliant, a technique that Nevin referred to as "rape." Under questioning by Nevin, Mitchell said that what the CIA was doing to the detainees rectally was not among the approved interrogation techniques, and he did not personally employ them.

"It sounds crazy to me," Mitchell said.

Once the CIA transferred Mohammed to a black site referred to in court as Blue or Location 4 (in Poland), Mitchell got directly involved in his treatment. The March 2003 enhanced interrogations at Blue spanned twenty-one days and included slapping, walling, prolonged nudity, sleep deprivation that at one point lasted six and a half days, and repeated sessions of waterboarding.

Mitchell, Jessen, and a third interrogator conducted all of the waterboarding of Mohammed, with Mitchell typically holding the cloth down over Mohammed's mouth. Mitchell referred to the third interrogator as "the Preacher," as he did in his book, due to the religious zeal he brought to at least one interrogation, or as "NZ7," which was his official UFI in the CIA's key. NZ7 was a covert CIA employee, and the government was keeping his identity top secret—and refusing to make him available as a witness, along with dozens of other UFI witnesses.

Mitchell testified that a "board-licensed physician" was in the room at all times to monitor Mohammed's condition and help track the pourings, which were capped at forty seconds. Mitchell explained that interrogators were more aggressive in waterboarding Mohammed than other detainees because he was effective at resisting the technique by diverting water with his lips and swallowing large amounts.

"I suspect he was a swimmer because he has lips like geoducks," Mitchell testified.

At one point, Mitchell said, the Preacher cupped his hands around Mohammed's mouth and nose so that the water would pool more in that area. After the sessions started, medical personnel decided that Mohammed should be waterboarded with a saline solution to prevent an electrolyte imbalance from causing "water intoxication," a potentially fatal condition. Mitchell said that he engaged in "fireside chats" with Mohammed after the sessions to discuss how the detainee viewed the experience. He would begin these chats by saying something like: "Let's just talk about your reaction to what happened." Mitchell said that Mohammed would often be naked during these conversations.

Over several parts of his testimony, Mitchell reminded everyone that all the enhanced interrogation techniques were approved by lawyers from the Justice Department—at least the EITs he used. One technique, Mitchell testified, was approved separately by CIA lawyers. This was revealed during his most heated exchange with Nevin, when Mitchell acknowledged that he threatened to kill Mohammed's son if the detainee failed to provide information that could stop another attack in which American children died.

"'I will cut your son's throat,'" Mitchell said he told Mohammed.

Mitchell said he justified the threat by reasoning that Mohammed had himself killed eight innocent children in the 9/11 attacks. He nevertheless acknowledged that, looking back, the threat was "distasteful."

"But it is what it is," he added.

Nevin asked if the psychologist had been trying to instill fear into Mohammed at the time.

"I don't know whether it did or not," Mitchell said. He turned his head from Nevin to the left side of the table where Mohammed sat.

"Look over there," Mitchell said. "He's smirking, so it may well not have done anything to him."

* * *

The next morning, minutes before he began his second day of examining Mitchell, Carol and I were standing at the window of the gallery and wondering why Nevin looked like Darth Vader. He was milling suspiciously around the podium with a black jacket on top of his suit, the collar turned up, and he had put on a pair of black gloves. Some of the newly arrived family members for week two used the pre-court time to come to our side of the gallery to get a better look at the defendants. Family members always sit behind the prosecutors; the media is positioned behind the defense. Occasionally, family members will hold up photos of the loved ones that the five men are accused of murdering, but I failed to notice if this was happening, confused by whatever Nevin was up to. Most family members generally describe the experience of seeing Mohammed and the other somewhat frail looking middle-aged men as anticlimactic. I didn't know if they were informed that an MRI conducted a few years earlier on the base confirmed that he had traumatic brain injury from his past abuse.

In any event, Mohammed did not disappoint them by hanging back at the camp: He was in his chair waiting for his former tormentor to return to the stand. Nevin later ditched the jacket but kept the gloves on as court began. It turned out that he was going to be handling evidence from a black site, referred to only as "Site A," and also from rendition flights that shuttled the detainees between the global network of secret locations. The government had made this evidence available to the defense as part of the discovery process. Moving from the podium to the side of the witness box where an irritable Mitchell sat, Nevin held up handcuffs, a couple of different chains, audio equipment, a box of diapers, goggles, various pieces of clothing, and other items for Mitchell to view. This was not as exciting as it initially promised to be. Mitchell had no way of knowing if these were actually the same items used at the sites where he ran interrogations more than fifteen years earlier. At one point, Nevin held up a five-foot-long chain with a blue clip at the end and a red lock on it.

"Is this familiar to you?" Nevin asked.

"Well, the chain is. I saw chains like that," Mitchell said, though he added that the clip and lock did not look familiar to him.

The morning picked up some steam when Judge Cohen allowed Nevin to play clips from *The Report*, the 2019 movie by Scott Z. Burns starring Adam Driver about the making of the Senate Select Committee on Intelligence's report on the CIA torture program. Driver played Daniel Jones, the report's lead investigator. At this point, the defense teams were still pursuing a motion to compel the production of the entire 6,700-page report and six million pages of information that Jones's team reviewed. While most of the movie focuses on Jones's diligent pursuit of the truth, several flashback scenes show Mitchell and Jessen at the black sites interacting with CIA personnel and torturing a captive presumed to be Mohammed. Mitchell hadn't seen the movie and was surprised by his character.

"They've got some fat boy playing me," Mitchell said of the accomplished character actor Douglas Hodge.

From my view, Mohammed sat motionless as Nevin played the scenes of Mitchell and Jessen, both wearing masks, waterboarding a struggling Mohammed while interrogating him. With the lights back on, Nevin asked Mitchell how the movie compared to reality. The witness saw numerous differences.

"Well, first off, we didn't wear masks," Mitchell said. "The water wasn't poured out of a bucket. The person's head wasn't moving around like that."

Mitchell said there were three interrogators, and that they used one-liter saline solutions instead of buckets. He also said they did not shout questions at detainees during waterboardings but instead between sessions.

"We're highly suspicious of anything they say to us during waterboarding," Mitchell said.

The examination was sputtering but building to something. Nevin attempted to ask Mitchell about some of the critical opinions about Islam expressed in his 2016 book, *Enhanced Interrogation*, which he had plugged intermittently throughout his testimony. Predictably, prosecutor Groharing objected. As the attorneys argued over the relevance of Mitchell's musings on Islam, an earthquake shook the courtroom. Nevin didn't know what was happening as he heard concerned grumbling around the room.

"It's an earthquake," a voice from Mohammed's defense table told him.

"Oh," Nevin said.

"If anyone wants to get under their desk right this second, they're welcome to do so," Cohen said calmly.

Connell, at the fourth defense table for al Baluchi, was the only person to do so. He stayed there until the last vibration stopped. We later learned that the US Naval Base was under a tsunami warning and that the entire court complex, which sits near the shore, should have been evacuated. This was one of many examples of faulty logistical coordination between the base's different entities. Connell explained his actions a few days later when meeting with some journalists and NGOs: "I decided that dying by a tsunami on Guantanamo Bay during a military commission proceeding was something I wanted to avoid."

Groharing eventually prevailed on his objection, and Nevin moved on to his last series of questions. He told Mitchell that he wanted to know more about the emotion that he had displayed in his earlier days of testimony, when he teared up on the stand.

"My emotion was a reaction to the fact that there were people who had to choose between burning to death or jumping off the top of a tall building," Mitchell said. "That there were people who went into those buildings to save lives and as a result died."

Nevin nodded. "Yeah," he said.

"It's a genuine reaction, and anybody who doesn't like it can kiss my ass," Mitchell added, raising his voice.

Nevin then began asking Mitchell if he knew that people in the Middle East have also suffered and "have died in gigantic numbers." Groharing objected again, but Cohen allowed Nevin to continue.

"I mean, are you familiar with the Iraq sanctions, with five hundred thousand children under the age of five perishing in Iraq as a result of our economic sanctions?" Nevin asked.

"I'm familiar with all those things but that does not abrogate his responsibility for voluntarily choosing to attack our country," Mitchell responded. "He should have stayed home and taken care of the problems there."

Nevin pressed on, explaining that his client has an acute emotional reaction to the events that trouble him—just as Mitchell does. "Can you grasp that?" Nevin asked.

"You're not going to shame me into forgiving that guy," Mitchell shot back.

This was riveting, and a bold move. After six days of questions and answers on the details of the torture program—both graphic and bureaucratic—Nevin's pivot somehow brought the broad contours of a decades-long global conflict, of incalculable and needless suffering, into court with a single exchange. But I had trouble making sense of Mitchell's response: Who's shaming who into what? I didn't get it.

Covering court is a constant battle between mindlessly scribbling notes and comprehending what's actually happening. I've come to conclude that, most of the time, it's better to avoid trying too hard to understand oral arguments and witness testimony in anything close to real time. If litigation is complicated, I can only assume that human behavior is more so. The most important task is to capture the events in a manner that enables you to ask questions later. When I read the transcript a week later, I saw that this exchange took place on page 31,563. I marveled at how much preceded it over the years since the arraignment, and how much I had missed from a single day that I had watched intently.

This particular exchange was over before I had anything to miss. Groharing objected again, and this time Cohen sided with him. The judge told Nevin that he didn't think it was relevant if Mitchell believed that Mohammed had "a right to feel a particular way" about certain global events.

"Fair enough," Nevin said.

He was finally done and looked back at Mitchell.

"Thank you for answering my questions," Nevin said and sat down.

* * *

Nevin's direct examination of Mitchell on Monday and Tuesday of the second week proved the colorful exception to the work of the four other teams. Unlike with the other defendants, Mitchell developed an intense relationship with Mohammed, violently abusing him and then engaging his intellect. As Mitchell explained in various parts of his testimony, most detainees broke pretty quickly, typically after a day or two of EITs. Mohammed, by contrast, lasted three weeks. Once Mohammed finally transitioned to "debriefing mode," Mitchell continued to visit him over the years at the circuit of black sites before Mohammed's arrival on Guantanamo Bay in 2006. These were what Mitchell described as "maintenance visits" that allowed him to check in with detainees and make sure they continued to work constructively with the debriefers, occasionally playing the role of peacemaker between the two sides. In Mitchell's telling, Mohammed had it pretty good at the later black sites, often holding court to share his wisdom with CIA personnel as a professor would, sometimes with the aid of a whiteboard.

He also enjoyed his halal food in the improved conditions and would "rub his belly" in satisfaction. But Mitchell also confirmed to Nevin that it was conveyed to detainees, including Mohammed, that they could return to the "hard times" if they stopped cooperating.

Once Ramzi bin al Shibh's lawyer, Jim Harrington, took over from Nevin during the afternoon of Tuesday, January 28, Mitchell was once again put in the position of answering questions about events he either was not around for or did not recall in detail. When showed cables he did not draft, Mitchell was at least able to confirm the baseline harsh treatment as likely to be accurate—the forced head and beard shaving, the nudity, the use of diapers, sleep deprivation and disruption through constant noise (usually loud music) and constant light, prolonged isolation, among others—all of those being "standard techniques" that did not even require special approval or legal permission. As for the enhanced techniques, Harrington read from a cable that stated the goal was to "reduce bin al Shibh to a state of infantile-like dependence" to condition him to answer questions—"and he is getting there," the document noted.

For bin al Shibh's legal team, something less dramatic like the forced shaving was important. Bin al Shibh had also been forcibly shaved by the guard force on Guantanamo Bay in January 2007 in the days prior to his interrogation by the FBI, as a disciplinary measure for his bad behavior. From his team's point of view, bin al Shibh's past treatment by the CIA would be very much on his mind during his supposedly "voluntary" statement to federal agents. This linkage to the past would likely be intensified by the fact that bin al Shibh, like al Hawsawi, had also spent time at the CIA's black site on Guantanamo Bay, the same location where the FBI sessions later took place.

Mitchell generally recalled bin al Shibh being "a pain in the ass" at the black sites, someone who was always complaining about something. Mitchell was at Location 4 in Poland in February 2003 during bin al Shibh's EIT sessions, but he did not personally administer the techniques. The interrogator who did so was "the Preacher." As established during Nevin's examination, "the Preacher" or NZ7 was the third interrogator who helped Mitchell and Jessen during Mohammed's waterboardings.

Mitchell recalled in some detail a particularly eerie scene at Location 4. He said that he and his colleagues came up with the idea to have the Preacher lead bin al Shibh by a room where Mitchell and Jessen were using the "enhanced" measures on Mohammed, which informed bin al Shibh for the first time that Mohammed had been caught and provided a glimpse of what was being done to him. The details of what bin al Shibh actually saw or heard were not disclosed in court. Mitchell only said that the Preacher then took a "visibly upset" bin al Shibh into a nearby closet, and Mitchell later stopped by.

"Ramzi was sitting in there in the closet in the lap of the Preacher, and the Preacher was kind of patting him like a child," Mitchell told Harrington. Mitchell said he told bin al Shibh, "We may be coming for you next."

Unlike with NX2, Mitchell worked constructively with NZ7, even though NZ7 was one of NX2's acolytes. Mitchell added, however, that NZ7 was the type of person who would be nice to you in person and then complain about you behind your back. NZ7 eventually told a federal grand jury investigating parts of the CIA program that Mitchell had tried to stomp bin al Shibh during the closet episode at Location 4. The Justice Department probed two areas of possible criminality with the RDI program beginning in 2008—the destruction of videotapes documenting early interrogations and the use of unapproved techniques. These investigations led by John Durham, an assistant US attorney in Connecticut, did not result in any charges. Mitchell told Harrington that NZ7's statement to the grand jury was a lie.

Mitchell's most extended period of time with bin al Shibh came at Location 5, after the detainee had been transitioned into debriefing mode. He said he went there to smooth over relations between bin al Shibh and a senior CIA "targeter," a woman who was leading the debriefing sessions. He and Jessen also later inspected a cell that bin al Shibh complained had a vibrating bed that prevented him from sleeping—a preview of the complaints that would come to dominate the rest of his life. Much to Mitchell and Jessen's surprise, the bed actually shook when they laid down on it. Mitchell told Harrington that they determined it was not some CIA "mind experiment" but the connection of the cell's support structure to a heavy piece of equipment at the black site.

Near the end of Harrington's brief examination, completed in just one afternoon session, Mitchell acknowledged that he believed the five defendants should have been summarily tried and executed, and that he viewed the defense lawyers in the courtroom as "al Qaeda defense lawyers." But he insisted he did not hate the defendants, whom he said viewed themselves as "warriors."

"I don't dislike them," Mitchell said. "I dislike what they did."

Cheryl Bormann, on behalf of Walid bin Attash, conducted the last direct examination over Wednesday and Thursday of week two. By this point, Mitchell was beginning to fray somewhat on the stand. Bormann, it turned out, had to retread some of the ground covered by Connell related to Mitchell's interrogations of Abu Zubaydah in the spring of 2002 in Thailand, with FBI agents Ali Soufan and Stephen Gaudin. That's because Gaudin was the government's most important witness for the admissibility of bin Attash's confessions. He led the "clean team" interrogations of bin Attash on Guantanamo Bay in 2007 and again in 2008 that the prosecution intended to use at trial. (Bin Attash was the only defendant who also was interviewed again in 2008 in additional FBI-led interrogations.) Gaudin was expected to testify at a future session later in the year.

Mitchell portrayed Gaudin, who stayed at Location 3 for a period after Soufan left, as interested in using SERE-based techniques even before the Justice Department approved them. Mitchell and Gaudin even discussed a "mock burial" plan in the hopes of convincing Zubaydah to resume his cooperation with interrogators. In this scenario, personnel at Location 3 would take Zubaydah to an open grave and pretend to plan to bury him alive, at which point two new FBI agents would come to his rescue—and hopefully earn his renewed cooperation in the process. The plan was not implemented.

Mitchell also recalled Gaudin's presence at the seminal meeting later in the summer, in July 2002, in which FBI Director Mueller told CIA Director Tenet that the FBI would not participate in enhanced interrogations. Mitchell testified that he and Gaudin chatted on the way out of the meeting, and that Gaudin said that he wished he could participate in the forthcoming EIT sessions that Mitchell and Jessen would later lead in their return to Location 3 in August 2002, following the Justice Department's approval. Mitchell said he believed that Gaudin himself had undergone SERE training.

Otherwise, Bormann was in the same position as most of her colleagues—asking Mitchell about cables and other CIA reporting that documented what NX2 ("the New Sheriff"), NZ7 ("the Preacher"), and other interrogators did to her client. Mitchell did not meet with bin Attash until Location 7, once he was out of EITs and participating in debriefing sessions. This wasn't particularly exciting court, as most of the documents describing bin Attash's harsh treatment were classified and were not shown to the gallery. At one point, Bormann asked Mitchell if one cable indicated whether interrogators in an NZ7-led session displayed "moral disengagement" with her client, a factor that can contribute to "abusive drift." Mitchell spent a half-minute or so reading the document.

"I would say there's a good chance that they let their emotions get ahead of them there," Mitchell eventually opined, looking over briefly at bin Attash sitting at the second defense table.

Bormann spent significant parts of her examination asking about the use of standing sleep deprivation on bin Attash, who wears a prosthesis from the knee down on his right leg. One cable suggested that interrogators removed the prosthesis as punishment for his refusal to cooperate. Other cables documented the use of sitting or prone sleep deprivation, apparently in response to massive swelling in bin Attash's left leg. Bormann showed Mitchell several classified photographs that documented the swelling along with cellulitis, blackened toes, and abrasions from shackles. At one point, bin Attash's ankle had a diameter of ten and a quarter inches. Mitchell, by now quite irritable, would not agree that the ankle was swollen.

"You don't find a ten-and-a-quarter-inch ankle pretty swollen?" Bormann asked Mitchell on the morning of January 30.

"I don't have any idea how big his normal ankles are," Mitchell shot back.

With another photo from mid-2003 we couldn't see, Mitchell finally acknowledged that bin Attash's left calf looked "swollen."

"Yeah, that would be an understatement," Bormann said.

She also led Mitchell through parts of cables that showed that NZ7 wanted to resume EITs on bin Attash even when he was cooperating. Mitchell said he could not interpret the summaries or descriptions in the cables, nor could he justify the continued interrogations of bin Attash in light of the injuries to his left leg, ankle, and foot following seventy-two hours of standing sleep deprivation.

"You'd have to talk to somebody who was there, not me," Mitchell said.

"Yeah," Bormann responded. "We've tried."

Throughout the questioning, Mitchell denied that the cables were evidence that the CIA withheld medical care as an enhanced technique. Bormann, however, showed him another cable by NZ7 in which he wrote that "the rest and solicitous medical care bin Attash received has restored his arrogance, mental will, and determination to resist interrogation." Once again, Mitchell said he was not there and could not provide Bormann with any more details. He told Bormann that the best information would be from the cable itself.

"Or from NZ7?" Bormann asked.

"I have no say in that," Mitchell responded.

With that, Bormann had made her case for additional witnesses—in particular for NZ7. Her examination was another reminder to Judge Cohen that the government's limitations on witnesses had compromised her presentation for suppression. While NX2 and his chief acolyte, MA2, were both dead, NZ7 was alive. All five teams wanted the so-called "Preacher" as a witness, along with dozens of other covert agents. At that point, the defense teams had no idea if Cohen, after sitting through the first rounds of CIA testimony, would grant defense motions to compel additional witnesses. If he did, the government could either refuse to produce him—and face sanctions—or come up with some arrangements for securing witness testimony from a covert agent.

* * *

Mitchell got a break with Groharing, who completed his cross-examination in less than forty-five minutes. His main task would be using Mitchell to support the government's position that the CIA program did not break the detainees to the point of shattering their will and rendering them incapable of participating voluntarily in future interviews. Of course, other than perhaps for Mohammed, Mitchell was not a particularly knowledgeable witness for the government.

Mitchell told Groharing that he may have spent between one to two thousand hours with Mohammed, given all the debriefing sessions and maintenance visits over the years. Mitchell said that they would sometimes hold hands during their talks. He said that Mohammed was "quite charming" and that the handholding "was part of his charm initiative." Mitchell said that Mohammed did not appear to be suffering flashbacks or other aftereffects from EITs, and instead was engaged in his Sufism studies and enjoyed lecturing to Mitchell and others in attendance at the black sites. Mitchell said that he also knew of instances where Mohammed either lied or withheld information during debriefing sessions, even if he was overall cooperative.

"Throughout all of your interactions with Mr. Mohammed, did you observe any behavior that suggested to you that Mr. Mohammed had lost the ability to voluntarily determine whether or not he would cooperate when questioned?" Groharing asked.

"Not that I saw because he either cooperated or didn't cooperate, he either lied or he didn't lie, based on his choices," Mitchell responded.

Groharing then led him through a series of similar questions about Mohammed's codefendants. He said he did not see evidence of either flashbacks or apathy, or generally any signs of psychological distress, with any of them. Mitchell noted that al Hawsawi expressed distress about his rectal problems when Mitchell spent time with him at the CIA's black site on Guantanamo Bay in late 2003—but that was about it.

On redirect, the defense lawyers attempted to poke holes in these breezy conclusions. Connell read from descriptions of al Baluchi's physical and mental conditions contained in various CIA reports and cables that completely undercut Mitchell's assessment—that he suffered from panic attacks, depressed mood, anxiety, chronic fear, sleep problems, and that he had "vivid memories of his earlier interrogations."

"Did you know that some debriefers had described him as having major psychological issues?" Connell asked.

"I never read anything like that," Mitchell said.

"Did you know that he believed that what he had been through was only 10 percent of the torture that he could experience?" Connell asked.

"I never had that conversation with him," Mitchell responded. "I don't know what's in his mind."

When it was his turn, Nevin asked Mitchell to think about why Mohammed would be so "charming" with him during the debriefing sessions and maintenance visits. In doing so, he presented Mitchell with the list of abusive techniques and conditions endured by his client. Mitchell, clearly exhausted, defaulted to denialism.

"And you were the one who caused him to be nude?" Nevin asked.

"I think that was a condition of initial confinement," Mitchell said.

"You're the one that manipulated his diet?"

No, Mitchell said, the diet was part of the larger interrogation plan to which he only had "input" but not responsibility.

"And you were the one that gave him a bucket for his human waste?"

"Nope, that was the guards."

"Ah, the guards did," Nevin said, his tone dripping with sarcasm. "But they did that at your direction, right?"

"No, they didn't," Mitchell insisted.

Nevin asked him if he was the person to receive Mohammed at Location 4 after his "anal rape" at Location 2.

"No, he can't be transferred and received by a contractor," Mitchell said quickly. "He's not in my custody. He was never in my custody. I never received him."

Mitchell acknowledged that he threatened to kill one of Mohammed's children and subjected him to sleep deprivation, constant noise and lights, and 183 waterboardings—but he denied they were near-drownings, as Nevin characterized it.

"My question is: Can you think of a reason why he would want to charm you?" Nevin asked.

"I can think of a dozen reasons why he would want to charm me," Mitchell responded.

The reason, Nevin said, was that he associated Mitchell with the techniques he just read through—and the possibility that he could always return to them, right?

"I don't know what was in his mind," Mitchell said.

"Really? I mean, you have some idea of what was in his mind, right?" Nevin said. "I mean, you just answered fifteen questions from the prosecutor about what was in his mind."

* * *

Early in his testimony on Friday morning, Dr. Bruce Jessen looked over at the defense side of the courtroom with a sense of wonderment, or perhaps with the lingering pride of an estranged father—it was hard to tell. Judge Cohen had just noted for the court record that Mohammed had entered the court, and al Baluchi had recently left.

"I don't recognize these guys anymore," Jessen said. "They've all grown up. Is it okay if I know who's who?"

Alka Pradhan, Connell's second-in-command on the al Baluchi team, appeared unfazed by what could have been interpreted as a twisted expression of ownership. She listed them in order, noting that her client, Ammar al Baluchi, had recently left, and the defendant sitting farthest in back, Mustafa al Hawsawi, had chosen not to attend.

"So, Ammar and al Hawsawi are . . . okay," Jessen said, nodding. "Thank you for that."

"Of course," Pradhan responded.

Jessen would not even get a full day on the stand, as the end of Mitchell's redirect examination took up the first hour of Friday. All of the defense teams told Cohen that they still had a significant amount of ground to cover with Mitchell in closed sessions—probably at least a week between the five defense teams—so his testimony also remained vastly incomplete. The defense and the prosecution team would need to complete the bulk of both their open and classified examinations of Jessen at some future session, probably lasting close to two weeks. The 2020 court calendar, as grueling as the schedule appeared, was beginning to look woefully inadequate given the early pacing of the agreed-upon witnesses—not to mention the NZ7s of the world. The suppression hearing was becoming more unwieldy as it moved forward, signaling yet again the staggering challenges of running a five-defendant death penalty case in which all five had been violently abused and held for years in incommunicado detention.

Jessen, too, had worked at the Air Force's SERE school but was in a leadership position at JPRA at the time of the 9/11 attacks. Later that year, the CIA asked him and Mitchell to review the so-called "Manchester Manual," an al Qaeda training document seized by British authorities in a May 2000 raid of a suspect's home and computer in Manchester, England. While Pradhan had to remind him of the details, Jessen confirmed that he and Mitchell wrote a paper for the CIA in late 2001 that recommended countermeasures to al Qaeda techniques for resisting interrogations. Jessen's memory also proved weak when it came to his role for the JPRA in late 2001 in drafting protocols for creating what he called "an interrogation captivity facility" on Guantanamo Bay. He did not recall what he knew at the time about the conditions of Camp X-Ray, the first location where detainees were held, or whatever became of the memo.

Jessen recalled with greater clarity being at the start of the seminal meeting at the CIA in April 2002 to discuss how to interrogate the recently captured Zubaydah, after which Mitchell boarded a plane with the interrogation team while Jessen went home. He was eventually detailed to the CIA from the JPRA by the time of the July 2002 meetings at CIA headquarters, during which he and Mitchell developed a list of SERE techniques for use on Zubaydah before heading to Location 3.

"We went into a room, a ubiquitous carrel, and sat down and we typed out a list," Jessen said. He estimated it took them forty-five minutes.

"Those techniques have been used for decades effectively with no problems," he added. "So I was completely comfortable and confident with recommending those, and still am."

Pradhan spent much of the late afternoon asking Jessen about his time at Location 2, or Cobalt, the notorious site in Afghanistan that he visited in the fall of 2002 after his time interrogating Zubaydah in Thailand. Jessen confirmed that he compiled a list of improvements for the poorly run facility, including the need for heaters and other climate control measures, the replacement of indigenous guards with US personnel, and the development of protocols for diet and medical attention. He said he wrote a cable specifically about his concerns over Gul Rahman, who soon died of hypothermia.

In fact, when the CIA Office of Inspector General called him later in the year to discuss Rahman, Jessen said his response was: "He's dead, isn't he?"

"That's just the first thing that came to mind," Jessen said.

Not long after that chilling detail, Jessen was done for the day—and no one knew when, or if, he might come back, at least in person. Near the start of his testimony Friday morning, Jessen had made a not-so-cryptic remark in response to Pradhan's preliminary questions about his conversations with the prosecution about his testimony—that he would give two weeks, and that's it. After he departed the courtroom late Friday, Sowards urged Cohen to order Jessen to return for the March 2020 session. (The February session was already scheduled for testimony by FBI witnesses.) Cohen said that he did not have the power to do so. He said that he hoped Jessen would "realize the importance of what's going on" and agree to return to Guantanamo Bay—otherwise, he would have to testify by videoconference. Sowards disagreed. Because Jessen was currently under Cohen's jurisdiction on Guantanamo, the judge could order him to return under the threat of contempt of court. Sowards said that "there is a qualitative and important difference" between in-person and remote testimony, which had already proven in many prior sessions to have technical problems. After Cohen rejected the contempt idea, Sowards told the judge that he was not doing "all that is reasonably necessary to ensure the attendance" of a critical witness.

Ruiz, on behalf of al Hawsawi, said he joined Sowards in his request.

"You can join all you want," Cohen said.

After Bormann also joined the request, Cohen—who was proving himself to not be entirely unflappable—gave a terse "We're in recess" and quickly left the courtroom, abruptly ending what had been the 9/11 case's biggest hearing in several years.

CHAPTER 23

The Long Goodbye. February 2020.

Jim Harrington had spoken from the podium many times since the May 5, 2012, arraignment, including on one of the case's most momentous days almost two years later when he told Judge Pohl that the FBI had infiltrated his defense team. As time went on, Harrington spoke less than his colleagues, at least on substantive legal issues. His team was initially gutted by, and then often preoccupied with, the FBI probe and its fallout, and then even more preoccupied by Ramzi bin al Shibh's declining mental health over the alleged noises and vibrations at Camp 7. Still, Harrington was beloved by his colleagues for more than his humor and calming presence. He was regularly the most effective with the fewest words, serving as a defense-side closer by sensing which areas of a dispute needed a finer point—what a judge might miss in the preceding avalanche of words. Now, Harrington had another bombshell, one that would turn the case, yet again, on its head.

"My trial days are over," Harrington told the judge on February 18, 2020.

At least, that was his plan.

Things were more or less back to normal at the start of the two-week February hearing, with Carol and I as the only reporters who showed up at Joint Base Andrews on Saturday, February 8. This wasn't too surprising, given that the grueling January trip had just ended; I myself had only arrived back in Brooklyn on February 1 before having to drive to DC again on February 7. And March was set to be another blockbuster with the bulk of Jessen's testimony remaining, even if it took place by video; most reporters would wait for that. The February hearing nevertheless had important witnesses, with the first week devoted to the testimony of FBI Special Agent James Fitzsimmons. He was involved in the interrogations of defendants Ammar al Baluchi and Walid bin Attash after their capture in Karachi, Pakistan on April 29, 2003, shortly before their transfer to CIA custody.

No one flinched when someone at the air terminal informed the large crowd of about 125 travelers that a mechanical issue had rendered the plane inoperable. We would have to fly out on Sunday. Judge Cohen postponed the start of court until Tuesday morning to give the defense teams a day of prep on base and the opportunity to meet with their clients.

Looking back, Harrington may have previewed his looming departure with Carol and me in the recent prior trips, hinting that the strained relationship with bin al Shibh was becoming irreparable. Too much time had passed in which Harrington simply could not help his client with his most pressing need—to stop the noises and vibrations. We also knew that, at age seventy-five, Harrington couldn't keep going forever. But it still felt like a shock to hear him put his request on the record, which he did near the start of court on February 11. This was a major turn in the proceedings: The government would have to accept severance of bin al Shibh from the case—and transition to the two-trial track it desperately wanted to avoid—or possibly face a lengthy postponement as Harrington's replacement got up to speed on the case.

Cohen told Harrington to file a written motion requesting his withdrawal within forty-eight hours, and he gave the prosecution twenty-four hours to respond to that pleading. On that timeline, the arguments would not take place until week two. Court went dark, and another week in the 9/11 case was lost.

On the morning of February 18, Harrington told Cohen that he was "not about to drop dead" in court, but that his health issues had become a serious hindrance. Between 2018 and 2019, Harrington fought through two knee surgeries and a heart procedure, and his cardiologist had recently recommended that he leave the case. Harrington said the exhausting two-week January session convinced him that he was no longer up to the task, even if he could continue practicing a more laid-back version of law up in Buffalo.

"I have reached the realization that I really shouldn't continue in this case," Harrington said.

Harrington said he could probably try a weeklong case. But the 9/11 case had more than a year of pretrial litigation left—possibly closer to two—which would be followed by a trial lasting a year or longer. From the point of view of Harrington and the chief defense counsel, Gen. Baker, this situation was entirely foreseeable. For years, Baker had sought funding for a second learned counsel for each team, and he also specifically tailored his request for the bin al Shibh team once he understood Harrington's declining health. Each time, the Pentagon official overseeing funding decisions for the military commissions, the convening authority, rejected the request. Harrington said he would stay as a "resource counsel" for the defense team as his replacement, whoever that was, learned the case.

In its response pleading, the government tabulated what Harrington had been paid as learned counsel in his long history on the case—a minimum of $3.2 million, using the $195 hourly rate for contractors in his role. The implication was that, having earned his millions, Harrington owed it to the court system to keep going.

"For the life of me, I don't understand why that's in there," Harrington told Cohen. "I consider it to be petty, and I consider it to be vindictive by them. And I don't say those words very often."

He noted that his contractual rate is less than half of that charged by his firm, Harrington & Mahoney, a boutique firm with five lawyers (including his son, Ian)—a rate that itself is far below what the firm would charge if operating in a major city. Harrington also said the money he receives goes into the firm's expenses, including salaries for attorneys and support staff, office supplies and equipment, health insurance, and a 401(k) plan, among others. He noted, with a hint of irony, that Dr. Mitchell made similar comments about the $81 million he received from the government.

Harrington then read a list of eight names to Cohen as references: the four Republicans and four Democrats who had served as US Attorneys for the Western District of New York, which includes Buffalo, over the past several decades. He said all of them would describe him as a curmudgeon, an iconoclast, and a well-prepared trial lawyer with "a very twisted sense of humor" who "gets away with murder in the courtroom." Above all, though, they would say you can trust him, Harrington said.

"In the end, Judge, I'm sad," Harrington said. "I'm disappointed in myself, but that shouldn't matter to anybody but me."

He could not discuss the details of the breakdown of his relations with bin al Shibh in open court; that would have to wait for an ex parte session with the judge. But Harrington said his removal was the right thing for his client.

"It's the right thing for the commission," Harrington added. "It's the right thing for the prosecution—even though they don't agree with it right now—and for the other accused in this case that I be permitted to withdraw."

Once Harrington hobbled back to the third defense table, Ed Ryan was anything but chastised as he took his turn at the podium. He told Cohen that the scheduled witness, Special Agent Fitzsimmons, was himself seventy-four with his own health issues and yet continued to work a demanding, international career. In fact, Fitzsimmons couldn't stay for the second week because he had a medical appointment long in the making, Ryan said. He expressed his despair that the parties didn't take the agent's testimony during the prior week, in which the bin al Shibh team was self-admittedly planning to work as normal while Harrington's request played out.

"So last week we accomplished about eight minutes or so on the record, and for no good reason that I can see, we lost a week when we don't have weeks to lose," Ryan said.

He referred to a recent filing by the al Baluchi team regarding the need to reschedule Fitzsimmons. In that pleading, the lawyers predicted that they could not finish witness testimony in time for the January 2021 trial date.

"So that drumbeat has just began," Ryan said.

The prosecution team was operating somewhat in the dark about the breakdown between bin al Shibh and Harrington, but Ryan told Cohen that the standard for finding "good cause" to remove a defense lawyer is quite high—and one addressed earlier in the case with the difficulty between Walid bin Attash and Cheryl Bormann, which preceded Cohen's arrival on the case. That relationship eventually smoothed itself out, Ryan informed Cohen. Ryan surmised that the reason for the breakdown was related to the noises and vibrations over which Harrington had vigorously and futilely litigated. If true, then finding cause to remove Harrington on these grounds would be setting the case up for failure, as the next learned counsel would also fail to satisfy a client who was complaining about conditions that "don't exist."

Ryan urged Cohen to hold off removing Harrington as learned counsel until a new one—with help from the other seven lawyers on the team—was ready to take over. In making his final plea, Ryan invoked the memory of Lee Hanson, the ailing victim family member who testified earlier in the case to preserve his testimony at trial. That happened in 2017 before the case's first judge, Army Col. James Pohl.

"He sat about six feet from where you sit right now, sir, and was the picture of grace and dignity as he talked about the murder that he watched on television of his son, his daughter-in-law, and his granddaughter, Christine, the youngest victim of them all," Ryan said. "Within a year of his appearance on this island, we lost him."

He added: "We have many, many Lee Hansons in our midst."

Ryan was effective, as always, but Cohen was in a bind. It would probably take a few months to get a new learned counsel on the case, give or take, depending on the process of that person getting the necessary security clearances. It would take far longer for that lawyer to be familiar enough with the record to play any type of lead role in examining the most important witnesses in the case. That meant that Cohen would have to force Harrington to do the two things he wanted to avoid: extended travel and grueling days of witness testimony. And Harrington made that point in his rebuttal: He simply was not ready to come back in three weeks in March and resume questioning witnesses. The long-distance commuter court had finally become too much.

"What's your ideal scenario?" Cohen asked him, in a tone of deference from a young man to his respected elder.

"To call my wife tomorrow and tell her that I'm coming home and I'm not part of this," Harrington responded. He added, more seriously, that his client deserved "a change of situation" that included a new learned counsel.

* * *

Cohen returned to court the next morning with one heck of a speech, one that went far beyond releasing Harrington from his role. For the first several minutes, Cohen gave a passionate defense of the military commissions system—and his role in it as the relatively new judge. He said he had succeeded in providing a "structure on a process that for over seven years had none." He softened the implied criticism of his predecessors by noting that federal and state death penalty cases often take several years to fully litigate, and that this was a very rare five-defendant death penalty case with the associated challenges of a joint trial.

"Although the decision to execute a death sentence may take less time in the heat of battle, Lady Justice demands more when such penalties are executed in her name," Cohen said.

Unlike his predecessor, a marine who had portrayed managing the case as a straightforward task of using a rule book to move through a process, step by step, Cohen recognized this had a complication far larger than the number of defendants: the vast amount of classified information, which he said had "simply no equivalent or precedent." Despite the difficulties of doing so, he praised the parties for working through the CIPA-like processes to move the case forward. Before turning his attention to Harrington's request, Cohen had one final boast.

"There is no doubt that this case is on the best footing and has the best opportunity to get to trial that it has had in the past eight years," he said.

That was a dangerous claim, even if tethered to reality. It was a statement that could only be made by someone who had been on the case for eight months. For many of us watching, it felt like a tragic jinx.

Cohen told the court that he was convinced Harrington's request to withdraw was not "a delay tactic" to throw the case off schedule. He said that he had been observing Harrington in and out of court over the past several months and that it was clear he was "no longer the marathon runner" of years past.

"He moves slowly, clearly gets tired more easily," Cohen said.

He praised Harrington for swallowing his pride and acknowledging a difficult fact—"that he is not the attorney he once was and will never be again." The timing was bad, Cohen acknowledged, but he agreed with Harrington that a serious health event happening later on—such as on the eve of trial—would be far worse for the case. Cohen said he did not have to consider the breakdown of the attorney-client relationship in his decision; he easily found good cause in Harrington's "physical and mental fatigue." Somewhat gratuitously, the judge added that Harrington was not only well past retirement age but also in "his statistical twilight years."

Cohen ordered Harrington, as offered, to stay on the case as a resource counsel and to review all court filings by his team until he was eventually discharged. Cohen also ordered updates from the team and Gen. Baker on the process of finding a replacement learned counsel, along with the filing of a transition plan once that lawyer was on board. He canceled the March hearings and estimated that a new learned counsel could be on the team by April, a timetable that seemed unlikely if not delusional to those who had been around the case for a few years or longer. Cohen said he would not entertain severing bin al Shibh from the case until receiving the team's transition plan, and at that point he might request briefing from the parties on severance.

Ever the optimist, Cohen explained how the path toward a 2021 trial remained plausible. He said he would use the remainder of the week to hear oral arguments on pending discovery motions, and that he would try to issue rulings on them before the next session—with March canceled, that would be June. He also said he would issue a series of "findings of fact" from the witness testimony and documentary evidence thus far, which would streamline what was needed from future witnesses. He said he would do that by March 18. Cohen confessed to the parties that he had always suspected that June 2021 was a more realistic trial date; he had chosen January 2021 as a target date to build in a buffer. He thought it was not impossible to keep things on course—once again recklessly taunting the Guantanamo gods.

Cohen told Harrington that he could call his wife and tell her he no longer had to come back to Guantanamo, even if he wasn't completely off the case.

"Judge, she's used to disappointment from me," Harrington said.

The next night, the defense teams had a celebration for Harrington in the conference room at the Navy Gateway Inn & Suites. The room was packed and booze flowed freely, though Harrington himself didn't drink. Carol and I were allowed to attend the event. I told Harrington that Cohen really laid it on pretty thick in the comments on his health.

"He was doing me a huge favor," Harrington said, clearly in a state of relief.

Members from all five teams toasted Harrington's great skill, kindness, and wit, and there were many laughs that shook the room. There was, of course, a sense of sadness, an acknowledgment that an era was ending. Carol had told me some time ago that Harrington was the glue that helped keep the five defense teams working as well together as possible, a bridge across competing legal positions and egos. The love for him was intense.

The island didn't want Harrington to leave. The departing flight on Saturday also had a mechanical problem and was canceled. He would have to stay one more night. Of course, on that Sunday return flight, none of the lawyers knew they wouldn't be returning to Guantanamo Bay for a very long time.

* * *

Even in a two-week hearing that ended up having little to do with the CIA program, the agency was very much in the courtroom—literally, as we found out. During Mitchell's testimony in January, members of Connell's team at the fourth defense table noticed one of the prosecutors, Christopher Dykstra, monitoring a silver tablet. On at least three occasions, they saw Dykstra react to the tablet by alerting another prosecutor to tell Cohen and his security officer to cut the public feed, triggering the hockey light over a possible classified spill. On February 7, shortly before the start of the next session, Connell's team filed a "Motion to End Apparent Intelligence Agency Disruption of Courtroom Proceedings."

In court on February 19, it became clear that this latest move by the government infuriated Connell. He raised his voice, which even cracked a bit, as he pointed over to the silver screen while airing his complaints to Cohen. He said it appeared as though Cohen had "authorized the installation of a CIA device in the courtroom to allow the CIA externally to assist" the prosecution team.

"Which flies in the face of every idea, not just of due process, but of an adversarial system and democratic values," Connell argued.

In January 2013, after the CIA remotely cut the public feed, Pohl issued an order prohibiting any outside agency from doing so. However, he said it was appropriate for "original classification authorities," or OCAs, to observe the proceedings in real time to watch for spills, so long as they themselves could not shut the court down. Pohl noted that the OCA in the January 2013 episode had not assisted the prosecution with its case—another red line that could not be crossed.

Connell told Cohen that the government now appeared to be crossing that line because the CIA had directed prosecutors to interrupt witness testimony that did not constitute a spill. In one hockey-light interruption of Mitchell's testimony, the prosecutors acknowledged that they did not know why the CIA had told them to cut the feed. Connell was mystified that the judge would acquiesce to the prosecution's request for the communications device through an ex parte hearing without the defense teams participating—driving "suspicion" instead of creating "transparency" over what was sure to be a sensitive topic.

Cohen was clearly taken aback and became defensive. He acknowledged that he allowed the government to have the tablet in court after an ex parte presentation prior to the January session. He insisted that the outside agency was not providing "litigation advice" to the prosecution but merely helping all the parties do what they are all required by law to do—prevent spills. Cohen said that, as a judge, he's long since accepted that every decision would upset someone, but he did not expect this one to blow up the way that it had.

"And that's on me, because I have never seen this level of distrust and skepticism in any case I've ever tried in twenty-one years," Cohen said.

He quickly added: "I'm not saying it's not warranted."

Cohen continued on for a few minutes, toggling between apology and defiance. He insisted that there was no evidence the government was spying on the defense teams—an issue that Connell had not even raised.

"And you have my absolute word if I ever had evidence that the defense was being actively listened to at this point in the trial, I would dismiss the charges without thinking twice about it," Cohen said. "That absolutely cannot go on, and it will not go on in my courtroom."

Gary Sowards rose to comment on Cohen's contention that he was merely using modern technology to make the proceedings more efficient.

"It is twenty-first-century technology in service of covering up fifteenth- and sixteenth-century torture," Sowards said. "That is 99 percent of the classified information in this case."

He also challenged Cohen's position that it was the judge, with input from the security officer sitting to his right, who was making the decisions about what was allowed in open court.

"The proceedings I observed was a relay of information to you to turn on that light, and that's what happened," Sowards said. "You did not say to them, 'Why am I turning on the light?'"

He requested a transcript of the ex parte hearings in which the use of the tablet was requested by the prosecution.

"Not going to happen," Cohen said.

Sowards said his team also wanted the courtroom schematics that defense teams had first requested in 2013.

"Counsel, I'm inclined to let you have a ladder and let you walk all over this place," Cohen shot back. He also disputed Sowards's contention that the government was still covering up torture.

"They did a really horrible job of covering it up when we had nine days of testimony on these allegations of torture, not to mention hundreds and thousands of pages of documents that you guys have on the issue," Cohen said.

He said he would take the schematics request under advisement. Sowards said his team would decline to participate in proceedings until he made a decision.

"That is your choice," Cohen said.

"Your Honor, it's compelled by my ethical obligations, not my choice," Sowards responded.

Once again, the defense team for the accused 9/11 mastermind would not be actively participating in the 9/11 case. Given that Cohen was still awaiting Harrington's formal motion to leave the case, along with the government's response, this otherwise bizarre fact was again lost in the litigation shuffle. Cohen called a recess.

* * *

The February hearing was consequential, but slow. My wife and I used it for a few lengthy, painful talks in which we formalized plans to separate. I would move in with my friend, Gabe, who lived a few neighborhoods over from us in Brooklyn. Fiona needed more time to get the apartment ready for my departure, and Gabe needed more time to prepare for my arrival. Luckily for all of us, the two-week 9/11 hearing was followed by a one-week hearing in the military commission against Majid Khan. He had pleaded guilty in 2012 to crimes related to his role as a courier for al Qaeda and was expected to be sentenced later in the year. I stayed for the third week.

I ran into the chief prosecutor in the Camp Justice laundry tent on the Friday afternoon before the 9/11 teams took off. Gen. Martins was in good spirits despite the Harrington hiccup, still feeling the momentum of a suppression hearing that had seen several critical witnesses. In the Guantanamo bubble, neither of us discussed the coronavirus that was becoming a bigger issue outside of the US Naval Base. We shook hands in a "see you soon" way—heck, we'd be sick of each other by the end of 2020, given that both of us would be on the base for more than half of the year.

The Khan case did not consume much court time, just several hours across a few different days as the parties discussed the details of his sentencing. I worked in a few hikes along the Ridgeline, some visits to the beach, and caught a few movies at night. The week went too fast. On the last evening, I walked with my friend Alexandra, one of the NGO observers who had come for the Khan case, down to Glass Beach. We found the Khan team wading in the water with bottles of beer and, like us, waiting for another magical sunset. I wish I had appreciated it more, but I was preoccupied. I would be going from three weeks in a tent to one final night in my apartment, though I didn't know at the time that it would be the last night I would ever spend there.

The apartment in Carroll Gardens was the first one Fiona and I looked at after deciding to move in together in the fall of 2012: A one-bedroom apartment on the ground level of a narrow four-floor, four-apartment building, with a spacious backyard culminating in a comically large tree that our landlord would one day have dismembered. But the inside was small, and we began looking at apartments farther out in Brooklyn. Eating lunch during our search a few days later, we realized our folly: How could we pass up that yard? We called the broker from the restaurant, and our future home was still available. We jumped on it. It's where we built our life, hosted parties, planned trips—including our 2015 elopement—and planned starting a family.

To give Fiona a few more days, I hung out with Jeff in DC for a few nights, drinking heavily while discussing the split. We saw a show at the 930 Club and hit up a few bars, not quite believing that these packed-in crowds could soon be a thing of the past. On the drive back to Brooklyn from DC, I listened to podcasts to stay awake. A recent episode from the *Times*' *The Daily* detailed the growing global concerns over the coronavirus and the general panic that appeared to be descending on the world, not least of all New York City. But I still had no idea of what I was getting myself into, nor did Gabe. My planned stay of a few weeks would turn into a virtual quarantine of six long months.

Fittingly, the last indoor event he and I attended was a March 4 book talk and signing at Pioneer Works in Red Hook, Brooklyn, featuring Neal Katyal and his book *Impeach: The Case Against Donald Trump*, which he coauthored with Sam Koppelman. The mood in the crowded space was ominous given the subject matter and looming pandemic, but Katyal struck a hopeful tone for America. After all, he told the audience, he had represented Osama bin Laden's driver, Salim Hamdan, in his seminal case against the Bush administration. In 2006, the Supreme Court sided with his client by a 5-3 majority in *Hamdan v. Rumsfeld* by invalidating the Bush administration's first attempt at a military commissions system on Guantanamo Bay, a decision that led to the creation of the court I was now covering. His point was that the rule of law prevails in America, even against the most unlikely odds—even for people like bin Laden's driver.

Katyal was one of just a dozen or so lawyers who had made my company's annual best-of guide, "The Lawdragon 500 Leading Lawyers in America," each year since we launched it in 2005. For this reason, I waited in line to shake his hand—which he refused, wisely—and chat briefly. When I mentioned all the time I was spending on Guantanamo, Katyal was apologetic for not staying up on the subject.

"I burned out on that stuff," he told me.

So, apparently, had Judge Cohen. He dropped a St. Patrick's Day bombshell by notifying the parties by memorandum that he was retiring from the military, with a final day of active service of April 24.

"My very recent decision to retire is based on the best interests of my family and was not impacted by any outside influence from any source," Cohen wrote in the memo.

Among his parting shots was canceling the June session as the US Naval Base went into lockdown. He also denied the long-pending defense motion to compel the production of the full Senate torture report and all of its underlying information—something that was both an afterthought and a ruling of great significance.

Cohen's abrupt departure would have been the topic of intense discussion over drinks at the Camp Justice picnic table. Instead, we talked about it at some of the early pandemic Zoom "happy hours" attended by me, Carol, Flesvig, and some of the semi-regular Gitmo journalists. We speculated that maybe Cohen had reason to suspect that spying had taken place—and didn't want to be forced to dismiss the case, as promised. But that seemed like a stretch. Another speculation: While he clearly liked the action of court, the negativity and animosity seemed to be getting under his skin; maybe it was proving to be too much for him. My conclusion was that Cohen, upon some reflection, finally sensed how impossible the whole thing was—getting through many more months of suppression hearings followed by other evidentiary battles only to arrive at a trial that itself would last twelve–eighteen months. Just thinking about it was exhausting, and you could never separate that hellish schedule from personal or family issues; the schedule itself was incompatible with sanity. Whatever drove him away, you couldn't blame the guy.

CHAPTER 24

Pandemic and Return. March 2020–August 2021.

Overall, the pandemic was difficult for me, as it began with a separation that I agreed to but was more ambivalent about than Fiona. It took a few months to realize that she had come to view this as the beginning of a divorce and not an attempt to work things out. This brought a genuine anguish, one that included feelings of humiliation as I came to grasp how far behind her I was in processing where our relationship was. I couldn't really complain about what I was going through, however. Even within my narrow world, a looming divorce was justifiably lost in the shuffle—as the military might say, it was "OBE," overtaken by events. Gabe's place was basically right in the middle of a downtown Brooklyn area that had sirens going all day and night as hundreds of people around us died each day. We were in the epicenter of the epicenter.

We also were just a few blocks from the Barclays Center, which became one of the central meeting and departure points for the Black Lives Matter protests and confrontations with police. While not covering the protests for Lawdragon, like any journalist I could not keep myself away from the marches and capturing what I could with my phone. (I wore a media badge in case it lessened the chance of me getting bashed in the head.) After one particularly tense protest and police standoff by the Manhattan Bridge, Gabe and I arrived back at his place and watched CNN's split-screen coverage of the various protests nationwide projected onto the wall of his outdoor patio. The chaos and sirens from our streets ricocheted off the images and sounds from the TV.

All of this happening in a condensed period—the death of my marriage, the chaos and tragedy of the pandemic, and the frenetic energy of the protests—left me with some version of a low-grade emotional scarring that probably hasn't gone away. Whatever you call it, I am not quite the same person I was in 2020. Still, I had it easy. While we had wanted children just a few years back, not having any made the divorce about as uncomplicated as it could be. Fiona and I decided to use New York State's do-it-yourself (DIY) online system, which we eventually learned was not so simple. But with the help of a specialized paralegal service, we got it done.

My health allowed me to exercise furiously. Gabe's outdoor space allowed us to socialize with other folks relatively early. I also had a car, which meant I could drive to the Boston area to see my mom and other family members, even if I now stayed at a hotel and would only go so far as a backyard deck. My friend and colleague from Lawdragon, Alison, started dating Gabe after a few hangouts in his patio space. She eventually moved in with Gabe and I subletted her place in Prospect Lefferts Gardens, right on the eastern side of Prospect Park, one of the best urban parks in the world—which quickly became my new backyard during the fall.

The best part of the pandemic year took shape at the same time and was something I could not have predicted when Gabe agreed to take me in eight months earlier. He and Alison convinced me to try a few online dating apps, including Hinge. My second date was with Allison (spelled with two Ls instead of one), an installation artist and professor I first met at an outdoor area of a bar/coffee shop in her Brooklyn neighborhood, Sunset Park. We hit it off, then moved slowly in an old-fashioned way. With COVID-19 still raging, we did not even hug until the fourth date. Soon, however, we would split time between her place and mine, with use of my car to take day trips for hikes outside the city as the winter took hold. It might be a better story if I had met my future wife on my first date in about a decade, but finding her on the second one was, as I said, lucky.

The pandemic was also a good time to start thinking about a book. My Guantanamo life had otherwise been limited to Zoom happy hours with Carol, Ron Flesvig, and some of the regulars—Lisa Hajjar and Terry McDermott from Southern California, Kasey McCall-Smith from Scotland, Margot Williams from DC, and Leila Barghouty, who was just a neighborhood away from me in Brooklyn. Early in 2021, I was accepted into the Logan Nonfiction Fellowship Program, which provides mentoring and workshop sessions for book authors and documentary filmmakers. The normally in-person residency program, based in upstate New York, was held virtually for my cohort. I began chipping away at what felt like a massive undertaking, attempting to make sense of the case and also the dominant role it had played in my life.

* * *

On the late afternoon of January 29, 2021, I called Allison, and said something like: "If you want to hang out at all, we have to do it now."

It was a confusing time, but Gitmo was calling. Among the under-the-radar developments of the new Biden presidency was that the convening authority approved a new military commission for three of the former CIA detainees held in Camp 7. The timing was odd. Years earlier, Gen. Martins's team had drafted charges against Encep Nurjaman, also known as "Hambali," an Indonesian suspected of being a leader in the terrorist group Jemaah Islamiyah, as well as the two Malaysian detainees, Mohammed Nazir bin Lep and Mohammed Farik bin Amin, that he allegedly recruited to assist in terrorist activities in Indonesia. But the Pentagon officials who previously served in the role of convening authority refused to approve the charge sheet. That changed the day after Biden's inauguration when Jeffrey Wood—an army colonel with the Arkansas National Guard, who had been the convening authority for less than a year—did just that.

Given how slowly the commissions move, the new case did not appear consistent with the administration's stated intent to close the Guantanamo Bay detention facility. Absent any waivers, under commission rules the three defendants had to be arraigned within thirty days, which placed the date of the court hearing at some point in late February. Initially, the Pentagon was not going to allow attendance by any journalists. Carol raised the issue with John Kirby, then the chief Pentagon spokesman. She pointed out that none of the new defendants had been seen since their capture and incommunicado detention by the CIA; this would be the first time they would appear in "public." The Senate torture report contained a chilling anecdote in which a CIA interrogator told Hambali that he would never have a court case because "we can never let the world know what I have done to you." Kirby agreed that barring the media would be a bad look, and Carol and I received approval to attend.

Carol was already in DC, where she had been spending most of the pandemic. I was planning to drive down on February 3 for the February 4 flight.

But Flesvig, who remained the court's spokesman, informed me by email on January 29 that—according to the latest guidance he had received—travelers to the Naval Base had to be in "restriction of movement," or "ROM," for five days prior to the flight. By any plausible interpretation, this meant I had to be in the DC area for five days prior to getting to Joint Base Andrews. My quarantine would have to begin on January 31 at 10 a.m., which really meant I had to drive down on January 30 to be safe.

That's why I called Allison to come over and watch me throw as much crap as I could think of into a large duffel bag, giving her an early taste of the absurdity of Gitmo travel. This episode ranked high. The February 4 flight was actually for a February 22 arraignment because all travelers to Gitmo had to quarantine on the base for two weeks, even with the required negative PCR COVID test prior to flying. At the time, the plan was for Carol, Flesvig, and I to all stay in the FEMA-like CHU trailers in Camp Justice, where we would be brought takeout meals and perhaps other delivery items (whiskey, one hoped) from the Naval Exchange. On the return side, I would have to deal with multiple reentry requirements for both DC (is the Naval Base a foreign country?) and New York. All told, I would be traveling for close to a month for a court hearing that would probably last a few hours or half a day.

The whole thing, of course, was completely idiotic, and I was more than a little nervous about being trapped in a trailer for two weeks. Still, I was filled with a sense of excitement and adventure as I drove to DC on January 30 with an AirBnb reserved about a ten-minute walk from Jeff and Kristin's place. Because getting food was an allowable activity within ROM, Jeff and I walked—spaced several feet apart in case anyone was watching—to get takeout lunch on January 31. On my third day of DC quarantine, however, the judge in the case issued a continuance of the arraignment, canceling the trip. The next night, I met Carol and Flesvig for a heated outdoor dinner at Zaytinya in the Penn Quarter, which was a blast. That had to suffice for commissions-related media activity for the time being.

Still, the COVID shots that were beginning to roll out meant that the US Naval Base on Guantanamo Bay would be able to start accepting visitors without requiring the two-week quarantining on base. The loosened "ROM" policies would finally make resuming court hearings feasible. My Logan fellowship program ended in early June, just a few weeks before I was set to return to my second home, after more than five hundred days away.

* * *

The first of the four commissions in pretrial proceedings to resume was the first I ever attended, the still-pending case against Abd al Hadi al Iraqi. We had to arrive at Andrews on Monday, July 12, with our vaccine card and printed-out proof of a negative PCR test within three days of the flight time. Allison and I were keeping tight COVID-19 protocols so I stayed at a hotel in DC instead of with Jeff and Kristin, though we hung out in their backyard area. It felt good to get the old routine back in place—almost, at least. At Andrews early Monday morning, everybody boarding the flight had to do a self-swab rapid COVID test in a large room and wait fifteen minutes for negative results before making their way to the terminal. Masks were required.

The media contingent was a fairly robust group of nine, but interest in the resumption of the commissions was mainly a foreign affair—two reporters from UK papers, a three-person team from Sky News, and two from Japan's NHK public broadcasting organization. Carol and I represented the United States. As expected, life on the base was different upon our arrival in the COVID era. Masking was still required at all Department of Defense facilities, regardless of vaccination status, which meant we were supposed to wear masks in court and in the media center. I quickly learned that strict enforcement of this and other COVID protocols was basically impossible and, therefore, inconsistent from day to day and location to location. As in many US locations, masks were not required when actively eating or drinking. I was the lone reporter to eat essentially all my meals outside or in my hotel room, though I joined my colleagues at O'Kelly's and lowered my mask for sipping drinks or sneaking bites of food.

Staying at the Navy Gateway Inn & Suites was, by far, the biggest difference, when compared to the tents. The plan was for us to return to the tents at some point, but they had not been maintained during the pandemic. The NGIS, as it's called, is a short walk to the coffee/ice cream shop and the jerk chicken stand, which is on the way to the complex with the Tiki Bar, the officers' club Rick's, and the Bayview restaurant. It's also about a half-mile walk in the opposite direction to the bowling alley, with its food court and beer options, and only slightly longer to O'Kelly's and the Windjammer. The gym is close by, as is the main entrance to the Ridgeline, the popular hiking trail with good views of the bay and the base.

We were effectively in the center of town, allowing for more adult freedom of movement. Instead of being driven into town after court for meals and errands, the process was reversed: Flesvig had contractors driving us in vans from town into Camp Justice on workdays. The NGIS was not immune from the hazards of humidity and intense storms, but the rooms—at the time between forty and eighty-seven dollars a night, depending on whether you wanted a full-sized fridge and kitchenette—were nice. Above all, of course, they were private, with normally functioning bathrooms and showers, and with mostly reliable Wi-Fi. I knew after just the short Hadi trip that returning to the tents would be a challenge.

Court, as it always seemed to be for the Hadi case when I showed up, was uneventful, though the proceedings showcased some of the system's underlying problems that had gotten worse with time. Hadi, then sixty, had had five surgeries in recent years for a degenerative spinal condition. (Hadi's lawyers say his name is Nashwan al Tamir and refer to him by that name in court and in pleadings.) His first day of court was delayed because his large therapeutic chair was missing and then again later because someone had forgotten his pain medication, which included Percocet and Valium. As always, a hospital bed was available for him at the back of the courtroom, in the event he needed to lie down. The judge, Marine Lt. Col. Michael Zimmerman, had been assigned to the case the prior September; neither the prosecution nor the defense sought to challenge him after a brief voir dire. The real mystery, however, was how he would decide to handle the complex process of reconsidering the prior rulings of his predecessors. The US Court of Appeals for the DC Circuit had ordered this, as it did in the military commission over the USS *Cole* bombing, because an earlier judge on the Hadi case had sought employment with the Justice Department as an immigration judge while he was still on the case—which at the very least was a potential conflict of interest.

Hadi's lead lawyer, Susan Hensler, told reporters after the hearing that her client's case should be dismissed because his alleged crimes had taken place during the war in Afghanistan, which the president was now ending in the clearest possible terms. Biden had said in April that he was pulling out all US troops by September 11, 2021, the twentieth anniversary of the attacks. Dismissal of the case was not going to happen of course, but Biden's policy—the need to end "America's longest war"—created another complication for endless detentions on Guantanamo, whether legal or symbolic, or both. In support of his closure policy, Biden renewed what Trump had halted: the transfers of detainees to host nations after their approval for release by the interagency Periodic Review Board, or PRB. As Carol and Charlie Savage soon reported for the *New York Times*, the first transfer of the Biden administration occurred the following week, bringing the total detainee population down to thirty-nine.

Hensler told us that the medical facilities on the base were not sufficient for her client. This was true generally for the aging detainees but especially so for Hadi.

"Nashwan should be sent to a country where he can receive adequate medical care," Hensler said outside the media center on a sweltering summer day.

I included that quote in "Military Commissions Resume on Guantanamo Amid Biden Closure Plans and Pandemic Uncertainty," my first write-up of proceedings since February 2020. In court, I realized how out of practice I was. It also hit me for the first time in years how ill-suited I was for this type of job, given the nerve damage in my right arm. I had just passed the twentieth anniversary of my June 2001 car accident in Mexico, almost certainly the most harrowing experience of my life. I had not been in touch with my girlfriend, Liz, from that time, since we broke up in 2005. But I had emailed her a few weeks earlier, thanking her for saving my life and getting me out of Mexico with my spleen still inside my body. My near-constant hip and back pain when running was a regular reminder of the accident, as was court once again when it came to my arm: If I did not type up my notes right after court, understanding them was basically impossible.

I went on a brief return trip in late July for a hearing in the military commission for Majid Khan, who was expected to be sentenced later in the year. The end of August brought a third trip to finally hold the arraignment in the three-defendant Indonesian "Hambali" case, which became the fifth active military commission. But I was mostly eyeing the resumption of the 9/11 case on September 6, a two-week trip during which the middle Saturday would be the twentieth anniversary of the attacks.

CHAPTER 25

Twentieth-Anniversary Reboot. September 2021.

Seymour Hersh begins his memoir *Reporter* by describing himself as a "survivor from the golden age of journalism"—a time of profits and endless resources for travel and in-depth reporting that preceded the era of layoffs and closures. That was never my life. Though I started in the tail end of this age, I never quite got a taste of its benefits, nor did I ever arrive at one of the few well-resourced news institutions that would have approximated the experience. After about five years at my first job with the *Los Angeles Daily Journal*, it felt like time to move on, and in prior eras of journalism a talented reporter at a small paper would have transitioned to a bigger paper. Because I had good clips and won some awards, that was still technically possible for me, but major papers were beginning to shrink. I had a friend and former editor who worked at the *Los Angeles Times*, but she didn't think she could get me in; she also did not recommend me trying at the time. Looking at the landscape, I decided to join Katrina on her new venture of launching a legal media company, Lawdragon, which would be more online focused without some of the legacy burdens of larger print operations.

By staying on the fringes of journalism, I've operated more or less anonymously—in other words, like most journalists, which suits me okay. In fact, the only reason I've been able to stay on the Guantanamo beat is because of my place outside mainstream journalism. No news outlets, with the exception now of the *New York Times*, can or will invest the time and resources to cover the story. No editor wants to send a reporter to a remote location where nothing immediately interesting happens—where it might take several trips for a story to emerge. Hersh was right: There's just not the staff to do it. Co-running a small business has brought enormous stresses unrelated to my journalism work, but I am mostly my own boss and mostly in control of my own schedule. With Katrina's support for our Guantanamo project, my fate was sealed. If you have the type of freedom we have, and if you believe the material is worth it, you might just feel the need to see the story out to its conclusion, even if one never seems to appear on the horizon.

But there are drawbacks, including the occasional humiliation. Among them was being informed on August 23 by Flesvig's deputy for media relations, a navy lieutenant commander, that I would not be traveling for the 9/11 trip, which I later learned was because Lawdragon was not "major media." I would be an "alternate," allowed to travel if a reporter from a major outlet dropped off. Apparently, the Pentagon had agreed to provide twenty slots for journalists, down from a more than decade-long commitment to support sixty media representatives (around that many had attended the May 2012 arraignment). Many big outlets wanted to mark the occasion with twentieth-anniversary stories or segments, live from Guantanamo Bay. Flesvig also later told me that his overseers at Office of the Secretary of Defense public affairs division wanted to make sure all mediums (TV, print, radio, online) had the opportunity to attend.

To make matters worse, I was already traveling to the base for the August 30 arraignment in the Indonesian case. This meant I would have to leave Guantanamo Bay when the big media contingent showed up; they would be entering the Gitmo air terminal as I waited to board the same plane out. I would have to watch the first week of proceedings from Fort Meade, then return to the Naval Base once everybody cleared out for the second week. That would happen on Sunday, September 12, as September 11 was reserved for memorial events. (Someone had made the wise decision to not make family members travel in and out of the base on the twentieth anniversary of the attacks.) Understandably, most journalists did not need two weeks of court to get some color for their pieces, so I'd be granted the luxury of sitting mostly alone in court again for week two.

Katrina and I were discussing possibly getting a lawyer to lodge a protest with the Pentagon, and Carol and Terry McDermott (who had been approved to attend for the *Los Angeles Times*) were considering sending memos in support of my attendance. To be honest, I thought about skipping the whole thing. Flesvig was not too concerned, however, in part because he was expecting pullouts, which became increasingly likely as news outlets focused their attention on the disastrous withdrawal from Afghanistan. By the time I arrived at my hotel room in DC on August 25, the day before the flight for the Indonesian case, Flesvig's deputy had moved me from the waiting list to the travel list for the 9/11 case. Like Carol, I'd get to stay on Gitmo and wait for the media swarm to arrive, which included representatives from NBC, ABC, CBS, CNN, and Fox, among others, for a total group of nineteen.

Still, it was a sign of what could happen at the start of a trial or a sentencing hearing: No matter my commitment, I might be denied access to the Naval Base on some of the biggest news days. Also, the humiliation lingered. On the first day of court for the 9/11 case in a year and a half, the front row of the gallery was apparently reserved for the "major media." For the first time ever, I was relegated to the second row, typically reserved for NGOs.

* * *

In a few different meetings before court, James Connell told us how hard the pandemic was for his client, Ammar al Baluchi, and the other detainees, for exacerbating their sense of isolation. At Camp 7, the detainees were split into two tiers, but within those tiers they had been allowed to live communally over the past few years—a mutually beneficial arrangement that, among other things, allowed Hadi to be taken to the bathroom by his "brothers" rather than guard staff. But the pandemic had interrupted communal living due to COVID protocols. In addition, meetings with legal teams were the detainees' connection to the outside world. Pre-pandemic, with regular commissions' flights and the rotator options, the five legal teams sent representatives down on a weekly or near weekly basis. Beyond talking about their cases, detainees could discuss current events with their lawyers, hear about developments at home and air complaints about their conditions. Those meetings had a relationship-building aspect to them, and they stopped during the pandemic.

The guard force and court personnel arranged for remote client meetings by video between a Virginia location, which was being established as a court annex, and the Camp Justice courtroom. But when one of the teams discovered that someone could listen in, that became a less desirable option. Another difficultly, we learned, was the April 2021 closure of Camp 7 and the transfer of all the high-value detainees to Camp 5, the maximum-security wing of the prison that had not had any detainees since late 2016.

Camp 7 had fallen into extreme disrepair, with a litany of serious maintenance and sewage issues, but the detainees still found the move disruptive.

None of this was apparent from my partially obstructed seat for nonmajor media in row two of the viewing gallery on September 7. I was surprised to see during the pre-court socializing that the defendants did not look too much different from before the pandemic. All I noticed was Mohammed appearing a bit smaller—thinner maybe—and some more gray in the dark beards of his four codefendants; KSM's beard remained orange. As before, they generally appeared happy to be in court.

Only a handful of reporters appreciated just how new of an era this was for the 9/11 case. First was the judge, Air Force Col. Matthew McCall, who was either the fourth or eighth judge on the case, depending on how you counted the placeholder judges or temporary appointees. McCall was actually first appointed to the case in October 2020, but he was only on the case for a short while. The prosecution protested his appointment for being outside the court's own rules: He had not yet been a military judge for two years, a prerequisite. He was reappointed in August 2021, once he had finally met the threshold as a judge.

It was odd, of course, that the new judge on the biggest case in US history could only assume the position because a global pandemic had delayed the case long enough for him to qualify for the job. But that's the military. McCall, who was fifty, had served in a number of legal roles since getting his law degree twenty years earlier. During voir dire, he became the only person in court who was not wearing a mask; McCall felt it was important for lawyers to see his face when answering questions. Like Cohen, he appeared friendly but was noticeably less intense. He told the lawyers during voir dire that he was a patient judge, and that he believed this reputation contributed to his appointment.

"I think this case requires some patience, right?" McCall said.

He would have to draw on his patience immediately. Walter Ruiz could not make the trip for personal reasons, which left Mustafa al Hawsawi without his learned counsel. His team would have to study the transcript and decide if it wanted to voir dire the judge later, either in person or writing. McCall indicated that he would curtail the substantive scope of the hearing with Ruiz gone, though he planned to hear some oral arguments.

An even bigger change was the absence of Army Brig. Gen. Mark Martins, who had been the chief prosecutor since 2011. He had announced his retirement earlier in the summer and was stepping down effective September 30. I had talked with Martins on the recent prior trips—he was friendly, as always—but he was not on the base for this one. As Carol reported for the *Times*, Martins had butted heads with some members of the new Biden administration over the prosecution's intent to use a limited amount of torture evidence in the pretrial phase of the case against Abd al Rahim al Nashiri, accused with planning the USS *Cole* bombing. While the law barred its use at trial, the prosecution wanted to use a statement al Nashiri made to CIA interrogators to rebut one of the defense's theories—this type of pretrial usage was untested and controversial. The Biden administration soon came out against the use of torture at any phase of a military commission. Whether Martins retired or was fired, the public face of the commissions was now gone. In court, the government's case would now flow through the longtime managing trial counsel, Clay Trivett, a civilian. Trivett's thick mane of hair remained intact, without a trace of gray, proving to be one of the case's consistencies from the pre-pandemic era. Trivett had been on the case since its beginning in the Bush era, having joined the commissions as a junior navy lawyer. Ed Ryan may have been the prosecution's most dangerous weapon, but Trivett had proven himself adept at calmly and effectively punching back against the flurry of arguments from his five learned opponents.

The absence of Martins overshadowed the fact that Jim Harrington was also gone. He remained on the team for Ramzi bin al Shibh as "resource counsel," providing support from the United States, but would no longer be traveling to Guantanamo Bay. His replacement as learned counsel, David Bruck, was a legend in the field of death penalty law who had argued some of the seminal capital cases before the US Supreme Court. Prior to joining the commissions, Bruck had served as the director of the death penalty clinic at Washington & Lee University School of Law for sixteen years. His recent cases included representing Dzhokhar Tsarnaev, the convicted Boston Marathon bomber, and Dylann Roof, who killed nine people at a church in Charleston, South Carolina.

On the Sunday before the hearing, Bruck stopped by the NGIS conference room to meet with the nineteen journalists, giving a mostly prepared statement about the torture that he said his client continued to suffer. By this point, bin al Shibh was complaining not only about noises and vibrations but also about stabbing sensations that he claimed were remotely directed at his body, including his genitals. Bruck said the ongoing misery was causing a sleep deprivation that had now gone on for close to two decades. He said his team's most important job was to "solve the mystery" of what was happening to bin al Shibh.

"The torture program for him never ended, and in fact it's getting worse," Bruck told us.

When voir dire resumed on Wednesday, September 8, Bruck engaged in a brief exchange with McCall. He told the new judge that so much of the case was uncharted—in fact, Bruck said, the United States had never had a five-defendant death penalty case tried to verdict. Beyond that, of course, was the CIA program and the government's decision "to disappear people into an information-extraction program for so many years." Bruck said that many people assumed that the government had made this choice at the exclusion of criminal prosecutions, until 2006, when it decided to transfer the men to Guantanamo Bay for a trial.

"It could be that this second stage of the process cannot be done, period, it's impossible," Bruck said. "That the die was cast when they were first put into the RDI program run by a secret intelligence agency whose identities by and large we are not permitted to know, and that's really the end of the possibility of a fair trial. And my question is: Can you remain open to that possibility?"

McCall didn't miss a beat. He knew what he had stepped into.

"Absolutely," he said. "Absolutely."

* * *

At the end of week one, only two victim family members decided to meet with the media. Dr. Elizabeth Berry, a clinical psychologist, and her husband, Paul Berry, a retired lawyer, sat on our faux leather couch surrounded by a swarm of journalists, several of whom had cameras. Dr. Berry's brother, William "Billy" Burke, a captain in the New York City Fire Department, died during rescue efforts in the North Tower. The Berrys had both attended before and were interested in returning as the case moved forward. They remained poised as the questions came from multiple faces scattered about the room.

"As you know, the world has moved on," Dr. Berry said. "And a lot of people in the United States today, especially young people, were not even born on 9/11. So it's not something that you hear a lot about in the media."

The next day was the twentieth anniversary. I took part in the annual 9.11-kilometer run, which this year was held in the early morning hours to mitigate the heat. I performed admirably, I thought, but was blown away by Willy Lowry, a correspondent with *The National,* a publication based in the United Arab Emirates, who glided effortlessly in a way that made me feel old and feeble. We were able to shower and get ourselves to the 9/11 memorial service held later that morning at the chapel, a beautiful building on a hill high above Sherman Avenue. It was a nice event, but the base prohibited media from getting any visuals or audio. At the day's end, most of the journalists, myself included, found our way to Glass Beach to wade in the warm water and drink beers. The next morning was a rare Sunday departure for the commissions. I walked down to see my eighteen colleagues off to the ferry, then returned to the hotel alone, but for Flesvig. In another rarity, Carol, expecting a slow week, decided to head stateside for a wedding and watch proceedings remotely from Fort Meade.

We did not have a lot of court to watch. McCall used much of the week to hold ex parte meetings with the defense teams (other than Ruiz's for al Hawsawi) to learn their theories of the case. McCall wanted to be educated. Alone with my thoughts in the gallery, I began to think about how weird it was to spend so much time sitting behind the five 9/11 defendants, whom I had come to accept as regular figures in my life. They knew who we were, and we knew at least a few read our stories and occasionally commented on them through their lawyers; they also occasionally looked back at the gallery to see us looking back at them. Many things separated us, including glass, but we had spent a lot of time together. I wondered what they thought of me going to their case more than they do, but I never asked anyone.

A groundbreaking moment came when Alka Pradhan, from al Baluchi's team, presented oral arguments from a remote site. Prior to the hearing, McCall had designated the so-called "Remote Hearing Room"—established during the pandemic in the Virginia offices to lessen travel burdens—"an extension to the well of the courtroom." The setup of the "RHR" mirrored that of the Guantanamo courtroom, with the prosecution on one side and the defense teams in the same order on the opposite side. Team members from each courtroom could communicate via headset, and Pradhan spoke from a podium that was displayed on the courtroom monitors. The remote facility also had a witness box.

Pradhan and I both made our first 9/11 trip together in October 2015, and we had a long-running competition to see who could accumulate the most Guantanamo Bay souvenirs. This took on an even more absurd quality in the pandemic when the main souvenir store on the base began selling Disney-themed T-shirts, including a "Guantanamo Dad" option with Mickey Mouse ears. Neither of us were above wearing such items or buying them for family members and friends. Pradhan told me by email that the remote system worked well—that she could see and hear the judge and communicate with her team. She added that the team had concerns "about Confrontation Clause issues at trial if the intention is to continue its use beyond pretrial proceedings."

McCall planned to hold a last day of court on Friday, but a complication arose the prior evening when a reporter who attended week one emailed Flesvig that he had tested positive for COVID after becoming sick in the days after his return. The defense lawyers and staff who met with the media would have had significant exposure. So, of course, did Flesvig and I, and before dawn broke on Friday morning he drove us to the base hospital to get COVID tests. We were rebuffed because we did not meet the base's standards for needing one—a curious response to two people who, among other things, shared a crowded van with the sick reporter. After Flesvig made a few calls, we drove back to the hospital parking lot and waited for someone to swab us. A young medic in what appeared to be a Halloween costume of a hazmat suit came out with tubes and swabs, which he collected through open windows.

"Is this a PCR or a rapid test?" I inquired, but he didn't know what I was talking about. As he walked back to the hospital juggling tubes between his hands, Flesvig and I agreed that, if either of us tested positive, we would retest before starting a two-week quarantine, which could have caused us to miss a return flight. A few hours later, we learned that both tests were negative. Members from a few different defense teams felt sick and were taking the morning to get COVID tests. As well. McCall made the obvious move by canceling the Friday session.

Carol rejoined me on Saturday to attend hearings in the last case to resume, that against al Nashiri for his alleged role in the USS *Cole* bombing. She came with photographer Erin Schaff to take photos for what would become "Guantanamo Bay: Beyond the Prison," published in late November. It was a fun week with Schaff on base; the military suddenly offered up an abundance of photo opportunities. We did a tour of the cemetery and the secret Blue Beach, a boat cruise helmed by Flesvig, a night at the base's Octoberfest event in the Windjammer ballroom, and even a late-Friday-night stop at the Tiki Bar, the thundering party scene that I claimed to be "too loud" but had secretly been making a regular part of pandemic-era Gitmo life. I also produced a story on the USS *Cole* case, explaining how al Nashiri's lawyers were still seeking additional information about the hidden microphones in the attorney-client meeting room that had derailed the case years earlier.

Twentieth-Anniversary Reboot. September 2021.

Carol stayed for week two of the al Nashiri hearing while I headed back with Schaff, ending what had been a whirlwind for me. I left for DC on August 25 thinking I might be coming back in a week, and instead stayed for more than a month—my longest trip, surpassing the three-week suppression hearing of September 2019. I would be returning to Allison in a major fog, but I would not be a stranger. The privacy of NGIS for phone calls and Zoom hangouts made longer trips easier, a luxury I hoped I could continue to rely on.

CHAPTER 26

The Silent Treatment. March 2022–September 2023.

One could hardly blame Majid Khan for being nervous on the afternoon of October 28, 2021. After all, he would soon be admitting to a panel of eight military officers his various crimes for al Qaeda, which included delivering $50,000 to the Southeast Asian terror group Jemaah Islamiyah for the August 2003 bombing that killed eleven people and wounded more than one hundred others at the J.W. Marriott in Jakarta, Indonesia. He also would be the first Guantanamo Bay detainee to speak in a military commission in detail about his past torture by the CIA. After an evening break, Khan, dressed in a black suit and light tie, finally walked to the podium at 7:34 p.m. He swiveled the podium to face the jury and took a deep breath before speaking in accented but clear English. Early in his statement, the forty-one-year-old Pakistani said he forgave his CIA torturers, just as he had to forgive his younger self for his crimes.

"For those who tortured me, I forgive y'all," Khan said. "All y'all."

Sitting to the right of Carol and me were Khan's father and sister, who began sobbing almost immediately and would do so intermittently during his two hours at the podium. Khan's family fled from Pakistan to the Baltimore area in 1996, when he was sixteen. He traveled back to Pakistan in 2002, during a tumultuous time in the year after his mother died, and he fell under the influence of extended family with ties to al Qaeda. Pakistani authorities captured Khan in Karachi in March 2003. Khan said that they subjected him to violent beatings in the presence of American interrogators before his transfer to CIA custody, which he said happened even though he immediately confessed his terrorist activities.

He described his CIA torture in graphic detail: the prolonged sleep deprivation; being hung by chains and doused with cold water with a fan blowing on his naked body; being submerged in ice water while wearing a hood; and violent forced feeding. On one occasion, CIA personnel sharpened the end of a feeding tube and doused it with hot sauce before inserting it into his nose. At another time, Khan said, personnel used a syringe to force-feed him down his throat. Khan also said he endured numerous sexual assaults and rapes when CIA personnel rectally fed and hydrated him as punishment for his hunger strikes. At one point, he said, a green garden hose was inserted into his rectum and attached to a faucet.

"I could feel the gush of water going into my rectum," Khan said.

Khan said his transfer to Guantanamo Bay in September 2006 ended the severe physical torture but brought a continued mental anguish like "death by a thousand paper cuts." He said he first met his lawyers in October 2007 and immediately proposed cooperating with the government.

From an actual sentencing perspective, the stakes for Khan were not so high. Under the pretrial agreement, the judge would instruct the jury to sentence Khan to twenty-five to forty years; however, the convening authority would not approve a sentence of more than eleven years if Khan was found to have fully cooperated with the government—which his lawyers said he had for many years. This meant that Khan was likely to be eligible for release in early 2022, with credit for time served. His team, led by Wells Dixon for the Center for Constitutional Rights, had secured significant leverage the year before when the prior judge on the case ruled that he had the authority to reduce Khan's sentence "as a remedy for illegal pretrial punishment" based on his time in CIA custody. That set the stage for an evidentiary hearing at which defense lawyers could call witnesses—including covert CIA employees identified only by their UFIs—with knowledge of Khan's torture to make a case for a lesser sentence. Prosecutors agreed to a greatly reduced maximum sentence to avoid this.

The next day, after closing arguments and three hours of deliberations, the panel returned with a sentence of twenty-six years and a handwritten letter recommending clemency. It was signed by seven of the eight jurors, each using a number instead of a name. The panel members said that Khan's treatment "in the hands of US personnel should be a source of shame for the US government" and was "an affront to American values."

It was, by one measure, a resounding rejection of the torture program and of the government's legal position that past abuse could be successfully "attenuated" from subsequent criminal proceedings. By another measure, however, it felt like something of a government victory, proof that hiding past conduct was possible—that the out-of-sight, out-of-mind Gitmo project had worked: Carol and I were the only two journalists to show up for the historic event, something we marveled at later. A handful of NGO attendees sat behind us, including Terry Rockefeller, who regularly attended the 9/11 case as a member of September 11th Families for Peaceful Tomorrows. It seemed like one of those days—and there have been many—when the lessons from Gitmo would remain trapped on the island.

Then again, there were more important observers of these proceedings, among them the prosecutors and defense lawyers from the other pending cases.

* * *

Judge McCall guaranteed that Khan would remain the highlight of 2021 by moving cautiously with his stewardship of the 9/11 case. He and his predecessor, Judge Shane Cohen, may have both been Air Force colonels—and shared polite demeanors—but their strategies for assuming control of the case were worlds apart. McCall was not going to dive into witnesses. While September was a nonstarter with Ruiz gone, McCall could have conceivably resumed the case's mammoth suppression hearing during the three-week session in November 2021. Instead, he decided to work his way through the discovery motions that had accumulated in Cohen's final weeks and after. Not surprisingly, defense teams had found additional areas of inquiry and potential new witnesses following the testimony from FBI witnesses and from Mitchell and Jessen—both of whom still needed to finish their testimony.

McCall told the parties in November that his focus on discovery motions would provide some "clarity" to the remaining suppression hearings. Even so, they also revealed the staggering complexity of the case. McCall gave each defense team and the prosecution great leeway in presenting their arguments—encouraging as much background information as possible to help educate him about the case's many intersecting issues. As arguments unfolded, each side of the courtroom once again blamed the other: Prosecutors contended that the defense teams were gumming up the system with endless discovery motions, while the defense teams accused the government of causing the delays by withholding evidence—even ignoring the prior judge's discovery order related to evidence of CIA and FBI coordination. The case felt like it had returned to square one when defense lawyers insisted to McCall that the twenty-three thousand pages of discovery from the RDI program was "a drop in the bucket" compared to the six million pages of documentation that went into the Senate report.

"I get some of the frustration from both sides," McCall said on Wednesday of the first week.

By the end of the third week, the interagency picture had become even more muddled—both for seasoned observers, and surely to a newcomer like McCall. James Connell told McCall something previously unknown to the public—that nine FBI agents actually became CIA agents for an undisclosed period of time during their time at the black sites.

"FBI agents stopped being FBI agents and became CIA agents temporarily," Connell said. "This really is unheard of."

Connell said that the FBI agents' switch to the CIA might have been a tactic of "deniability" or "strategic ambiguity" to obscure the FBI's involvement in the black-site program. While the defense teams had learned this fact from discovery, the government had only recently declassified it for public consumption. Connell warned McCall that he should be wary of the government's use of "distortion" during pending discovery disputes "because all may not be as it seems."

Connell came up to me after court with a smile, as I had been asking about this topic for years now. Finally, we could stop dancing around the information.

"That's about as clear as I can make it," Connell told me.

McCall also had to wrestle with discovery disputes that went far beyond the RDI program. Defense lawyers and the prosecution were still arguing over evidence related to "hostilities"—the dispute over whether an armed conflict existed between the United States and al Qaeda at the time of the 9/11 attacks. Defense teams wanted a vast amount of information from both the Clinton and Bush administrations about how the US government dealt with the al Qaeda threat—decades of material from a wide array of government agencies. As far as I could tell, I was still the only reporter in the world who cared about the hostilities issue.

McCall ended the November session by asking for input on how to structure the scheduled two-week hearing in January. Several FBI agents and analysts still had to testify, including some of those who conducted the 2007 "clean team" interrogations that were the subject of the suppression

The Silent Treatment. March 2022–September 2023.

hearing. As it turned out, nothing happened in January. McCall canceled the session as the Omicron COVID variant spread like wildfire. Before the three-week March session, McCall issued a docket order in which he listed about thirty-five motions he wanted to get through, most of them discovery disputes, without yet determining if he wanted witness testimony. Even if he had, it's likely no one would have taken the stand.

* * *

The decommissioning of the media tents brought enormous quality of life benefits. Even after new tents were built in Camp Justice later in 2021, we maintained the option of staying at the NGIS hotel. I was never one to complain too much about the tents, but the choice was not difficult. In my view, sharing a tent with other media was a COVID risk, even if we were in separate living compartments. Though the old latrine and tent bathrooms had been replaced by individualized units in metal trailers, using them would still involve breathing someone else's leftover air. Beyond safety, having a private room with a comfortable bed, TV, clean bathroom, and kitchenette was impossible to pass up, even if it added to the expense of travel, especially because the round-trip airfare had also increased to eight hundred dollars in October 2019. That I could end a workday on Guantanamo Bay by watching an old TV show with Allison through a Hulu "Watch Party" was nothing short of a Gitmo miracle. For reasons still not entirely clear, we began making our way through *Doogie Howser, M.D.*

NGIS living also shifted the locus of life to what is the best area of the base for anyone without a car, and for anyone looking for the most outdoor options. If you had told me back in early 2020 that I would be spending more time at the Tiki Bar than O'Kelly's in my future Caribbean travels, I wouldn't have believed you. The Tiki Bar can be a relaxing place to grab a drink on an early evening, before the younger crowds show up. Even with our press badges flopping down our front torsos, we'd occasionally get a fellow patron to chat us up.

"I really admire what you guys do here," a middle-aged woman, sitting across from us on the other side of the bar, told us one June night in 2022.

Carol and I were pleasantly caught off guard and gave our thanks. We have our share of friendly interactions on the base, but seldom with such positive expressions about the media's role on Guantanamo.

"You guys are teachers, right?" she asked.

Oh well.

The hotel is a four-story structure about eighty yards in horizontal length, the entire back of which is filled with patio furniture and chairs. Though bugs remained a constant menace, this was a great area either for eating takeout or using the nearby charcoal grills. The socializing behind the NGIS was great fun, as many civilians associated with the commissions—not to mention a wide assortment of contractors and other random folks—stayed at the hotel. On most nights, you'd find some combination of people hanging out in the back, sometimes until very late. I often marveled at the mix of people at the table with me and the few other journalists: lawyers, intelligence analysts, interpreters, paralegals, audio engineers who handled the courtroom sound, you name it—once in a while, even a prosecutor from one of the pending cases would join us. On other random nights, a Coast Guard ship would come in and "coasties" would fill up the Tiki Bar and O'Kelly's before stopping by our tables at the end of the night. A highlight of this era was being joined on occasion by Bobby Hendricks, a contractor who worked on the audio systems for the courtroom and the remote hearing facility in Virginia. Hendricks is a string musician with many recording sessions to his name. He also toured with the likes of Stevie Wonder and Hank Williams Jr. I've spent much of my discretionary income over the decades on live music, including seeing Bob Dylan at least seventy-five times. That Bobby knew a few musicians who have been part of Bob Dylan's endless touring troupe seemed to make this whole Gitmo reporting project worth it.

It wasn't too uncommon for NGIS staff to come out to the patio after receiving complaints and implore us to move farther away by the grills. Even on slow nights, we were joined by the area's swarm of "banana rats"—officially hutia, a type of rodent—and stray cats, which NGIS patrons could not help but feed despite admonitions to the contrary. The cats were desperately hungry, and we might have more than a dozen swarming around the area looking for leftovers. The hutia, named banana rats for the shape of their feces, were generally content with Cheetos or other snacks. "Operation Git-Meow," a volunteer organization established to spay and neuter the base's cats and help with finding foster and adoptive homes, had first gained attention in 2017—when Carol profiled it for the *Miami Herald*. But the cat population apparently exploded during the pandemic.

The hum of friendly activity made the silent treatment Carol and I received at the March session all the more noticeable. Most of the civilians on the 9/11 case stayed at the hotel during this phase, and all of them were ignoring us. Carol had an inkling of what was happening, but I was clueless. Even when she told me her suspicions, I wasn't buying it.

As usual, the first of the three weeks began with something that was either a stunning twist or a predictable déjà vu moment—and one that prevented us from even getting into court. In the days before the hearing, Cheryl Bormann, the lead lawyer for Walid bin Attash, had requested to leave the case due to an internal investigation into her "performance and conduct" by the Military Commissions Defense Organization. McCall used the first day of court, March 7, to hold an ex parte hearing with Bormann, and he used subsequent days to have ex parte meetings with other members of her team. He also set a March 14 deadline for the other parties to file anything if they wanted to weigh in on Bormann's motion to withdraw.

By this point, the longtime chief defense counsel, Marine Brig. Gen. John Baker, had departed the commissions and was on his way to becoming the federal public defender for the Western District of North Carolina—yet another big sign that the commissions had entered a new era. His replacement, Army Brig. Gen. Jackie Thompson, who started on the job in January 2022, stopped by the media center on March 10. He could not discuss the details of the investigation, but it appeared to be a personnel or employment type dispute within the bin Attash team—not the type of supposed national security investigation involving outside agencies that had earlier derailed the case. Thompson recited his predecessor's refrain: We'd all be in court if each team had a second learned counsel. Now, instead, the case could face several more months of delays to find a replacement learned counsel, as required by the law, if Bormann left the case.

"This would not be an issue," Thompson lamented. "We would be moving forward."

The bin Attash team had a lot of good lawyers, and the prosecution would soon argue that William Montross, a team member since 2017, qualified as a learned counsel. Montross had worked on death penalty cases at the Southern Center for Human Rights, but Thompson did not think Montross qualified, and he would soon begin a search for a new learned counsel.

It made sense that no one wanted to talk to us about the situation involving Bormann, who by the end of the week had left the case unceremoniously after a decade of zealous advocacy. But that was not the reason why everyone was avoiding us. The real reason emerged in the downstairs laundry room of the NGIS on the afternoon of Sunday, March 13, before the start of the second week. Carol and I were transferring our loads from the washers to the driers and had started discussing what to do for dinner and, more generally, how to kill time in the coming week. That's when a lawyer from the case casually strolled in and told us what was going on: The government and the five defense teams had entered into plea negotiations.

After the brief meeting, we stumbled out of the laundry room and onto the outdoor patio to process the stunning news that the government was willing to take the death penalty off the table in exchange for guilty pleas. The second iteration of the 9/11 case was less than two months from the ten-year anniversary of the May 2012 arraignment. Now, unbelievably, a conclusion to the case finally appeared plausible—the end was not yet in sight, but the road there might be taking shape.

We learned that, as the Bormann situation was blowing up, Clay Trivett emailed the five teams to propose using the remaining time to iron out plea agreements. The defense teams agreed, and McCall signed off on the parties and the defendants using the courtroom to begin negotiations, which eventually carried into the second and third weeks. Because Carol and I had obtained our confirmation of the secret negotiations at the same time, in the laundry room encounter, we agreed that Lawdragon and the *New York Times* would break the news at the same time: March 15 at 10:30 a.m.

The convening authority, who was still Jeffrey Wood, would have to sign off on any pretrial agreements, but the complexity of the deal would take it far past his office. Our sources told us that the terms sought by defense teams would need ratification by the most senior levels of the Biden administration. One issue was that at least some of the defendants would prefer to stay on Guantanamo Bay, where they had built a predictable life for themselves—even if the move to Camp 5 had disrupted that somewhat. This desire would run contrary to the Biden administration's plans to close the detention facility. Even more important were securing guarantees for conditions of confinement to include communal time, which they had enjoyed since 2019, and improved physical and mental healthcare, with rehabilitation services tailored to torture victims. The teams also wanted guarantees that could be invoked even if a new administration didn't like the deal, something in writing that could be considered a contract. In the parlance of the case, these became known as "the policy principles"—agreed to by the teams and the prosecution and supported by the convening authority, but perhaps ultimately out of their hands.

We learned in our reporting that several factors led to the prosecution finally pulling the trigger on what had seemed like an obvious move for years. First was the absence of Gen. Martins, who had retired just as the 9/11 case was restarting the prior September. We believed Martins wanted a trial and a death sentence for at least Mohammed, even if it was unlikely to stand up on appeal—though I guess we don't know what he would have done if faced with the Bormann situation. Even if the bin Attash team did not need a new learned counsel, the case had probably close to two years of pretrial litigation left—and that's if it moved smoothly, without the loss of additional lead lawyers or judges. If the case made it to trial, the Khan jury suggested that securing the long-sought-after death sentences would be far from a guaranteed outcome. The prosecution also sensed—accurately, as it turned out—that McCall would take a friendly view toward many of the defense's discovery motions, which could be a harbinger for other rulings.

A sentencing trial in the 9/11 case would be a much longer affair than Khan's. The government would put on a lengthy case to outline the alleged conspiracy and to show the horrors of 9/11, with many victim-impact witnesses testifying. The defense teams would be given significant leeway to present past torture and other mitigating evidence. Most lawyers estimated that a sentencing trial would take several weeks or months, with no guarantee that it would take place at the same time for all five defendants.

Bormann's absence did not prevent her team from participating in negotiations. For this reason, the departure of such a powerful presence in the case became something of an afterthought. In the middle of the third week, McCall granted her request to leave the case, though he made "no findings regarding the adequacy" of the investigation into Bormann "or of the veracity of the allegations." In fact, he noted that Bormann had only received a redacted version of the investigative report "and that she had not been interviewed or offered an opportunity to respond to the investigation." Still, McCall concluded that the team could not function effectively in "its current configuration." He ordered Thompson to find a new learned counsel "expeditiously" and to update him every two weeks until the next session, a three-week hearing set to begin on May 9.

For me, the timing of the 9/11 case beginning to find its way toward a resolution could not have been better. Late the prior year, Allison and I decided to try IVF, and we were in the thick of it. Our fingers were crossed that we'd have the best of all possible reasons for me to slow my Gitmo travel, even if the cases were still going on. But it seemed like there was now a good chance I would not be missing an actual 9/11 trial.

If Carol and I received the silent treatment, however, so did the parties to the 9/11 case when it came to "the policy principles," which officially sat with the Department of Defense's Office of General Counsel. Even as it seemed clear the Biden administration didn't want to touch the proposed deal, McCall and the parties were going to wait it out. McCall canceled the May session and then a monthlong session that would have spanned parts of June and July. As the fall loomed, Walter Ruiz broke from the pack and proposed moving forward with the four-week session starting in September 2022. He contended that the parties could move forward with the pretrial litigation while still supporting plea deals. McCall nevertheless canceled the session, though everybody traveled to Guantanamo Bay during the last week of September so that the judge could hear ex parte updates and other concerns from the parties.

Carol and I were allowed to join on the September trip on the .05 percent chance that McCall held any open court, such as a status update or to put new lawyers on the record, but that did not happen. We at least got to meet with Bormann's replacement as bin Attash's learned counsel, Matthew Engle, a longtime capital defender in Virginia, though one on the younger side, having received his law degree in 2001. Like Bruck, he had also taught at Washington & Lee's law school and served as a director of its Virginia Capital Case Clearinghouse; before that, he taught at the University of Virginia's law school and directed its Innocence Project. Engle still had to finish a few of his pending cases before representing bin Attash full-time.

Weeks later, McCall canceled the November session—making 2022 the first year in the case's long history to not have any days in open court. McCall kept ruling on discovery motions, however, siding with the defense in many areas—including on evidence related to FBI-CIA coordination and on CIA records related to the former Camp 7. The prosecution began filing a long stream of motions asking for additional time to comply with McCall's orders. In one filing, the prosecution said that completing its obligations with McCall's recent discovery orders—which "have caused the prosecution team to have to review approximately 24,625 pages of material"—would take until spring 2023. In addition, the prosecution would have to seek substitutions and summaries for significant tranches of the new evidence.

Before the end of 2022, McCall canceled the three-week session scheduled to start January 16, 2023, but he was beginning to lose his patience. He ordered the prosecution to update him on the status of the proposed policy principles every two weeks. Each time, Trivett filed the same notice: "The Prosecution has been advised that US government officials are continuing to discuss the proposed policy principles. It is anticipated that these discussions will continue for some time."

* * *

But I kept busy. The USS *Cole* commission provided the action throughout 2022 and 2023 that the 9/11 case did not—and like Khan's case, its progress would prove relevant to the 9/11 case. The legal team for Abd al Rahim al Nashiri, led by Anthony Natale, a death penalty lawyer from South Florida, moved forward with its motion to suppress the statements that al Nashiri made to his "clean team" in early 2007. This was, in a sense, a miniature version of the suppression hearing in the 9/11 case, covering some of the same ground with testimony from Drs. James Mitchell and Bruce Jessen—but also going into new territory.

This included testimony from the team's medical consultant, Dr. Sondra Crosby, who often traveled with the team. Crosby, a professor of medicine at Boston University, testified in February 2023 about the ongoing effects of the CIA's rectal abuse of al Nashiri, which she said he experienced "as painful sexual assaults or rapes." She said that al Nashiri told her that personnel at a CIA black site stripped him naked, shackled him at his feet and ankles, bent him over a chair, and inserted liquid food into his anus. He described another incident to Crosby in which personnel inserted a broomstick into his anus while he was naked with his arms shackled above his head.

Natale handed Crosby an endotracheal tube so that she could demonstrate how the device is typically used to help an individual breathe. Crosby said that CIA reporting showed that personnel used the device to rectally infuse al Nashiri with Ensure for thirty minutes, then left the tube in for an additional ten minutes. Crosby testified that medical science had debunked the potential benefits of rectal feeding by the 1930s. She said that 95 percent of digestion is completed by the time food moves through the small intestine, and that nutrients are not absorbed in the rectum or colon.

"It's not a two-way street," Crosby said.

The more disturbing highlight came a few months later, in April 2023, when one of al Nashiri's civilian lawyers, Annie Morgan, examined Dr. Jessen and had him reenact some of his "enhanced interrogation techniques." At one point, Morgan asked Jessen to step down from the stand to demonstrate what were considered the "least intrusive" measures, such as attention grabs, that he and Mitchell would have used on al Nashiri prior to starting the harsher measures. Jessen did so reluctantly, saying that he felt like he was "beating up" his own daughter. Morgan also asked Jessen to show the court how he would order someone into a confinement box. He began by telling Morgan, in the role of her client, that he was disappointed that she was not being "helpful" in the interrogation.

"We're going to give you time to think about this," Jessen said calmly. "Get into the box."

Morgan complied by sitting on the floor in front of a rectangular plywood structure about thirty inches tall, then scooting backward into the box. She pressed her knees against her chest and held her arms over her shins, while another defense lawyer closed the box's door. Morgan sat in there for several seconds, which seemed uncomfortable; al Nashiri would spend up to two hours in the box. Her presentation was creepily effective, though less so because it took place from the remote hearing room in Virginia; we had to watch it on a screen in the Guantanamo court. The defense lawyers and prosecutors in the al Nashiri case preferred to question witnesses in person, which made the Gitmo courtroom nearly empty at times, or at least devoid of any real action. Clearly, there was no reason for all the staff from defense and prosecution teams to travel to Guantanamo Bay for weeks at a time. Nevertheless, with all the COVID restrictions lifted by that point, it felt like the remote facility had morphed into something that was not intended.

After completing her memorable examination, Morgan caught the Saturday commissions' flight for the hearing's second week. Hours later, she met Carol and me at the Tiki Bar for beers. Morgan was spent, physically and emotionally. It occurred to me, as it did in the Khan hearing, that the government or at least the CIA had "won" this latest round. Carol and I produced the only articles that week on Jessen's testimony, and we were the only journalists to watch from court. No one seemed to care.

As with Khan, however, the government lost in court. On August 18, 2023, Army Col. Lanny Acosta issued his suppression ruling just a few weeks before his planned retirement, siding overwhelmingly with the defense. He ruled that the CIA's past torture of al Nashiri "presumptively tainted" any of his subsequent statements unless the government could prove they were "sufficiently attenuated" from the prior torture. Acosta said that the government failed to prove that attenuation, even though he determined that the FBI and NCIS agents treated al Nashiri with respect in the early 2007 sessions on Guantanamo Bay. He said al Nashiri's resistance had been "intentionally and literally beaten out of him years before." The judge explained that al Nashiri understood there was a "contract" with his interrogators—that he would return to the "hard times" if he ever stopped cooperating. He said al Nashiri had no way of knowing in early 2007 that he wouldn't suddenly be "shipped back to a dungeon" or that his prior tormentor wasn't lurking outside "with a pistol, a drill, or a broomstick in hand in the event he chose to remain silent or to offer versions of events that differed from what he told" the CIA.

The ruling was damning. It also provided a noteworthy backdrop to Judge McCall's decision to resume suppression hearings in the 9/11 case, scheduled to last a month beginning September 18, 2023. McCall had hinted at this when canceling the other sessions in 2023—that at some point, he would have to resume pretrial hearings if the Biden administration continued to avoid a decision on the plea deals. McCall asked the government to propose witnesses for the hearing. Among them planned for September was former FBI Special Agent Frank Pellegrino, who might finally testify about his interrogations of Mohammed in early 2007.

Allison's and my IVF efforts had not been successful, a devastation that we had been working through since our last attempt. I would have loved to have been a new dad and skipped the resumption of the 9/11 case, reading Carol's coverage and maybe watching a small part from Fort Meade if we could make it work. Instead, it looked like I'd be heading back to Gitmo for a new phase of intense coverage. But our plans to get married at City Hall in the fall gave us something to look forward to.

The afternoon Acosta's ruling came down, I got Connell on the phone after his return flight from Guantanamo Bay, where he had gone for a client meeting. Connell noted that Acosta's ruling did not rely on any evidence about FBI-CIA coordination. He ignored that whole area of possible taint, relying instead on the CIA's brutality that conditioned al Nashiri into being a cooperative subject—rendering attenuation impossible. Connell said the ruling rejected the "the foundational argument" behind all the prosecutions on Guantanamo Bay, that "a sharp line" existed between CIA torture and the subsequent FBI interrogations.

"That is the whole reason we are in the military commissions," Connell said. "The ruling rejected that foundational principle of these prosecutions."

CHAPTER 27

Suppression II—The "Flaming Bag of Crap."

As the Biden administration sat on its hands, opposition to the plea deals grew suddenly, seemingly out of nowhere. The course of events was odd. Some of the lawyers involved in the March 2022 plea talks felt that it needed a quick buy-in and sign-off well before the months leading up to the November mid-term elections. That, of course, never happened. But while the Office of the Chief Prosecutor began outreach with the victim family community immediately in March 2022, the groundswell of opposition did not mount until nearly a year and a half later, after a letter about the potential deals reached a wider number of family members.

In August 2023, about two thousand relatives sent a letter to President Biden opposing any deal that took the death penalty off the table. A bipartisan group of lawmakers also sent a letter of opposition to Biden, after which Republican Sen. Ted Cruz of Texas and Rep. Nicole Malliotakis, a Republican representing parts of South Brooklyn and Staten Island, sent a letter to Secretary of Defense Lloyd Austin that opposed the proposed deal and posed several queries about it. By September 6, less than two weeks before the case was set to resume, Biden had formally declined to accept the terms of the plea deals, the so-called "policy principles." He did not oppose plea agreements, which was the sole discretion of the convening authority—then still Jeffrey Wood in his last month on the job—Biden only rejected the list of conditions related to confinement, which included the guarantees of continued communal living, better communications with families, and improved medical care. Even so, defense teams began preparing motions for unlawful influence in light of the advocacy against the deal by lawmakers. In a public statement, Cruz proudly took credit for his role in the deal falling apart.

Judge McCall's resumption of the case was a double gut-punch. Few involved in it wanted to return to the witness-intense suppression hearings, an endless grind of long examinations in court followed by nights preparing for the next day of testimony, while also working in oral arguments on any pending motions during "white space" between witnesses. And this would be the case's longest pretrial hearing since it began more than eleven years before, the first-ever four-week session, to last from September 18 to October 13. The hearing would be another stress test for a possible trial, but also one for the participants' physical, mental, and emotional stamina—the challenge to stay sane as the case reentered its most difficult and important phase, one that could drag on for another year with no end to the case reasonably in sight. McCall's role in all of that remained uncertain, as he informed the parties immediately before the session that he was planning to retire in April 2024. He acknowledged in a brief voir dire at the start of the session that the failure to reach plea deals played a role in his retirement plans, as it would have been logical for him to guide that process through the entry of guilty pleas.

Before returning to suppression, however, McCall would have to deal with the declining mental state of Ramzi bin al Shibh. David Bruck, who replaced Jim Harrington during the pandemic, had made his client's mental competency the core focus of the team's defense effort. Earlier in the year, McCall had ordered an evaluation of bin al Shibh by a three-member team of military mental health professionals referred to as a "Sanity Board" in commission rules. In August, that panel found that bin al Shibh suffered from post-traumatic stress disorder "with secondary psychotic features" and a delusional disorder that prevented him from effectively participating in his defense. But McCall had the final say.

On Tuesday of the first week, McCall gave the prosecution and defense teams a chance to provide oral arguments on the competency issue. On behalf of the prosecution, Clay Trivett gave what sounded like an argument that recognized he knew where the judge was leaning. Trivett acknowledged that bin al Shibh, with his endless complaints of noises, vibrations, and stabbing pains inflicted remotely, was delusional, but he maintained that bin al Shibh remained competent to stand trial and had repeatedly proven himself capable of working with his lawyers.

Suppression II—The "Flaming Bag of Crap."

Nevertheless, Trivett told McCall that the government supported severing bin al Shibh from the case if he found him to be incompetent, rather than put the proceedings on hold while trying to restore him to competence.

Bin al Shibh sat calmly in court, sipping Pedialyte and occasionally chatting with his codefendants as Bruck replaced Trivett at the podium. Bruck told McCall that his client was, once again, in disciplinary status at the prison for disruptive behavior—a punishment that only exacerbated his mental health problems, as the isolation and harsher conditions reminded him of the CIA's incommunicado detention. Bruck explained that the CIA had destroyed bin al Shibh's ability to sleep and that his ongoing torment was an "omnipresent" factor in the defense's relationship with him. He told McCall that the judge now faced "a moment of truth" in confronting the fallout of the CIA's program of "human experimentation."

On Thursday, McCall did as expected: He issued a ruling that found bin al Shibh incompetent to assist in his defense and that removed him from the case. The five-defendant "Trial of the Century" was now down to four accused; McCall had ushered the case into another new era just as he was returning it to the suppression hearing that began four years earlier. The ruling did not mention the CIA by name or blame bin al Shibh's condition on his time in US custody, but Bruck did when he stopped by the media center to discuss the matter with the handful of journalists who attended. He portrayed it as historic.

"This decision by the military judge today does mark the first time that the United States has formally acknowledged that the CIA torture program produced profound and prolonged psychological harm," Bruck said.

Bin al Shibh could be charged again if he was determined to be competent, but his course of treatment remained very much in doubt. One major complicating factor was that the Biden administration had just declined to implement a torture rehabilitation program as part of the plea deals. Bin al Shibh would need to be treated while in the restrictive custody of the government that had tortured him.

"We've reached a really mysterious point in these proceedings," Bruck said, a quote I used to end my article on the day's events.

* * *

We met with Bruck in the new media operations center, which had been planned for a few years. Like just about everything else in Camp Justice, the new MOC was constructed of long metal trailers, in this case five of them, conjoined to form a large metal box of an office of about 3,400 square feet, or about four times the size of our prior office. The MOC was part of the ongoing construction in Camp Justice, which included the expanding footprint of the Expeditionary Legal Complex (ELC). Instead of a drab and somewhat depressing military tent for the first TSA-like security check to get into the ELC, pandemic-era construction had given us a large, brightly lit, and new-smelling screening room—also made of several fused metal trailers—that on the back side opened to the walkway leading to the court. Of greater consequence was that, immediately adjacent to the current court, the Pentagon was building a second courtroom that could hold a three-defendant trial. This way, the Office of Military Commissions could hold two hearings at once. Dust and noise, as ever, filled the air, and both Camp Justice and the ELC either became more secure or less so, depending on the time of day, whether court was in session, and who (if anyone) was guarding one of the available gates when someone attempted to enter.

Visually, the biggest change to Camp Justice was the endless expanse of single-occupancy "tiny houses" from a company called Boxabl. These units, more than a hundred of them, covered much of the area that was previously filled by tents, including those for the media and NGOs. It's quite a sight to gaze at the land of Boxabls, which are mostly intended for senior-level civilian lawyers and staff for the eventual trials or perhaps other lengthy hearings. A year earlier, Carol had reported that the Boxabyl units were uninhabitable due to mold and other defects. One of the Boxabl owners told her that they didn't even have a factory to build the homes when the massive Pentagon contract came in. A year later, as the 9/11 case resumed, they remained unused, their fate uncertain.

Like the old MOC, the new one was divided into two rooms with screens for the courtroom feed, though the new one only had desks on one side; the second was a large open space reserved for press briefings or, if no one was around, body-weight exercises and naps. In addition to a sparkling new break room with two refrigerators, the MOC came with four bathrooms with working sinks and flushing toilets; gone, at long last, were the days of trailer bathrooms with nonexistent or dubious air flow. The bathrooms alone constituted an upgrade of immeasurable proportions. I'm not going to say I cried after returning to my hotel room after the first day of working in the new MOC, but it was a momentous turn in our Guantanamo lives. Carol and I assumed the positions we had in the old space: I stayed at a desk in the back row on the far left of the viewing room, she stayed next to

Suppression II—The "Flaming Bag of Crap."

me in the back center, with the back right reserved for Terry McDermott, whenever he showed up.

McDermott was a lock for this hearing. The reboot of the suppression hearing in week two came with a blockbuster witness, retired FBI Special Agent Frank Pellegrino, the star of McDermott's book *The Hunt for KSM*, which he coauthored with Josh Meyer. As recounted in their book, a genuine page-turner, Pellegrino unsuccessfully pursued Mohammed around the world while investigating many pre-9/11 terrorist activities. He was the logical choice for the "clean team" agent to re-interrogate Mohammed after his arrival on Guantanamo Bay from the black sites. The government was calling Pellegrino, as it did the FBI witnesses before him, to testify that the early January 2007 interviews were voluntary, regardless of what the CIA had done to the detainees before, and therefore admissible. The third week was slated for Brian Antol, the former FBI intelligence analyst who worked with Pellegrino for many years and also participated in Mohammed's interviews, which took place over parts of four days in January 2007.

The Pellegrino week also brought Sarah Koenig, the famed *Serial* host and cocreator. The planned season four was titled "Guantanamo," and in fact she and cohost Dana Chivvis had accompanied me and Carol on a July 2022 trip in the USS *Cole* case to get some local color. Their witnessing me nodding off in court that week—and getting reprimanded by one of the new guards—became an embarrassing claim to fame once the season was released nearly two years later. The episode captured an important element of a court reporter's life on Guantanamo: Hostile or overly tense guards in and around the courtroom gallery can make life miserable. Since that guard was replaced, however, the uniformed security personnel—who generally are replaced by a new unit every nine months—have been consistently friendly and laid back. Occasionally, a guard might also provide some useful intel. When we noticed one day that part of the gray, worn carpet in court appeared to be in fitted squares that could be removed, a guard told us it was to clean or replace areas where dogs had urinated during security sweeps.

On the second week of the trip, Koenig was following around Colleen Kelly, my friend and semi-regular fellow traveler from September 11th Families for Peaceful Tomorrows. Kelly would eventually be the subject of her own "Guantanamo" episode that focused on the 9/11 case. Peaceful Tomorrows, which was increasingly sending a new generation of members in their twenties in addition to regulars like Kelly and Terry Rockefeller, was strongly in favor of plea deals. These family members knew that pleas would involve detailed stipulations in which the defendants would have to admit to their crimes, and that the prosecution would put on a lengthy case about the 9/11 plot and its devastating impact at the sentencing trial. This is the type of closure that some family members desperately wanted.

The week was a fun one for hanging out in back of the NGIS, with all of us wondering what remarks Koenig might choose to incorporate in some upcoming episode. But the ratio of lawyers and other staff from the various cases participating in the socializing at NGIS had declined significantly. The defense side of the operation had taken over a long tract of refurbished trailer units near the Naval Exchange called "Bay Hill," soon dubbed MCDO-ville, using the abbreviation for the Military Commissions Defense Organization.

Sadly, McDermott was not going to have beers with Pellegrino at O'Kelly's or the Tiki Bar; more consequentially, Mohammed and his longtime pursuer were not going to be in the same courtroom, which muted the week's drama. Ed Ryan conducted his direct examination of Pellegrino from the Remote Hearing Room in Virginia; Mohammed's lead lawyer, Gary Sowards, conducted his cross-examination through a screen connecting him from Gitmo to the remote witness stand. Antol and many of the upcoming witnesses were also scheduled for the remote court. The 9/11 case was moving in the direction of the USS *Cole* case, in which the remote facility had become a fact of life. Given the unpredictability of Guantanamo travel, not to mention the proceedings themselves, one cannot blame witnesses for forgoing the ridiculous travel regimen, or the government for acquiescing to these preferences. But it made court less court-like.

Even if he had been in court, Pellegrino wouldn't have noticed what I had started processing from week one: How different the defendants looked, in particular KSM, from the last time we saw them in November 2021. I saw a much bigger difference this time than I did after the long pandemic-induced gap. Other than with the orange-bearded Mohammed, the graying of hair and beards had increased, but more noticeable was the slower and more frail movement of the defendants—except for maybe the youngest of the bunch, Walid bin Attash, now in his mid-forties. Mohammed, now fifty-eight, looked like he had shrunk a size. I also saw that he was no longer wearing any battle fatigues over his clothing, which perhaps was a symbolic gesture of his continued willingness to reengage with plea talks. JTF-GTMO seemed to be going along with the positive vibes: Guards no longer escorted the defendants to their seat with light touches to both elbows and wrists. The defendants walked on their own with a guard trailing casually behind with their legal bins and prayer rugs.

Suppression II—The "Flaming Bag of Crap."

Pellegrino was one of the government's most important witnesses. The prosecution had the burden of establishing the voluntariness of the four remaining defendants' statements, an effort based in significant part on establishing the details of the so-called "clean team" interrogations. All of the FBI agents who led these sessions (including bin al Shibh's) had testified, save for Pellegrino and former FBI Special Agent Stephen Gaudin, who interviewed Walid bin Attash. Gaudin was expected to testify at one of the next two sessions.

Pellegrino's testimony was a retread of his colleagues' in core ways: Under direct examination, he portrayed the interviews as friendly and cordial; under cross, he acknowledged the oddities of the sessions, such as having to take notes on CIA laptops and having to write up a separate memo to document any allegations of CIA abuse, so that these details would not be included in the written statements that the government hoped to use as its most critical evidence. But Pellegrino, as expected, was a colorful witness, telling Ryan that by the time he finally sat across from Mohammed he felt like he had been preparing for the interview "my entire life." He recounted how his exchanges with Mohammed were peppered with humorous banter. Pellegrino said he told Mohammed that the Toshiba computer seized during his arrest in Pakistan in March 2003 was nicer than the one he used for the FBI.

"He goes, 'Frank, if you join al Qaeda, I can get you a good computer,'" Pellegrino told Ryan.

Pellegrino also effectively cast the conversations as the product of a genuine give-and-take between him and Mohammed, in which they worked out a plan of talking for about half a day at a time, with breaks. Mohammed declined to meet for interviews for one of the days. After what turned out to be the final session on January 16, Mohammed told the guard force to inform the agents that he was done with the interviews—even though they had hundreds of questions remaining. In the government's view, this was ironclad proof that Mohammed's participation was voluntary.

When questioned by Gary Sowards, Pellegrino said that the CIA briefed him and the other agents prior to the January 2007 sessions that it had used EITs on detainees, but he did not know the full course of Mohammed's abuse—the 183 waterboardings, being hung naked by chains for days at a time, the anal rape, or the threats of murdering his children. Pellegrino seemed genuinely disturbed when hearing about the threat to Mohammed's sons and repeatedly indicated throughout his testimony that he did not support the CIA's approach to interrogations.

Sowards made effective use of a CIA cable in which personnel from a black site reported that they would not have to return Mohammed to enhanced measures because he had resumed cooperating with debriefing sessions in which he openly volunteered information and used "appropriate interludes of humor." Pellegrino acknowledged that parts of the cable were similar to how he described his own exchanges with Mohammed. In fact, the whole goal of the CIA program, Sowards explained to the witness at one point, was to condition detainees into engaging in the type of cordial, open-ended discussions that Pellegrino described as having with Mohammed on Guantanamo Bay.

"Did anyone explain that to you?" Sowards asked.

"No," Pellegrino replied.

Throughout various parts of his cross-examination by defense teams, Pellegrino, who had a law degree from St. John's University in addition to an accounting degree, acknowledged being uncomfortable with aspects of the clean-team sessions. Putting aside the past abuse, FBI agents pretty much always read suspects their *Miranda* rights and provide them lawyers upon request. Not only did Mohammed ask Pellegrino for a lawyer, he had already been charged with a crime: A federal grand jury had indicted him for his alleged planning role in the planting of bombs on commercial planes in the so-called "Manila Air Plot," which never came to fruition. Pellegrino said he discussed his concerns with superiors.

Rita Radostitz, a former lawyer for Mohammed who had months earlier joined the team of his nephew, Ammar al Baluchi, elicited the week's most memorable response when she asked Pellegrino to elaborate on his disapproval of the CIA's RDI program.

"I think the whole thing from the beginning, you know, was a flaming bag of crap that we got stuck with," Pellegrino said.

With that, the witness might have been speaking for just about everybody in the traveling court system.

James Connell, still the lead on al Baluchi's team, decided to travel back to the DC area for the third week to conduct the cross-examination of analyst Brian Antol, operating on the belief that it was better to be in the same room as the witness. But the government's shifting and intensifying classification guidances made the process far more cumbersome. Much of the cross-examinations of both Pellegrino and Antol involved the defense lawyers huddling with Trivett and the other prosecutors about what could be asked in an open session. Some of this happened with Mitchell and the earlier FBI witnesses, but the huddling was becoming a more dominant

Suppression II—The "Flaming Bag of Crap." 323

element of the proceedings—even if it involved evidence that had been previously discussed in open court.

For example, it was a published fact in the unclassified portion of the Senate's report on the RDI program that the CIA had "operational control" of the Camp 7 facility for a period after the detainees arrived, which was a major complicating factor for the government's attenuation argument. But for some reason Sowards's attempts to probe this area with Pellegrino set off the red hockey light, at one point causing a delay of two hours. The subject also stopped the proceedings when Antol testified. This time, McCall decided to recess for the day rather than to wait for guidance. Four times between October 2 and 3 Antol's testimony on cross-examination led to security delays over possible spills, even with all the huddling that preceded the questions. Connell triggered it the fourth time when asking Antol about how he and Pellegrino had to type their notes from the sessions on CIA laptops. There was confusion in both Guantanamo and Virginia as to who requested the interruption, and for what reason; McCall called another open-ended recess to let the parties discuss the matter.

"Does that mean I leave?" Antol, clearly confused, asked from the remote witness box as McCall left the bench in Guantanamo.

"You can if you want to," Connell said, leading to audible laughter arriving in the Guantanamo courtroom from the Virginia feed.

Now that the courtroom had an annex, prosecutors and defense lawyers had to talk with one another in the Guantanamo court and also by headset to Virginia to convey whatever the decision or guidance was. Twenty minutes later, Connell was allowed to ask Antol whether the areas where the FBI wrote up their memoranda on Guantanamo Bay on CIA laptops were "FBI spaces."

"It was not," Antol said.

This was not the most exciting court, and defense attorneys lodged ongoing complaints about the security interruptions, most of which were apparently being demanded by the CIA communicating with the prosecution table via the tablet. McCall acknowledged his own frustrations with the complications posed by classification guidances and the government's use of the national security privilege. At this rate, the suppression hearings would never end—especially if the defense teams successfully litigated for more witnesses not agreed to by the government.

But McCall, it turned out, had a plan. The judge had used the lengthy delay caused by plea negotiations to read the record of the case. This became clear when he discussed intricate details of the past hearings with the lawyers, and also when he ruled on the many objections during the witness examinations. During the final week, he told the court that he might have—or might soon have—what he needed to rule on suppression. Based on the litigation regime inherited from his predecessors, McCall knew he could rule in at least two different ways: By determining whether the CIA's torture program and the FBI's role in it rendered the 2007 confessions inadmissible; or whether the investigative restrictions in Protective Order #4 coupled with the government's use of its classification and national security privileges unfairly hindered the teams in making their case. He ordered the defense teams and the prosecution to submit updated filings on those two areas, taking into account all of the witness testimony and evidence since the suppression hearings began in September 2019. McCall, in a sense, wanted something of final—or close to final—written positions that would enable him to determine if he could rule or needed additional evidence.

On Tuesday of the last week, the parties had fully adopted a role reversal that was incredibly striking to anyone who followed the case—the defense teams supported the push ahead toward a ruling, while the government wanted to hit the brakes. The prosecution team sensed danger in a ruling by McCall, who had sided with the defense on many discovery orders and was openly expressing frustration with the government's strict control of information. In a bold move, Trivett told McCall that he saw "no scenario" in which the judge could rule on suppression before his retirement. He said the government had the burden to establish the voluntariness of the defendants' statements, and that McCall could not cut that process short. This came off as a bit odd, given that the government did not have too many witnesses left of the agreed-upon set. Trivett told McCall, however, that they would want to add witnesses to bolster their positions due to the ruling in the USS *Cole* case, in which Judge Acosta suppressed al Nashiri's 2007 confessions. He told McCall that the judge at least had to wait until the Court of Military Commission Review ruled on the government's appeal in al Nashiri, which would be binding case law in his court.

The defense teams, in sharp contrast, sensed they had a friend in McCall. Even though they still believed they were entitled to a hundred or more witnesses, they told him he had enough to rule on suppression or to fashion some sanction against the government. If the statements remained "unsuppressed," Sowards told McCall, then the defense would need testimony from the covert CIA agents from "within the torture chambers."

The day before, Walter Ruiz had referred to the suppression hearing as "a fool's errand" five times during arguments to McCall. He told McCall that his attempt to resume suppression hearings had only proved how impossible it was—and that Judge Pohl was right in preemptively suppressing the FBI statements back in 2018.

"It's a fool's errand that has consumed time and energy," Ruiz said.

With that line, Ruiz, too, was surely speaking for most of the courtroom.

* * *

The attending journalists were a little surprised at Trivett's transparent admission that the government was hoping to wait McCall out. It could have been interpreted as disrespectful to the robe. Carol and I both wondered if the judge could postpone his retirement. But his apparent leanings provided some hope that a resolution was in sight. In addition, both the defense teams and the prosecution said near the outset of the hearing that plea negotiations could soon resume. They just had to wait for Wood's replacement as convening authority, Susan Escallier, a retired brigadier general who had been a lawyer in the Army for more than three decades, to get up to speed on the various cases. Some defense lawyers believed that a convening authority could agree to the "policy principles" related to the conditions of confinement without seeking approval from more senior-level officials. It would always be a risk, of course, that a potential second Trump administration or new prison commander would not abide by the terms, but presumably the detainees could pursue remedies through their lawyers.

A McCall ruling in favor of the defense on suppression—and a likely government appeal, depending on how the al Nashiri appeal shook out—would maybe induce the parties to finally get something done during the lengthy appellate review. And McCall was not limited to suppressing the FBI statements: He could also remove the death penalty as a sentencing option to sanction the government. Beyond that, McCall had other defense motions to find an "out" as Pohl had five years earlier, including a motion to dismiss the case for "outrageous government conduct" and a growing raft of constitutional challenges to the court and its underlying legislation and rules. The government still claimed that the due-process protections of the Fifth and Sixth Amendments did not apply to Guantanamo's "alien unprivileged enemy belligerents." And the DC Circuit, which sits above the commissions' appellate court, still had not ruled decisively on the issue. In April 2023, the circuit avoided the decision in en banc review of a habeas petition by a Yemeni detainee, Ali Abdulrahman al Hela, whom had been cleared for release but not yet found a transfer country. The majority held, in an opinion criticized as wishy-washy, "We assume without deciding that the Due Process Clause applies," before returning the case to the lower court. Maybe McCall would finally decide the issue was "ripe" in the 9/11 case and rule on the applicability of the Constitution with a decision that the government would have to push through the appellate process, another possibility for a lengthy delay to reach plea agreements.

These were the scenarios playing out in my mind as I sat in the air terminal on Friday the 13th, having gotten a seat on the rotator flight to leave a day early. I wanted to attend Allison's "Open Studios" event in our Brooklyn neighborhood of Sunset Park, in which dozens of artists open their workspaces to the public. Of course, after about twenty minutes, the familiar female voice at the terminal announced that the plane coming to get us had mechanical problems and would not be arriving until the next day. In these situations, a rational traveler (like Carol) might stay on the Leeward-side NGIS to avoid lugging baggage back and forth on the ferry again. But I made the trip back to the Windward side to see a country rock concert in the large stage area across from the Tiki Bar. Rodney Atkins was, after all, one of the bigger shows to come to Guantanamo Bay that overlapped with my time on the base. It was also keeping with my informal policy of doing as many community, or Moral, Welfare, and Recreation, events as possible. After checking back into the hotel and taking a shower, I walked down to the Tiki Bar, ordered a beer, and waited for the show. I eventually noticed the small crowd and empty stage, and asked the bartender what was up.

"The band was on the flight that didn't come," he told me, casually pointing out the idiocy of my decision, which I attributed to heat and exhaustion. I lost about ten pounds of water weight for nothing. The next morning, I got the regular commissions flight out of Gitmo, which itself was predictably delayed. I stayed overnight in DC and made it to Allison's studio for the final "Open Studios" hours on Sunday afternoon. I'd be driving back to DC for the next trip on November 3.

The main event of the brief interlude back home was keeping the important reservation we had made at City Hall in Manhattan that Friday, October 20, at 10:45 a.m.—to get married. Our friend Benjamin served as the witness, and Allison's friend Sena Clara watched by iPhone and took photographs from Northern California. We did a mini-honeymoon in upstate New York, then had a party the following Friday in Brooklyn with mostly local friends (we had celebrated with our families during the summer.) It was true that the court schedule was, to a large extent, dictating these life events, but it was also true that we were not letting the court schedule prevent us from moving forward with our lives together. We eyed a later date for a longer trip.

Connell saw our City Hall wedding picture on Instagram and had a member of the al Baluchi team put it on a cake. He couldn't resist showing me at the terminal on Andrews on the Saturday morning of November 4; I cut into it later that night at the NGO barbeque hosted by the team at the "Bay Hill" CHU trailers. Among many first experiences on Gitmo over the years, I could add being doused by two bottles of champagne while being chewed alive by bugs.

* * *

McCall had a gift for the defense side of the courtroom near the start of the November session as the parties discussed upcoming deadlines: He announced that he was extending his retirement, at least past the middle of 2024, which would allow him to preside over the first two sessions of the next year. Carol and I looked at each other and smiled, smugly: We had called it. Trivett turned in his chair, away from the judge, and lowered one side of his exasperated face to his palm. McCall quickly added that this decision was not a guarantee that he would rule on suppression.

"I am not making any decision on whether this issue is even ripe to address," he said.

That may have been true, but it sounded like McCall was going to be the one to wait out the government—and not the other way around.

McCall seemed meditatively aware that he was unable to quicken the case's pace, as hard as he pushed. Witnesses had complicated schedules, and prosecutors didn't seem to know exactly when everybody was available. They also kept providing the defense teams with discovery relevant to the witnesses either shortly before or even after their testimony—one of those details that might sound shocking to newcomers but had long since become one of the case's many oddball characteristics. This happened with Pellegrino, leading defense attorneys to tell McCall they might need to recall him soon. In the November hearing, in fact, much of the time was taken up by testimony from FBI Special Agent James Fitzgerald and Abigail Perkins, a retired FBI special agent, both of whom had testified twice before—during the first suppression hearing in September 2019 and before that during Mustafa al Hawsawi's jurisdictional hearing in December 2017. I was excited to see David Nevin, long since in the background on the KSM team, examine Perkins. He deftly elicited some of Perkins's own frustrations with the CIA program, which I could still work into a future profile of Nevin. Perkins told Nevin that he and her colleagues had argued to their superiors that they should have access to the detainees at CIA black sites, only to be unwisely rebuffed.

"We were the experts at interviewing in these sorts of circumstances," Perkins said.

Our planned departure on November 18, the Saturday before Thanksgiving, was delayed by a day. That plane, too, had unspecified mechanical issues and did not make it to Guantanamo to pick us up. Once again, the announcement was not made until after we had been waiting in the air terminal for a lengthy period. And, once again, I traveled with most of the court system back to the Windward side. This time, however, I confirmed that the magic show scheduled for that night was still happening—the magician was already on base. After checking back into NGIS and taking a shower, I made my way over to the Windjammer complex and took my seat in the mostly full ballroom to watch the show. Along with many of the two dozen or so children in attendance, I was completely mesmerized. *But how did he do that?* I wondered at various points. It's the little things that get me through these trips.

CHAPTER 28

2024 — Trifurcation.

Allison and I took a proper honeymoon to Grenada in mid-January, which caused me to miss one of the more important court events in recent years: The guilty pleas and sentencings of Mohammed Farik bin Amin and Mohammed Nazir bin Lep, the two Malaysians who, along with Encep Nurjaman or "Hambali," had been charged at the start of the Biden administration with conspiring in terrorist plots in Indonesia. They decided to plead guilty to roles in the 2002 terrorist bombings in Bali, Indonesia, and agreed to testify against Hambali, whose case remained pending in pretrial hearings. The lawyers for bin Amin and bin Lep had orchestrated a resolution to their clients' cases in remarkably quick fashion.

As in Majid Khan's case, the jury of military officers gave a sentence—this time twenty-three years—within an instructed range that was far outside the deal that the defense teams reached the prior year with the convening authority, who at the time was still Jeffrey Wood. The maximum sentence was an additional six years, which was later reduced by about a year due to discovery violations by the government. The State Department could repatriate them prior to the completion of their sentences at Guantanamo Bay. The only reporters covering these events in person were Carol and John Bechtel from *BenarNews*, whom I had met once at Fort Meade when watching the Hambali proceedings remotely. Several relatives of those killed in the Bali bombing had come from Europe to testify, and two older brothers of bin Amin were flown in from Kuala Lumpur to ask the jury for lenience. Bin Amin's lead lawyer, Christine Funk, projected drawings on the courtroom screen that bin Amin had made of his torture by the CIA.

"This is, frankly, un-American," she said.

I was sorry to miss it. Still, I arrived on Guantanamo Bay somewhat refreshed on February 10, 2024, which was a good thing: The year looked daunting. Judge McCall was pushing ahead with this four-week hearing—just the second in the case's long history—and then a first-ever five-week hearing to begin April 15. Virtually all of these days would be taken up by witness testimony related to the suppression motion. Beyond these first two hearings, 2024 had three additional sessions scheduled for four, five, and three weeks, respectively. What a nightmare.

Predictably, tensions flared almost immediately over security interruptions with the first witness, former FBI Special Agent James Fitzsimmons. Fitzsimmons had been scheduled to testify and was on the island in February 2020 before Jim Harrington's departure from the case gutted the last pre-pandemic suppression hearing. Fitzsimmons, who showed up in person again, was a key witness for defense efforts to establish the FBI's early collaboration with the CIA. Fitzsimmons and two CIA officers questioned Ammar al Baluchi and Walid bin Attash in Pakistan after their capture in April 2003 and before their transfer to CIA black sites. Fitzsimmons, we would learn, was also one of the FBI agents later formally detailed to the CIA's RDI program. He debriefed Mustafa al Hawsawi when the CIA held him in its secret black site on Guantanamo Bay in late 2003 to early 2004.

Three defense teams examined Fitzsimmons on his first day of testimony, which came on Wednesday of the first week. Their exchanges set off the hockey light nine times, a record in my time on the case. The first one occurred when Connell used the coded unique functional identifier, or UFI, for one of the CIA officers involved in the Pakistan interrogations. After a fifty-minute break, Trivett told McCall that any use of these UFIs would have to take place in a closed session. McCall had the same perplexed reaction that I had, asking: "Isn't that why we have UFIs, so that we can use UFIs in open court?" The judge had another thought, which he conveyed with a sharper-than-normal edge: "Would it be useful to have equity partners here in the courtroom? Like, I don't want to yell at you, but I sometimes feel like I should yell at somebody."

"You feel free to yell at me," Trivett said, convincingly. "That's my job for the whole United States."

Walter Ruiz had finally had enough in the afternoon, after setting off the light when asking Fitzsimmons about an unclassified document that was only shown to the witness, judge, and lawyers, not to the gallery. He told McCall that proceedings set up to "appease" the government were rendering his team's work ineffective, and yet it all had become "the normal course of things."

"I'm not doing my job," Ruiz said. "I'm simply taking the road that's least traveled, you know, and I can't do that anymore."

McCall said he understood. He said, however, that his role was as the "gatekeeper" of information. He had to follow the government's determinations on what was classified or allowed for discussion in open court.

"There are other remedies, as you're aware," McCall said. "And again, perhaps the commission will have to take those remedies."

This was a fairly clear indication of McCall's thinking on the impact of the restrictions on the defense teams. But Ruiz wasn't satisfied.

"You say there may well come a time where there's a remedy for this," Ruiz said. "I'm going to tell you right now that there may very well come a time where we just stop playing this game. And if we do, we'll face whatever consequences there are."

It would soon emerge that the stop-and-go restrictions on Fitzsimmons's open-court testimony were even more egregious. Ruiz and the others could not question Fitzsimmons in open court about something we would learn later: He had been detailed to the CIA's RDI program and had done his debriefings of al Hawsawi at the agency's black site on Guantanamo. All of that had to take place in a closed session. During Wednesday of the second week, long after Fitzsimmons had left the stand, Trivett told McCall that, in fact, those details had been declassified. He said the government had failed to make those declassifications clear in the guidance provided to the defense teams prior to the testimony. Defense attorneys were outraged that once again the public had been denied important information about the CIA program and the FBI's role in it. Trivett, appearing somewhat sheepish, said he took full responsibility.

"I understand how it happened, but it was unacceptable that it happened," Trivett said.

Fitzsimmons's time on the stand was emblematic of the ongoing suppression hearings in other ways. He was older and, while still sharp, did not always have the clearest recollections, a common issue with recent witness testimony. (Fitzsimmons, who lawyers said was in his late seventies, also wore a hearing aid and had trouble understanding certain questions.) Many tidbits were interesting, including the fact that al Baluchi and other detainees had been cooperating with interrogators in Pakistan, which made their transfer to CIA custody for "enhanced" measures even more unnecessary and tragic from the defense teams' point of view. But lawyers had trouble drawing out these and other details in any coherent fashion due to the stilted nature of the testimony. Most of the interruptions were coming from defense attorneys themselves, self-censoring as they paused their own examinations to check with Trivett or another prosecutor what they could ask. In addition, Fitzsimmons and many of the other witnesses for the hearing would have to spend about as much time in a closed session as they did in open, if not more. Even in open sessions, the attorney-witness exchanges were often rendered opaque because the parties were referring to documents that could not be seen in the gallery.

I concluded at that time that the 9/11 case had become "trifurcated." The parties often talked about bifurcating testimony and arguments between open and closed sessions. But many parts of the open sessions were not truly open, as attorneys asked "yes" or "no" questions about documents I could not see. That's where trifurcation came in. With trifurcation came the realization that, as much as I knew about the 9/11 case—perhaps as much as any member of the public looking in—there was much more I did not know. I was haunted by something James Connell had told me during an interview in September when we were discussing torture evidence: He guessed that he knew maybe 1 percent of what had happened to his client at the black sites. My percentage would be just a small fraction of his.

An example of trifurcation came on Monday of the first week, which McCall set aside for Mustafa al Hawsawi's motion to have the case dismissed for "outrageous government conduct." As with al Hawsawi's jurisdictional challenge in 2017, Ruiz was the first to move forward with this motion, which the other teams had not yet filed. Ruiz told me before court that he felt his team had enough to prevail, using essentially the same set of disturbing facts that drove the suppression cases; he also wanted to give McCall another avenue to sanction the government and possibly speed up resolution to the case.

In court, he told McCall that the CIA's torture program met the US Supreme Court standard for outrageous conduct claims because it included a long pattern of illegal behavior that "shocks the conscience." In laying out the vast "international criminal enterprise" of human trafficking and the "depravity" inflicted on his client, Ruiz walked McCall through dozens of documents that only the judge and the other parties could see on their monitors. Ruiz would refer McCall to a certain line or paragraph of text, then move to the next, using brief unclassified explanations for material we could not see. Even so, at 10:50 a.m., Ruiz's reference to a secret document set off the security light.

I was a little annoyed to realize later, when rereading some of the recent transcripts, that McCall and the parties already had used "trifurcated," and that this term had been used in other cases. They weren't doing it my way, but instead to refer to situations where a defendant might be allowed to attend part of a closed session—so where one half of the bifurcation was split, thus creating three distinct sessions. I concluded, then, that the 9/11 case had more accurately entered "quadrifurcation."

* * *

So much time had passed since his first time on the stand that Dr. James Mitchell had actually forgotten what many people considered to be his most dramatic testimony from January 2020. That was when he recounted telling Khalid Sheikh Mohammed that he would execute one of his sons if Mohammed failed to provide intelligence that would stop another attack in which American children died. "I will cut your son's throat," Mitchell famously said on January 27.

His failure to remember that line surprised me and others watching. My article on that earlier day in court, the aptly titled "CIA Psychologist Threatened to Cut Throat of KSM's Son in Quest to Stop More Attacks," had been nominated for a best news article award by the Society of Professional Journalist's New York Chapter, the Deadline Club. (I lost to a *Bloomberg News* article about the day Trump got COVID.) Under direct examination by Gary Sowards, Mitchell denied making the threat.

"Nice try, though," he shot back, apparently confident it never happened.

Mitchell declined to make the trip to Guantanamo Bay that time. As with Pellegrino, Sowards had to ask his questions through a screen. He presented Mitchell with a transcript from his 2020 testimony about the proposed throat-slitting. Mitchell quickly changed gears, acknowledging that he wanted KSM to "picture" the attack on his child "in his mind."

Mitchell's testimony over nine days in 2020 was all in open court; his return to the case was primarily intended for his closed testimony. However, in the intervening period, some declassifications, new discovery, and revelations from other witnesses created additional areas of questioning suitable for open court. As in his first testimony, Mitchell sought to repeatedly emphasize that the detainees were only put through "enhanced interrogation techniques" for narrow periods, early in their confinement; the rest of the time was spent in debriefing mode, without the EITs, when they were treated much better.

From many interviews over the years, we knew that these claims, which were occasionally echoed by prosecutors, irked defense attorneys to no end. They pointed out that the "standard" techniques or conditions that did not require any approval from higher-ups—such as standing sleep deprivation for up to seventy-two hours (the crossover point at which it became "enhanced") or being chained to the floor for weeks or even months at a time, often while nude, either in total darkness or constant light—were clearly tortuous. Even worse, lawyers said, was the endless nature of the incommunicado detention, the maddening unrelenting contemplation that this was likely how you would spend the rest of your life, completely cut off from family members who would have no idea what happened to you.

Still, in his testimony Mitchell used the condensed periods of EITs to move into important new ground. He said that Mohammed and the other detainees would have undergone a process of "fear extinction" by the time they participated in the January 2007 sessions with the FBI on Guantanamo Bay. The use of EITs was "classical conditioning" to instill "conditioned fear" in the captives, but this would have dissipated in the lengthy debriefing phase in which "operant conditioning" provided improved conditions for cooperative detainees. He said the intermittent threats of sending uncooperative detainees back to the "hard times" would have supported the dissipation of fear because those threats were not acted upon. He compared this dynamic to a parent making repeated threats to take away a teenage child's cell phone but never doing it.

Sowards asked Mitchell why he hadn't mentioned "fear extinction"—a common concept in scientific and academic literature—in January 2020, wondering if he was influenced during his preparation for the testimony by one of the prosecutors, Jeffrey Groharing. The implication was clear: The prosecution was recalibrating after the judge in the al Nashiri case had suppressed that defendant's FBI statements on the grounds that the negative effects of the CIA torture lasted a long time. Fear extinction—which we quickly agreed after court was a great band name—was a good way to refute that conclusion. But Mitchell said this was his initiative, that he decided on its relevance after reflecting upon how lawyers and the general public always failed to understand the point of the RDI program: It was to transition to more conversational debriefings as efficiently as possible.

For me, the highlights of this session came in week three, when we heard from James Hodgson, a longtime investigative agent with the US Army. Hodgson was a self-described "glorified mailman" who had served as the go-between for defense teams and the prospective covert CIA witnesses identified only by UFIs. Initially, when prohibited from independently contacting CIA witnesses, the defense teams had to make their requests for UFI witness interviews through the prosecution team. Later, under the lightly amended terms of Protective Order #4, they were able to send sealed letters delivered by government agents. Testifying from the remote hearing room, Hodgson said he played the lead role in delivering interview requests from the al Hawsawi team to eighty-eight UFI witnesses. At one point, twelve of the witnesses were gathered at an amphitheater in CIA headquarters to receive the al Hawsawi letters and an additional letter from the agency's Office of General Counsel, which explained it was their choice whether to talk to the defense team.

"These people were none too pleased to be there," Hodgson testified.

As a seasoned investigator, Hodgson made no effort to defend the process, other than to say he felt that lawyers from the CIA Office of General Counsel engaged with it in good faith. When questioned by Ruiz, Hodgson said he always prefers to talk to his own witnesses and to visit crime scenes in person. Ruiz asked him if he had ever conducted a "mass mailing" as the foundation of one of his own criminal investigations.

"I have not, sir," Hodgson testified.

Matthew Engle, the still relatively new lead lawyer for Walid bin Attash, was getting some of his first action in court. He had replaced Cheryl Bormann several months after her March 2022 departure but then waited around with everyone else for the Biden administration to decide on the proposed plea deals. Taking questions from Engle, Hodgson testified that he personally would never rely on "a legal adversary" to contact critical witnesses in his own criminal investigations.

"That's no way to conduct an investigation, is it?" Engle asked on Friday morning of the third week.

"No, sir," Hodgson said.

These were new and important details as McCall assessed the impact of the investigative restrictions. He had made it clear that he was considering all manner of limitations imposed on the defense teams—including the increasing use of the national security privilege—but the biggest were still contained in Protective Order #4, which had led Judge Pohl to preemptively suppress the FBI statements and avoid the whole mess that McCall was now dealing with. Hodgson's testimony could be layered on top of other problems identified with the UFI discovery. Earlier in the hearing, another lawyer for bin Attash, Anisha Gupta, had argued to McCall that the defense should be given access to additional UFI witnesses because the pool of prospective witnesses was implausibly low. The government had provided each team with an "RDI Index" to help organize the CIA discovery by listing which UFI witnesses had "direct and substantial contact" with each detainee in each black site. But Gupta told McCall that her team's index contained no listings for about two-thirds of bin Attash's time in CIA custody, which made no sense. She said that CIA cables during these periods revealed that bin Attash was being interrogated and providing information that was being disseminated to the intelligence community.

Both the bin Attash and al Hawsawi teams had only spoken to three UFI witnesses; al Baluchi's had interviewed five; and Sowards wouldn't tell me how many his team had interviewed, keeping with the team's policy of not engaging with the media. It was clear that testimony from even a smaller number of these witnesses—if McCall ever ordered the government to produce them—would be powerful: Gupta told McCall that the UFI witnesses who met with the bin Attash team wept when discussing their roles in the CIA program and described having PTSD symptoms, including nightmares.

Perhaps the biggest moment of the third week came when McCall announced that he was delaying his retirement again—now through the end of the year. Though he continued to push, McCall clearly sensed that the suppression testimony would last the better part of the year, even just to get through the agreed-upon witnesses. Most of that set of twenty-eight were done, but the government had three additional for its case—a longtime FBI analyst on the 9/11 prosecution team, a terrorism expert, and a forensic psychiatrist. There were also health issues that had caused delays in the testimony of Dr. Bruce Jessen, who had only testified for one day in January 2020, and with the first army commander of the Camp 7 facility after the detainees arrived from the black sites.

"That gives us a little bit more white space to get in these other witnesses and, again, allow the government to call the witnesses that they have," McCall said on February 29.

That McCall was really going to wait the government out and rule on suppression—almost no matter what at that point, it seemed—led to an uncharacteristic complaint by Trivett at the start of week four. He said he wanted to voir dire the judge about his shifting retirement plans but wasn't prepared to do it yet. He instead told the judge that the prosecution would be seeking an extension to respond to the defense teams' updated suppression motions, which McCall had ordered late the prior year.

"But we've been crushed," Trivett said. "The last two months have been a crushing Op-Tempo that I don't know has ever been—at least from the prosecution's perspective—ever been this high during the last decade of the litigation."

In my article on week four, I initially had "up-tempo" until Connell read it in the air terminal before our departing flight and informed me that Trivett was clearly using "Op-Tempo," military shorthand for operational tempo. McCall would grant the extension on the filing deadlines, but he told the parties that he was going to continue to push. He said it was the government's decision to hold such a complex case on Guantanamo Bay.

"Talk to your leadership and get more people on your teams, both for the defense or the government, if need be, because we're going to continue at this pace, at least while I'm the judge," McCall said.

Trivett then took the discussion in an odd direction, candidly telling McCall that his team was making strategic decisions based on when the judge was going to retire. He said the government wanted to file a renewed motion for a trial date and other motions, but it was waiting for the judge who was going to preside over the actual trial. He added some urgency: "If this case doesn't go to trial in 2025, it may never go to trial."

I wasn't alone in having trouble following Trivett's reasoning. The government had thus far succeeded in getting the most streamlined version of a suppression case as was possible—at least compared to what the defense teams wanted—and now it was the side calling for additional witnesses. Beyond that, some judge was going to rule on suppression at some point, and in McCall they had a judge who had a full understanding of the record. In any sequence of events that I could play out in my head, getting a new judge to come on the case and rule on suppression would only delay proceedings. Trivett wanted two things that seemed to be completely at odds: McCall to retire before ruling on suppression, and a trial to start faster.

Connell rose to say that his team was willing to keep pushing. He added, however, that five team members had gotten sick during the hearing, which he blamed on the location. This was Connell's first monthlong session on the base; he had spent a week of the prior one between September and October working from the remote hearing room.

"It's just Guantanamo is a toxic, corrosive environment, and people are away from everything that they know," Connell said. "This four weeks marks the longest that I have ever been away from home in any case in any situation since I got married twenty-five years ago."

The government's witness for week four was one of its add-ons, Kimberly Waltz, an FBI supervisory intelligence analyst who had been on the case since the Bush era. Because Waltz watched the so-called "clean team" sessions in January 2007 from a nearby observation room, she was another witness to testify that the interviews were cordial, constructive, and by all appearances voluntary. But the main area of her testimony was in support of the government's efforts to pre-admit intercepted phone calls between some of the defendants in the months before and the month after the 9/11 attacks, in which they allegedly discussed the plot.

Defense lawyers objected on the grounds that the calls had nothing to do with suppression—either with the voluntariness of their clients' statements to the FBI or the negative impact of the investigative restrictions. McCall, however, was going to let the government try to meet its burden of voluntariness however it wanted. Under direct examination by Trivett, Waltz said the government had intercepted 118 calls between the alleged 9/11 coconspirators, twenty-six of which it identified for "affirmative use" at trial. (One of the defendants, Walid bin Attash, was not on any of the calls.) Most of Waltz's direct testimony would have to take place in a closed session, as the means of intercepting the phone calls was a secret and had its own protective order—Protective Order #3, which came before the prohibitions on CIA witnesses in Protective Order #4.

Judge Pohl signed off on #3 in July 2018, restricting any team from referencing the calls or asking questions in ways that could reveal or "conceivably elicit information regarding the classified source or method" associated with them. This was, as Connell argued back then, "Kafkaesque" to say the least. But McCall appeared to be eyeing the stringent terms of the order as another defense-side limitation that the teams could exploit. On the concluding Friday, after two days of direct testimony by Waltz in a classified session, McCall suggested that the defense teams submit their proposed questions to the prosecution team so that it could determine what lawyers could ask during their cross-examinations, which would have to wait until the session starting April 15.

"It creates a very nice record for how the defense is being impaired potentially by Protective Order #3 and especially how potentially vague Protective Order #3 is and overbroad it might be," McCall said.

* * *

Presumably everybody agreed with Connell and Trivett's informal joint stipulation of fact that the second monthlong hearing was both "crushing" and "corrosive." I would throw in the word "isolating," as well. The NGIS area had become less social over the past half year, in large part because most of the defense team members were now living in units at the Bay Hill CHUs. But the more important factor was that the bugs had evolved to a staggering level of power and animosity, with DEET-products having almost no repellant power. I had noticed during the prior November trip that, unlike in years past, good weather—cooler and breezy—had no effect on whether your body would be chewed to bits. Slow-moving mosquitoes did not pose much of a danger, which came instead from no-see-ums that could ravage a limb in seconds. I went to bed both reeking of DEET and incredibly itchy, and woke up bleeding from scratching in the night.

The new year continued a media trend from 2023 in which Carol and I were joined mainly by foreign journalists dropping in for a week at a time—representatives from Spain, Germany, Japan, Poland, Sweden, and Mexico—most of them DC-based US correspondents trying to work in a Gitmo-update piece among all their other responsibilities. We had some fun, including the Friday-night goodbye dinners at the Bayview, but there would have been more late-night socializing in past years. The plurality of journalists were from TV outlets, which was odd given the photo and video restrictions on the base. For years, Flesvig or one of his deputies could approve footage taken around the base or Camp Justice, but this authority ended during the pandemic era. Now Flesvig or his deputy had to set up appointments for the media to have their material inspected at the base headquarters or with a security specialist at Camp Justice's Washington Headquarters Service. And there was still no getting into the detention zone, the best area for B-roll.

By week three of that trip, the group was down to me, Carol, and Terry McDermott, a great cook who used the NGIS kitchen to diversify the maddeningly limited meal options. By week four, it was just me and Carol. My preferred option for killing time had become the bowling alley: a giant, air-conditioned space with a decent food court and large three-sided bar situated between the bowling lanes and the Dave & Buster's–type game room. The seating was plentiful and often mostly empty. This matched the growing vibe of the base, which only grew sleepier in the pandemic and post-pandemic eras. The detention facility was down to about a thousand personnel, less than half of what it was when I started showing up. The Coast Guard also had pulled out of Guantanamo Bay in the summer of 2023, formally ending its post-9/11 mission of patrolling the bay for the detention zone commander and leaving those duties to Navy police who were already on patrol for the base. Aside from isolated settings and events—bingo night at the Windjammer ballroom, the bowling alley on league night, the galley on days with Surf n' Turf, or the Tiki Bar after 10 p.m. on weekend nights—the base felt empty.

Key personalities were also missing from the case. Carol had broken the news prior to the trip that Ed Ryan, the prosecution's most accomplished trial lawyer, was stepping away from the case for personal reasons. His departure reminded me that another stalwart from the Bush era, Robert Swann, had left the case shortly after it resumed during the pandemic. Army Col. George Kraehe, then the interim chief prosecutor, commended Swann in a February 2022 filing that updated McCall on changes in the government's team: "No one in the United States government worked harder, or sacrificed more in the cause of justice in this case, than he did." The same, of course, could be said of Ryan, who was also a great guy and fun to talk to, even if he could never say anything on the record. He was missed immediately.

David Nevin also did not show up for any part of the four-week session, though he was still on the KSM team. Before starting his examination of Dr. Mitchell, Sowards told the witness that Nevin—who conducted the memorable January 2020 examination—was "fighting for justice" in Idaho. I included this line in my article on Mitchell's February testimony. That Nevin would be taking part in a different trial many worlds away during such a key phase of the 9/11 case was hard to process. I emailed him my article after it went live on Lawdragon.com. "I hadn't heard that Gary ratted me out as working on another case," Nevin wrote back, continuing an email correspondence that had started back in March 2015.

But the biggest absence from court were the four remaining defendants. Other than showing up for the first day, as required for a formal reading of their rights advisement, they chose to skip court, though one or two would occasionally travel to the legal complex to meet with team members in the holding cells outside court, where they could also watch a feed of the proceedings. The defendants were avoiding court to protest stricter security protocols at the prison. The commander of JTF-GTMO, Army Col. Matthew Jemmott, had formally passed the reins to his replacement, Army Col. Steven Kane, shortly before the hearing. Though leadership changes at the prison regularly caused hiccups, we had heard that Jemmott had actually been the one to make the changes to the standard operating procedures or "SOPs" in the later part of his tenure. Jemmott had been elevated from leader of the detention group to full JTF commander in June 2023, when the United Nations special rapporteur for counterterrorism and human rights, Fionnuala Ní Aoláin, issued a critical report that concluded Guantanamo detainees were still being held in conditions amounting to

2024—Trifurcation.

"cruel, inhuman, and degrading treatment under international law." In it, she accused the prison staff of arbitrary and inconsistent implementation of the SOPs, and some defense lawyers viewed the new stringent imposition of old SOPs as retaliatory. The Biden administration pushed back, contending that the detainees lived communally, communicated with family members, and had access to quality healthcare.

Lawyers raised concerns about the changes to McCall in mostly veiled terms during the hearing, as many of the security protocols are classified, though more restrictive "movements" of the detainees appeared to be part of the problem. The changes were complicating the teams' ability to adequately meet and prepare for the proceedings, the lawyers said. From my point of view, the biggest implication was on the potential for plea deals. By one analysis, the defendants would need lasting guarantees that their communal living and any improvements in conditions would carry over from one administration to the next. Yet these problems seemed to spring out of nowhere, within the same administration.

On the flight home, I scrolled through the photos approved by the base's public affairs officer, which included those taken during another tour of Radio GTMO. I had no idea how many of these tours I had done, but this was only the second time I pulled a card from the towers of vinyl card catalogs seeking karmic guidance or insight. On March 6, 2024, my random selection was "Hard to Say Goodbye, My Love," by Sheryl Lee Ralph.

CHAPTER 29

Fives Are Wild.

Unbeknownst to me, as I was driving down to DC on April 12, packed for five weeks, Judge McCall issued a notable order in the motion-to-suppress series for Ammar al Baluchi, the first team to file its motion five years earlier. That initial filing was AE628. The pleadings were so voluminous by now that nine letters attached to AE628 in the series, so that AE628AAAAAAAAA was followed by AE628BBBBBBBBB. In his order, officially AE628OOOOOOOOO, McCall said that the tracking had "become unwieldy" and directed that "all future filings in the AE628 series be filed in the newly designated AE942 series."

The order was an apt expression of the madness that had consumed the suppression case. And this was just one of four (with Ramzi bin al Shibh severed from the case) suppression motions in the case's docketing system. The hearings had thus far largely dealt with the thirty or so witnesses agreed to by the al Baluchi team and the prosecution. A good number of witnesses overlapped with the three other defense teams, but they were only willing to forgo their own client-specific witnesses—at least for the time being—so that McCall could rule on suppression prior to leaving the bench.

The order highlighted another data point—the number of motion series was approaching a thousand. I was not alone in the military commissions in hoping that the crossover to four digits would trigger a massive Y2K-type event that would shut down the entire court permanently, and we could all go home to our families.

Connell's team was the only one to send a proposed list of questions for Kimberly Waltz to the prosecution, many but not all of them relating to the intercepted phone calls. This process pushed the case back into Kafkaesque territory. Connell told McCall on the opening Monday morning that the government had fully or partially redacted 175 questions, which meant that the judge himself had not seen—and perhaps would never see—the full set of questions. Connell said he was entirely cut off from probing the "provenance and reliability" of the phone calls, due to both Protective Order #3 and additional classification guidance provided by the government. The parties had to go into a closed session in the afternoon to continue ironing out what lawyers could ask Waltz. According to a partially un-redacted transcript of that closed hearing, Connell raised again his concern that McCall couldn't see what questions he was prevented from asking the witness. The judge responded that the limitation was "another arrow" in Connell's "quiver" to argue either to him or a future judge against the admissibility of the phone-call evidence.

In reading this exchange over questions known to the defense and the prosecution but not the judge, I wondered if the case had moved from quadrifurcation into pentafurcation. When questioning Waltz in open court during the first week, Connell would occasionally turn to McCall to say he "would have asked" a certain prohibited question. As with prior witnesses, the exchanges with Waltz were stilted due to the restrictions and the fact that lawyers had to cite each document's location with the unprecedentedly long record. Connell gave Waltz a preface like this dozens of times: "Ma'am, I'd like to show you MEA-WALTZ-00000001, which is found in the record at AE628 sextuple R (RRRRRR), triple A (AAA), attachment F." Even with all the prep work and huddling, defense lawyers and Waltz set off the security light several times. Occasionally, when declining to answer a question, it wasn't clear to Waltz or any of us watching—except perhaps certain members of the prosecution team—whether the prohibition was due to Protective Order #3, a related guidance, or the national security privilege, or parts of both or all three.

Walter Ruiz earned widespread praise on the defense side of the courtroom by having Waltz compare language from CIA cables to her written analyses of the phone calls. The prosecution initially objected, but McCall allowed Ruiz to go forward, as the public would not see any of the documents, and Waltz would not be asked to discuss the details of their contents. When going through about twenty different examples put forth by Ruiz, Waltz confirmed that certain "terms" or "explanations" from CIA cables generated from interrogations were also used in her analyses and explanations of the phone calls. This was somewhat cryptic to us in the gallery, but

Ruiz's point was clear: Torture-derived evidence, otherwise prohibited in the case, may have infected the phone-call evidence.

But the real whopper from Waltz came when she discussed, with multiple defense teams throughout the week, her role on a government team that reviewed potential criminal cases in 2009. That was when the administration of President Barack Obama sought to determine whether certain Guantanamo detainees should be tried in civilian courts or military commissions. The Obama administration decided to hold the 9/11 case in lower Manhattan federal court and obtained a federal indictment against the five suspects, before political opposition sent the case back to Gitmo. Waltz testified that prosecutors from US attorney offices in New York and Virginia decided that the statements taken on Guantanamo Bay by the FBI in 2007 would not be admissible because the defendants had not been read their *Miranda* rights. Prosecutors would instead rely on other evidence, including the phone calls.

In other words, prosecutors in the federal case were not going to use the evidence that everybody on Guantanamo Bay had been fighting over for five years in the suppression litigation—a fact that could twist the brain in knots. The Office of the Chief Prosecutor still had a policy of not speaking with the media, so we couldn't ask Trivett any questions about it. The biggest one would have been: Why not just dump the January 2007 statements and get on with the case? Trivett's team had the intercepted phone calls; the secret recordings of the defendants from Camp 7; the so-called "Islamic Response" from the first case; statements made by Khalid Sheikh Mohammed and Ramzi bin al Shibh in a highly publicized Al Jazeera interview from 2002; the statements the defendants made to the Combatant Status Review Tribunals in 2007; and lots of financial documents and records showing money transfers and assistance given to the hijackers. It was true that all of these categories of evidence would face challenges to their admissibility, but why spend years and years defending use of the FBI interrogations? If all that other evidence was good enough for a federal case, why wouldn't it be good enough for a military commission where the evidentiary standards were lower?

Among the defense teams, none of this was too surprising. Prosecutions in the military commissions were built on the concept of using FBI interview teams to clean up whatever happened before at CIA black sites—it was a principle the government apparently lacked the mindset or courage to abandon. The point, defense lawyers suspected, was sticking to a system that laundered torture-derived evidence, that it was still possible to do it. That was more important than more swiftly pursuing justice for the 9/11 attacks.

Waltz's testimony also reminded us of how broad the concept of voluntariness was. McCall could weigh years of testimony and millions of pages of documentary evidence about the torture program, along with the elaborate nature of the FBI's previously concealed role in it. Or, he could simply find that the defendants did not voluntarily confess in 2007 because they hadn't been given the rights advisement that is the bedrock of American criminal law.

The last clean-team leader was scheduled to testify in week two. That was former FBI Special Agent Stephen Gaudin, who interrogated Walid bin Attash. But Trivett told McCall on Thursday that Gaudin was too sick, explaining that "he could barely talk last night." He added that the first Camp 7 commander scheduled for week five was also too ill to testify. McCall was frustrated, telling Trivett that the government needed to get more witnesses "in the queue" to avoid losing time, even with plenty of unrelated motions ready for oral argument.

In fact, the prior day, McCall squeezed in his first-ever arguments over defense motions to compel additional witnesses, including one of the key covert CIA officers. Teams for bin Attash and al Baluchi pushed McCall to compel testimony from an officer known only as "SG1." Even with the deficiencies of the RDI indexes cited by defense lawyers, SG1 was regularly listed as having "direct and substantial" contact with the detainees at CIA black sites. If McCall ordered the testimony of a witness the government refused to produce, it could bring the case to another impasse or give McCall another reason to sanction the government.

McCall declined to quickly rule on whether to compel SG1, eventually acceding to the prosecution's preference to wait until the defense teams questioned Dr. Bruce Jessen—to see if SG1 was really necessary or instead "cumulative" to what Jessen and Mitchell had provided. Jessen was also too sick to testify, but prosecutors expected him to be ready for the monthlong hearing set to begin July 15.

* * *

The trip had a few historic events, at least to the few people who cared about these things. One happened when the Office of Military Commissions finally opened its second court, the doors of which are maybe a hundred feet from the first. Carol and I, along with a pair of colleagues from Germany and Spain, took part in history on Tuesday, April 16, by attending a pretrial hearing for Hambali, which meant we missed the start of Waltz's testimony. In fact, at least a few of us wanted to switch to the 9/11 case after getting a taste of the new court, but we were not allowed to make the move. The official policy, as given to us by Flesvig, was that we could only switch courtrooms at lunch or perhaps if one of the two cases was done for the day. The reason was for unspecified security concerns.

Reporters and NGOs are monitored in court by "escorts" with security clearances, who also have to leave with us if we go to the bathroom. Bathroom breaks have occasionally led to all of us either having to leave court at the same time—even if we didn't want to—or having to wait outside court until the last of us finishes up. Still, with the current staffing of escorts, movements between the courtrooms were entirely feasible. Defense lawyers complained about the negative impact on their clients' rights to a public trial, and McCall took their side and ours, though he didn't think there was much he could do about it. During the third week, when the Hadi case had resumed in the second court, the policy changed: Public affairs would now "generally support media movement between the courtroom galleries at any time during the proceeding, subject to availability of seating and escorts." It therefore remained unclear if the chaperone-to-the-toilet bureaucracy would allow reporters on Gitmo to do what they do in courthouses around the country—move between courtrooms.

But the more dramatic event occurred in week two. Confronted with "the white space" created by Gaudin's unavailability, McCall decided to conduct a site visit to Camp Echo 2, the location of the CIA's former black site on Guantanamo Bay and where the FBI interviewed the defendants in January 2007. While only Mustafa al Hawsawi (and Ramzi bin al Shibh, now severed from the case) spent time at the black site, defense attorneys had long claimed that the interrogation huts in Echo 2 were eerily similar to other black sites. Lawyers hoped that the similarities, which the judge could see in classified images of other black sites, would further undercut the government's claims that the January 2007 interrogations were sufficiently attenuated from those during coercive CIA custody.

Carol and I were the only reporters on the island for the second week. We put in a request to Flesvig to accompany the visit, which we knew was a long shot. The detention zone had not had media visitors since 2019. JTF-GTMO policy had barred journalists from entering the area once the prison had decided to relocate the high-value detainees from the secret Camp 7 location to Camp 5, where we used to visit during the earlier tours. The *New*

York Times sent a letter to McCall two days before the visit requesting that Carol and I be allowed to attend or, alternatively, to "accompany the group to and from the Camp and wait outside" Echo 2 during the visit.

The next day, Connell told McCall that allowing the journalists to wait outside Echo 2—which he likened to reporters waiting outside a known location where a grand jury was meeting—was reasonable and supportable. McCall agreed.

"I think the more public we can make any aspect of this proceeding, the better," McCall said.

However, on Friday morning before the visit, Trivett told McCall that the JTF-GTMO policy barring journalists remained intact. Instead, Carol and I—accompanied by Flesvig's deputy, Navy Lieutenant Commander Adam Cole—waited in and around Cole's truck Friday afternoon about a hundred yards from the entrance to the detention zone gate. We watched as the judge and representatives from each of the defense and prosecution teams drove themselves in for the site visit starting at 1:41 p.m. We noted down that McCall entered the detention zone at 1:46 p.m., and he left at 2:18 p.m.

It felt a little silly, but it was fun—like a field trip. Also, it really was historic. As far as anyone knew, this was the first time an American judge had visited a former CIA black site.

* * *

In another historic first, at least for me, I would be spending a week of hearings away from the Guantanamo court, watching remotely before returning in-person for the final two weeks. Allison and I devised a plan in which she would come down to DC, and we would spend the middle week together to avoid five full weeks apart. Being apart for four weeks for the prior hearings had been painfully difficult for us, even with the benefits of hotel life. At some point, Hulu watch parties can only get you so far. The mid-session rendezvous with Allison was fun—and perhaps a model for other lengthy hearings or a trial—but it added to my physical exhaustion, given the two additional weekends of travel on either side of the middle week. The military's hurry-up-and-wait approach to commission travel, which for the media starts before dawn at Andrews—with four or more hours passing before we even get to our seats by the toilets—was enacting a greater toll.

I alternated watching court from Fort Meade and the Pentagon, which has a viewing room near the complex's library. In both locations, I was the only attendee other than a minder. The star witness of the week was the government's second add-on witness, Evan Kohlmann, whom the government has used as a terrorism and al Qaeda expert in prior military commissions and federal court cases. With his thick mop of hair and large head, I saw something of my doppelgänger in Kohlmann. One attendee at the remote hearing room, where Kohlmann testified, did a double take, wondering for a moment how a reporter had made it into the facility, which is off-limits to us.

For me, the week will best be remembered for the release of episode 7, titled "The Forever Reporter," of *Serial*'s "Guantanamo" season. The episode is an excellent exploration of Carol's dedication to covering Guantanamo since January 2002, though some fans of Lawdragon's work felt it may have overly minimized our role in covering Gitmo. I listened to it after court on Friday afternoon on the drive from Fort Meade to the hotel where Allison and I were staying. The episode included the incident from July 2022 when a guard angrily confronted me for nodding off in a hearing in the USS *Cole* case. As Sarah Koenig narrates it, the incident is extremely funny—and I can't deny that it happened. But I had to accept the sad fact that, after nearly a decade of covering Guantanamo, many people would only know me as the guy who fell asleep during court.

My return to Guantanamo on Saturday, May 4, was well-timed, as I was able to make the base's "Derby de Mayo" community event in the Windjammer ballroom. The promotional poster for this event had been so confusing—"$20 to own a horse; Must be 18+ to own a horse; Max 36 horses; Owners must provide their own jockey; $10 wager per horse"—that I viewed my attendance as a journalistic obligation. In the end, it proved to be a fairly pleasant mash-up of Cinco de Mayo and the Kentucky Derby, which was broadcast on a giant screen. Many attendees dressed up in ponchos and sombreros, and the "horses" were the wooden-stick type horses that both adults and kids had decorated. I bought myself a Mint Julep and a beer and watched the "parading" of horses but did not stick around to see the winner, which I assumed would be based on the quality of the horse design and not by people actually racing. Sadly, as I was alone without a public affairs officer present, I could not take any photos.

I was fraying by the end of week four, which featured the testimony of Dr. Charles Morgan, a psychiatrist and consultant for the al Baluchi team. As Alka Pradhan walked the witness through the details of al Baluchi's torture, many of them contained in the oft-referenced CIA Office of Inspector General report on his mistreatment, I wondered how many more times in my life I would have to sit through this depressing material, a feeling I also had when Dr. Mitchell testified again in February. Morgan testified that al Baluchi would have been suffering the effects of PTSD at the time of his FBI interviews on Guantanamo Bay, and that he would not have been able to "meaningfully distinguish" between the FBI agents and his prior CIA interrogators. Morgan, who testified on Guantanamo, ridiculed Dr. Mitchell's "fear extinction" conclusions, which he said ran contrary to decades of scientific research and literature on the profound effects of intense stress and trauma on the functioning of human brains.

In fact, Morgan performed much of this research studying the SERE programs from which Drs. Mitchell and Jessen hailed and which they used as the basis for their development of the CIA's "enhanced interrogation" program. Morgan told Pradhan that the data collected over many studies showed conclusively that the stress of the SERE program led to dramatic impairments of cognition and memory on trainees. He said some SERE participants developed PTSD even though it was only a controlled "taste" of what service members might encounter if captured—a far cry from "the uncontrollable stress" inflicted on al Baluchi and other CIA captives. What made Morgan's testimony even more dramatic is that he worked as a psychiatrist for the CIA on a part-time basis between 2003 and 2010 on various projects within the Office of Medical Services; he was not involved in the RDI program. He recounted running into Mitchell at a CIA location in 2003 and warning him against using SERE techniques on detainees because doing so would produce "false memories."

Morgan also recalled a CIA employee involved in the RDI program expressing concerns to him at his office within the agency several years later. He said the person was "terrified" and sat in his office "and cried."

"'These people are Nazis,'" Morgan testified the employee told him. "'I don't know how to get away from them because I'm afraid of what they will do.'"

Morgan said he provided advice on how the individual could "extricate himself from the program." He said he "never heard from that person again."

McCall filled the fifth week with a replacement for former FBI Special Agent Stephen Gaudin—Robert McFadden, a former naval criminal investigator who also participated in the January 2007 interviews of Walid bin Attash, which were followed up with additional sessions in October 2007 and February 2008. With McFadden's testimony, which he gave from the remote site in Virginia, the government had finally called at least one witness for each of the "clean team" sessions. McFadden said that bin Attash participated voluntarily—controlling when the sessions began and ended—and proudly took ownership of his roles in 9/11 and other plots. McFadden's cross-examination was expected to take place at the July 15–August 15 hearing, along with testimony from Gaudin, whom the government expected to be ready.

Prosecutors also told McCall that they expected the first Camp 7 Army commander to be healthy enough for testimony in the midsummer session. In 2019, the commander testified that he had control of Camp 7, even though the Senate report of the CIA program said that the agency maintained "operational control" of the facility. On Friday morning, the last day of the five-week marathon, James Connell rose to put on the public record that the prosecution had cut off his oral arguments related to that forthcoming testimony during a classified session the day before. He said prohibiting oral arguments in a session that was closed to the public was "a new and radical evolution" of the national security privilege.

"That is the death of the adversarial system," Connell said.

It was another line that would have been dramatic in any other case but barely raised an eyebrow on Guantanamo Bay. Everybody was preoccupied with the next day's flight, praying that the plane would show up.

* * *

The terminal on Saturday was crowded, as participants in both the 9/11 and Hadi cases were on the way out. I was exhausted along with everyone else. The humidity was brutal, transforming a mild hangover into abject misery and what felt like a dangerous electrolyte imbalance. I contemplated the stupidity of returning home with another satchel of notebooks from court that neither I nor anyone else would ever read again. They'd be dumped on top of the dozens and dozens of other notebooks in one of several different boxes in my apartment. If anyone later examined my life from these archives, they'd claim to possess the indecipherable manifesto of a lunatic from another planet, which would at least be in the ballpark of the truth.

The terminal got even more crowded as lawyers and staff from the USS *Cole* case, which was set to resume in a week, entered from the arriving flight. Members from the al Nashiri defense team were amazed that people had made it through a five-week session. I told al Nashiri's lead lawyer, Anthony Natale, what a predecessor on the case told me back in

2017: There could never be a trial on Guantanamo Bay because people would snap.

"Snap?" Natale, who himself was planning on retiring from the case in September, said. "They would be running wild and naked in the streets."

This, I realized, or hoped, was what McCall was doing. He was pushing people to their limits, getting them to embrace the fundamental truth that there could be no trial. Of course, this view was already held by many people, and had been for years. But you could ignore that truth by holding a one- or two-week session every once a while, which had been the case's pattern for most of its long history. McCall had cracked the code by holding what was effectively a massive trial every other month—a schedule that would shatter the court participants' mental and physical will, well before the actual trial was even scheduled. This is what it took. McCall wasn't being cruel; he was actually looking out for everybody.

His plan was a source of hope. In fact, in week three, as I watched from the Pentagon, Trivett told McCall that plea negotiations were continuing. The lead prosecutor made the remarks when arguing against a defense motion to dismiss the case for "unlawful influence" over the opposition to the deal by Sen. Cruz and other elected representatives. Trivett told McCall that he didn't even want to make his argument because he didn't want to draw attention to the negotiations.

As I waited to board, I decided that the most memorable line from my return for the final two weeks—maybe other than the one about Nazis—came on Wednesday, May 8, when McCall was discussing the witness lineup for the next two sessions, scheduled to last four and five painful weeks.

"I have not asked to extend my retirement a third time," McCall told the court. "But I still have not applied for any jobs, and I have a lot of flexibility. And so, if I have to adjust, I can."

He quickly added: "I would rather not."

Those were my sentiments exactly. The day after McCall's threat of sorts—that he might be prepared to wait everyone out, even into 2025—Allison and I celebrated her forty-fifth birthday via Zoom. A week later, we celebrated my fiftieth birthday by Zoom, along with many friends that Allison had invited to the call. Carol had kicked off the day in style with a gift display awaiting me on my desk in the MOC—an inflatable teddy bear cradling a bottle of Jameson. She also got a cake, which we cut with others later at night in the NGIS conference room. I appreciated the effort by Carol, whose research determined that the best cake-maker was the guy who ran the base's Auto Port. I also felt lucky making it to half a century;

many people do not. Still, turning fifty on Guantanamo forced me to confront the fact that my ability to keep covering each session, no matter how long, resulted from my never having been a partner to a pregnancy or having any kids, despite all best efforts.

I had turned fifty during the fifth week of the fiftieth pretrial hearing in the 9/11 case—a case that was still consumed by a motion to suppress that had been filed five years earlier, on my birthday, May 15, 2019, back when I had turned forty-five. Recognizing how unlikely this was, I decided to go back and count just how many trips I had made to Guantanamo Bay since 2015. As it turned out, this trip was my forty-ninth. I counted a few more times, but still hit forty-nine, which was frustrating—fifty would have been perfect. For a moment, I considered telling people that this was my fiftieth trip. Who would know the difference? But truthful journalism is important to me. I believe in accurately reporting what happens on Guantanamo Bay, as best I can. And let's face it, forty-nine was plenty.

CHAPTER 30

End in Sight.

Of course, I would make my fiftieth trip, even as the challenges of the longer trips were becoming more obvious, both for me and my company. I applied for funding from the Pulitzer Center to take some of the burden off Lawdragon. Prior to my departure to DC on July 12 for another monthlong trip, the center agreed to cover much of the travel costs for the remainder of the year. At that point, I was also staring down a five-week trip between mid-September and October and a three-week trip in November. All told, that would be twelve of eighteen weeks on the Naval Base between mid-July and Thanksgiving. Judge McCall was intent on finishing the suppression hearing before retiring, and he was going to make everyone—including, in fairness, himself and his staff—suffer through it.

The anticipated schedule is why I skipped out on June's big event—the two-week sentencing trial of Abd al Hadi al Iraqi, who had earlier reached a plea deal. The Hadi case was my first military commission back in September 2015, and I really wanted to see its conclusion, but I had to leave it to Carol's excellent coverage. The jury of eleven military officers gave Hadi a sentence of thirty years for his work for al Qaeda in Afghanistan, though under the plea deal he would spend an additional eight years in prison. Among the important news of the session was that the jury stayed in the Boxabl homes, which otherwise had remained mostly unused.

This 9/11 hearing should have been a "blockbuster," a term I had started using either ironically or sarcastically knowing full well that few people would care or watch—even though Dr. Bruce Jessen would finally be testifying again, after a few health-imposed delays. Only Carol and I made the trip, though Terry McDermott flew into DC from Los Angeles to watch from the closed-circuit site in Fort Meade. Jessen had testified for less than a full day before the pandemic, on January 31, 2020, at the conclusion of a two-week session that featured Dr. Mitchell's nine-plus days in open court. Jessen had more recently taken the stand in the al Nashiri case, in April 2023, where he famously reenacted some of the less violent enhanced interrogation techniques on Annie Morgan, a defense lawyer whom Jessen ordered into a small confinement box. That all took place in the court's remote hearing room in Virginia, where Jessen would testify from again the week beginning on July 15. Lawyers from all four defense teams questioned him from Guantanamo, however, which once again did not make for the most exciting court, with all the key players staring intently into screens.

As with Morgan, Jessen was mostly a cordial presence on the stand with defense lawyers, as the would-be antagonists had long since adopted a shared, mutually beneficial narrative: that the former CIA contract psychologists were just two figures in a giant interrogation machine, and that they stayed within the approved techniques, unlike "NX2" and his acolytes. With the lawyers for bin Attash, al Baluchi, and al Hawsawi, Jessen testified that he didn't have much knowledge about how their clients were treated, particularly during their periods of enhanced interrogations. Jessen, like Mitchell, told the lawyers that they'd have to talk to the actual witnesses to get this information—another buttress to defense-side claims that any fair suppression hearing would require access to covert CIA officers. Jessen only met with those three defendants during the so-called "maintenance visits" at later black sites when he worked as an "advocate" to hear detainee concerns and facilitate good working relationships with the CIA debriefers. Jessen wasn't as prone to crankiness as his former partner in Mitchell & Jessen Associates, and he gave off a more thoughtful, patient, and grandfatherly vibe, contrived or not. Still, it all felt pretty familiar.

Jessen had more to talk about with Gary Sowards. The witness acknowledged that even the most intense version of SERE training would not come remotely close to the type of abuse inflicted on Mohammed over three weeks—the forcible sodomy, the dozens and dozens of rounds of waterboarding, and intense sleep deprivation, which at one point lasted a staggering full week.

"I know you didn't get to join us this time, but some of us flew down on the flight Saturday," Sowards told Jessen on Tuesday, July 16. "So, if we try to replicate that, it would mean that upon our arrival in Guantanamo, if we stayed awake until next Saturday, that would equal the time Mr. Mohammed was sleep deprived at the time of this report, is that correct?"

Jessen seemed impressed, almost amazed, at the comparison.

"That's a long time, isn't it," Jessen said.

Jessen portrayed Mohammed as unusually resilient during the EITs and also extremely intelligent and charismatic in the lengthy debriefing periods that followed. He described Mohammed as "a prolific thinker and writer and orator" who once wrote a poem for him, unrelated to their interrogation relationship—what Jessen described as "a personal thing." The next day, Sowards followed Morgan's lead and had Jessen reenact a technique—this time walling—on a lawyer from his team, Nicholas McCue, in the remote facility. McCue wore a purple ski mask as a hood, which looked a little silly with his suit and was clearly much different than being naked or wearing just a diaper. The dynamic was nevertheless unsettling, especially as Jessen came within inches of McCue's face.

Some of Jessen's best lines came during the prosecution's cross-examination, which took place during an unusual Thursday-night session. McCall was keeping his foot on the gas for a few reasons, one being his ongoing push to have the parties confront the existential dilemma of their future lives absent a resolution of the case. The other was that Jessen had a long-planned trip starting on the weekend that he really wanted to keep. Jeffrey Groharing began questioning Jessen just before 5:30 p.m. on Thursday and finished a little after 9 p.m. Similar, again, to Mitchell, Jessen explained how he had developed an intense relationship with Mohammed beginning with the torture and continuing through his years of confinement. He recalled that Mohammed was particularly concerned about the status of one of his children. Jessen used his contacts in the CIA to find out what the child's situation was, and he gave the update to Mohammed personally.

"He cried, and I held him," Jessen said. "And, you know, even in the most austere and unpleasant circumstances, humanity can still exist."

In fact, Jessen told Groharing that he didn't like waterboarding Mohammed but felt like it "had to be done."

"It exacts a great toll on the recipient, but also on the people who are doing it, if they have any moral bearing," Jessen explained. "It's a nasty thing."

Jessen said that he himself disliked being waterboarded during SERE training, which he acknowledged was of an intensity "infinitely less" than Mohammed's. But he nevertheless backed up Mitchell's claim that the much lengthier debriefing phase—involving hundreds of cooperative conversations in which waterboarding and other EITs were not used—would have resulted in a process of "fear extinction" for Mohammed and other detainees. Jessen testified that he saw nothing in any of his later interactions with the defendants that suggested they could not make voluntary decisions to speak with law enforcement agents in 2007, after they arrived on Guantanamo Bay from the black sites.

"Is it accurate to say that achieving extinction was a goal of the RDI program?" Groharing asked.

"That's one way to put it, yeah," Jessen said.

Groharing concluded his cross-examination by returning to an issue that Sowards had touched on—that Jessen, as one of the few publicly known participants in the CIA program, had received credible threats against his safety. At one point, Jessen and his daughter and her family, who were living with him at the time, had to leave their home within fifteen minutes and stay away for "a prolonged" period. This testimony was presumably elicited in support of the "Protective Order #4," the prohibition on contacting CIA witnesses that Judge Pohl concluded had unfairly hampered the defense teams' suppression cases.

"Were CIA personnel concerned about detainees or other terrorists seeking retribution for their participation in the RDI program?" Groharing asked.

"I believe so, yes," Jessen said.

* * *

McCall would have more "white space" to fill for the second week. The judge had set aside Monday for a possible ex parte session with the bin Attash team, then he planned on hearing testimony from the next suppression witness, Maria Jocys, a former FBI supervisory special agent who had been detailed to the CIA. But that couldn't happen once Mohammed tested positive for COVID. The entire week was gone, a reminder of how even McCall's best-laid plans were subject to many matters beyond his control.

The third week would begin in a closed session with the testimony of the "First Camp 7 Commander," which was frustrating but would also make for a good story. The witness had testified for the government in open court near the start of the suppression hearing, back on November 1, 2019, when he rebutted the Senate torture report's statement that the CIA had "operational control" of Camp 7 after the detainees arrived in September 2006. McCall's predecessor, Air Force Col. Shane Cohen, had agreed with the defense teams that they should be able to cross-examine the witness in public about his claim—a process that was now impossible due to the government's latest classification guidance. To me, this was an example of the government drawing more attention to a topic it wanted everyone to avoid—the CIA's role in Camp 7. As the former commander returned to the stand for his secret testimony, this time in the remote hearing room, I began working on an article on the long history of this litigation from my hotel room, eventually putting together about a thousand words. But my effort was, as the military says, overtaken by events; I never completed the article.

McCall had called for the open session to resume on Wednesday afternoon, which I attended while Carol hung back to watch from the media center—for a reason that would become clear. I thought the parties had maybe found a carve-out of testimony the commander could give in open court, or that the witness was done and they would now be fighting about any guidance related to Jocys. Instead, I just waited as I watched lots and lots of huddling between the defense teams and the prosecution. A guard soon informed the gallery that court was delayed, so I headed outside to bake in the sun and see if I could find an attorney to talk to. No one approached me. I went back into court to watch more huddling, then was told minutes later that there would be no court at all for the day. I flagged down Matthew Engle, bin Attash's lead attorney, to see if he could enlighten me—off the record, just for planning purposes—on what was happening: Something to do with Maria Jocys, perhaps?

"I'm sorry, I really can't say anything," he said and walked off.

Something very weird was going on, which was confirmed when I got back to the media center with plans to finish off my article on "operational control": Three of the 9/11 defendants were pleading guilty. The al Baluchi team led by Connell was still going to pursue a suppression ruling, at least for the time being, but Mohammed, bin Attash, and al Hawsawi were all pleading guilty to their roles in the September 11 attacks in exchange for the government removing the death penalty as a possible sentence. I popped into Flesvig's office, and he confirmed with a smile that the convening authority, Susan Escallier, had signed the agreements earlier that afternoon. He even had a short press release ready to go, one that did not mention any of the terms—such as the removal of the death penalty. Just like that, seemingly out of nowhere, the case was ending.

I was dumbfounded. The defense and prosecutions teams has been open about plea negotiations continuing, but the timing caught me completely off guard. I texted my wife the news, called Katrina to give her a heads-up, and began working on an article in something of a haze of excitement, delirium, and panic, as I wasn't sure I could get my hands to coordinate with my brain. For this news, coverage of the 9/11 case would not be limited to just a few reporters—there would be dozens upon dozens of articles and news segments. I published my article at 6:43 p.m. on July 31. At nearly the same time, Lester Holt—whom Allison and I try to watch most nights we are together, a ritual we developed during the pandemic—included a brief segment on the deals in *NBC Nightly News*, with reporting by Courtney Kube. Allison took a photo of the segment and sent it to me by text. Suddenly, the world was watching. I was more than happy to have my article drowned out by other coverage, especially by Lester.

We did not learn many details of the deals, but it was clear that the legal teams had concluded that the convening authority did not need approval from senior Biden administration officials on every provision related to conditions of confinement. It seemed that a few of the more controversial aspects of earlier proposed deals—other than removing the death penalty—were not included. For example, Connell told me that al Baluchi was interested in a plea deal but was not able to secure what was most important to him. This was "an official recognition" of his past torture, which could have included the prosecution agreeing to not use al Baluchi's January 2007 statements to the FBI against him during any future sentencing hearing. Above all else, al Baluchi wanted a guarantee for improved healthcare tailored to torture rehabilitation.

The prosecution team sent a letter to victim family members that day informing them that the three defendants had agreed to plead guilty to "all of the charged offenses." The defendants also agreed to answer questions submitted by family members "regarding their roles and reasons for conducting the September 11 attacks," which I knew for some family members was an important component of any conclusion to the case. The letter predicted that the guilty pleas would be entered during the following week—the fourth and final week of the ongoing hearing—or the subsequent hearing, set to begin September 15.

The letter stated that the sentencing trial would not occur before Summer 2025. This sounded like a long way away, but the gap made sense. The 9/11 sentencing would not be a short hearing; it would be a lengthy trial that would take several weeks, maybe a few months. Under commission rules, regardless of what is agreed to by the defendants and the government, a jury of military officers hears the case before returning with their

End in Sight.

recommended sentences. The 9/11 sentencing trial would take place at some point in the summer or fall of 2025. Getting to it would take a lot of work, but the end was in sight.

Carol and I ordered a pizza after publishing our articles and ate it on the patio area on the front of the hotel. I sipped whiskey, still in a state of disbelief. Trivett also seemed somewhat dizzied as he walked by us on the way to his room an hour or so later. He declined whiskey or pizza but told us with a grin that he had just heard coverage of the news on ABC radio while driving back from the court complex. This was really happening. If anyone had any doubt, Trivett made an official pronouncement at the start of court Thursday morning:

"Sir, I rise to announce that the convening authority has reached pretrial agreements in this case with Mr. Khalid Sheikh Mohammed, Mr. Walid bin Attash, and Mr. Mustafa al Hawsawi," he told McCall.

Trivett said that the prosecution and the defense teams were jointly requesting that the documents be filed under seal. He said that Mohammed and bin Attash were prepared to enter their pleas next week, with al Hawsawi expected to follow in September. It was clear now, and I had learned during my reporting, that the parties were close to making this announcement the prior afternoon—which explained all the intense huddling while I watched from the gallery. Now I was back in the gallery, more than a little slaphappy as I processed that, in less than a week, I would be hearing KSM plead guilty to planning 9/11. Terry McDermott had already been approved to travel to Guantanamo Bay, so he was going to be able to get the Saturday flight down. Every other reporter interested in watching the proceedings would have to do so from Fort Meade. As my recent career had proved, half of journalism is just showing up.

McCall wasn't convinced it could happen so quickly. He knew from reading transcripts of other commission cases that the inquiry, or colloquy, he was required to conduct with each defendant would take significant planning to get right. He and his staff would need to read the plea agreements and work with the parties on ironing out any problematic areas, including what legal rights the defendants would be waiving, all of which would require collaboration to get every aspect scripted out for the entry of pleas. McCall said his team would work the weekend to try to make it work; Trivett promised that he and the defense teams would provide joint filings to prepare the judge as best as possible.

"Perfect," McCall responded. "I also understand the reason that the parties would want some alacrity with getting this done."

In a truly anticlimactic move, both Trivett and Connell then told McCall that they were ready to move forward with the next witness, Maria Jocys. The other three teams would now merely observe, as they agreed to waive pending motions as part of the plea agreements. Al Baluchi's suppression case had two witnesses for the next week, but Connell told McCall that the team would agree to postpone any testimony if needed.

"We don't want to do anything to interfere with the pleas," Connell said.

The assumption, as we came to understand it, was that it would be "all hands on deck" to have Mohammed plead guilty before the end of the session. In a sense, no one else really mattered: Once KSM pleaded guilty, the case's final phase was set into motion. It was nevertheless interesting to think how al Baluchi's case might play out. After all, so much of the case over so many years had been devoted to determining the admissibility of confessions given to the FBI following years of torture and incommunicado detention by the CIA. Maybe McCall would rule on this, but only if al Baluchi did not first reach his own plea deal. When Connell inquired about the scope of the plea agreements' sealing, none of the teams objected to the al Baluchi team having access to them. Sowards also offered this tantalizing tidbit: "We think that would probably facilitate disposition globally of the case." I interpreted this as the deals containing terms that might heighten al Baluchi's interest in a deal.

Minutes later, Defne Ozgediz, a civilian lawyer on al Baluchi's team, began questioning former FBI agent Jocys. I know I sat in court and took notes—the topic of CIA-FBI coordination had been endlessly fascinating to me—but I have no memory of doing so. I was distracted by the idea of getting my life back. I knew that the next hearings would not need to be five weeks and three weeks, respectively, with just one defendant remaining. The next year would go from being about 50 percent of my life on Gitmo to maybe 15 percent, depending on when al Baluchi reached a plea deal. The sentencing trial would be long and intense, but I'd be well-rested for it.

My wife, Allison, didn't use the word "alacrity" in her phone conversations with me, but the idea was clearly on her mind. She was happy about the news but not as buoyant as other people associated with the case. Her point was a simple one: KSM hadn't pleaded guilty yet. It wasn't over. There was so much news coverage of the deals that I had trouble assessing the full extent of the opposition. I knew some family members opposed the deals, and that Sen. Mitch McConnell and several other prominent political figures issued highly critical statements. Sen. J. D. Vance, by then Trump's running mate, criticized the new Democratic nominee, Vice President Kamala Harris, and President Biden at a campaign event in Arizona, calling the agreements a "sweetheart deal." Sen. Tom Cotton introduced legislation, the "Justice for 9/11 Act," which would purport to require a trial in the 9/11 case and keep the death penalty as a sentencing option.

The main opposition was that the planners of 9/11 deserved the death penalty. Sen. Cotton was clearly disingenuous in his public statement claiming that they might "go free," but taking death off the table was understandably a difficult step for many to accept. Others wanted a full trial on the belief that the public would learn more about the 9/11 conspiracy. Family members were still pursuing civil claims against entities with alleged culpability in the attacks, the most high-profile being the case in New York federal court against the Kingdom of Saudi Arabia. Of course, many critics, whether expressing genuine concerns about the ramifications of plea deals or merely scoring political points, probably did not understand just how difficult getting to a trial had become—with still no trial date on the calendar after more than twelve years of litigation. Some of the family members who had been traveling to Guantanamo Bay and following the proceedings were exceptions, and some of them still wanted a trial.

On Friday morning, Trivett told McCall the government and the defense teams now believed that all three guilty pleas could take place the next week—out of a shared "desire" by both sides of the courtroom to have the guilty pleas done before leaving.

"You know, we want to ensure that we insulate the proceedings from any unlawful influence," Trivett said. "There's obviously a lot of attention on this right now, and we do think that the faster that the pleas are entered, the better we're able to insulate the commission from that."

Ruiz rose to say that, when it came to unlawful influence, the ship had effectively sailed with the signing of the deals by Escallier. He noted that the teams had already begun "specific performance" under the agreements by not examining the latest witness and by continuing to not participate in the case.

"So in terms of that aspect, we're confident that if something were to be pulled back, Mr. al Hawsawi would be entitled to the benefit of the bargain, at least from a legal standpoint," Ruiz said.

"Sure," McCall said with a nod.

The day was over quickly. Ozgediz finished her examination of Jocys before 11:30. It must have been interesting: Significant portions of the public transcript would be completely blacked out. But I don't recall watching it.

Carol and I planned to have dinner with Ozgediz and another of al Baluchi's civilian lawyers, Rita Radostitz, at the Bayview Friday night. The only people from the case we could hang out with on this day were members from the al Baluchi team; anyone involved in the deals wouldn't want to be seen with us, even if they trusted us to not hound them for information. Carol and I normally walk to the restaurant together, but she texted me to go ahead without her. Ozgediz, Radostitz, and I were seated at a four-person table by the window overlooking the bay. A few tables away from us, the large Mohammed defense team was finishing up its traditional Friday-night dinner, and several members came over to chat with us before heading out. Everybody was in great spirits.

I ordered a Manhattan, and we began to talk about the "what's next" in our lives. Al Baluchi was still litigating suppression, but the case had made a clear and decisive turn toward its conclusion. Carol texted me for us to go ahead and order, and eventually our food and my second Manhattan arrived while she was still at the hotel. I assumed she was working on a story, I just didn't know how big. A few minutes later, she called me.

"Secretary Austin revoked the plea deals," she said.

"No fucking way," I responded.

Carol told me that she had gotten the tip a few hours earlier and had just published a story on the *New York Times* website. I looked around and saw that the restaurant was now empty except for a table maybe thirty feet away. I put the phone on speaker and placed it in the center of the table to let her explain it herself.

"No!" Radostitz gasped.

I finished my Manhattan and stood up, asking Radostitz to cover my portion of the bill, for which I later Venmo'd her. On the walk back to my room I talked first to Allison and then to Katrina, both of whom had just heard the news. Less than forty minutes later we published what I thought was a solid first take that we would add to over the weekend: "In Shock Move, Defense Secretary Kills 9/11 Plea Deals." My wife's skepticism had been proven justified. Perhaps I had been naive, or a fool, not to worry about the timing of the plea agreements, but the mostly Republican opposition to the deals did not seem that intense to me, more like the normal bluster that would eventually be lost in America's even-shorter-than-normal attention span. On the other hand, it was an election season where the outcome would likely be decided by a razor-thin margin. As little as most people cared about Guantanamo, publicity over the deals could conceivably help Trump at the margins by portraying the

Democrats as soft on terror, all while the war in Gaza was raging. Maybe Austin didn't want to be blamed for anything that could help Trump return to the White House.

Of course, if that is why Austin did what he did, it would constitute "unlawful influence," which could lead to dismissal of the case or another serious sanction. In his short memo to Escallier on Friday evening, Austin only said that he was taking responsibility for approving plea deals in the 9/11 case "in light of the significance of the decision," and that he was doing so as the designated "superior convening authority" under the Military Commissions Act of 2009. He was not removing her as convening authority of the military commissions or the 9/11 case; he was only withdrawing her ability to enter into plea agreements for the case. He then concluded the memo by stating that he was withdrawing from the three agreements, "Effective immediately."

Austin briefly elaborated on his thinking when taking questions from reporters at an event in Annapolis, Maryland, the following Tuesday, saying: "What I have long believed is that the families of the victims, our service members, and the American public deserve the opportunity to see the military commissions trial." The sentiment, if genuine, meant that he probably had not been educated about the fraught course of the 9/11 case and the prospects of actually having a guilt-or-innocence trial. By then, Carol had already published a postmortem—"How the 9/11 Plea Deal Came Undone"—which explained that Austin had been caught off guard by the agreements when traveling in Southeast Asia. He withdrew from the agreements without having read them. In my reporting, lawyers told me that the secretary of defense was indeed the superior convening authority under the law, and that he could legally assume an oversight and dispensation role for any military commission. But they expressed doubt that he could do so at this late stage, after appointing a convening authority and after that person had signed plea agreements.

Connell also told me that his team had found no precedent for a superior convening authority taking on one responsibility—such as reaching plea deals—while leaving the rest of the oversight responsibilities to a subordinate convening authority. The al Baluchi team had taken the lead on the most recent prior round of unlawful influence allegations, which followed the Biden administration's decision in 2023 to not endorse the "policy principles" from the earlier negotiations. In fact, that motion to have the case dismissed for unlawful congressional interference was still pending before McCall. Now the teams would have additional claims.

Court did not resume until Wednesday, a delay that gave the defense teams additional time to meet with their clients about the unlikely turn of events. Near the start of court, McCall told the parties that he knew any new unlawful influence claims could involve fights over what evidence the defense would have access to. He asked the teams to give him a status update in the weeks ahead so he could set deadlines for the litigation schedule. Getting to the bottom of Austin's decision, and whether that constituted unlawful influence, was going to take a long time, almost certainly well into 2025.

But the Mohammed team had filed a simpler motion the day before, one that urged McCall to move forward with the guilty pleas. Sowards told McCall on Wednesday that the issue of unlawful influence, while "very, very prominent and substantial," was not necessary to resolve any dispute over the deals. He said it was a straightforward matter of basic contract law and a reading of the section of the Rules for Military Commissions that deals with withdrawals from plea agreements. The rules state that a convening authority can only withdraw from a pretrial agreement if a defendant has not yet started to fulfill its terms, or if there appeared to be disagreements over provisions, among some other factors—none of which applied to this situation. Echoing Ruiz's point from Friday, Sowards told McCall that Mohammed had already begun his required performance under the agreement, which in addition to not participating in the pending motions included signing the stipulation of fact admitting to his crimes. Sowards said that Austin had no lawful basis for withdrawing from the contracts, which therefore remained enforceable.

Otherwise, Sowards said, Austin had effectively doomed the case to years of additional pretrial litigation without any end in sight. At the sentencing trial, he added, the government would "have carte blanche to introduce all the evidence they have"—including the long-disputed FBI confessions—and the defendants had to give information to victim family members, who had already begun sending questions. Now Austin had jeopardized all of that.

"He intervened in this most unusual way and threatens total chaos from this point forward because he thought he was ensuring a trial is tragically just the opposite of what he was trying to achieve," Sowards said. He told McCall that he could hear the entry of pleas by the end of the week if he ordered expedited briefing of the matter to conclude within twenty-four hours. Sowards said his team was prepared to extend the hearing if needed.

"We're prepared to remain on the island—to not leave—until we can resolve this very important issue," Sowards said.

Trivett was clearly in an awkward position. He had labored for more than two years as the government's lead prosecutor to reach the plea agreements. Defense attorneys had repeatedly praised his work on the deals both in court and in talks with the media. Trivett's team represented the United States, however, and as far as he knew the government's position was what Austin said in his August 2 memo to Escallier.

"We do not have our position fully articulated and coordinated throughout the US government on this," Trivett said. "We shouldn't be expected to only a couple of days after the fact."

McCall sided with Trivett, saying he did not want to make a "rash" decision. He instead would allow the normal briefing cycle on whether plea agreements should be enforced. While the unlawful influence claims would take longer, McCall said he could hear arguments on the legality of Austin's move at the next hearing.

In another anticlimactic move, McCall, ever the calm steward of this mess, asked for the next witness in the suppression case, former naval investigative agent Robert McFadden. The proceedings would now be even more dismembered going forward. Connell had some questions for McFadden, but the government had called him as a witness against bin Attash because McFadden had taken bin Attash's "clean team" statements in early 2007 and after. He was a stand-in witness for his partner in the interrogations, former FBI Special Agent Stephen Gaudin—who remained unavailable for health reasons, a status that was now not expected to change. But Engle's team would not be cross-examining McFadden about his interrogations of bin Attash. All three teams with plea deals believed that the agreements remained valid, and they were not going to do anything that might appear to violate them.

Understanding their position, McCall did not order them to participate. He said that, going forward, each team would have to have one attorney either in court or in the remote facility to observe the proceedings. Now, however, if the judge ever decided that the three teams needed to rejoin the litigation—if Austin was found to have acted lawfully in killing the deals—lawyers for those defendants would be entitled to recall certain witnesses. The end to the 9/11 case was evaporating, which McCall seemed to acknowledge the next day when he said he could always delay his retirement a third time.

"I still have not applied for any jobs," McCall said.

The day before we departed, I ran into William Montross on the hotel's front patio. Montross was a longtime member of the bin Attash team, an important part of the connecting thread from the days of Cheryl Bormann to the current Engle era. Because the bin Attash team did not speak on the record about the case, I normally talked to Montross—a serious Yankees fan—about baseball or other general life topics, but on that occasion I had to tell him about a dream I had the night before. In it, Montross had two young sons, maybe late elementary- or middle-school age, and I ran into them on a subway ride home. Montross told me that he and his kids were going to have dinner at a gourmet pizza place near my stop, and he suggested that I join them. I told him I had plans but that he should come up to my loft to get a bottle of red wine, as I knew the pizza place had a bring-your-own-booze policy.

He and his sons came up to my loft, which was a giant, endlessly sprawling place with couches, tables, painting canvases, and other assorted items spread around haphazardly. I got him a bottle of wine, and we all proceeded to get on the elevator to leave. Right around this part of the dream—and it was fuzzy in my memory—I realized that the elevator to my loft was a dumbwaiter, a tiny freight elevator, and I was trapped in it, crunched. But then suddenly I was on the bottom floor, and I looked up and saw that Montross was in the dumbwaiter; he was the one stuck. I said, perhaps to his kids, "Oh no, now William is stuck." Then I woke up.

Montross laughed heartily.

"That doesn't even need interpretation," he said.

The one highlight from the final week was the reappearance of David Nevin, who decided to make the trip after Mohammed reached his plea deal. Nevin, who had represented KSM since 2008, wasn't going to miss the historic event, and he was already in DC from Boise by the time of Austin's reversal. Nevin hadn't been to a hearing since the prior November. We vowed to catch up a few different times during the week and finally did so while waiting for the Saturday-morning ferry to take us to the other side for the flight. He was carrying a guitar with him, packed in its case, which had been on the island for many years. Now he was taking it back for his grandson. That would be another great detail for the profile.

CHAPTER 31

Ghost Town.

My wife and I did about as much late-summer city activity as we could between my return to Brooklyn and the next drive to DC on Friday, September 13, for another Saturday flight to Gitmo—this time for five long weeks. On the drive down, I thought back to the Sunday after the Friday-night plea-deal reversal by Austin, when I decided to go to the brunch buffet at the Bayview. This is a popular weekend activity among base residents and visitors that I typically avoid, unless I can't resist the pull of having as much bacon as I want—eight, ten, fifteen, even forty pieces, they won't stop you. I was able to get one of the tables with the prime view of the bay, and in fact sat at the same table and the same seat as Friday evening.

Sitting there, I replayed the events in my head. I well understood the desire of many people, most notably victim family members and survivors, to see a trial and to hear a sentence of death for those accused of planning 9/11. The United States, after all, still had the death penalty—and if any case deserved to be capital, you'd think this would be it. I knew that Austin's move was celebrated by a bunch of people I had met over the years. But I had to acknowledge the genuine excitement I felt at the prospect of the case coming to an end. I wished Carol hadn't called with the news, that we could get back to the place before she did. The feeling reminded me of the fall of 1986, when I was in sixth grade, when my brother and I recorded each Red Sox playoff game by VHS. For months, I would watch the last inning of Game 6 against the Mets to see if something different would happen. As I ate my bacon, I accepted the sad truth that most important things in life are out of your control.

Then it hit me: "Where the hell is everybody?" I was the only customer. The entire indoor and outdoor areas were completely empty. True, it was a bit late: Brunch lasts from 10 a.m. to 2 p.m., and I showed up at 1:20 p.m. But it still felt unlikely that I would be the only person here; surely, another table would be finishing dessert or at least paying their bill. The waitress who refilled my coffee assured me that there had been people there earlier, that the spread in the adjoining room that could feed hundreds of people had been visited by others. The eerie feeling nevertheless confirmed something that Carol and I had been discussing for several months: Guantanamo Bay had become a ghost town. It just felt more and more empty. On my very first trip there back in September 2015, I felt that the Jamaican and Filipino workers were the biggest demographic; that feeling was greatly amplified by now. Over nine years, the total base population had dropped from more than six thousand to what we suspected was closer to four thousand, but it felt like it had been cut in half. Even the cats outside NGIS had stopped providing company, a development likely spurred by the efforts of "Operation Git-Meow."

The long trips had become isolating and maddening. I used to think that all the downtime with the proceedings—the classified court sessions, the delayed witnesses, the positive COVID tests—helped by reducing the court-imposed exhaustion of sitting and taking notes for several hours at a time. But trying to live a normal 9-to-5 life on the base is a challenge, even if I always have plenty of other work for my job. There just isn't enough to do, a point driven home by our reliance on drivers, the intense heat and bugs, and the occasional tropical rainstorm. It's a lot of time indoors, a lot of time in the hotel room, a lot of time eating the same meals in the same places; it's a lot of time feeling stir crazy, a lot of time feeling like I have too much time on my hands but can never seem to get enough done.

Maybe it's just getting older, but the humidity started wearing me down more than in years past. One thing I didn't recall noticing during the pre-pandemic days of living in Camp Justice were the rotating flags—from white to black, with yellow and red in between—set high above the intersection of Sherman Avenue and Kittery Beach Road by the athletic complex. White signified that outdoor activity was safe, and black meant it was very dangerous. I found it depressing how often a black flag was put up, an oddly prominent display on a US naval base of what is also an ISIS symbol. I tried to take heart in how the base was putting this misery to good use through the solar panels that had been proliferating on the base—and presumably operating better than the still-static wind turbines looking down on us.

I had begun incorporating a few new activities, including the occasional weekday evening at the base's recreational pool, followed by a short walk to either O'Kelly's or the bowling alley bar. But those things got old fast. I realized with some concern that I had started finding "joy," or something close to it, in oddities like the intermittently recurring "club soda crisis," induced by inadequate ordering for the barge shipments, because it allowed me to take a daily walk to the Naval Exchange to see if club soda had arrived. I might even ask one of the warehouse guys what the deal was with the club soda. I also could get a van ride to the convenience store on Marine Hill to check there. That was my reporting work.

The September trip marked a full year since this phase of the 9/11 case started—a year since the earlier round of plea talks failed and McCall resumed the suppression hearings with a monthlong bang, first by severing Ramzi bin al Shibh from the case and then resuming testimony in the form of former FBI Special Agent Frank Pellegrino. A year where I spent basically half of my life on Guantanamo Bay, after several years in which I would only spend a week or two there every six weeks or so. How quaint that seemed now: A one-week hearing. When I checked into the NGIS on Saturday afternoon, September 14, there was a feeling of misery but also normalcy, like I was at home. That was the problem of having Brooklyn and Gitmo life split close to 50-50, an endless tug-of-war between which side was the normal side. As much as Allison and I did in my month away, I always had one foot on the island; at times, in fact, the crowds of city life felt stranger to me than the isolation and boredom of Gitmo. As Jeffrey Groharing, one of the prosecutors, might have suggested, I was becoming less "tethered to reality," and I worried that the long Gitmo trips were rotting my brain from the inside out.

To make matters worse, McCall showed little interest in hearing arguments on the disputed plea deals once court started. By the start of the session, the defense teams and prosecution had submitted most of their competing briefings on whether Austin had the authority to legally withdraw from the agreements. The defense teams presented relatively straightforward "read the rules" and "basic contract law" cases similar to Sowards's oral arguments from the prior month. The filings by the prosecution team predictably contended that Austin had broad authority to act as he did, given his statutory role as "superior convening authority" of the commissions. The brief by the bin Attash team contained a reference to *Bleak House* by Charles Dickens, arguing that Escallier—the lawfully appointed subordinated convening authority—had appropriately decided that plea deals were the best way "to resolving this real-life *Jarndyce v. Jarndyce.*" The *Jarndyce* case is the fictional dispute over conflicting wills that runs through the book. In March 2019, I gave a talk at a "Dean's Roundtable" event at my alma mater, NYU's Gallatin School of Individualized Study. The dean of Gallatin at the time, Susanne Wofford, said that my explanation of the case reminded her of *Bleak House*, which I had not read. After the editor at Skyhorse who acquired this book said the same thing after reading an early draft, I decided I had better start reading the Dickens epic.

But the briefing cycle on the plea-deals dispute was not yet complete, as some late pleadings were filed to which one side or the other could respond or reply. McCall, instead, turned his attention to the final suppression witnesses for al Baluchi, which absent the case's other developments would have been significant news—the completion of witness testimony for a hearing that began five years prior. This included the psychiatrist who treated the defendants on Guantanamo Bay in late 2006 and early 2007, after their arrival from the CIA black sites. During the prior session, she had given her direct testimony for the government under the alternating pseudonyms "Dr. 1" or "WK5I." In her view, al Baluchi suffered anxiety, panic attacks, and depressive symptoms but did not have PTSD; she also noted that he had not reported any problems with his FBI interviews in January 2007. She said that al Baluchi was into self-help and that he particularly liked the book *Mind Over Mood: Change How You Feel by Changing the Way You Think*. The witness had given him a copy of the book after he told her that he had found it helpful during his time in CIA custody. During her cross-examination, Defne Ozgediz told WK5I that al Baluchi still had the same copy of the book from about seventeen years earlier. The witness smiled.

"It's encouraging that he still has it," she said.

The rest of the first week and the start of the second week were taken up by competing expert testimony on whether al Baluchi suffered a traumatic brain injury, or TBI, from his intense bouts of walling. The defense witness, Dr. David Hanrahan, a retired navy doctor who had evaluated thousands of American service members for brain injuries, diagnosed al Baluchi with TBI, post-concussion syndrome, and PTSD after interviewing him in October 2018. The government called a neuropsychologist, Dr. Thomas Guilmette, to rebut this position. Guilmette never met with al Baluchi but testified that he could not be diagnosed with a TBI because there was no contemporaneous medical report that documented him suffering a loss or alteration of consciousness during the walling. Al Baluchi himself told Hanrahan he had passed out during the walling and later woke up naked and chained in his cell, but Guilmette did not see any evidence of that happening in the CIA's medical reporting. These were narrow points, but the testimony was interesting. Hanrahan gave perhaps the most memorable line when explaining why, as a navy doctor, he'd agreed to evaluate al Baluchi, whom he referred to as "a 9/11 terrorist" and "the enemy." Hanrahan told Connell that he was guided by the philosophy of one of his mentors, who had served during World War II.

"Treat first, then execute," Hanrahan said from the remote facility.

The line dangled for a bit, and Hanrahan—who seemed like a nice guy—succeeded in casting a cold chill in the Guantanamo courtroom from about 1,200 miles away.

But the real star witness was Dr. Michael Welner, the forensic psychiatrist who was batting cleanup for the government and serving as its final rebuttal witness to defense contentions that their clients' confessions to the FBI on Guantanamo Bay could not have been voluntary. Like the other three witnesses, Welner, who had testified in person on Gitmo for al Nashiri's suppression hearing the prior year, would participate from the remote facility. His testimony would mark the end of the government's case and allow for oral arguments on admissibility of the January 2007 statements during the November hearing. Even though he had been watching most of the proceedings from the remote courtroom, Welner wasn't available for week two, which meant that court concluded before noon on Tuesday, after Guilmette left the stand. Welner also wasn't available for week three and instead was scheduled to take the stand in week four. The five-week trip was already starting to fizzle.

But we had Gitmo work to fill the end of the second week, as Carol and I broke important news related to the plea deals. The tip came in a late-night meeting with a source away from Camp Justice, and it took two full days of reporting to iron it out: The plea agreements contained "a poison pill" that rendered the case noncapital if the government withdrew from the deals without proper cause. As one source explained to us: "The death penalty is off the table no matter what." We reported that the agreements for Mohammed and al Hawsawi contained this penalty provision; the deal with bin Attash did not. We later learned, however, that bin Attash's deal contained a provision that removed the death penalty in the event of a "breach" of the agreement, which would allow his legal team to present a similar argument.

This was huge. McCall could always rule that Austin acted unlawfully, that he had no right to withdraw from the agreements. But even if he decided that Austin's move was valid, the death penalty would be removed from the case going forward. Lawyers familiar with the agreements told us that the penalty provision was straightforward and basically impossible for the government to maneuver around. It was included in the agreements out of a fear that a future Trump administration would try to kill the deals, but it would clearly apply to the current situation, as well. Perhaps the biggest cause of opposition to the plea deals—that KSM could not be sentenced to death—was now firmly entrenched in the case. Presumably, this would contribute to everybody seeing the wisdom of just going ahead with the plea agreements. Then again, maybe not: Austin had said in August that he wanted a trial; he never specified a death penalty trial.

The satisfaction of getting our stories published by about 4:30 p.m. on Friday, September 27, was heightened by getting a week away from Gitmo, as McCall had decided to cancel the third week. For me, going home for week three was not an obvious decision, despite my interest in remaining tethered to reality. It would involve the travel back to Andrews, a drive to Brooklyn on Sunday followed by a drive back to DC five days later, with then another trip starting out of Andrews at 5:45 a.m. on the next Saturday. It would be doubling my Gitmo travel for the session, with four weekends of the exhausting muscle movement instead of just two at the front and back ends. Allison and I agreed that if the Saturday flight back was delayed until Sunday, I would just stay at Gitmo for the week and avoid the hassle.

Luckily, the Saturday afternoon flight was on time, even a little early. Most people on the case stayed on the island, which made the flight on Global Crossing—a relatively new contractor for commissions flights—mostly empty, with about thirty travelers. About twenty minutes into our flight, a crew member announced that the plane had a problem with its cabin pressurization system. We had to descend to ten thousand feet and make an emergency diversion. The plane landed at Miami International Airport at just about 5 p.m. The pilot told us that they would take "five minutes" to determine if someone could fix the problem; if not, a new plane was waiting for us at the next gate.

One of the odd things we'd learned about Global Crossing from the past few flights was that their planes had intense "misting" systems—before taking off and after landing, a white smoky mist would billow out of the sides of the length of the plane. The mist was particularly dense as we sat on the tarmac, cutting off visibility after four or five feet, and we all began taking pictures of it. It was disconcerting, both looking and smelling a little funny, but the "learned helplessness" of Gitmo travel prevented anyone from asking any questions—even as we waited for close to two hours instead of five minutes. Just before 7 p.m. they finally let us off at a concourse that seemed to be a mostly empty area for random charter and international flights. We waited in the seating area and could see our new plane at the gate, but they weren't letting us on it. A customs official was talking to the crew, and a representative from Global Crossing showed up. They apparently didn't know what to do with an "international flight" that was not really international. The staff at Andrews were used to us; Miami International Airport was not prepared.

Someone eventually made the decision that we had to go through customs, and a Customs and Border Protection (CBP) agent led us on a long walk—maybe three-quarters of a mile or so—to get there. They created a few dedicated lines for us, but it took a good forty-five minutes to bypass the waiting masses and eventually arrive at an area where they had dumped our bags. A Global Crossing agent led us on another long walk that ended with us at their ticketing desk, but they had never ticketed a flight like this before, so that took close to an hour. Then we had to go through the TSA screening again before walking back to the gate at which we started. We began boarding at around 10:40 p.m. for an 11 p.m. flight, which meant we had spent six hours going in a giant circle. At this point in my life, I didn't need another metaphor for the 9/11 case, but there it was, kicking dirt in my face. I got to Jeff and Kristin's at around 2 a.m.

* * *

One of my new weekend activities on Guantanamo was taking a three-mile midmorning walk from the hotel to Glass Beach, a journey that takes you through most of town by way of Sherman Avenue. The heat index is well into the hundreds by this time of the day. Consistent with Gitmo's small-town charm, several cars will pull over and ask me if I want a ride to wherever I'm going. I decline, preferring to work up a real sweat before jumping in the water and then making my way into the shaded park overlooking ferry landing. I arrived at this peaceful spot during the second weekend of the September–October trip, finding shade under a canopy at one of the park's grilling areas. At around 12:15 p.m., I saw a disturbance in the water—a ripple or tight cord-like wave that extended horizontally hundreds of feet in both directions. It appeared to move closer, slowly, in a long line parallel toward the shore, before disappearing. Knowing nothing about the ocean, and perhaps influenced by a touch of heatstroke,

I concluded that some alien vessel was now likely resting off the shores of Guantanamo Bay. It was waiting to strike at an opportune moment, a long-planned attack that would make the sad affairs of this strange little island ever more trivial. I returned there two weeks later, after arriving on Guantanamo Bay for Dr. Welner's testimony. There was no evidence of the vessel; perhaps it had sensed my earlier surveillance and moved locations. I decided that this would be my "what's next" after the 9/11 case, becoming a correspondent covering UFOs or "UAPs" and perhaps a global war implicating the fate of humanity.

McCall had already informed the parties that he was willing to go well into the night to make the most of the week, as Welner was not available the following week. But, as it turned out, there would be no Welner. The witness lives in South Florida and had to return there to help his family prepare for Hurricane Milton. The parties discussed him returning later in the week, but that would prove to be impossible. We would have no court until the very end of the week, Friday afternoon on October 11, which McCall had set aside for oral arguments on a motion by a consortium of media organizations to unseal the three plea agreements. This was frustrating beyond belief: Now Welner could not testify until November, which meant oral arguments on suppression couldn't take place until January—after McCall was already scheduled to retire.

Thankfully, McCall canceled week five, which confined the task of killing time to a single week. In addition to continuing to run down the club soda crisis, we bought a palm-tree-style tropical Christmas tree at the NEX and set it up in the office. We did not find any ornaments at the Radio GTMO souvenir store, but we found plenty of decorations at the thrift store, the Trading Post. During the week, a few ships came in port to refuel, which added some crowds to the drinking establishments as I barhopped—including one near-fight I witnessed outside the Tiki Bar. On another sweltering night, I was one of maybe twelve base visitors and residents to watch *Joker: Folie à Deux* playing at the outdoor cinema. I noted with interest when newscasters in the movie referred to the Joker's trial for his string of murders from the first movie as the "Trial of the Century." Without a trial date set for the 9/11 case, it was hard to quibble with the characterization.

We finally got about two and a half hours of court on Friday. The media consortium was represented by David Schulz, whom I had first met in Guantanamo Bay in February 2016 when he came down to argue against the government's redacting of public transcripts. This time, he argued from a room in an office building in Northern Virginia. He and his cocounsel apparently were not allowed in the remote hearing room, which is a SCIF whose location is apparently a secret, though we all know where it is. The prosecution and the defense teams presented a unified front against Schulz's contention that the public had a First Amendment right to see the agreements—or at least parts of them—while McCall considered whether Austin could legally withdraw from them.

The real news came after, when McCall announced what he had hinted at before: He was postponing his retirement again, this time for another six months. He wanted to hear arguments on the disputed plea deals at the start of the next hearing, November 4, which would be the day before the presidential election, and then finally move into Welner's testimony. The hearing was scheduled for three weeks, which in my mind allowed for the possibility that McCall would hear guilty pleas in the final week if he sided with the defense that the agreements must be enforced. Regardless, this meant McCall could hear oral arguments on al Baluchi's suppression case in January 2025. He was going to keep guiding the case to whatever conclusion might be in store for it.

"So that should make sure that we're able to accomplish at least what we have for now," McCall said. "And once we get past the decisions on . . . the way forward with the various cases."

This was surely music to the ears of the defense teams. Still, Connell couldn't resist putting on the record again his position that the government had used its add-on witnesses, most notably Welner at the end, to delay resolution of the suppression hearing. Connell reminded McCall that he had started predicting back in May that this type of delay—whether caused by a health problem or other event—would happen if the government kept insisting on having Welner testify after everybody else. Connell added that "this could easily come up again in November."

The canceled fifth week meant that I would be both home and well-rested for my one-year wedding anniversary on October 20, which felt like a luxury, even though my return to Gitmo was lurking on the horizon. On October 15, the general manager of the Navy Gateway Inn & Suites emailed me to thank me for my review of the hotel. It was a nice note, but I had not actually written a review. I surmised that it was written by the "other John Ryan," who had been attending the proceedings regularly as part of the victim family member group. That John Ryan is the real John Ryan, and I am the "other John Ryan," given that he is a former Port Authority Police lieutenant who helped lead rescue and recovery efforts at Ground Zero for nine months after the attacks. Ryan had been meeting with journalists over several of the past sessions, proving to be a fountain of knowledge of numbers and anecdotes—people who were either killed or saved by randomly being in the wrong or right place on 9/11. Ryan told us that he hated it when people said that "nearly three thousand people died" in the attacks, given the incalculable ripple effects of each loss of life; this was not a number to round up.

The night after receiving the NGIS email I had a dream in which I played for the New England Patriots and had a chance to win the Super Bowl with a game-ending field goal. But the playing field wasn't a field, it was Times Square, and I would have to kick the ball—which wasn't a football but tightly folded up articles of clothing—over the top of the famous red "TKTS" stairs, right in the center of one of the city's most crowded tourist spots. Holding the "ball" for me at the bottom of the stairs was Suzanne Lachelier, the longtime member of Mustafa al Hawsawi's defense team. I looked into the crowd and saw the leader of that team, Walter Ruiz, there to support me. He was in a ridiculous, head-to-toe green leprechaun Boston Celtics outfit, and he gave me a thumbs-up as I approached the kick. But I knew it was impossible. Lachelier and I positioned the clothes-ball as advantageously as possible, but my kick only made it to near the stop of the red stairs—not over. The game would have to go into overtime, though it would not take place in Times Square. Tens of thousands of people, myself included, began walking down the street to play the rest of the game in a parking lot of a Holiday Inn Express, per the accepted rules of this version of the NFL. But as we got closer to the hotel, I knew it was a Navy Gateway property.

* * *

James Connell was, of course, proven right. Storm activity in the Caribbean led to a postponement of the November 2 flight to November 6, the day after the election. I had already driven down to DC on Friday, November 1, when the news came. If it had been just a few hours earlier, I would have turned around mid-trip. Instead, I stayed the night and drove back to Brooklyn on Saturday to have a few more days with Allison. I already had cast my vote the prior weekend, which allowed me to work a half-day on Election Day before driving back down to DC on Tuesday. I walked by the cordoned-off Capitol and hit a few Irish bars before watching the results with Jeff and Kristin. I went to bed knowing the outcome, confident that its decisive nature would lessen the chance for chaos in the city from which I was departing and elsewhere.

The scene at Andrews was subdued, no mourning or outward celebration; I didn't even hear discussions about the election, though people had to be thinking about what a Trump presidency would mean for the court system and the detention facility. Aside from the court cases, sixteen of the thirty detainees had been approved for release, and most of them were set to go to Oman before the Hamas attack on Israel on October 7, 2023—a resettlement plan halted out of security concerns. The fate of the low-value detainees remained unclear.

Once on the base, Carol and I were in a van, en route to check on the club soda crisis, when we received word that McCall had just given his ruling on the disputed plea deals—without needing to hear oral arguments. We skipped the Naval Exchange and went to our hotel rooms to write up the story. The judge's twenty-nine-page ruling was, in the clearest possible terms, an overwhelming victory for the Mohammed, bin Attash, and al Hawsawi teams. McCall agreed with them on every big point, finding that Austin could not withdraw from the plea agreements after a lawfully appointed subordinate convening authority had reached them. None of the criteria that allowed for withdrawing from a plea agreement were met; McCall agreed with the teams that, quite the opposite, the teams had been actively performing under the deals by signing their stipulations admitting guilt and by not participating in the ongoing suppression hearing, now limited to al Baluchi. In a footnote, he referenced the penalty provision that rendered the case noncapital in the event of a withdrawal. He said the parties would need to litigate this if an appellate court overruled him and decided that Austin had acted lawfully.

The deals were back on, and McCall wasn't messing around. In court the next morning, he told the parties that he wanted to finish Welner's testimony by the middle of the second week and then to hear "one or more" of the guilty pleas during the third week—starting, as planned before, with Mohammed. McCall said he would issue an order related to the clarifications he needed for KSM's plea agreement by the end of the day, and he would get to the other two agreements in short order. Lead prosecutor Clay Trivett was silent, which meant the government had not decided to appeal. In what would have otherwise been a big moment, Welner finally took the stand in the remote hearing room. At about 9:40 a.m., Jeffrey Groharing, also working from the remote site, began examining the government's final witness in the suppression case, at least for now.

Trivett's silence on Thursday and again on Friday boded well for the possibility that Mohammed would plead guilty before Thanksgiving. Most lawyers I talked to put the chances of an appeal at about fifty-fifty; I found that entirely reasonable but put the odds slightly lower. Presumably, by now, Austin would have been better educated about the endless nature of the pretrial litigation, and that a trial was either unlikely or the path to it so unpredictable that it risked the case never ending. And the election was over; the Biden administration had nothing to lose. On balance, allowing the pleas to go ahead was the logical move.

On Friday evening, I had dinner with members of the al Baluchi team and the attending NGO observers at the Windjammer restaurant. I was about halfway through a Manhattan when, at 8:03 p.m., Terry Rockefeller from September 11th Families for Peaceful Tomorrows texted us from the continental United States: The prosecution had just notified family members that it was appealing McCall's ruling. I told the table. For the second time in three months, guilty pleas made possible by Wednesday developments were overtaken on a Friday night. Rita Radostitz and I looked at each other in disbelief: Once again, we were sitting directly across from each other when the news came. We vowed to avoid having dinner together the next time the plea agreements were pending.

Trivett put the decision on the record in court on Sunday, as McCall was holding court then and on Monday's Veterans Day to make up for days lost to the storms. Trivett said the government would be seeking a writ of mandamus from the Court of Military Commission Review. McCall's ruling was not technically subject to a regular interlocutory appeal, which is limited to certain categories of decisions like the dismissal of charges or exclusion of evidence, so the prosecution had to seek a writ to stop the pleas. Mohammed's lead lawyer, Gary Sowards, referred to the move as "the second of one of the Friday-night specials from the Secretary of Defense." He and his cocounsel from the other teams urged McCall to stick to his schedule, contending that the government's appeal had little chance of success.

McCall decided to split the difference: He would give the government time to file its appeal, canceling the third week of the hearing. But he did not see the need to wait until the next scheduled session, set to last two weeks beginning January 20, the day of Trump's second inauguration. He told the parties to find a time before that for the entry of guilty pleas, in the event his ruling was upheld. McCall said that he could do it Christmas week if needed.

"My wife may not be very happy with me, but I am willing to do it," he said.

After getting input from the teams, McCall decided on hearing guilty pleas during the first two weeks of January, which would make the first hearing of 2025 a monthlong session. We would fly down on January 4 for Mohammed to enter his plea the week of January 6, with bin Attash and al Hawsawi expected to follow in the week after. Then McCall could move into oral arguments for al Baluchi's suppression case.

I was kicking myself for having gotten my hopes up again. Putting aside the idea of winding down my Gitmo life, KSM pleading guilty would be the biggest journalistic event of the case's history—it was tantalizing to think about covering it. Of course, if my own internal roller-coaster ride was exhausting, it paled in comparison to what victim family members were going through. After Austin's revocation in August, the Peaceful Tomorrows organization put out a statement referring to the developments as "emotional whiplash." Now it had happened again. During the final week, Carol and I met with eight of the attending family members in the media center. While they differed in their views of the plea deals, they agreed that the last several months had been agony—what Jessica Trant called "mental warfare." Trant's father, Daniel Trant, worked for Cantor Fitzgerald and was killed on 9/11. She opposed plea deals, as did Julie Boryczewski, whose brother Martin Boryczewski was also killed while working for Cantor Fitzgerald. Boryczewski said that the threat of jihad remained—as the October 7, 2023, attack on Israel made clear—and that a failure to seek the death penalty against KSM and the others would "send the wrong message."

Just to Trant's right sat Colleen Kelly, of Peaceful Tomorrows, whose support for plea agreements was the focus of the final episode of season four of *Serial*, "Guantanamo." Kelly did not speak too much during this meeting. She noted, however, how interesting it was that Austin's August 2 reversal would have been met with joy by the folks sitting immediately to her right, but with extreme disappointment by herself and many others she knew. Sitting closest to Carol and me were Maureen Basnicki and Deborah Garcia, who were also strongly in favor of plea deals. Basnicki's husband, Kenneth, and Garcia's husband, David, both died in the World Trade Center. Garcia also attributed the 2020 suicide of one of her sons to the earlier loss of his father. Garcia had initially wanted the death penalty for the defendants but had come around to wanting a conclusion to the case.

"Justice right now, at this point, is finality," Garcia said. "The sooner it comes, the better." Her biggest concern was that KSM and the others would die "innocent" if the case never had a resolution. She wanted them "to die guilty."

This, we had learned in recent years, was a fairly common perspective—a gradual acceptance among many family members that plea deals were probably the best way out. Also present at this meeting was John Ryan, who mostly expressed his disappointment with the poor communication from the government to the family members, which he said "further victimizes everybody again." Carol used the meeting as the basis for her November 22 article, "Twists and Turns in Sept. 11 Plea Process Are Agonizing, Families Say."

I personally found a few things striking about the meeting. One was that people on both sides of the plea-deal debate were livid that politics had infected the court process. The other was that each side seemed to suspect, at least at times, that the other side was the more vocal and listened-to viewpoint. Garcia had said this at a few different meetings in recent sessions—that family members and groups who were not familiar with the protracted nature of the pretrial proceedings had joined the loud chorus of mostly Republican opposition. She was concerned this was the "loudest voice" in the dispute. But my sense was that the opponents of the deals—including those who had followed the proceedings—felt that the pro–plea deal side was getting more attention, at least in mainstream news outlets.

In any event, it was a rewarding, if depressing, meeting—proof again of the benefits of showing up in person for court coverage. I asked somewhat jokingly to the group if anyone was excited by Dr. Welner finishing his testimony earlier in the week—which meant that the suppression testimony was now over. No one seemed to share my level of enthusiasm, at least outwardly. A few had suggested they were irked by the proceedings' focus on al Baluchi's claims of PTSD, a diagnosis that applies to them and so many other victim family members.

McCall pushed the parties through Sunday and Veterans Day, which allowed Groharing to finish his direct examination of Welner on Tuesday morning of the second week. They spent much of his four-plus days on the stand going through medical reporting of al Baluchi from his time in CIA custody and then at Camp 7. Welner said the reporting did not support defense claims that al Baluchi suffered from a condition that would have prevented him from making a voluntary statement to the FBI in January 2007. Welner said it was significant that al Baluchi expressed no concerns to his treating psychiatrist, WK5I, either before or after his FBI interviews in January 2007. He said the medical records showed they had a trusting relationship, leading him to believe that al Baluchi would have told her or a member of her team if the FBI sessions had triggered traumatic memories from the black sites.

"Do you have an opinion based on all the information you reviewed whether [his] statements to the FBI were voluntary?" Groharing asked on Tuesday.

"My professional opinion, they were," Welner said.

Connell had initially told me that his cross-examination would take two days. But he pulled a dramatic move by telling McCall after a 15-minute break that he had no questions for the witness.

"All right, too easy," McCall said in a surprised tone. "All right. Well, thank you, Mr. Connell."

This wasn't a giant surprise: It's hard to control a voluble witness like Welner, and Connell already had been stepping on the gas to get through suppression. He had, in fact, suggested to McCall earlier in the hearing that the judge could give his ruling based on the forthcoming, final written briefs instead of holding arguments in January—though McCall indicated he still wanted them. Multiple participants from the remote site said that Welner appeared irritated that he didn't get a chance to tangle with a single defense lawyer.

Connell's move made writing my final article of the hearing a good deal easier. To Katrina's credit, we published a 2,300-word piece, "Suppression Testimony Completed in Sept. 11. Case," that we felt was worthy of its historic significance—after all, it was five years in the making. The article was, as far as we knew, the only journalistic work to sum up what had happened in court other than the disputes over the plea deals. I'd rather have written an article about Mohammed pleading guilty, but this was still a good example of why Lawdragon's work was important, filling what would have been a gap in the journalistic record.

CHAPTER 32

2025—Game of Inches.

Judge McCall's scheduling of Mohammed's guilty plea for the week of January 6 likely contributed to the US Court of Military Commission Review (CMCR) moving at a relatively fast clip. For me, the appellate court's ruling came about sixteen days into holiday travel between my family in the Boston area and my wife's outside of Chicago. I was at my sister Mary's house on the night of December 30, just a handful of hours after Allison and I arrived at Logan International from the Chicago leg of the trip, when an attorney forwarded me the ruling: The guilty pleas were back on. I notified Katrina and began writing an article we published around midnight. The three-judge panel concluded that Sec. Austin could assume responsibility for entering into any future plea agreements, but he could not legally withdraw from the ones that Escallier had already reached as his duly appointed subordinate. The judges agreed with McCall's reasoning that Mohammed, bin Attash, and al Hawsawi had already started "performance" under the contracts by not participating in al Baluchi's suppression hearing.

Allison and I headed to Brooklyn on New Year's Day, which gave us a few nights at the apartment before I drove to DC on January 3, in preparation for the flight out of Andrews the next day. As I was driving, McCall denied the prosecution's request for a continuance of the plea proceedings. The government had wanted a delay until January 27 as it considered whether to challenge the CMCR's ruling to the civilian court with oversight of the military commissions—the US Court of Appeals for the DC Circuit.

In his denial, McCall said that he would delay Mohammed's guilty plea until Friday, January 10, to account for a snowstorm that was expected to hit the capitol region on Monday and also for the National Day of Mourning planned for Jimmy Carter on Thursday. I was not alone in expecting that McCall would finish Mohammed's guilty plea on Saturday or Sunday if he did not finish it on Friday.

Still, the extra time helped the government. The Justice Department filed its petition for a writ of mandamus with the DC Circuit on Tuesday, asking it to find that Austin "validly withdrew" from the agreements and to prohibit the entry of guilty pleas. It also filed an emergency motion for a stay of the proceedings while the DC Circuit considered the mandamus petition. Of course, I wasn't shocked at the move, but I also would not have been surprised if the government had decided to leave the CMCR ruling alone. The day before, the Department of Defense announced the massive detainee transfer that had long been in the works by sending eleven low-value detainees to Oman—reducing the prison population to fifteen, with three of those remaining already recommended for transfer by the Periodic Review Board. I thought, perhaps, the Biden administration was embracing a spirit of closure. We later learned that some Justice Department lawyers opposed Austin's pursuit of an appeal.

Regardless, time was running out, as McCall was not going to wait for the DC Circuit. He used Wednesday to finalize the plea colloquy with Gary Sowards and Clay Trivett—a brisk ninety-minute hearing in which the judge and the two lead lawyers ironed out a few dozen changes and updates to the 103-page script. January 8 was about as close to a guilty plea as a defendant could get without actually pleading guilty.

"Can you confirm that Mr. Mohammed is pleading guilty to all charges and specifications without exceptions or substitutions?" McCall asked Sowards on Wednesday morning.

"Yes, we can, Your Honor," Sowards said.

In what felt like a deliberate move, Trivett also drove home just how substantial a future sentencing trial would be: He told McCall that the government would need longer than ten months to prepare for the sentencing, which meant it would probably not happen until 2026. Trivett explained that the government's presentation would last several months as it sought to build "a historical record" of the 9/11 attacks. He said hundreds of victim family members had expressed interest in participating. Sowards asked McCall if the judge could push forward a quick production of the day's transcript, so that defense teams could attach the document to its responses at the DC Circuit. Trivett's words, Sowards said, were proof that the government's petition for a stay inaccurately claimed that guilty pleas would prevent a public trial.

While the fate of the case remained with the DC Circuit, Katrina felt we should do an article when I explained to her what had happened in court. With Mohammed's plea tantalizingly close, we published "Stage Set for 9/11 Suspect's Guilty Plea on Friday" later that afternoon. Her instincts were proven right on Thursday evening when we met with victim family members in the conference room of the hotel. They, too, said that Wednesday felt historic or at least deeply meaningful: The accused mastermind of the 9/11 attacks had acknowledged in open court, albeit through his lawyer, that the government could prove every charge against him beyond a reasonable doubt.

The victim family members who attended were mostly regulars or semi-regulars who were unanimously and strongly in favor of the plea agreements—for whom finality through unappealable guilt, whether or not that brought closure, was the most important outcome. This included Stephan Gerhardt and Deborah Garcia, whom I had interviewed in recent trips; Garcia was with her son, Dylan, who was having his twenty-eighth birthday. Also present were Thomas Resta and his wife, Cherie Faircloth, who had made several trips over the years. Terry Rockefeller and Elizabeth Miller, members of September 11th Families for Peaceful Tomorrows, were traveling as family members on this trip. On her first trip was Claire Gates, whose uncle, New York Fire Department Lt. Peter Freund, was killed at the World Trade Center. (Gates was traveling with her mother, Carol Freund, who was not at the meeting.) They sat with me, Carol, Terry McDermott, and two first-timers with the media group, Alice Cuddy from the BBC and Eleanor Watson from CBS.

KSM was about fifteen hours away from beginning his guilty plea when Carol alerted the room she had heard by text: The DC Circuit had granted the government's motion for a stay of the proceedings. The emotional roller coaster of the plea dispute was by that point so ingrained that no one expressed much surprise; dejection was now thoroughly mixed with resignation. Gates began to cry as she lamented how the case's lack of finality would affect her mom and the other families—that a trip "that was supposed to be a time for healing for us" would end in continued pain and uncertainty. The DC Circuit called for full briefing on the government's petition with a final deadline of January 22. The delay meant the Biden administration had succeeded in punting the controversy to the incoming

Trump team, which brought even more uncertainty. Gerhardt made it clear to all of us that we could quote him saying that "the Biden administration has failed the families of 9/11."

The week ended with a perfunctory nine-minute hearing on Friday morning. McCall canceled the second week of the hearing, as the closing arguments for al Baluchi's suppression case were planned for week three. McCall noted that the litigation at the DC Circuit could be resolved by the time of the two-week session scheduled to start February 17. McCall told the court that he would hear Mohammed's guilty plea then, or possibly a week earlier if the Circuit moved faster. He still had hope.

* * *

I decided to do the exhausting Gitmo-DC-Brooklyn-DC-Gitmo travel loop, which gave me and Allison almost five full days together. I'm sure I listened to a lot of podcasts, probably a bunch of them about Trump or the state of American democracy, or climate change given the wildfires ravaging my former home of Los Angeles, but my brain did not retain any information. I did not appear to be operating at full capacity, as excited as I was for closing arguments for litigation I had been covering since 2019, or since 2015 if one counted all the evidentiary and witness disputes that preceded actual testimony.

McCall now had time to spare and decided to not hold court on Monday, which was both Martin Luther King Jr. Day and Trump's second inauguration. We decided to watch the inauguration at the bar at the bowling alley. Carol and I were joined by a few friends who made the trip. Lisa Hajjar, a sociology professor at the University of California, Santa Barbara, and author of *The War in Court*, had been looking forward to the suppression arguments as much as I had. Michelle Shephard, the renowned Canadian journalist and author of *Guantanamo's Child*, was on her first Gitmo trip since 2017.

Trump's big day did not get the respect one might have expected. The staffer working the bowling alley initially told us that she was not allowed to turn down the music. Eventually she lowered the music a little and amplified the sound of the TV behind the bar, but it was still hard to hear. Trump's swearing in was accompanied by Ini Kamoze's "Here Comes the Hotstepper," and the early part of his speech was drowned out by Cher's "Believe" and DJ Jazzy Jeff & The Fresh Prince's "Ring My Bell." Earlier in the day, Trump had issued a proclamation that all flags—including at foreign military bases—would be flown at full-staff for his inauguration before returning to half-staff on January 21, in the ongoing recognition of Carter's passing. But compliance with this edict was inconsistent, at best, around the base, with even flags at the Camp Justice sign still at half-staff on January 20. Once again, Guantanamo was living up to its reputation for lawlessness.

My travel fatigue was evident the next morning, when Carol and I approached the court with a sense of excitement.

"First time in court since November," I remarked.

"What?" Carol responded, a tinge of concern in her voice. "We were here like a week ago."

The suppression hearing, from my point of view, did not disappoint. Jeffrey Groharing, who generally hung back at the remote hearing room, showed up in person for his closing argument. He gave it over the entirety of the Tuesday session, burning through an approximately two-hundred-page slide deck by 4:15 p.m. Groharing also had a giant piece of poster board on display near the witness box, facing the courtroom, with a quote from the day Ammar al Baluchi first met FBI Special Agents James Fitzgerald and Abigail Perkins on Guantanamo Bay for his so-called "clean team" interviews in January 2007: "Yes, let's get down to business," al Baluchi told the agents after they explained their interest in talking to him.

The quote underscored an important point: The government's suppression case had always been a relatively simple one. Before the FBI meetings took place, the Army commander of the Camp 7 detention facility told detainees they could either go to their scheduled meetings or skip them (on the first day, the detainees did not know they would be meeting with the FBI.) Once they arrived at the meetings, the FBI agents told the detainees their participation was voluntary and that they would not be returned to the custody of the CIA, regardless of whether or how they answered the questions. The FBI agents gave this "modified rights advisement" for each day of the sessions, which for al Baluchi took place on January 17, 18, 19, and 30. Groharing drove the point home numerous times during his presentation: The interviews were, by definition, voluntary; therefore, the statements were given voluntarily and admissible under the law. As portrayed by Groharing, the sessions were about as far from the CIA's "enhanced" approach as possible, with cordial and businesslike discussions mixed with prayer breaks and shared lunches from McDonald's. (Al Baluchi apparently really liked the apple pies.)

Groharing reminded McCall that the government never challenged the defense team's portrayal of al Baluchi's past treatment, that it had always been open to any descriptions that were "tethered to reality"—my favorite phrase, which Groharing used three times on Tuesday and McCall once himself. The prosecutor also acknowledged that the treatment was "undeniably harsh," particularly during al Baluchi's three and a half days of enhanced interrogation techniques or "EITs" at Cobalt, the most brutal of the black sites where he spent four months. Groharing said that the abuse and lengthy stay at Cobalt would have "no doubt had an impact" on al Baluchi, but not the type of impact that would have made him unable to talk voluntarily with law enforcement agents.

He referred to the testimony of WK5I, al Baluchi's first psychiatrist at Camp 7, and Dr. Michael Welner, the government's forensic psychiatrist, both of whom did not see any evidence that al Baluchi suffered from a mental illness preventing him from participating in the interviews voluntarily. Groharing said that al Baluchi's behavior during the sessions proved that he was not experiencing "conditioned fear" at the time. Groharing noted that al Baluchi told the agents that the United States deserved the 9/11 attacks so that Americans could feel the pain felt by Palestinians, and that he would do it again to stop the US support of Israel.

"Your Honor, those are not the statements of a broken man," Groharing said. "Those are not involuntary statements. Those are the statements of a man who believed what he did, who wasn't hesitant to explain why he did what he did."

James Connell had meant it when he told McCall in late 2024 that the judge could rule on the written pleadings. On the trip down, both he and Alka Pradhan told reporters that they were still not exactly sure how they would handle oral arguments. As it turned out, they split their presentation, with Pradhan going first on Wednesday before passing the baton to Connell in the mid-afternoon. Pradhan began with various historical examples of torture and comparing them to that inflicted on al Baluchi—the water torture, the nude shackling and stress positions, the walling, the prolonged sleep deprivation, the isolation—noting that "very little changes about the brutality of torture from century to century." She described al Baluchi's treatment as both torture and "nonconsensual human experimentation." Al Baluchi attended the start of the session but left once Pradhan began referring to the CIA's Office of Inspector General report that documented how new CIA interrogators at Cobalt gained their "certification" by "practicing" EITs on al Baluchi, which included his oft-referenced two-hour bout of walling.

As defense attorneys had many times in the past, Pradhan took issue with the prosecution's argument that the condensed period of EITs meant that the detainees could not suffer from permanent or lasting damage. She said that the medical science was clear that just a single traumatic event can cause PTSD and other severe symptoms.

"You would never, I hope, hear the government or their witnesses dismiss a single instance of rape or a single experience of being in an IED explosion," Pradhan said.

But she also said that her client's misery and torture were yearslong, not mere days. She reminded McCall, as Groharing had, that al Baluchi spent four months at Cobalt, a place that CIA personnel had described as a Nazi concentration camp, a dungeon, and one of "Dante's Circles of Hell." Detainees were kept in total darkness in cramped cells described as horse stalls, with loud music blasting constantly and a bucket provided for human waste. She said that al Baluchi's treatment at subsequent black sites—constant light and solitary confinement, with the only human contact provided by debriefers—also constituted either torture or cruel, inhuman, or degrading treatment. Pradhan said that the discovery provided by the government revealed that CIA personnel interrogated or interviewed al Baluchi at least 1,119 times between 2003 and his transfer to Guantanamo Bay in September 2006. Once there, he was kept in solitary confinement and interviewed by FBI agents in a cell that closely resembled the types of rooms in which he was interrogated by the CIA. Pradhan told McCall that these similarities were why, to this day, al Baluchi and his team members always sat on the floor of the cells during their attorney-meetings, avoiding the table and plastic-chairs setup that had been used at the black sites.

"International and US law is clear," Pradhan said. "He was tortured. He lives with his torture to this day. The torture irrevocably changed his brain. And his statements in 2007 were involuntary."

In his presentation, Connell began by noting that the Military Commissions Act prohibits not just involuntary statements but also those actually "obtained" by torture or cruel, inhuman, or degrading treatment. He said that al Baluchi's 2007 FBI meetings met this second definition of being obtained by torture, even though the agents used standard rapport-building interview techniques. Connell referred to the wealth of evidence and testimony showing the "information loops" between the CIA and the FBI that culminated in the January 2007 sessions: FBI agents had first sent "intelligence requirements" or questions to the black sites for CIA personnel to ask detainees; they took investigative steps based on this intelligence and submitted follow-up questions; then they reviewed the CIA reporting before conducting their reinterrogation of al Baluchi on Guantanamo Bay—covering the same topics that the CIA had earlier asked him about at the black sites.

"How is that not information obtained by torture?" Connell asked.

Connell spent most of Thursday on the separate legal arguments over "voluntariness," portraying the government's position on attenuation as essentially absurd. He told McCall that the parties might have "overcomplicated" the issue by focusing so much on the "fact-rich" details of al Baluchi's torture. He said that US Supreme Court case law is clear that incommunicado detention can never be followed by voluntary statements if "prophylactic measures" such as *Miranda* warnings are not given to detainees. Al Baluchi's statements would still clearly be inadmissible even if he hadn't been subjected to intense violence, Connell said.

Nevertheless, he added that the violence and isolation provided another pathway to suppression because it caused the type of psychological damage that would render al Baluchi's future statements involuntary. He said his team had made a "pretty good" case that al Baluchi had PTSD but that it didn't matter because the cluster of symptoms—anxiety, depression, nightmares, headaches, sleeplessness, memory loss, and many more—were all present. While WK5I did not diagnose al Baluchi with PTSD, future Camp 7 psychiatrists did. Connell displayed for the court a chart that showed, by my count, about forty psychotropic drugs that al Baluchi had been prescribed since his arrival to Guantanamo Bay. He said that any distinction between the CIA and the FBI wouldn't have mattered to al Baluchi by early 2007, comparing it to an American being captured by North Korea and assessing which of the nation's five security agencies was interrogating him. In the end, Connell argued, the CIA used violence to change his client's "decision-making matrix."

"When the government talks about how pleasant Ammar was and how friendly [he was] or makes fun of him for finding an apple pie delicious, they're really just expressing how much violence and isolation drove Mr. al Baluchi's decision to follow the approach he had taken the last 1,100 times he was questioned," Connell contended.

McCall had said at the outset of oral arguments that he wanted the parties to focus on the voluntariness dispute, as opposed to Protective Order #4 or other restrictions imposed on the defense teams. This signaled to me that

McCall felt he could rule on suppression without necessarily making the same analysis that Judge Pohl used when preemptively suppressing the FBI statements back in 2018. Still, he allowed the lawyers to discuss the restrictions as it related to the main dispute. Connell told McCall that the law required that the judge's determination of whether al Baluchi confessed voluntarily be based on "the totality of the circumstances"—which was impossible in light of how the prosecution had blocked access to CIA witnesses.

"We've never heard from a single witness who was present or even nearby for the application of physically coercive techniques to Mr. al Baluchi, right?" Connell said. "How is that the totality of the circumstances?"

Connell was—as he often is when at his best—both technical and blistering in his remarks, combining a carefully planned outline with off-the-cuff examples that conveyed a mix of sadness, outrage, and disbelief. He ended by reading a lengthy quote from *Ashcraft v. Tennessee*, the 1944 Supreme Court case in which the justices held that the Constitution barred the use of coerced confessions. The opinion stated that, while the world had other governments that would use secret detention and torture to extract confessions, "So long as the Constitution remains the basic law of our republic, America will not have that kind of government." Connell told McCall that al Baluchi's motion to suppress presented a fundamental question.

"Does America have that kind of government?" Connell asked.

In his rebuttal, Groharing accused Pradhan and Connell of "judge nullification" and told McCall that he "should be offended" at their attempt to "manipulate" him into making "an emotional decision." He also accused them of "larding" up the record with historical examples of torture and experiences of other detainees that had nothing to do with al Baluchi's case. But Groharing made his own emotional closing pitch in what was a clever and effective return to the portrayal of the black site Cobalt as a circle of hell. He said the real circle of hell was the North Tower after a hijacker that al Baluchi gave money to flew a commercial plane into it.

"People had a choice: Am I going to stay here and be burned alive and die or am I going to jump?" Groharing said. "That's Dante's seventh circle of hell. Whatever Mr. Ali experienced paled in comparison."

* * *

The next day, Lawdragon published "Judge Set to Rule on Admissibility of 9/11 Confessions," a close to 3,500-word article on the week's events. That's another benefit of staying outside the mainstream of journalism—the freedom to go deep in ways that almost no other news outlet would for three days of court. The article explained more than a few complications, including the multipronged caveat that this might not be the end of suppression. The obvious wrinkle was that the other three defendants might have to rejoin the pretrial litigation if the government prevailed in withdrawing from the plea deals. (McCall had already told the parties to begin thinking about severing al Baluchi's case from the others.) But another complication resulted from the confusing litigation regime that McCall inherited from his predecessors, which simultaneously required him to assess the fairness of the suppression hearing because of the investigative restrictions. In Connell's view, al Baluchi should get to move forward with motions to compel dozens of additional witnesses—including covert CIA officers—if McCall determined that the government met its "initial burden" in establishing that the statements were voluntary. Groharing disputed this, telling McCall on Thursday that the defense was "stuck with the record they have right here."

Regardless, it appeared that McCall was closing in on his own version of finality. He told the parties at the end of court Thursday that he would probably have his suppression ruling completed in about a month. He also said he would cancel the two-week February session if the guilty pleas weren't happening. McCall told Connell that he wanted al Baluchi's motion to dismiss the case for outrageous government conduct—one that was long-planned but still unfiled—ready for oral arguments in the coming months, as it would be based on a similar set of facts as the suppression case. (Al Hawsawi's outrageous government conduct motion, the only other one filed, was still pending.) The next session after February was not scheduled to begin until April 23, which felt light-years away. That hearing would almost certainly be McCall's last.

"I am not anticipating that I'm going to extend again," McCall said. "I think my wife would kill me."

But McCall also said that he would stick around for the fourth week of the current hearing—just in case the DC Circuit ruled quickly and lifted the stay. He told the Mohammed and prosecution teams to also be ready, though the timing was implausible. Oral arguments were set for Tuesday of the final week, January 28, in Washington, DC. The three-judge panel of the DC Circuit would have to find for the defense teams almost immediately on Tuesday or Wednesday. Then, the government would either have to decide not to seek an en banc review by the full DC Circuit or to decide not to appeal to the US Supreme Court; or, if it did take any additional appellate steps, those courts would have to deny any stay requests in quick fashion. I understood why McCall didn't want to miss the chance at pleas, but I was a little annoyed, as I initially told Allison I'd likely come home a week earlier. Now Carol and I agreed that we had to stay for the final week of January—just in case.

Once again, we would be alone if the historic event happened. In addition to Hajjar and Shephard, we were joined for the suppression hearing by Catherine Herridge, a veteran of Fox News and CBS News who was now independently producing her own segments under "Catherine Herridge Reports." (She came with a cameraman/producer, Kalen Eriksson.) All of them would depart on Saturday. Hajjar had made two other trips in the McCall era of the 9/11 case, but she had been more of a semi-regular in the pre-pandemic days. Back then, we would hang out into the late hours, drinking Jameson whiskey at the picnic tables by the tents. On this trip, during our final hangout on the patio of the NGIS, Hajjar brought me her leftover wine and liquor—most of which I would just end up storing at the media center. Times had changed; our stamina was not what it once was.

"I was buying booze like it was 2018," Hajjar said with her signature throaty laugh.

Even during the third week, I had begun annoying Carol, Hajjar, and Shephard by stating that anything we did—a group dinner, drinks at the bowling alley, shopping for souvenirs—"could be our last" time. It was a joke, but one that was clearly tethered to reality. I assumed two things: The defense would eventually prevail in the plea-deal dispute, and the Trump administration would at least consider shutting down the court to block the pleas from happening—especially if fresh uproar over the removal of the death penalty gained traction. The 9/11 defendants would then return to being law-of-war detainees without criminal cases, which had been the experience of most of Gitmo's nearly eight hundred detainees over the past two-plus decades. Even without pleas on the verge of happening, the Trump administration could postpone all court proceedings while it performed a general review and plan for the military commissions. After all, that's what Obama did when he took office in January 2009.

Carol and I planned something like a real court day for the otherwise-dark fourth week by going to the media center for the arguments, as the DC Circuit broadcasts its audio live on its website and YouTube. The arguments, which dragged on for about four hours, suggested that a quick ruling was not very likely. The discussion between the three judges and the attorneys got way more muddled than I expected for what seemed to me—and to McCall and the CMCR, for that matter—to be a relatively straightforward issue. The judges were Patricia Millett and Robert Wilkins, two Obama appointees, and Neomi Rao, a Trump appointee, all of whom took some level of skepticism toward Austin's unusual move of withdrawing from the plea agreements reached by a competent subordinate. After all, Austin had appointed Escallier without any restrictions on reaching plea agreements, even though he was well-aware of her successor's earlier approval of the deals that fell apart in September 2023. Melissa Patterson, a longtime appellate attorney at the Justice Department, and Michel Paradis, the appellate specialist for the Military Commissions Defense Organization, handled the arguments; Matthew Engle, the lead lawyer for Walid bin Attash, added brief additional argument for the defense. It was clear that the judges did not have a complete understanding of the record of the case from the moment Escallier signed the agreements—a confusion apparently triggered, at least in part, by al Baluchi's ongoing suppression hearing. The judges wanted additional supplements and transcripts; KSM's guilty plea would not happen that trip.

The bigger news happened the day after the arguments, January 29, when Trump directed the Departments of Defense and Homeland Security to expand the migrant operations on Guantanamo Bay for "high-priority criminal aliens unlawfully present in the United States." The current migrant operations had space for maybe a hundred or so individuals; Trump said he wanted to build out the capacity to thirty thousand. The move got an enormous amount of media attention, even with all the other news created by Trump's first few weeks—perhaps more attention than the plea deals had during the summer. I even went on the *Don Lemon Show* podcast to discuss the news. This development, to me, was another sign that this trip might be our last, as the Trump administration might decide against having any journalists on the base during the migrant surge.

The migrant operations center—which oddly has the same MOC acronym used for the media operations center—is on the nearly empty Leeward side of the base past the air terminal. On Saturday February 1, the morning of our departure, several people associated with the case stayed on the Leeward bus instead of getting off immediately at the terminal. Our purported destination was the convenience store, but the quick loop around the area gave us decent views of the large green tents being erected for a new migrant tent city. I saw at least three dozen tents. As we flew out later that morning, perhaps never to return, Guantanamo Bay appeared to be embarking on its next phase, though we knew Trump could abandon this plan as quickly as he announced it.

In what seemed both unbelievable and totally predictable, and also fitting, the current phase had not quite ended. For me, the phase had dominated about a decade of my life; for others, it was much longer. On the flight home, I thought back to our hangout on Thursday night, January 9, several hours after our meeting with family members had been interrupted by the DC Circuit's stay. Carol and I and a few others were still in the hotel conference room when Terry Rockefeller of Peaceful Tomorrows rejoined us for a final nightcap or two. She told us that September 11, 2001, was also her parents' sixtieth wedding anniversary. At the time, her sister, Laura, was an actress and singer living in New York City. Like many people living a life in the arts in the city, Laura took on freelance work, which included intermittently helping a risk-management firm run conferences. That's why on the morning of 9/11 she was at Windows on the World on the 106th floor of the North Tower.

After the towers were hit, Rockefeller called her parents to see if they had heard the news, blanking on the fact that it was their anniversary. She also tried Laura, her only sibling, not knowing that Laura had been working at the World Trade Center that day. It wasn't until later in the afternoon that she grew more concerned about not having heard back. Rockefeller eventually spoke to people who lived in Laura's building on West 85th Street, who told her that they thought she had been working at the towers—a fear that the company, Risk Waters Group, mostly confirmed but without complete certainty. Early the next morning, Rockefeller left the Boston area and began her drive to New York. That was about fourteen years before I first showed up to the Guantanamo Bay courtroom to see the five men accused of planning the attacks.

CHAPTER 33

An "End."

The return stateside was accompanied by much waiting, more than I expected. The DC Circuit seemed intent on wading deeper and deeper into the plea-deal dispute. On February 7, 2025, the panel replaced its temporary administrative stay of the plea proceedings with a full stay pending the resolution of the government's petition for a writ of mandamus. The brief order stated that one of the judges, Robert Wilkins, would have denied the stay, allowing the pleas to go forward, because the government had "not demonstrated a likelihood of success on the merits." Defense lawyers cautioned that this did not necessarily mean that the other two judges felt the government had met this standard—and was therefore likely to prevail on its argument that Sec. Austin acted lawfully—only that perhaps the judges felt they should fully assess the merits given the significance of the case. After all, this was the biggest case in US history over the worst-ever attacks on American soil. Three days later, Judge McCall canceled the February 17–28 hearing, with the next session scheduled to start April 23 and last until May 16.

McCall himself did not seem in any particular rush to rule on the matter squarely before him—suppression. He said on the last day of court, January 23, that he was hopeful for a ruling "sometime within the next month," but a month came and went, as did six weeks, then two full months and then ten weeks. It was a two-track waiting game, with McCall issuing orders in late March and early April canceling the first and second weeks of the upcoming hearing because the DC Circuit had yet to rule on the plea agreements. Absent guilty pleas, there wasn't a whole lot to do in the spring session.

As the waiting continued, I had begun to wonder if maybe McCall did not view suppression as clearly as most of us thought he did—that maybe he was finding a way to conclude that the government had met its burden. But his ruling, when it finally came on April 11, confirmed our earlier instincts. McCall had used the time to craft a 111-page opinion that was a complete rejection of the prosecution's theory of "attenuation," that the statements to the FBI in January 2007 could somehow be separated from the years of abuse and isolation at CIA black sites through the RDI program. McCall concluded that the government failed to prove by a preponderance of evidence that the statements by al Baluchi were voluntary, and it also failed to establish that the statements were not the products of torture or cruel, inhuman, or degrading treatment.

"Mr. Ali was tortured during his time in the RDI program," McCall wrote in one of several damning passages, using (as he and the prosecution always did) the defendant's given name. "The goal of the program was to condition him through torture and other inhumane and coercive methods to become compliant during any government questioning. The program worked."

Luckily, due to a miserable early spring day of rain, wind, and cold, on April 11 Allison and I had abandoned plans to go out to dinner and were waiting for delivery when I received a text about the ruling from one of the attorneys on Friday evening at 7:14 p.m. The lawyer apologized for not letting me know earlier, as the ruling came out around 3 p.m., which meant that Carol would beat me to the punch by publishing first. I had prewritten significant parts of the background, however, which allowed Lawdragon to have a solid 1,100-word article published shortly after 8 p.m. The ruling was not yet public, but I received important sections by text before publishing and later received a copy of the document.

McCall noted in his findings of fact that the FBI repeatedly sent questions into the black sites for CIA personnel to ask al Baluchi and that the agents later had access to this information prior to interviewing him on Guantanamo. But McCall didn't focus on the "information loops" or "feedback loops" that al Baluchi's lawyers highlighted during various parts of their suppression case. In his view, it didn't matter if the FBI agents based their questions on their own investigative work or on what they learned from CIA reporting. What mattered was the relentless and brutal conditioning that went on for three and a half years at the black sites. For al Baluchi, this conditioning included answering questions on every topic related to his role in the September 11 attacks and other plots that he later admitted to during the FBI sessions: He was trained to give the answers he gave.

In fact, the longest section of McCall's ruling—more than thirty pages—was devoted to a detailed description of al Baluchi's conditioning and treatment at five different black sites, beginning with his especially brutal four-month stay at Location 2, or Cobalt, where he was subjected to "enhanced interrogation techniques." In his concluding summary of this section, McCall noted that al Baluchi was questioned more than a thousand times at the various sites by about thirty different agents who were his only human contact during his entire time in CIA custody.

"He did not know how long he would be held," McCall ruled. "He did not know what would happen to him when he no longer had intelligence value to the Americans."

McCall said that it was "easy to focus" on the torture because it was "so absurdly far outside the norms of what is expected of US custody" but that the prolonged period of incommunicado detention and solitary confinement was just as "egregious." Rather than supporting attenuation, the judge saw the four-month break between al Baluchi's time in CIA custody and his FBI interviews "as a short lapse in time" given the protracted period of misery that preceded it. He agreed with the defense team that the conditions of the Camp 7 detention facility "were markedly similar to those at previous RDI locations" and that the FBI agents conducted their early 2007 interviews similar to how the CIA did its debriefings—and they had done so in a former CIA black site that the agency had previously used for debriefings. (A special agent from the Department of Defense was also present during the sessions.) Echoing James Connell's closing arguments from January, McCall said that al Baluchi would have seen the agents as "just the latest iteration of American officials who wanted answers." If he didn't give answers, McCall said, al Baluchi would understandably think that his conditions would worsen; he had no reason to believe the rules had changed and that he was free to remain silent.

"All of this would have indicated to Mr. Ali that he was still in the RDI program, and he needed to answer the way he had been trained," McCall ruled.

That, to me, was perhaps the clearest rejection of the government's case. As far as al Baluchi knew, he was renditioned into a torture program and never truly left. McCall said that the government would have had a better argument for attenuation if the FBI agents had given al Baluchi a *Miranda* rights advisement, as they had in other terrorism investigations and as they normally would in the course of their jobs. Instead, the agents read "a carefully constructed" script that avoided telling al Baluchi that the government could not use his prior statements to the CIA against him. McCall also noted that the prosecution declined to call as witnesses the medical professionals who examined al Baluchi during his time in CIA custody, relying instead on cables that hid the identities of the observers and possibly other key details. McCall referred to the testimony from competing defense and prosecution medical experts, but he declined to make any findings regarding al Baluch's "possible mental disorders." He didn't need to.

McCall also did not rule on the facet of the litigation that had been entwined with suppression for more than seven years—whether the investigative and witness restrictions on the defense teams unfairly hindered their cases. These burdens are what led the first judge, Army Col. James Pohl, to preemptively suppress the FBI statements in August 2018 before his successor reversed him and forced the defense teams to file their suppression motions. McCall deferred ruling on this dispute; it remains pending for al Baluchi and his codefendants, should they rejoin the case.

While I expected al Baluchi to prevail, I would have personally been intrigued by a ruling that said the government had met its initial burden of voluntariness but that the defense teams were entitled to interview and eventually examine covert CIA witnesses involved in the RDI program. I was always curious to see if the government would produce certain witnesses, or if it would refuse and create a standoff that could derail the case, possibly leading to a dismissal of the charges or an abeyance of all proceedings. But such drama was not in the cards. In the end, McCall didn't see this as a close call. As he pointed out in his ruling, and as Connell and Alka Pradhan said in their closing arguments, the situation confronting him was basically unprecedented in American law—US agents conducting law enforcement interviews of a suspect whom the US government had tortured and kept in incommunicado detention for more than three years. McCall said the only "comparable" case was the military commission against Abd al Rahim al Nashiri, and the US Court of Military Commission Review had recently upheld the suppression decision in that case. Despite that *al Nashiri* precedent, the government filed a notice with McCall that it would appeal his ruling.

Near the end of the 111 pages, McCall gave what may have been my favorite line when he referred to the seemingly endless debate—still unresolved, as far as the public knows—over the extent to which the CIA may have had "operational control" of Camp 7 after the detainees arrived from the black sites. For all the time the parties spent litigating the issue, McCall wrote, "the Commission does not believe it actually matters." Al Baluchi

An "End." 403

knew he was still in the custody of the United States when he gave his confessions to the FBI. That was all that mattered.

McCall's ruling provided a conclusion to the litigation I had been covering for the past decade—at least for the time being, with the fate of the plea agreements still uncertain. As of this writing in early May 2025, the DC Circuit was expected to rule any day, but even if the panel sided with the defense the government was expected to seek a rehearing by the full Circuit or a review by the US Supreme Court. Lawyers hadn't fully discounted the possibility that the Trump administration would drop the matter and simply blame Biden and Austin for deals that got rid of the death penalty. However the dispute resolved, it was expected to take a while, which would push any actual guilty pleas to later in the year. Seeing the writing on the wall, McCall ended up canceling the entire April–May hearing, with the next session to start July 14. By then, of course, McCall would be long gone, assuming he stuck to his plans of finally retiring—which in my view was not a foregone conclusion.

My guess is that McCall could never have predicted the plea-deal dispute would drag on for so long—that he really would never get to hear KSM plead guilty. He had delayed his retirement, in part, to guide that process to a conclusion, and he had come ever so close on January 8 when he finalized Khalid Sheikh Mohammed's script with Gary Sowards and Clay Trivett. Not taking the next step must have been an enormous disappointment for McCall. Then again, he always seemed like a guy who could take things in stride. And anyway, the affable Air Force colonel—the judge who had pushed the parties down a "crushing" and "corrosive" path for more than a year, generally with a smile on his face—had truly left his mark.

If he was still reluctant to walk away, I can sympathize. There is never a good time to end a story that may have no end.

*　*　*

Allison had an art installation going up at the University of North Carolina Asheville, in early April, so I joined her on the trip and ended up guest "lecturing"—really just taking questions after giving some introductory remarks—on Guantanamo issues at an undergraduate human rights class. I did the same at a national security class at Fordham University School of Law in mid-April, the week after McCall's suppression ruling. The questions from students and faculty in both forums were excellent, proving again that fresh eyes are often better than trained ones. One that stuck with me was from a student at Fordham who asked about other evidence the government might have against al Baluchi (and the other defendants) aside from the now-suppressed confessions. Given how much the suppression hearing had dominated my life, this was something I had been thinking about ever since the FBI intelligence analyst Kimberly Waltz had testified a year earlier, in April 2024. Waltz said then that federal prosecutors in New York and Virginia had decided in 2009 not to use the FBI confessions for their case, back when the Obama administration was planning to prosecute it in Manhattan. Never mind all the prior torture by the CIA, these prosecutors thought that the lack of *Miranda* warnings would likely render the confessions inadmissible. The government had other evidence at its disposal, a fact that the suppression hearing had paradoxically both obscured and promoted with red flashing lights.

The media consortium's challenge to the sealing of the three plea agreements (which Lawdragon had joined in January) led to the public release of less-redacted versions of the documents in early February. Pages four through eight of Mohammed's agreement list twenty-six categories of evidence that the government planned to present at his sentencing trial—the FBI statements from January 2007 are but one. Not all of the evidentiary categories directly implicate the defendants, such as the first category, which includes the 2,976 death certificates of the victims, or the fourteenth, which is evidence collected at the World Trade Center crime scene. But the categories also include the intercepted phone calls between four of the defendants in the months before and after the attacks (Walid bin Attash was not a participant in the calls), along with the secret recordings made of the defendants at Camp 7. There is the "Islamic Response" from the first case in which they purportedly bragged about the attacks as a group, as well as statements made by three of the defendants (not including al Baluchi) during their Combatant Status Review Tribunals in 2007. The government also had a significant quantity of financial records and other documents allegedly linking the conspirators to the hijackers, which was particularly relevant to al Baluchi's case.

Still, despite all this evidence, the government refused to let go of the FBI statements once the case returned to the Gitmo military commissions. From Obama to Trump to Biden and back to Trump again, the government has held firm in its belief that the FBI "clean-team" system established in 2006 and 2007 to reinterrogate the 9/11 suspects had successfully laundered their previous experiences from the CIA black sites. This position has now been firmly rejected by two military judges and the commissions' appellate court. Whether or not the Guantanamo court is "a regularly constituted court" as required by Article 3 of the Gevena Conventions remains a matter of dispute; perhaps it always will be. But the court has spoken decisively: No matter how many hundreds of millions of dollars America spends to prove otherwise, there is no going back from torture.

The other categories of evidence underscore the stubborn complexities that will accompany the 9/11 case if it moves toward a trial. The admissibility of the FBI statements was the biggest and most witness-intensive pretrial hurdle, but the defense teams will file additional motions to suppress for several of the other categories. And, of course, the effort to suppress the FBI statements is far from over if the government is allowed to withdraw from the three plea agreements and Mohammed, bin Attash, and Mustafa al Hawsawi rejoin the pretrial litigation. It remains unclear if the case against Ramzi bin al Shibh, who has remained severed from the proceedings, will resume; it's possible the 9/11 prosecution could go on three separate tracks, with al Baluchi and bin al Shibh going solo and the other three defendants proceeding together. The case or cases will have a new judge (or judges) before jury selection could ever begin along with the attendant changes in legal teams due to age, retirement, or other professional and personal obligations—the constant threat of these complications and delays will continue once the trial (or trials) start, given their estimated length.

McCall was always seen—accurately as it turned out—as a relatively defense-friendly judge, and it's possible the case could get a new judge who moves the proceedings faster. But there's no reason to bet on that. A no-nonsense judge might be just as likely to order the prosecution to produce relevant witnesses—covert status or not—that pushes the case to a standstill. Or a judge might rule, as Pohl had, that the investigative and witness restrictions were too severe for a fair trial. A future judge might also be tempted to rule on the legal challenges that McCall and his predecessors left unaddressed, including whether the due-process guarantees of the Constitution apply to commission defendants. With all of these unresolved motions, including those alleging outrageous government conduct, the next judge or judges will have any number of avenues to sanction the government through suppression of evidence, dismissal of charges, or the removal of the death penalty as a sentencing option.

In fact, if the government can withdraw from the three plea agreements, the first motion of real consequence will be those defense teams seeking enforcement of the "poison pill" provision that renders the case noncapital upon a withdrawal or breach. Beyond that, Austin's reversal and all the political opposition to the plea agreements have set the stage for perhaps the case's biggest battle over unlawful influence, with relevant events spanning multiple years; disputes over discovery could last several months or longer. To top it off, Secretary of Defense Pete Hegseth's first comment on the 9/11 case was to tell Laura Ingraham on Fox News that he felt Mohammed deserved the death penalty—another drop in the unlawful-influence bucket. Defense lawyers have already begun scouring other public comments Hegseth has made throughout his career. It always remains possible that Trump or Hegseth will decide to halt court operations, as Obama did after he took office.

After I spoke at the Asheville class, the professor sent me a nice note about my journalistic style—that it was good for students to hear balanced commentary on controversial topics. I hadn't thought much about coming off this way, though it was consistent with some of the praise Lawdragon has received for our articles over the years. I've played it pretty straight in my coverage, firm in the belief that accurate reporting about the Guantanamo court lets the events speak for themselves; no need for me to get in the way. For all the reasons outlined, however, I'm honest when people ask me about the prospects of actually having trials, or whether the government should still try. The events of McCall's tenure support the position that plea deals followed by lengthy sentencing hearings are the best way out of a mess that has no other guaranteed way of ending. Much of the political commentary and opposition to this path has been riddled with ignorance and opportunism.

Still, I understand why many victim family members want a trial even while fully understanding all of the challenges involved. I might want the same thing in their shoes. Surely, additional information about the 9/11 attacks would come out in a contested guilt-or-innocence trial. On April 27, *60 Minutes* aired a segment on evidence that had recently surfaced in the family members' civil case in New York federal court against Saudi Arabia over its alleged role in aiding the 9/11 hijackers. (As of this writing, the Kingdom's motion to dismiss was pending.) The evidence was a video of the Capitol and surrounding areas in DC made by Omar al Bayoumi, a Saudi national who provided assistance to two of the 9/11 hijackers in Southern California. (Al Bayoumi was never charged and is living in Saudi Arabia.) In checking my past articles, I saw that James Connell gave his oral argument on a motion to compel evidence on al Bayoumi in October 2023, during a break between suppression witnesses. McCall later ruled for the defense, ordering the government to provide evidence related to al Bayoumi "currently or formerly in the custody of the FBI."

Connell told me that his team has received significant amounts of discovery on al Bayoumi, and more was on the way, given that the prosecution has filed several motions asking for an extension of time to comply with McCall's order. It's hard not to be intrigued. Information flows out of court proceedings. I saw so much sitting in court for about a decade that I felt compelled to put as much as I could into a single source. If the defendants had tried to plead guilty in May 2012, as many people predicted they would, I never would have even come to this strange place.

* * *

Due to a mix of personal and other work obligations, I only dipped my toes into coverage of the legal mess that followed Trump's January 29 directive to expand migrant operations on Guantanamo Bay. Tempted as I was, I did not see the need: Unlike the rest of America's operations on Guantanamo, the journalistic and public interest in the story was high. I told the students at Fordham that the plea agreements and Austin's reversal led to more national and international news coverage of the 9/11 case than the prior several years combined—a nonscientific, gut-level estimate—and that the news coverage of Trump's migrant operations on the base exceeded that of the plea agreements by a large margin. Put another way: Most Americans knew that Trump had sent migrants to Gitmo, but very few knew that the FBI agent who investigated the accused 9/11 mastermind referred to the CIA's interrogation program as "a flaming bag of crap" or that KSM wrote his former waterboarder, Dr. Bruce Jessen, a poem.

The Trump administration had started building a new tent city on the Leeward side of the base, but it ended up using the existing dormitory-style housing on Leeward as well as empty cells in the Camp 6 detention facility. According to administration lawyers, migrant detainees remained in the custody of ICE, but the Department of Defense provided for their "safe and humane care and control" through the newly created Joint Task Force Southern Guard or "JTF-SG." The ACLU, the Center for Constitutional Rights, and other groups sought to provide or at least facilitate legal representation for the detainees, which the administration technically allowed but made practically impossible with the first groups by deporting them to Venezuela before any assistance could be provided. The administration claimed that the migrants sent to Gitmo were serious criminals, but lawyers and family members of the detainees presented contrary information. The Guantanamo operations became one of the many due-process controversies confronting the Trump administration's efforts to deport migrants.

As it turned out, the tent city was abandoned (at least as of this writing). Thirty thousand migrants would not be coming to Guantanamo Bay, which anyone who had spent time on the base in recent years knew would be impossible. The plan had morphed into using the base as a temporary holding facility for migrants prior to their removal to other countries. Carol reported in the *Times* on March 31 that, in the first few months of JTF-SG, the base held about four hundred detainees, mostly Venezuelans and Nicaraguans, at a cost of about $40 million in the first month alone. The experiences of the detainees were, by some news accounts, harrowing, but one couldn't help but think that the fifteen law-of-war detainees were marveling at the speed at which the latest detainees came and left.

The *Times* article stated that operation had only added about a thousand new workers to Gitmo, nine hundred of them members of the military. Even so, this was a sizable increase given that the base population had previously been down to about 4,200 people. For that reason, I thought I would see for myself what changes, if any, the operations brought to my second home—which in 2025 was starting to feel less like a true second home. With the 9/11 case tabled until at least midsummer, I set my sights on a May 5–9 hearing in the USS *Cole* case, until something of an emergency medical situation forced me to skip it. Sadly, this meant I would also miss what would have been my second "Derby de Mayo" event at the Windjammer ballroom. (Unbelievably, it's possible I would have had to miss KSM's guilty plea if it happened in May.) A June hearing in the Hambali case would be up next.

Guantanamo Bay was always pulling me closer while pushing me away. Not having been there since February 1, a part of me really missed the place while another part thought I was crazy—that I should enjoy the time away while I could get it. Still, as much as Gitmo defies logic, there is always a logic to another trip. With all the chaos and busyness of the 9/11 case from the past year, I had mostly ignored the other cases, which suddenly felt regrettable. Also, as I had in my very first trip to the Hadi case in September 2015, I thought some lawyers from the 9/11 case might travel down for client meetings. If the weather cooperated, it might be nice to sit outside at night in the Caribbean breeze with Carol and some of the other participants in the traveling court system. If the bugs or heat were oppressive, we could always go to O'Kelly's or the bar at the bowling alley. It would be nice to catch up, share a few laughs, and discuss the various scenarios that might unfold in the year ahead.

Acknowledgments

A book based on fifty-five trips over ten years is bound to have too many people to thank, starting with those not directly involved in the reporting: my family, including my parents, siblings, and their families, and too many friends to list here. My Guantanamo coverage was made possible by Katrina Dewey and my other colleagues at Lawdragon—Alison, Carlton, Michelle, and Emily, among them. Not far behind are Jeff and Kristin for providing soft landings on the front and back ends of almost every trip, and my first wife, Fiona, for her support and patience during the first half of this journey. More recently, I am grateful to Tom Hundley and the Pulitzer Center for their support of our coverage.

Though this book makes the point that most news organizations have tended to ignore the proceedings on Guantanamo Bay, the best part of this assignment has been getting to know the journalists and media-adjacent folks who have been a part of the journey in some way. In addition to Carol Rosenberg, to whom I feel indebted for her friendship and incalculable help over the years, I am grateful to Terry McDermott, Lisa Hajjar, Leila Barghouty, Margot Williams, Kasey McCall-Smith, Ben Fox, Arun Rath, Janet Hamlin, Sarah Koenig, Dana Chivvis, Jeffrey Stern, Michelle Shephard, Dru Brenner-Beck, Karen Greenberg, Mark Fallon—and too many others to name who have made a particular trip, day in court, or night at O'Kelly's more bearable or even fun.

It's also impossible to thank all the participants, named in this book and otherwise, who have played roles in this traveling court system and given me their time—the public affairs officers (from Gary Ross through Ron Flesvig) and their support personnel, members of the legal teams and commissions staff, the victim family members, NGO attendees, Naval Base leadership and personnel, not to mention those who work at the base shops, bars, restaurants, and the Navy Gateway Inn & Suites. For brevity here, I give sincere credit and thanks to all the individuals who have led the Office of the Chief Prosecutor and the Military Commissions Defense Organization—as well as the lawyers who have led all the individual legal teams on both sides of the courtroom—for creating an environment of respect and collegiality for my reporting efforts. While not everyone spent as much time taking my questions as James Connell and other members of the Ammar al Baluchi team—or for that matter, as Mark Martins (now in private practice) did during my early years on the case—each team has been helpful in its own way. Sometimes a friendly conversation during an interminable day at the air terminal makes all the difference. I would be remiss to not thank by name David Nevin for getting me into this mess and for his continued patience as I endeavor to complete the profile I began in March 2015.

When it comes to this book, my fellowship at the Logan Nonfiction Program was a big boost at the outset of the writing process. Among many people who made that experience possible, thanks to program manager Zan Strumfeld, mentors Rafil Kroll-Zaidi and Samanth Subramanian, and my cohort partner-in-crime Amanda. My friend Gabe, who took me in during my pandemic separation and read early proposal drafts, was also critical in this phase, as was attorney Ryan Fox when eventually ironing out the book contract.

I am grateful to Mark Gompertz, executive editor at Skyhorse, and publisher Tony Lyons for recognizing that the absence of a trial—at least for now—did not mean there was not yet a story to fill a book. In addition to Mark's early guidance, I give great thanks to my editor Caroline Russomanno and the rest of the Skyhorse team for taking this complex and still-evolving tale home to completion, a process that included adding many pages after the book was first "done."

It's no coincidence that the proposal that led to Skyhorse's interest was the one that my wife, Allison, had edited and improved immensely. Allison has been the not-so-secret ingredient to my ability to stick with this story despite the ever-increasing uncertainty and absurdity, keeping me as sane and happy as possible. Completing this book is a small part of the luck I feel for having met her during that first pandemic summer.

Sources and Bibliography

I wanted the reader to experience the events of *America's Trial* much the way that I did. For this reason, the book is based mostly on my observations and interviews with sources during the court trips, many of which I did in the presence of other reporters on Guantanamo Bay. I read or reread court transcripts and pleadings to check my notes, flesh out reporting, and come to fuller—and occasionally somewhat different—understandings of the events. The transcripts and pleadings can be found at the website for the military commissions (mc.mil) by using the "Cases" navigation tool and selecting the 9/11 case.

My articles for Lawdragon (all freely available at lawdragon.com/guantanamo) and Carol Rosenberg's for the *New York Times* are probably the best sources for reading about the court proceedings, though of course online searches will pull up some of the excellent work done intermittently by friends and colleagues over the years at a wide range of publications.

Throughout *America's Trial*, I occasionally refer to books and reports that served as essential background or other relevant reading. Those materials and other select sources are listed below.

Bravin, Jess. *The Terror Courts: Rough Justice at Guantanamo Bay*. Yale University Press, 2013.
Denbeaux, Mark P., and Jonathan Hafetz, eds. *The Guantanamo Lawyers: Inside a Prison Outside the Law*. New York University Press, 2009.
Fallon, Mark. *Unjustifiable Means: The Inside Story of How the CIA, Pentagon, and US Government Conspired to Torture*. Regan Arts, 2017.
Greenberg, Karen. *The Least Worst Place: Guantanamo's First 100 Days*. Oxford University Press, 2009.

Greenberg, Karen, and Joshua Dratel. *The Torture Papers: The Road to Abu Ghraib.* Cambridge University Press, 2005.

Hajjar, Lisa. *The War in Court: Inside the Long Fight Against Torture.* University of California Press, 2022.

Hamlin, Janet, and Carol Rosenberg. *Sketching Guantanamo: Court Sketches of the Military Tribunals, 2006–2013.* Fantagraphics Books, 2013.

Klaidman, Daniel. *Kill or Capture: The War on Terror and the Soul of the Obama Presidency.* Houghton Mifflin Harcourt, 2012.

Koenig, Sarah, and Dana Chivvis, hosts. *Serial* Season 4: Guantanamo. https://www.nytimes.com/interactive/2024/podcasts/serial-season-four-guantanamo.html.

Mayer, Jane. *The Dark Side: The Inside Story of How the War on Terror Turned into a War on American Ideals.* Doubleday, 2008.

McDermott, Terry. *Perfect Soldiers: The 9/11 Hijackers: Who They Were, Why They Did It.* Harper, 2005.

McDermott, Terry, and Josh Meyer. *The Hunt for KSM: Inside the Pursuit and Takedown of the Real 9/11 Mastermind.* Back Bay Books, 2012.

Mitchell, James, and Bill Harlow. *Enhanced Interrogation: Inside the Minds and Motives of the Islamic Terrorists Trying to Destroy America.* Crown Publishing Group, 2016.

National Commission on Terrorist Attacks Upon the United States, The. *The 9/11 Commission Report.* Government Printing Office, 2004.

Paglen, Trevor, and A. C. Thompson. *Torture Taxi: On the Trail of the CIA's Rendition Flights.* Melville House Publishing, 2006.

Rejali, Darius. *Torture and Democracy.* Princeton University Press, 2007.

Rodriguez, Jose, and Bill Harlow. *Hard Measures: How Aggressive CIA Actions After 9/11 Saved American Lives.* Threshold Editions, 2012.

Rosenberg, Carol. *Guantanamo Bay: The Pentagon's Alcatraz of the Caribbean.* Herald Books, 2016.

Savage, Charlie. *Power Wars: Inside Obama's Post-9/11 Presidency.* Little, Brown and Company, 2011.

Scott-Clark, Cathy, and Adrian Levy. *The Forever Prisoner: The Full and Searing Account of the CIA's Most Controversial Covert Program.* Atlantic Monthly Press, 2022.

Shepard, Michelle. *Guantanamo's Child: The Untold Story of Omar Khadr.* HarperCollins, 2014.

Slahi, Mohamedou Ould. *Guantanamo Diary.* Little, Brown and Company, 2015.

Soufan, Ali, and Daniel Freedman. *The Black Banners (Declassified): How Torture Derailed the War on Terror After 9/11*. W. W. Norton & Company, 2020.

U.S. Central Intelligence Agency. *Comments on the Senate Select Committee on Intelligence's Study of the Central Intelligence Agency's Former Detention and Interrogation Program*. June 2013.

U.S. Library of Congress. Congressional Research Service. *The Military Commissions Act of 2009 (MCA 2009): Overview and Legal Issues*, by Jennifer K. Elsea. R41163. 2014.

U.S. Congress. Senate. Senate Select Committee on Intelligence. *Committee Study of the Central Intelligence Agency's Detention and Interrogation Program*. 113th Cong., 2nd sess. S. Report 113–288. December 2014.

Wright, Lawrence. *The Looming Tower: Al-Qaeda and the Road to 9/11*. Vintage Books, 2006.

Index

abaya (body cloak), 23–24, 109–110
Abdulmutallab, Umar Farouk, 196
ACCM (alternative compensatory control measure), 25–26
ACLU. *See* American Civil Liberties Union
Acosta, Lanny, 312–313, 324
AE (appellate exhibit) docketing system, 29–31, 133, 343
A Few Good Men, 13, 192, 194
Afghanistan. *See also* Location 2 facility
 discussion, 7–8
 Taliban, 63–64
 withdrawal of US forces, 127, 288–289, 292–293
al Baluchi, Ammar. *See* Baluchi, Ammar al
al Hawsawi, Mustafa. *See* Hawsawi, Mustafa al
Ali, Ali Abdul Aziz. *See* al Baluchi, Ammar
alien unprivileged enemy belligerents
 discussion, 11, 136–137, 325–326
 military commissions for trying, 62–65
Al Jazeera, 76, 345
al Nashiri, Abd al Rahim. *See* Nashiri, Abd al Rahim al
al Qaeda
 discussion, 7–8, 11, 36, 269
 hostilities arguments, 137–138, 183–184, 304–305
 promotional videos, 136, 140

alternative compensatory control measure (ACCM), 25–26
American Airlines Flight 11, 57, 135–136, 138
American Civil Liberties Union (ACLU)
 discussion, 16, 86, 240
 John Adams Project, 7, 217–218
 representation of migrant detainees, 407–408
"American Taliban," 63–64
Antol, Brian (FBI), 319, 320, 322–323
Aoláin, Fionnuala Ní, 340–341
appellate exhibit (AE) docketing system, 29–31, 133, 343
Article 3 of the Geneva Conventions, 36, 234–235, 404–405
Ashcraft v. Tennessee (1944), 393
Atkins, Rodney, 326
Atta, Mohamed, 57
attention grabs, 311
audio-video delay in courtroom
 discussion, 9–10, 16, 56, 151
 intelligence agency tablet in courtroom, 277–278
Austin, Lloyd
 discussion, 315
 revocation of plea agreements, 364–367, 371–374, 385–386, 379, 396, 406
author
 journalistic background, 2, 45, 291–293
 transitional justice studies, 73–76

Bad Boys II, 196–197
Bahlul, Ali Hamza al, 129
Baker, John
   discussion, 26, 111–115, 307
   on Harrington motion for removal, 272–273
Bali, Indonesia, bombing. *See* Indonesia terror plot
Baltes, Joanna, 4
Baluchi, Ammar al. *See also* Connell, James; suppression hearing; suppression hearing, continued alleged financial role in 9/11 attacks, 211–213
   capture and interrogations, 330
   CSRT statements, 220
   discussion, 22, 25, 40–41, 293
   hostilities arguments, 183–186
   jurisdictional challenges, 137–138
   McCall suppression ruling, 399–403
   PTSD suffered, 267, 349–350, 372-373, 391–392
   relationship with Connell, 53–56
   representation in *Zero Dark Thirty*, 51–52, 55–56
   requests for UFI witnesses, 159, 336
   torture of, 246–247, 372–373, 390-391
Barghouty, Leila, 187, 284
Basnicki, Maureen and family, 381
Bayoumi, Omar al, 406–407
Bechtel, John, 329
Bernstein, Assaf, 227
Berry, Elizabeth and Paul, 296
Biden administration
   conflicts with Martins, 294–295
   discussion, 127, 285, 363
   plea discussions, 308, 315–316
   withdrawal of US forces from Afghanistan, 127, 288–289, 292–293
   writ of mandamus for plea agreements, 387–388
Bigelow, Kathryn, 51
Bin al Shibh, Ramzi. *See also* Bruck, David; Harrington, James
   Al Jazeera interview, 345

   complaints of ongoing torture, 57–59, 67, 95, 118, 295–296
   discussion, 5–7, 22, 38, 51, 76, 230
   enhanced and standard interrogation techniques used on, 262–266
   interrogation at black site, 231–233
   mental competency concerns, 75, 316–317
   motions on decommissioned black site, 82
   occasional disruptions to proceedings, 69
   severance of case, 317, 371
Bin Amin, Mohammed Farik bin, 285, 289, 292, 329–330
Bin Attash, Walid. *See also* Bormann, Cheryl; Engle, Matthew
   capture and interrogations, 330
   discussion, 22–23, 310, 320
   disruptions to proceedings, 69, 85–86
   FBI interview of defense team paralegal, 177–179
   plea agreement and revocation, 359–365, 371-374, 379-381
   requests for UFI witnesses, 335–336
   request to remove counsel, 23–25, 31–32, 85–86
   use of EITs on, 264–265
Bin Laden, Osama
   discussion, 22, 52, 129, 140, 143
   hostilities arguments, 137, 138, 183–184
Bin Lep, Mohammed Nazir, 285, 289, 292, 329
Black Banners (Soufan & Freedman), 243
Black Lives Matter protests, 283–284
black sites. *See also specific black sites*
   detainee transfer to Guantanamo Bay from, 21–22
   discussion, 4, 35, 37–40, 96
   instant messenger chats on, 205–206
   McCall tour of, 347–348
   motions on decommissioned, 79–84, 147–150
   use of Guantanamo as, 144, 208, 233, 330–331

Bleak House (Dickens), 371–372
Blue location. *See* Location 4 facility
Boal, Mark, 51
Borger, Julian, 240
Bormann, Cheryl
    arguments for FBI-CIA coordination discovery, 161–163
    Bin Attash motion to remove, 23–25, 31–32, 85–86
    discussion, 42, 51, 109–110, 187
    examination of Mitchell, 263–266
    FBI interview of defense team paralegal, 177–179
    filing of suppression motion, 203
    MCDO investigation into, 307–309
    use of abaya, 23–24, 109–111
    wrist injury, 107, 112, 217
Boryczewski, Julie and family, 381
Boston Marathon bomber, 295
Boumediene v. Bush (2008), 13
Brady v. Maryland (1963), 44
Bravin, Jess, 3
Brenner-Beck, Dru, 86, 175
Brosnahan, James, 64
Brown, Gary, 180–183, 226–227
Bruck, David, 295–296, 310, 316–317
Burke, William, 296
Burns, Scott Z., 259
Bush administration
    al Qaeda-US hostilities, 137–138
    discussion, 2, 35, 41, 180, 241
    military commissions, 62–63, 75–76
    war-on-terror detainees, 13–14, 36
Butsch, Michael (FBI), 231–234

Caggins, Myles, 7
Camp 5 facility, 48–49, 89, 293–294
Camp 6 facility, 48–49, 89, 407
Camp 7 facility
    alleged noises and vibrations, 57–60
    closure, 293–294
    discussion, 21, 27, 47, 56, 76–77, 293, 401
    secret recordings of detainees, 213, 345, 404
    top secret ACCM program, 25–27
Camp Echo 2, 347–348
Camp Justice
    discussion, 12, 14–15, 50, 117, 223
    upgrades and construction, 317–319
Campoamor-Sanchez, Fernando, 23, 25, 28–29, 31
Camp X-Ray, 193–194, 197
Camp X-Ray (film), 194–195
Carter, Ash, 180
Carter, Jimmy, 388–389
Casey, Susan, 72
Castle, William, 181–183
Castro, Fidel, 13
Catch-22 (Heller), 179
Center for Constitutional Rights, 302, 407–408
Central Intelligence Agency (CIA). *See also* black sites; enhanced interrogation techniques; interagency coordination; Jessen, Bruce; Mitchell, James; suppression hearing; suppression hearing, continued
    contacting of Mitchell and Jessen for post-9/11 interrogations, 241
    discussion, 35–41, 238, 241
    FBI agents detailed to, 208, 230, 232, 304, 330, 331, 358
    information in *Zero Dark Thirty*, 51–52
    interpreter on defense team, 6
    instant messenger chats on black sites, 205–206
    rebuttal to Senate Torture Report, 251
    rectal techniques, 95–97, 171–172, 174, 256, 302, 311
    restrictions on investigation of personnel, 150–152, 154–160, 334-335
    use of Guantanamo as black site, 144, 208, 233, 330–331
Charleston, South Carolina, church attack, 295
Chivvis, Dana, 319
Cho, John, 195
CITF (Criminal Investigation Task Force), 139

Clarke, Peter J., 89
Classified Information Procedures Act (CIPA)
   CIPA-like provisions, 38–39, 44, 81–82, 122, 148–149, 151, 160
   motions on decommissioned black site, 81, 83, 84–85
   Pohl voir dire on decommissioned black site, 121–126
   classified information spills. *See also* audio-video delay in courtroom
   discussion, 4, 10, 113, 210, 323, 330–331
   intelligence agency tablet in courtroom, 277–280
Clinton, Hillary, 94, 106, 129
Clinton administration, 137–138, 196–197
CMCR (Court of Military Commission Review), 55, 113, 127, 385–386
Cobalt facility. *See* Location 2 facility
coercive physical pressures, 242, 244–245. *See also* enhanced interrogation techniques
Cohen, Shane
   approval of intelligence agency tablet in courtroom, 277–280
   on Harrington motion for removal, 271–277
   pre-suppression hearing matters, 208–213
   retirement announcement, 281–282
   suppression hearing scheduling discussions, 203–204, 222–223
   suppression hearing testimony, 211–217, 219–222, 231, 235
   trial date discussions, 204–206
   voir dire, 201–202
cold temperature torture, 233, 302
Cole, Adam, 348
Combatant Status Review Tribunals (CSRTs), 76, 219–222, 345, 404
conditioned fear, 334, 355–358
confinement boxes, 243, 311–312
Congress, 3, 64, 196
Connell, James
   Camp 7, 26, 234–235
   on Camp X-Ray, 194
   discovery arguments before Pohl, 40–43
   discussion, 41–42, 53, 67, 109
   examination of Mitchell, 237–247
   "explainer-in-chief" role, 30–31, 133–134
   FBI agents switched to CIA, 304
   hostilities arguments, 137–138, 183–184
   information in *Zero Dark Thirty*, 51–52
   on intelligence agency tablet in courtroom, 277–280
   jurisdictional challenges, 137–138, 145
   motion on constitutionality of military commissions, 93–94
   motions on decommissioned black site, 82, 147–154
   on Nashiri suppression ruling, 313
   on Omar al Bayoumi, 406–407
   on operational tempo of case, 337
   on Pohl suppression of FBI statements, 165, 173–174
   Pohl voir dire on decommissioned black site, 123–126
   pro se question, 25
   relationship with Baluchi, 53–56
   restrictions on investigating CIA personnel, 147–150, 152, 154–156, 159, 393
   security interruptions during testimony, 330–333
   suppression hearing testimony preparation, 208–211
   suppression hearing witness examinations, 214–217, 231–232, 237–247, 322–323, 343–344
   tracking of AEs, 30–31
   trial date discussions, 204–206
   unlawful influence motions testimony, 181, 183
Constitution
   applicability to enemy belligerents, 325–326
   discussion, 93–94, 149, 201–202

Index 421

convening authorities
   Austin plea revocation question, 364–367, 371–374, 379
   discussion, 110, 133, 285–286, 289
Convention Against Torture, 150
Cordry, Rob, 195
coronavirus pandemic
   discussion, 280–285, 293, 298, 305
   effect on case, 291–294
   quarantine protocols, 285–287
   Remote Hearing Room arrangement, 297–298
Cotton, Tom, 363
Counterterrorism Center (CTC), 241, 242, 246
Court of Military Commission Review (CMCR), 55, 113, 127, 385–386
covert agents. *See specific covert agents*
COVID-19 pandemic. *See* coronavirus pandemic
Cox, David, 192
Crawford, Susan, 110
Criminal Investigation Task Force (CITF), 139
Crosby, Sondra, 311–313
Cruise, Tom, 192
Cruz, Ted, 315–316, 352
CSRTs (Combatant Status Review Tribunals), 76, 219–222, 345, 404
CTC (Counterterrorism Center), 241, 242, 246
Cuba, 13, 191
Cuban service workers, 193
Cuddy, Alice, 387
Culpepper, David, 197

Darbi, Ahmed al, 129
"DC Sniper," 53
death penalty
   discussion, 3, 7, 109, 295
   guilty pleas and, 362–363
   military commissions, 113, 117, 150
   plea discussions, 307–310, 373–374
DeLury, Bernard, 219–223
detainee transfer
   ban on funds for, 3, 64, 196
   Camp 5 facility, 293–294
   Camp 6 facility, 407–408
   discussion, 35–36, 288, 386
   Obama administration, 14, 64, 345
Dewey, Katrina, 45, 92, 175, 291, 292, 383, 385, 387
Dickens, Charles, 371–372
Dixon, Wells, 302
Don Lemon Show podcast, 396
"Dr. 1" (WK5I covert medical professional), 371–372, 390, 392
Driscoll, Kevin, 25
Driver, Adam, 259
Drucker, Adam (FBI), 229–231
Dubose, Lou, 61
due-process provisions of Constitution
   discussion, 55, 93–94, 325–326
   migrant detainees, 407–408
   national security privilege versus, 150, 239–240
Dunford, Joseph, 180
Durham, John, 263
Dykstra, Christopher, 277–278
Dylan, Bob, 306

earthquake, 259–260
eavesdropping, 5, 27, 114, 298
Edwards, George, 86, 89
806 sessions, 132, 190
EITs. *See* enhanced interrogation techniques
ELC (Expeditionary Legal Complex), 14–15, 21, 318–319
embassy bombings (1998), 63, 137, 138
Engle, Matthew, 310, 335, 359, 396
Enhanced Interrogation (Mitchell & Harlow), 238, 239–240, 259
enhanced interrogation techniques (EITs)
   approved list, 243–244
   discussion, 4, 35, 41, 130
   fear extinction, 334, 355–358
   Jessen testimony on, 243–244, 269–270, 356–358

Mitchell testimony on, 244–247, 256–257, 262–266, 333–334
unauthorized techniques, discussion, 245–249
used on Baluchi, 246-247, 390–391
used on Bin al Shibh, 262–263
used on Bin Attash, 264–265
used on Hawsawi, 248–249
used on Mohammed, 6–7, 256–257, 321-322, 356–357
used on Zubaydah, 118–119, 263–264
Eriksson, Kalen, 395
Escallier, Susan, 325, 359, 363, 365
Espionage Act, 152
European Court of Human Rights, 13–14
Exile, The (Levy & Scott-Clark), 252
Ex Parte Quirin, 62–63
Expeditionary Legal Complex (ELC), 14–15, 21, 318–319

Fairben, Kenneth and family, 71, 73, 251
Faircloth, Cherie, 387
Fauda, 227
fear extinction, 334, 355–358
Federal Bureau of Investigation (FBI). *See also* interagency coordination; suppression hearing; suppression hearing, continued; *specific agents and analysts*
agents detailed to CIA, 208, 230, 232, 304, 331, 358
"clean teams" for Guantanamo interrogations, 35–37, 141–142
decision by Mueller to not use EITs, 243
discussion, 64, 404–405
infiltration of defense teams, 5–7, 23, 24, 28–30, 56–57, 113
interview of defense team paralegal, 177–179
McCall suppression of FBI statements, 400–403
Miranda warnings and lack of, 35, 64, 139, 196, 212, 322, 345, 392, 401, 404
Parrella reversal of Pohl suppression ruling, 184–185

PENTTBOM team, 135–136, 138–139, 143–145, 229–234
Pohl suppression of FBI statements, 164–165
rapport-based interrogation methods, 35, 143, 213, 242, 321, 391
voluntariness of "clean statements," 321–325, 345–346, 389–393
federal courts. *See specific federal courts*
female-guard dispute, 43–44, 56, 180
Fifth Amendment, 325–326
Filipino service workers, 190, 370
First Camp 7 Commander, 234–235, 358–359
Fitzgerald, James (FBI)
Hawsawi jurisdictional challenge testimony, 135–136, 138, 143–144
suppression hearing testimony, 211–216, 327–328
Fitzsimmons, James (FBI/CIA), 271–272, 274, 330–333
505 process, 39, 44, 81–82. *See also* Classified Information Procedures Act; Site A facility
Flagg family, 251–252
Flesvig, Ron, 228–229, 282, 284, 286, 287, 292, 298, 339, 347
forced feeding, 49, 89, 302
forced shavings, 174, 262
Fordham University School of Law, 404–405, 406, 407
Forever Prisoner, The (Levy & Scott-Clark), 252
Foster, Jodie, 195
Fouda, Yosri, 76
Fox, Ben, 19, 27, 105, 115, 119, 187, 193
Freund, Carol and family, 387
fruit of the poisonous tree concept
discussion, 140–145, 150
suppression hearing, 208–209
Funk, Christine, 329

Gabavics, Stephen, 89
Garcia, Deborah and family, 381–382, 387

Index

Gates, Claire, 387
Gaudin, Stephen (FBI)
    discussion, 242, 243, 252
    interrogation of Zubaydah, 263–264
    possible suppression hearing testimony, 321, 346, 351, 362
Geneva Conventions, Article 3, 36, 234–235, 404–405
Gerhardt, Stephan, 387, 388
Ghailani, Ahmed Khalfan, 63
Gibney, Alex, 252
"Gitmo brain," 87, 152–154, 299
Gladwell, Malcolm, 238
Greenberg, Karen, 13, 193
Greengrass, Paul, 21
Groharing, Jeffrey
    discussion, 144, 168, 169, 170, 211–213
    Mitchell suppression hearing testimony, 266–268
    oral arguments on suppression hearing, 389–393
    restrictions on investigating CIA personnel, 156–160, 170–174
    suppression hearing witness examinations, 214–217, 241, 247, 249–250, 259–261, 266–267, 357–358
"Guantanamo" (podcast series), 319–320, 349, 381
Guantanamo (television program), 115, 227
Guantanamo Bay (documentary), 89
Guantanamo Bay (Rosenberg), 88
Guantanamo Bay Naval Base
    Camp X-Ray, 193–194, 197
    court system, 10–11, 201–202, 404–405
    depiction in movies, 192–197
    detention centers, 12, 47–50, 88–90
    discussion, 2, 9, 191, 198, 306, 370
    due-process provisions questions, 325–326
    earthquake, 259–261
    environmental hazards, 14, 222–223
    media policy changes, 129–134, 153
    media tours, 47–50, 190–191
    migrant operations center, 396, 407–408
    minefields, 196–197
    monotony on, 189–191
    9/11 twentieth anniversary memorial, 291–293, 297
    Northeast Gate, 191–193
    physical description, 11–13, 189–191
    service workers, 190, 193, 197, 370
    use as black site, 144, 208, 233, 330–331
Guantanamo Diary (Slahi), 195
Guantanamo Review Task Force, 40
Guantanamo's Child (Shephard), 388
Guilmette, Thomas, 372–373
Gupta, Anisha, 335–336

habeas corpus, 13–14, 42
Hadi al Iraqi, Abd al. *See* Iraqi, Abd al Hadi al
Haim, Laura, 19
Hajjar, Lisa, 187, 252, 284, 388, 395
Hambali. *See* Nurjaman, Encep
Hamdan, Salim, 281
Hamdan v. Rumsfeld (2006), 36, 281
Hamlin, Janet, 240
Hanrahan, David, 372–373
Hanson, Lee and family, 68–69, 108, 109, 111, 274
Hard Measures (Rodriguez), 156
Harlow, Bill, 238
Harold & Kumar Escape From Guantanamo Bay, 195–196
Harrington, James
    Butsch suppression examination, 233
    Camp 7 alleged noise and vibrations, 57–60
    Cohen voir dire, 201–202
    discussion, 5, 23, 56–57, 109, 233, 295
    FBI interview of defense team paralegal, 178–179
    on limitations on investigating CIA personnel, 156
    litigation over FBI infiltration of defense team, 26, 28–29, 31

Mitchell suppression examination, 262–263
motion for removal, 271–277
motions on decommissioned black site, 125–126
Parrella voir dire, 168
Zubaydah testimony, 118–119
Harris, Kamala, 363
Harris, Kevin, 1
Harry Potter series, 49, 89, 195
Haspel, Gina, 130, 158
Hawsawi, Mustafa al. *See also* Ruiz, Walter
alleged financial role in 9/11 attacks, 139–140
colorectal damage, 22, 95–97, 99–101, 103, 267
discovery on interagency coordination, 139–144
discussion, 22–23, 59, 75, 294
at Guantanamo black site, 144, 208, 330–331
hostilities ruling, 183–184
jurisdictional challenge, 136–138
motion to dismiss for outrageous government conduct, 332–333
motion to sever case, 97–98, 103
plea agreement and revocation, 359–365, 371–374, 379–381
presence at Mitchell suppression hearing testimony, 247–248
requests for UFI witnesses, 335–336
unauthorized EITs used on, 248–249
hearsay statements, 54, 64
Heath, David, 44, 49
Hegseth, Pete, 406
Hela, Ali Abdulrahman al, 325–326
Heller, Joseph, 179
Henderson, Valerie, 92, 131
Hendricks, Bobby, 306
Henley, Stephen, 75
Hensler, Susan, 288–289
Herridge, Catherine, 395
Hersh, Seymour, 291, 292
Higgins, Sarah, 132–133, 228

hijab (head coverings), 23–24
hockey-light interruptions. *See* security interruptions
Hodge, Douglas, 259
Hodgson, James, 334–335
Holder, Eric, 3, 64
Hollander, Nancy, 195
Holt, Lester, 360
hostilities arguments, 137–138, 183–186, 304–305
hunger strikes, 49, 88, 89, 302
Hunt for KSM, The (McDermott & Meyer), 319
hurricanes, 169, 376

ICTY (International Criminal Tribunal for the Former Yugoslavia), 55
Impeach (Katyal & Koppelman), 281
Indonesia terror plot, 285, 289, 292, 301, 329
instant messenger chats, 205–206
Intelligence Identities Protection Act, 152
interagency coordination (FBI-CIA). *See also specific FBI agents and analysts*
discovery, 141–142, 161–164
discussion, 214–217
FBI agents detailed to CIA, 230, 232, 304, 331, 358
FBI intelligence requirements sent to CIA, 143–144, 214, 229, 392
FBI presence at Location 5 facility, 231–232
FBI review of CIA information and databases prior to interviewing 9/11 defendants, 143–144, 215–217, 231
FBI use of CIA laptops and workspace on Guantanamo, 144, 321, 323
fruit of the poisonous tree concept, 140–145, 150
interrogations of Zubaydah, 242–243
International Criminal Tribunal for the Former Yugoslavia (ICTY), 55
Iraqi, Abd al Hadi al
discussion, 7–8, 11, 70–71, 115
plea and sentencing, 355
pretrial proceedings, 287–289

Index

request for new lead defense, 15–17
"Islamic Response" document, 75–76, 345, 404
Islamiyah Jemaah terrorist group. *See* Indonesia terror plot
isolation. *See* prolonged isolation

Jamaican service workers, 190, 197, 370
Jemmott, Matthew, 340
Jessen, Bruce
   discussion, 156, 226, 238–239, 336
   examination at Nashiri suppression hearing, 311–313
   interrogation of Nashiri, 245
   JPRA position, 241–242
   suppression hearing testimony, 268–270, 355–358
   use of EITs on Zubaydah, 243–244
Jocys, Maria (FBI), 358, 362
John Adams Project, 7, 217–218
Joint Personnel Recovery Agency (JPRA), 241–242
Joint Task Force Guantanamo (JTF-GTMO)
   closure of Guantanamo Bay facilities, 88–89
   discussion, 20–21, 43
   media tours, 47–50, 89–90
Joint Task Force Southern Guard (JTF-SG), 407–408
Jones, Daniel, 259
jury selection, 118, 225
Justice for 9/11 Act, 363

Kaczynski, Ted, 217, 218, 219
Kammen, Rick, 114
Kampf, Lena, 89
Kane, Steven, 340
Kaplan, Lewis, 63
Karadžić, Radovan, 21
Katyal, Neal, 281
Kelly, Colleen and family, 32–33, 72, 108, 319–320, 381
Kelly, Wendy, 92
Kenya embassy bombing (1998), 63, 137, 138

Khan, Majid, 280, 289, 301–303
Kill or Capture (Klaidman), 213
Kingdom of Saudi Arabia, 363, 406–407
Kirby, John, 285
Klaidman, Daniel, 213
Koenig, Sarah, 319, 320, 349
Kohlmann, Evan, 349
Koppelman, Sam, 281
Kraehe, George, 340
Krause, Tammy, 72
KSM. *See* Mohammed, Khalid Sheikh
Kube, Courtney, 360

Lachelier, Suzanne, 59, 141, 378
Laden, Osama bin. *See* Bin Laden, Osama
Lang, Stephen, 192
Lawfare blog, 3
Lawrence, Martin, 196
learned counsel representation
   Bin al Shibh, 295
   Bin Attash, 307, 309
   Bormann, Cheryl, 107–108
   discussion, 7, 15, 111, 217
   Harrington motion for removal, 271–275
   Hawsawi, 97, 102, 104, 294
learned helplessness, 220, 222, 244, 374–375
Least Worst Place, The (Greenberg), 13, 193
Leboeuf, Denise, 217–218
Levy, Adrian, 252
Lindh, John Walker, 63–64
LinkedIn profiles, 156
listening devices, 5, 27, 114, 298
Location 2 facility, 96, 172–175, 245, 248, 256, 267, 269–270, 390, 401
Location 3 facility, 242, 244, 245, 264
Location 4 facility, 245–246, 248, 256, 262–263, 267
Location 5 facility, 232, 263
Location 7 facility, 264
Loftus, Karen, 72

Logan Nonfiction Fellowship Program, 284–285, 286
Lowry, Willy, 296–297

MA2 (covert agent), 246, 266
Maadi, Payman, 194
MacNaughton, Wendy, 226
Malliotakis, Nicole, 315
"Manchester Manual," 269
Manila Air Plot, 322
Marriot Hotel bombing (2003), 301
Martins, Mark
    discovery arguments, 42–45
    discussion, 10–11, 14, 19, 40, 280
    interview, 62–65
    media policy changes, 132, 133–134
    motions on decommissioned black site, 83
    Pohl voir dire on decommissioned black site, 124
    pretrial media statement, 67, 68
    restrictions on investigating CIA personnel, 147–152
    retirement from case, 294–295, 308–309
    ten category framework for CIA discovery, 37–38, 51
Mattis, James, 133, 180, 181–182
Mauritanian, The (film), 195
McAdams, Rachel, 226
McCall, Matthew. *See also* suppression hearing, continued
    Bin al Shibh competency ruling, 316–317
    Camp Echo 2 tour, 347–348
    ex parte meetings with defense teams, 297
    focus on discovery motions, 303–305, 310
    MCDO investigation into Bormann, 307–309
    operational tempo of case, 336–337, 351–352, 355, 358
    plea agreements and Austin revocation, 359–367, 371, 379–381, 385–388
    plea discussions, 308–310
    requests for UFI witnesses, 334–336
    resumption of suppression hearings, 313, 315–316
    retirement from case and postponements, 327–328, 336–337, 352, 367, 377
    security interruptions during suppression hearing, 330–333
    suppression ruling on FBI statements, 399–403
    suppression scheduling arguments, 323–325, 336–337, 346
    voir dire, 294, 296
    Waltz suppression testimony, 343–346
McCall-Smith, Kasey, 187, 225, 284
McConnell, Mitch, 362–363
McCue, Nicholas, 357
McDermott, Terry, 57, 115, 116, 187, 227, 252, 284, 292, 319–320, 339, 356, 361, 387
MCDO. *See* Military Commissions Defense Organization
McDonald, Kevin, 195
McElwain, Gregory, 48, 50, 60–62
McFadden, Robert, 350–351, 367
"Media Ground Rules for Guantanamo Bay, Cuba" document, 9–10
Media Operations Center (MOC), 15, 227–229, 317–319
media organizations
    access policy changes, 129–134, 153
    discussion, 16, 86, 225–229
    9/11 twentieth anniversary memorial, 291–293
    tours, 47–50, 89–90, 190–191
medical care, withholding, 265
Merriman, Justin, 89
Mexican American War, 62
Meyer, Josh, 319
migrant operations expansion, 396, 407–408
Mike Drop podcast, 250
Military Commissions Act of 2006, 35–36, 75, 184
Military Commissions Act of 2009, 35, 38, 40, 44, 54, 136–137, 164, 179–181, 184, 365, 391–392
Military Commissions Defense Organization (MCDO)

Index

discussion, 31, 112–113, 177, 320, 396
investigation into Bormann, 307–309
military commissions system
    alien belligerents, 2–3, 62–65
    annual cost, 112, 227
    applicability of Constitution to, 93–94, 149, 201–202, 325–326
    Bush administration, 35–36
    CIPA-like provision, 148–149, 151
    death penalty under, 113, 115, 150
    discussion, 10, 19–20, 31, 84, 110
    806 sessions, 132, 190
    learned counsel representation, 97, 102, 104
    media policy changes, 129–134, 153
    Obama administration calls for reforming, 63, 64–65
    Sanity Board, 316–317
    website, 132, 133
Miller, Elizabeth, 387
Millett, Patricia, 395–396
Mind Over Mood (Greenberger & Padesky), 372
Miranda warnings or lack of, 35, 64, 139, 196, 212, 322, 345, 392, 401, 404
Mitchell, James
    Bormann suppression examination, 263–266
    Connell suppression examination, 237–247
    discussion, 156, 203, 226
    Groharing suppression examination, 266–268
    Harrington suppression examination, 262–263
    Nevin suppression examination, 255–261, 267–268
    Ruiz suppression examination, 247–250
    Sowards suppression examination, 333–334
    threats of murdering Mohammed's sons, 257–258, 333
    use of EITs on Zubaydah, 243–244
MOC (Media Operations Center), 15, 227–229, 317–319

mock burials, 264
modified rights advisement, 212, 389
Mohammed, Khalid Sheikh. *See also* Nevin, David; Sowards, Gary
    CSRT, 76, 219–222
    discussion, 1, 4, 22–23, 38, 294, 319–320, 345
    early interrogations, 171–172, 173, 174
    EITs used on, 6–7, 256–257, 322, 356–357
    nuclear bomb statement, 69–70
    plea agreement and revocation, 359–365, 371–374, 379-381, 385–388
    threats of murdering sons made to, 257–258, 333
Montross, William, 307, 367–368
Morgan, Annie, 311–313, 356
Morgan, Charles, 349–350
"Motion to End Apparent Intelligence Agency Disruption of Courtroom Proceedings," 277–280
Moussaoui, Zacarias, 38
"Mr. Ali." *See* al Baluchi, Ammar
Mueller, Robert, 243, 264
Muhammad, John Allen, 53

Nashiri, Abd al Rahim al
    commission case, 37–38
    discussion, 114, 118, 351–352
    hearings, 295, 298–299
    suppression hearing and ruling, 311–313, 402
    torture of, 245, 246
Natale, Anthony, 311–313, 351–352
National Association of Criminal Defense Lawyers, 7
National Commission on Terrorist Attacks Upon the United States, 230
National Institute of Military Justice, 86
national security privilege
    discussion, 124, 209, 241, 324
    due-process provisions versus, 150, 239–240
    restrictions on defense team, 335–336
Naudet, Jules and Gedeon, 135–136
Nettleton, John, 131

Nevin, David
    discussion, 26, 44, 77, 109, 159, 170, 340
    FBI defense team infiltration, 29–30, 178, 185
    FBI interview of defense team paralegal, 178, 185
    Mitchell suppression examination, 255–261, 267–268
    on Mohammed nuclear bomb statement, 69–70
    motions on decommissioned black site, 79–84
    motions to record VFM testimony, 69
    Parrella voir dire, 167–168
    Perkins suppression examination, 327–328
    on Pohl suppression of FBI statements, 174
    Pohl voir dire on decommissioned black site, 121–126
    on pretrial events, 1–2, 5–7, 8, 92
    restrictions on investigating CIA personnel, 150–152, 154
    trial date discussions with Cohen, 206
    withdrawal as Mohammed learned counsel, 217–219, 222
Newman, Douglas, 181
"the New Sheriff." *See* NX2
NGOs (nongovernmental organizations), 19–20, 32, 42, 86
Nicholson, Jack, 192
9/11 attacks
    discussion, 67, 69, 135–136, 140, 170
    Planes Operation narrative, 22, 139–140
    twentieth anniversary memorial, 291–293, 297
9/11 Commission Report, 230
9/11 defendants. *See also specific defendants*
    discussion, 21–22, 49, 76–77, 320
    effect of pandemic on, 293
    interpreters, 69–70
    transfer to Guantanamo Bay, 35–36
    trial, 1–4, 225–226
9/11 Memorial Run, 170
9/11-related illnesses, 73
noise and light torture, 262, 267
noises and vibrations, 57–60, 118
nongovernmental organizations (NGOs), 19–20, 32, 42, 86
Northeast Gate Tour, 191–193
nude shackling, 311, 334, 390
Nurjaman, Encep "Hambali," 285, 289, 292, 329, 347
NX2 (covert agent)
    discussion, 256, 263–266, 356
    use of EITs, 245–249
NZ7 (covert agent), 257, 262–266

Obama, Barack, 10, 73–75, 129, 191
Obama administration
    decision to try detainees in civilian courts, 64, 345
    discussion, 2–3, 7, 63, 180, 196
    Guantanamo detention center policy, 36, 49, 64–65, 89
OCA (original classification authority), 39, 132, 278
October 7, 2023, Hamas attack, 379
Office of General Counsel, Department of Defense, 308, 309–310, 335
Office of Legal Counsel, Justice Department, 41, 243–244
Oman, 386
Omicron coronavirus variant, 305
Operation Git-Meow, 306, 370
outrageous government conduct
    discussion, 150, 248, 325, 352, 393–394
    Hawsawi defense team, 332–333
Ozgediz, Defne, 362–363, 372

panel selection, 118, 225
Paradis, Michel, 396
Parrella, Keith
    appointment to case, 167–168

Index 429

FBI interview of defense team paralegal, 177–179
hearing on Pohl suppression ruling, 170–174
hostilities arguments and ruling, 183–184
reversal of Pohl suppression ruling, 184–185
unlawful influence arguments and ruling, 180–183
voir dire, 168–169
Patterson, Melissa, 396
PCR tests, 286, 287. *See also* coronavirus pandemic
Peaceful Tomorrows. *See* September 11th Families for Peaceful Tomorrows
Pellegrino, Frank (FBI), 313, 319–323, 371
Penn, Kal, 195
Pentagon, 9, 136, 241
PENTTBOM team. *See* Federal Bureau of Investigation
Perfect Soldiers (McDermott), 57, 115
Periodic Review Board (PRB), 14, 49, 129, 195, 288
Perkins, Abigail (FBI)
    Hawsawi jurisdictional challenge testimony, 138–140, 143–144
    suppression testimony, 216–217, 327–328
Perry, Edwin, 111, 151
Pfeiffer, Sacha, 226–227, 240, 252
Planes Operation narrative, 22, 139–140
plea-agreement debate
    agreements reached, 359–363
    appeal to DC Circuit, 386-387, 394-396
    CMCR ruling enforcing, 385
    discussion, 399, 405-406
    earlier plea discussions, 180–181, 308-310
    evidentiary categories, 404–405
    McCall ruling enforcing, 379-380
    Mohammed script for entry of plea, 386-387
    opposers, 315–316, 363, 381
    poison pill provision, 373–374, 405–406
    revocation of plea agreements, 364–367
    supporters, 319–320, 381–382, 387-388
Pohl, James
    applicability of Constitution ruling, 93–94
    Bin al Shibh case severance, 5–6
    conflicts with Ruiz, 98–103
    discussion, 7, 20–21, 23, 51, 84–86, 278
    female-guard ruling, 43–44
    hostilities ruling, 183–184
    motions on decommissioned black site, 79–84
    motions to record VFM testimony, 68–69
    Nashiri case, 37–38
    pretrial motions, 84–88, 126–127
    pro se question, 23–26, 31–32
    retirement from case, 165–166, 167
    ruling on decommissioned black site (Site A), 126–127
    ruling on defense teams, 28–31
    ruling suppressing FBI statements, 164–165
    substitute-and-summary process, 38–40
    unlawful influence arguments, 180
    voir dire on decommissioned black site, 121–126
poison pill provision. *See* plea agreement debate
Poland. *See* Location 4 facility
policy principles, 308, 309–310, 315–316, 325
post-traumatic stress disorder (PTSD), 349–350, 372–373, 391–392
Poteet, Derek, 219
Power Wars (Savage), 196
Pradhan, Alka
    discussion, 42, 297–298
    Jessen testimony, 268–269
    motions on black site locations, 148–149

suppression hearing, continued,
  349–350, 390–391, 402
PRB (Periodic Review Board), 14, 49,
  129, 195, 288
"the Preacher," 257, 262–266
Priest, Dana, 36
prison standard operating procedures
  (SOPs), 43–44, 340
pro bono representation, 7, 27–28
prolonged isolation
  Baluchi, Ammar al, 390, 391
  discussion, 37, 141, 262, 317, 334
prolonged nudity, 256, 267, 311
pro se representation, 23–26, 31–32
Protective Order #3, 338, 344
Protective Order #4, 158–160, 164, 165,
  185, 232, 324, 334–336, 358, 392–393
protective orders, 4–5, 26, 156
PTSD (post-traumatic stress disorder),
  349–350, 372–373, 391–392
Pulitzer Center, 355

Qahtani, Mohammed al, 110

Radio GTMO, 106, 197–198, 341
Radostitz, Rita, 217–218, 222–223, 322
Rahim, Tahar, 195
Rahman, Gul, 245, 248, 269–270
Ralph, Sheryl Lee, 341
Rao, Neomi, 395–396
rapport-based interrogation methods, 35,
  143, 213, 242, 321, 391. *See also* Federal
  Bureau of Investigation
Rasul v. Bush (2004), 13–14, 195, 208
Rath, Arun, 89–90, 94, 140, 226
RDI (Rendition, Detention, and
  Interrogation) program. *See* Central
  Intelligence Agency; Federal Bureau
  of Investigation
rectal techniques used
  discussion, 171–172, 174, 233
  on Hawsawi, 22, 95–97, 99–101, 103,
    267
  on Khan, 302
  on Mohammed, 256

on Nashiri, 311
regularly constituted courts, 36, 148,
  404–405
Reiner, Rob, 192
Reitman, Janet, 9, 11, 12, 17, 112
Remes, David, 27–28
Remote Hearing Room (RHR),
  297–298, 312, 320
Rendition, Detention, and Interrogation
  (RDI) program. *See* Central
  Intelligence Agency; Federal Bureau
  of Investigation
Report, The, 259
Reporter (Hersh), 291
Reprieve organization, 42
Resta, Thomas, 387
restraint chairs, 21
RHR (Remote Hearing Room),
  297–298, 312, 320
Rishikof, Harvey, 133, 180–183, 226
Ritland, Mike, 250
Rockefeller, Terry, 303, 319–320, 380, 387,
  397
Rodriguez, Jose, 156, 242, 243, 251
Rodriguez, Phyllis and family, 72
Rohde, David, 29
Roof, Dylann, 295
Roosevelt administration, 62
Rose, David, 197
Rosenberg, Carol
  articles, 27, 131, 195, 226, 288, 298,
    364–365, 382
  book signing, 88–90
  buyout offer, 179
  discussion, 2, 3, 7, 8, 9, 12, 16–17, 27,
    68, 175, 197, 284, 292
  Nashiri hearing, 298–299
  plea agreements, 387
  Pohl profile, 84
  Silver Gavel Award, 114–115
Ross, Gary, 9, 10, 19, 20, 61–62
Ruby Ridge standoff, 1
Ruiz, Walter
  client claims of ongoing colorectal
    discomfort, 95–97

conflicts with Pohl, 98–103
discovery on interagency coordination, 140–142
discussion, 91, 104–105, 109, 294
examination of witnesses for jurisdictional challenge, 143–145
jurisdictional challenges, 136–138
Mitchell suppression examination, 247–250
motion to dismiss for outrageous government conduct, 332–333
motion to sever Hawsawi case, 97–98, 103
on plea agreements, 363
plea discussions, 310
on Pohl suppression of FBI statements, 185–186, 203–204
security interruptions during testimony, 330–333
suppression hearing, continued, 324–325
Waltz suppression examination, 344–345
Rwandan genocide, 2
Ryan, Ed
discussion, 67–68, 91, 320, 340
Drucker suppression examination, 230–231
on FBI-CIA coordination, 161–163
Fitzgerald examination for Hawsawi jurisdictional challenge, 135–136
Harrington motion for removal, 274–275
motions to record VFM testimony, 68–69, 108, 109
suppression hearing scheduling discussions, 222–223
trial date discussions with Cohen, 204–206
Ryan, John, 377–378, 382

Sakrisson, Ben, 131, 132–133
Salamone family, 140
Sanity Board, 316–317
Sattler, Peter, 194

Saudi Arabia, Kingdom of, 363, 406–407
Savage, Charlie, 196, 288
Schaff, Erin, 193, 298–299
Scholl, Christopher, 12
Schulz, David, 56, 376–377
Schwartz, Michael, 24, 85–87, 91–92
SCIF (Sensitive Compartmented Information Facility), 79–80, 156, 376–377
Scott-Clark, Cathy, 252
secret recordings of Camp 7 detainees, 213, 345, 404
security interruptions
CIA courtroom actions, 227, 278, 323, 330
Fitzsimmons suppression testimony, 330–333
self-censoring by defense teams, 331–332
suppression hearing, 322–323
Waltz suppression testimony, 343–346
Senate Select Committee on Intelligence, 251, 259
Senate Torture Report
defense teams desire to review complete version, 185, 206, 259, 282
discussion, 6–7, 95–96, 144, 251, 285
First Camp 7 Commander testimony, 234–235, 358-359
Senior Medical Officer (SMO) of Camp 7 testimony, 98–101, 103–104
Sensitive Compartmented Information Facility (SCIF), 79–80, 156, 376–377
sentencing trial, 301-303, 309, 329-330, 355, 360–361, 366, 386-387
September 11, 2001, attacks. *See* 9/11 attacks
September 11th Families for Peaceful Tomorrows
attendance at commissions, 86
discussion, 32, 72, 108, 303, 319
Mohammed guilty plea colloquy, 387
support for plea deals, 381
SERE program. *See* Survival, Evasion, Resistance and Escape program
Serial, 319, 349, 381

Sessions, Jeff, 181–182
SG1 (covert agent), 346
Shanksville, Pennsylvania, 136
Shephard, Michelle, 115, 388, 395
Site A facility. *See also* black sites
    discussion, 80, 84, 126–127
    motions surrounding, 79–84, 147–150
    Pohl voir dire on, 121–126
Sixth Amendment, 325–326
60 Minutes, 10, 29, 406
Slahi, Mohamedou Ould, 195
slapping, 171, 174, 233, 243, 247, 256
sleep deprivation
    Baluchi, Ammar al, 390
    Bin al Shibh, Ramzi, 57–60
    Bin Attash, Walid, 265
    discussion, 96, 233, 243, 262
    Khan, Majid, 302
    Mohammed, Khalid Sheikh, 7, 256–257, 267
standing, 171, 174, 265, 334
Smith, Will, 196
SMO (Senior Medical Officer) of Camp 7 testimony, 98–101, 103–104
sodomy. *See* rectal rehydration
Sorkin, Aaron, 13, 192
Soufan, Ali, 242, 243, 252, 263–264
SOUTHCOM (Southern Command), 47, 49
Southern Center for Human Rights, 307
Sowards, Gary
    DeLury suppression examination, 219–222
    discussion, 217–219, 239, 279–280
    Drucker suppression examination, 231
    Jessen suppression examination, 356–358
    Mitchell suppression examination, 320–323, 333–334
    on plea agreements revocation, 366, 380
Spanish American War, 13
Spath, Vance, 114–115

Special Category Residents, 190, 193, 197, 370
Special Review Team
    discussion, 23, 25, 70–71
    FBI defense team infiltration, 31
    FBI interview of defense team paralegal, 177–179
Spotlight, 226
Stahl, Lesley, 10, 29
standard interrogation techniques, 262, 333–334. *See also* enhanced interrogation techniques
Stern, Jeffrey, 92–93, 116
Stewart, Kristen, 194
Stone, Oliver, 21, 115, 227
stress positioning, 171, 174, 233, 246, 390
substitute-and-summary process, 38–40, 51, 79–80, 122-124
Sullivan, Emmet, 122
superior convening authority argument, 365–367, 371–372
suppression hearing (September 2019–February 2020)
    Bormann examination of Mitchell, 263–266
    Butsch testimony, 231–233
    classification guidance and arguments, 208–210
    Connell examination of Mitchell, 237–244
    DeLury testimony, 219–222
    Drucker testimony, 229–231
    earthquake, 259–261
    First Camp 7 Commander testimony, 234–235
    Fitzgerald testimony, 211–216
    Fitzsimmons testimony postponement, 274
    Groharing examination of Mitchell, 266–268
    Harrington examination of Mitchell, 262–263
    Jessen testimony, 257, 268–270
    media meeting with VFMs, 250–252
    media operations, 225–229

Nevin examination of Mitchell, 255–261, 267–268
Perkins testimony, 216–217
Ruiz examination of Mitchell, 247–250
testimony on unauthorized EITs, 245–249
suppression hearing, continued (September 2023–April 2025)
Antol testimony, 322–323
discussion, 315–316, 324–325
First Camp 7 Commander testimony, 358–359
Fitzsimmons testimony, 330–333
Guilmette testimony, 372–373
Hanrahan testimony, 372–373
Hodgson testimony, 334–335
interruption by plea agreements, 359–361
Jessen testimony, 356–358
Jocys testimony, 362, 363
Kohlmann testimony, 359
McCall ruling on FBI statements, 399–403
McFadden testimony, 350–351, 367
Mitchell testimony, 333–334
Morgan testimony, 349–350
operational tempo, 336–337
Pellegrino testimony, 321–322
Perkins testimony, 327–328
requests for UFI witnesses, 334–336, 346
scheduling arguments, 324–325, 336–337, 377
security guidelines and interruptions, 322–323, 330–331
Waltz testimony, 337–338, 343–346
Welner testimony, 373, 376–377, 379, 382–383
witness health delays, 346
WK5I covert medical professional testimony, 372
Supreme Court. *See also* Court of Military Commission Review
Ashcraft v. Tennessee (1944), 393

Boumediene v. Bush (2008), 13
Brady v. Maryland (1963), 44
death penalty case appeals, 113
Ex Parte Quirin, 62–63
Hamdan v. Rumsfeld (2006), 36, 281
Rasul v. Bush (2004), 13–14, 195, 208
rulings on Guantanamo detainees, 13–14
Survival, Evasion, Resistance and Escape (SERE) program
discussion, 241, 242–243, 247, 350
techniques based on, 249, 264, 269
Swann, Robert
direct questioning of SMO, 100–101, 103–104
discussion, 144, 340
First Camp 7 Commander testimony, 234–235
motions on decommissioned black site, 81–82, 125–126

Taliban, 13, 63–64
Talking with Strangers (Gladwell), 238
Tamir, Nashwan al. *See* Iraqi, Abd al Hadi al
Tanzania embassy bombing (1998), 63, 137, 138
Taub, Ben, 195
TBI (traumatic brain injury), 372–373
TCNs (Third Country Nationals), 12–13, 288, 386
ten category framework, 37–38, 51, 84–85, 149
Tenet, George, 156, 243, 264
Terror Courts, The (Bravin), 3
Thailand, 39, 130. *See also* Location 3 facility
Third Country Nationals (TCNs), 12–13, 288, 386
Thomas, Sterling, 42, 53, 55
Thompson, Jackie, 307, 309
threats of murder
discussion, 221, 267, 322, 343
made by Mitchell, 257–258, 333
Tidd, Kurt, 49

top secret classification, 6, 25–26
Top Secret documentary, 76
Top Secret Sensitive Compartmentalized Information (TS-SCI) clearance, 25
torture. *See* enhanced interrogation techniques; *specific kinds of torture*
"Torture Memos," 41
transitional justice, 73–76
Trant, Jessica and family, 381
traumatic brain injury (TBI), 372–373
Trivett, Clay
   Bin al Shibh competency hearing, 316–317
   Camp 7 alleged noise and vibrations, 59–60
   discussion, 62, 181, 295, 308
   examination of Perkins, 138–140, 143–144
   hostilities arguments, 183–186
   on operational tempo of case, 336–337
   plea agreements, 361–363, 367, 380, 386–387
   security interruptions during testimony, 330–333
   suppression hearing record of limitations, 208–210
   suppression hearing scheduling, 203–204
Trump, Donald J., 94, 106, 107, 115, 129, 192
Trump administration
   discussion, 130, 180, 362–363
   expansion of migrant operations, 89, 396, 407–408
   media policy changes, 130–133
   second inauguration, 388–389
Tsarnaev, Dzhokhar, 295
TS-SCI (Top Secret Sensitive Compartmentalized Information) clearance, 25
Tur, Christopher, 131

UAE (United Arab Emirates), 211–213
Unabomber, 217, 218, 219
unauthorized enhanced interrogation techniques (EITs), 245–249
Uniform Code of Military Justice, 179–181
unique functional identifiers (UFIs). *See also specific covert agents*
   discussion, 150–151, 155, 159, 165, 240
   information related to JPRA, 241
   interview requests, 334–336
   security interruptions during testimony, 330–331
   testimony for suppression of FBI statements, 170–171
United 93 (film), 21
United Airlines Flight 93, 136
United Airlines Flight 175, 69, 108, 136
United Arab Emirates (UAE), 211–213
United Nations Special Rapporteur for Counterterrorism and Human Rights, 340–341
unlawful influence allegations, 179–181, 364–367, 373, 399–403, 405–406
US Court of Appeals for the Armed Forces, 55
US Court of Appeals for the DC Circuit
   commission case appeals, 113, 115
   discussion, 55, 63, 127, 288, 402
   habeas corpus reviews, 13–14
   writ of mandamus for plea agreements, 386–388, 399, 403
US District Court for the Eastern District of Virginia, 38
USS *Cole* attack
   discussion, 114, 118, 137, 245, 311, 319
   hearings on, 295, 298–299

Vance, J. D., 362–363
victim family members (VFMs)
   desire for closure, 319–320, 406
   discussion, 19–22, 32, 67
   meetings with media, 71–73, 75–76, 250–252, 296, 381–382, 387–388, 397
   9/11 video evidence, 135–136, 140
   positions on military commissions, 71–73, 75–76

pretrial depositions, 68–69, 108, 109
victim-impact witnesses, 68, 309
Victim/Witness Assistance Program (VWAP), 72
Voll, Daniel, 115, 227

Waits, J. K., 15–16
walling
   Baluchi, Ammar al, 246–247
   discussion, 52, 233, 243, 256, 357
   TBI, 372–373
Waltz, Kimberly (FBI), 337–338, 343–346, 404
War in Court, The (Hajjar), 252, 388
waterboarding
   Baluchi, Ammar al, 390
   discussion, 130, 243–244, 249, 259, 357
   Mohammed, Khalid Sheikh, 6–7, 257, 267, 322
water dousing, 96, 171, 172, 174, 249
Watkins, Ali, 61
Watkins, Thomas, 116
Watson, Eleanor, 387
Watts, Sean, 137, 183–184
Welna, David, 89–90, 115, 140, 226
Welner, Michael, 373, 376–377, 379–381, 382–383
Wichner, Alaina, 57
Wilkins, Robert, 395–396, 399

Williams, Margot, 115, 116, 187, 252, 284
WK5I ("Dr. 1" covert medical professional), 371–372, 390, 392
Wofford, Susanne, 372
Women's March, 107–108
Wood, Jeffrey, 285, 308, 315–316, 329
Wood, Steve, 49
World Trade Center, 2–3, 387
World Trade Center (film), 21
World Trade Center North Tower
   American Airlines Flight 11, 57, 135–136, 138
   discussion, 32, 57, 73, 296
World Trade Center South Tower, 69, 108, 136
writ of mandamus on plea agreements
   DC Circuit, 386–388, 399, 403
   discussion, 380, 400–402

Zero Dark Thirty, 51–52, 55–56
Zika virus, 87–88
Zimmerman, Michael, 288
Zoom, 282, 284, 352–353
Zubaydah, Abu
   capture and interrogation, 241, 242–244
   possible testimony, 118–119
   use of EITs on, 263–264